VPN LCM A.

IS-IS Network Design Soluti

Abe Martey
Contributions by Scott Sturgess

Cisco Press

Cisco Press
201 West 103rd Street
Indianapolis, IN 46290 USA

rk Design Solutions

Cisco Press

Street
46290 USA

inted nited States of America 1 2 3 4 5 6 7 8 9 0

First P February 2002

Libra ngress Cataloging-in-Publication Number: 99-67938

ISBN: 0-220-8

War and Disclaimer

This bo esigned to provide information about IS-IS. Every effort has been made to make this book as complete accurate as possible, but no warranty or fitness is implied.

The inf on is provided on an "as is" basis. The author, Cisco Press, and Cisco Systems, Inc. shall have neither liability esponsibility to any person or entity with respect to any loss or damages arising from the information contain this book or from the use of the discs or programs that may accompany it.

The opi expressed in this book belong to the author and are not necessarily those of Cisco Systems, Inc.

Feedk Information

At Cisc ss, our goal is to create in-depth technical books of the highest quality and value. Each book is crafted with car d precision, undergoing rigorous development that involves the unique expertise of members from the professi technical community.

Readers edback is a natural continuation of this process. If you have any comments regarding how we can improve e quality of this book, or otherwise alter it to better suit your needs, you can contact us through email at feedback ciscopress.com. Please make sure to include the book title and ISBN in your message.

We greatly appreciate your assistance.

Trademark Acknowledgments

All terms mentioned in this book that are known to be trademarks or service marks have been appropriately capitalized. Cisco Press or Cisco Systems, Inc. cannot attest to the accuracy of this information. Use of a term in this book should not be regarded as affecting the validity of any trademark or service mark.

Publisher	John Wait
Editor-in-Chief	John Kane
Cisco Systems Management	Michael Hakkert
	Tom Geitner
	William Warren
Production Manager	Patrick Kanouse
Acquisitions Editor	Tracy Hughes
Development Editor	Howard Jones
Project Editor	San Dee Phillips
Copy Editor	Keith Cline
Technical Editors	Blair Buchanan
	Thomas Kramer
Team Coordinator	Tammi Ross
Book Designer	Gina Rexrode
Cover Designer	Louisa Klucznik
Compositor	Octal Publishing, Inc.
Indexers	Tim Wright
	Brad Herriman

CISCO SYSTEMS

Corporate Headquarters
Cisco Systems, Inc.
170 West Tasman Drive
San Jose, CA 95134-1706
USA
http://www.cisco.com
Tel: 408 526-4000
    800 553-NETS (6387)
Fax: 408 526-4100

European Headquarters
Cisco Systems Europe
11 Rue Camille Desmoulins
92782 Issy-les-Moulineaux
Cedex 9
France
http://www-europe.cisco.com
Tel: 33 1 58 04 60 00
Fax: 33 1 58 04 61 00

Americas Headquarters
Cisco Systems, Inc.
170 West Tasman Drive
San Jose, CA 95134-1706
USA
http://www.cisco.com
Tel: 408 526-7660
Fax: 408 527-0883

Asia Pacific Headquarters
Cisco Systems Australia,
Pty., Ltd
Level 17, 99 Walker Street
North Sydney
NSW 2059 Australia
http://www.cisco.com
Tel: +61 2 8448 7100
Fax: +61 2 9957 4350

Cisco Systems has more than 200 offices in the following countries. Addresses, phone numbers, and fax numbers are listed on the Cisco Web site at www.cisco.com/go/offices

Argentina • Australia • Austria • Belgium • Brazil • Bulgaria • Canada • Chile • China • Colombia • Costa Rica • Croatia • Czech Republic • Denmark • Dubai, UAE • Finland • France • Germany • Greece • Hong Kong • Hungary • India • Indonesia • Ireland Israel • Italy • Japan • Korea • Luxembourg • Malaysia • Mexico • The Netherlands • New Zealand • Norway • Peru • Philippines Poland • Portugal • Puerto Rico • Romania • Russia • Saudi Arabia • Scotland • Singapore • Slovakia • Slovenia • South Africa • Spain Sweden • Switzerland • Taiwan • Thailand • Turkey • Ukraine • United Kingdom • United States • Venezuela • Vietnam • Zimbabwe

About the Authors

Abe Martey, CCIE #2373, is a product manager at the Cisco Internet PoP Systems Business Unit (IPSBU), which is the home of the Cisco 12000 Internet Router Series. Abe focuses on high-speed IP routing systems and related technologies. Prior to this position, Abe held various support engineering positions, including time at the Cisco Technical Assistance Center on the IP Routing Protocols Team and later on the ISP Team (now Internet Engineering Services Team), where he developed special interest in the IS-IS routing protocol. Abe holds a masters degree in electrical engineering and has been with Cisco Systems for six years.

Scott Sturgess, CCIE #2346, is a technical leader within the Core IP Engineering's Deployment and Scalability Team, where he is primarily involved in the advancement of link-state routing protocols. Now in his sixth year at Cisco Systems, Scott held various roles from customer support to consultancy, focusing on IP routing protocols and Internet architecture, primarily within the Internet service provider arena. Scott holds a first class honors degree in electrical and electronic engineering.

About the Technical Reviewers

Blair Buchanan, CCIE #1427, is an internetwork architect who bases his consulting practice in Ottawa, Canada. For almost 30 years, Mr. Buchanan's career in data communication includes software development, standards participation, internetwork design, and education. Mr. Buchanan holds a bachelor's degree in computer science, has been a certified Cisco Systems Instructor since 1992, and earned his CCIE in 1995.

Thomas Kramer, CCIE #2662, has been working over the past seven years at Cisco Systems on IP routing and core technologies. After several years working in Brussels, he relocated recently to Mexico City, where he works in a consulting function for Cisco in the Latin American theater. He holds a master's degree in electrical engineering and telecommunication and is a recertified CCIE in IP routing and switching.

Dedication

This book is dedicated to my affectionate mom, Emelia, for giving me her best.

Acknowledgments

First of all, I'd like to express sincere thanks to Scott Sturgess for providing timely contributions to Chapters 7 and 8, helping to make the project deadline. Scott also reviewed some of the other chapters. The editorial team at Cisco Press was phenomenal, and many folks worked hard on various aspects of the book to bring it to fruition. I'd like to sincerely thank every one of them and also mention the following individuals with whom I interacted the most: Alicia Buckley encouraged me to take up the project; Tracy Hughes was always ready to forgive me yet another time whenever I fell behind schedule. Writing part-time was very challenging, and Tracy's extreme patience and understanding was very helpful. Many thanks to John Kane for his mentorship and also to Howard Jones and San Dee Phillips for their enthusiasm and thoroughness in reviewing the manuscripts.

The technical reviewers, Thomas Kramer and Blair Buchanan, were fantastic; and although their tough reviews compelled me to work harder and longer than I expected, I count myself very lucky to have had their knowledge and experience at my disposal! I wish to thank them for their time and great feedback for improving the text, and for making me a better writer.

Henk Smit influenced my interest in IS-IS while he was at Cisco as an IS-IS protocol development engineer, and I'd like to thank him for his tutorials and insights during our many interactions when I was a support engineer. I also want to acknowledge Henk's significant contributions to the enhancement of the IS-IS protocol while at Cisco Systems and as a current active participant in the IETF's IS-IS Working Group.

I'd like to thank several individuals, professional colleagues, and friends within and outside of Cisco Systems who have been resourceful and supportive in diverse ways, either throughout this project, or have generally helped shape my career. They are named in random order as follows: Jeff Zirker, Tony Bates, Bala Nagesh, Richard Harvey, Praveen Akkiraju, Chris Whyte, Ferdinand Sales, Scott Yow, Niklas Montin, Kevin Macaluso, Jean Nicolas, Heba Ibrahim, Hassan Kassem, Sampson Asiedu, Sandra Bell, Bill Ware, Tom Snyder, Bob Collet, Rob Saileanu, and many others. To all my many former colleagues in the Cisco TAC, thanks a lot for sharing your knowledge and expertise.

Finally, I'd like to express gratitude and love to my family for supporting this effort and for enduring many evenings and weekends without me, when I engulfed myself in this project. Thanks again for all the love, caring, and support!

Abe Martey

Contents at a Glance

Table of Contents

Foreword

With the Internet continuing to expand, the need for robust and flexible IP routing protocols to sustain the expansive global routing system can never be overemphasized. Of all the IP routing protocols that evolved alongside the Internet, only three of them survived the test of time and are currently widely deployed: BGP for exterior routing, and OSPF and IS-IS for interior routing.

The IS-IS Protocol has emerged as one of the universally adopted and widely used Interior Gateway Protocols, besides OSPF. BGP remains the de facto Exterior Gateway Protocol for interdomain routing. IS-IS is used as an IGP by most of the Tier 1 and Tier 2 Internet service providers for both practical and historical reasons. The wisdom and insight of the original protocol designers and subsequent pragmatic contributions by the IETF manifest in the protocol's flexibility can be easily adapted for many emerging applications, such as MPLS Traffic Engineering and IPv6. The scalability and extensibility of the IS-IS protocol made it an obvious choice for IGP when I directed the design and deployment of one of the largest existing IP backbones several years ago. Our high confidence and comfort level allowed us to run both IP and ISO routing in a single instance of IS-IS.

Many networking professionals have longed for a readable tutorial and design guide on this popular protocol. The original specification of the IS-IS protocol, ISO 10589, is a tough indoctrination for most people interested in grasping fundamentals of operation of IS-IS. Additionally, several enhancements to the original IS-IS protocol, including RFC 1195 and many recent related RFCs and IETF drafts, are not captured in one place for easy access by interested readers.

This book provides the first, most extensive coverage of the IS-IS protocol, written and reviewed by networking experts with many years of practical experience designing, deploying, and troubleshooting IS-IS-based networks and also working with advanced routing systems. Having firsthand experience with the challenges and fun in deploying and using IS-IS to its full potential, I only wish this excellent book had been available sooner.

IS-IS Network Design Solutions by Abe Martey certainly augments the list of excellent literature on internetworking technology brought to many networking professionals worldwide by Cisco Press in fulfilling one of its primary goals—sharing Cisco's networking expertise! This book is a key reference for anyone interesting in IGP deployment and evolution.

Tony Bates, VP/GM
Internet PoP Systems Business Unit
Cisco Systems, Inc.

Introduction

The Intermediate System-to-Intermediate System (IS-IS) Routing Protocol is a versatile and robust routing protocol suitable for both IP and CLNP applications. In the IP world, it has emerged as the only practical alternative to the Open Shortest Path First Protocol for Interior Gateway Protocol (IGP) applications in Internet Service Provider (ISP) networks. IS-IS is the IGP of choice in most tier one ISP environments and its significance certainly explains why it features in the CCIE Routing and Switching, as well as the CCIE IP recertification exams. Despite the importance of IS-IS in IP networking, it has received little coverage in the technical press and networking literature. Most users and networking professionals rely on scanty literature and the configuration manuals from Cisco and other major router vendors to boost their knowledge on IS-IS. Many routing protocol texts from Cisco Press cover IS-IS in sections, yet OSPF is covered in many book titles. This first book title on IS-IS breaks tradition of inadequate IS-IS coverage by focusing primarily on IS-IS. *IS-IS Network Design Solutions* follows the much-cherished Cisco Press approach of combining theory and practice within the setup of the Cisco Routing environment. The text also includes elaborate comparison with its competitor, OSPF.

Objectives

The overall objective of this book is to bring comprehensive knowledge about the IS-IS routing protocol to the IP networking professional at any career level. Coverage of the IS-IS protocol in this book stretches from basic to advanced concepts. Like most IP routing protocols, IS-IS is still evolving with various enhancements still being discussed and formalized within the IETF. This book builds a bridge between the original IS-IS protocol, which was specified for routing of the ISO Connectionless Network Protocol (CLNP), and all the recent IP-related enhancements. Its practical slant, which exploits the ubiquitous Cisco IOS environment, is designed to provide you hands-on experience for usage and configuration of the IS-IS protocol. In the grand scheme, the material presented should provide you with the necessary advanced skills for understanding, designing, and application of IS-IS as an IGP in IP environments. The numerous tables, references, and troubleshooting information makes this book an excellent reference.

Audience

The target audience of this book is networking professionals with diverse levels of experience. It is written for anyone who is new to IS-IS or has a decent level of familiarity, as well as the experienced routing protocol expert. The reader is expected to have knowledge of the basics of the TCP/IP Protocol suite, as well as IP routing concepts. The first chapter of the book provides an overview of IP routing and elaborates on how IP routers work and should be interesting to any networking professional. Even though a fair amount of the text is dedicated to the basics of IS-IS, a large section of the book covers advanced concepts including troubleshooting, design, deployment, and maintenance of IS-IS networks. The advanced sections are useful for networking professionals preparing for the Cisco Certified Internetwork Expert (CCIE) Routing and Switching Lab Exam, the CCIE IP Recertification Exam or similar professional certification tests.

Organization

This book is organized into three parts and two appendixes. Part I discusses IP routing technology and covers the theoretical foundations of the IS-IS protocol including protocol concepts, features, implementation specifics, protocol mechanisms, timers, metrics, and other parameters.

Part II builds on the material discussed in Part I and provides advanced information on IP network design strategies using the IS-IS protocol. This section also provides cases studies to elaborate and precipitate the design principles presented here.

Part III provides configuration and troubleshooting information with a hands-on approach using Cisco routers.

Appendix A is a collection of IS-IS packet formats and analyzer captures that are presented as supplementary or reference information to assist with understanding the material covered in Part I. This information is useful for studying and mastering complicated IS-IS problems, such as implementation or interoperability issues.

The following is a list of chapters in each major section:

Part I: IS-IS Protocol: Design Specification and Features

- **Chapter 1:** Overview of IP Routing
- **Chapter 2:** Introduction to the IS-IS Routing Protocol
- **Chapter 3:** Integrated IS-IS Routing Protocol Concepts
- **Chapter 4:** Addressing in Integrated IS-IS
- **Chapter 5:** The IS-IS Link-State Database
- **Chapter 6:** The Shortest Path First Algorithm

Part II: Integrated IS-IS Network Design for IP Internets

- **Chapter 7:** General Network Design Issues
- **Chapter 8:** Network Design Scenarios

Part III: Configuring and Troubleshooting Integrated IS-IS

- **Chapter 9:** Configuring IS-IS for IP Routing on Cisco Routers
- **Chapter 10:** Troubleshooting the IS-IS Routing Protocol

Part IV: Appendixes

- **Appendix A:** IS-IS Packet Formats
- **Appendix B:** Answers to Review Questions

How to Read This Book

This book is organized logically with the subject matter getting progressively advanced, yet flexible enough to allow readers to access sections or chapters of interest according to their level of IS-IS knowledge or interaction with the protocol. Advanced users might want to browse through Chapter 1 to refresh their knowledge on the fundamentals of IP routing and spend more time studying the chapters in Part I to master advanced knowledge about the IS-IS protocol. Other readers may combine the concepts presented in Part I with the design and deployment material presented in Part II. Readers interested in troubleshooting can focus on Part III and also review Part I in order to understand how IS-IS works. For the latter type of readers, the parameter tables in Part I and the packet formats and analyzer captures in Appendix A provide a good reference for regular troubleshooting situations and related responsibilities in operations environments.

This book also provides numerous references and Web links to relevant material that is not elaborated here because of space limitation or because it is beyond the scope of the book. Readers are encouraged to consult included references for additional information that augments the presented material.

Command Syntax Conventions

Command syntax in this book conforms to the following conventions:

- Commands, keywords, and actual values for arguments are **bold**.

- Arguments (which need to be replaced with an actual value) are *italic*.

- Optional keywords and/or arguments (or a choice of optional keywords, and/or arguments) are in brackets [ ].

- Choice of mandatory keywords and/or arguments are in braces { }.

- These conventions are for syntax only. Actual configurations and examples do not follow these conventions.

IS-IS Protocol: Design Specification and Features

CHAPTER 1

Overview of IP Routing

This chapter focuses on the general design and operation of routing protocols for the Internet Protocol (IP). It also provides background information on the IP protocol, as well as insights into how IP packets are routed through a data communications network. The ensuing discussions span IP routing principles and packet-switching mechanisms available on IP routers. Obviously, this chapter has a broader charter than the intended focus of this book. IS-IS-focused coverage starts in Chapter 2, "Introduction to the IS-IS Routing Protocol." This chapter covers the following major topics:

- IP routing and forwarding
- Essentials of IP addressing
- Classification of IP routing protocols
- Unicast versus multicast routing
- Cisco packet-switching mechanisms
- Comments on IPv6

The elaborate coverage of general IP routing issues should help remove many misconceptions held by most readers. For other readers, the material provides an excellent refresher on IP routing principles.

IP Routing and Forwarding

IP has emerged as the dominant Layer 3 protocol for connectionless networking. IP is part of a suite of protocols referred to as the Transmission Control Protocol/Internet Protocol (TCP/IP) protocol suite (or simply as the Internet Protocol suite). The IP suite embraces many protocols, some of which are listed in RFC 1800, "Internet Official Protocol Standards." This list of IP-related protocols continues to grow as new applications emerge. Some key IP protocols include the following:

- Internet Protocol (IP)
- Transmission Control Protocol (TCP)

- User Datagram Protocol (UDP)
- Internet Message Control Protocol (ICMP)
- Address Resolution Protocol (ARP)

TCP and UDP provide transport for applications and run over the IP layer. ICMP is a control protocol that works alongside IP at the network layer. ARP provides address resolution between the network layer and the underlying data link layer. Numerous applications use the transport services of TCP and UDP. Some common examples include the following:

- **Telnet**—A virtual terminal application that uses TCP for transport
- **File Transport Protocol (FTP)**—A file transfer application that uses TCP for transport
- **Trivial File Transfer Protocol (TFTP)**—A file transfer application that uses UDP for transport
- **Domain Name Service (DNS)**—A name-to-address translation application that uses both TCP and UDP transport

IP is largely responsible for the continuing success of the TCP/IP suite. The popularity of IP is mainly centered on its simplicity and high efficiency for data transfer. As a connectionless protocol, IP forwards data in self-contained routable units known as *datagrams* or *packets*. Each packet contains information, such as source and destination addresses, which is used by routers when making forwarding and policy decisions.

In connectionless networking, there is no need for prior setup of an end-to-end path between the source and destination before data transmission is initiated. A file can be transmitted from one end of the network to another by breaking it down into packets, each of which is forwarded independently along the best path by routers located between the source and destination. IP forwarding is primarily based on the destination address, even though the source address and other parameters in the IP header can be used for policy-based forwarding.

IP forwarding is, therefore, commonly referred to as *destination-based*. Routing and forwarding essentially mean the same thing with regard to IP, even though they've taken different shades in meaning along with the evolution of routers. A *router* is a network device that essentially consists of a collection of network interfaces linked together by a high-speed bus or a complex interconnection system, such as a crossbar-switch or shared memory fabric. A router has two functional planes: data and control. Frequently, both functions are performed by an intelligent subsystem known as the *route processor*. Most modern high-speed routers are designed with a clear separation between the control and data planes (see Figure 1-1). The control plane functions are centered on building the necessary intelligence about the state of the network and a router's interfaces. IP routing applications or protocols provide the framework for gathering this intelligence. The data plane handles actual packet processing and forwarding by relying on the intelligence of the control plane.

IP routing is the broader process of collecting routing information about the network, a function that is performed in the control plane. IP routing protocols process this information to determine the best paths to known destinations in the network. The known best paths are stored in the *routing table* or the *routing information base (RIB)*. The routing table is then used for forwarding packets, moving them out of the router onto the best paths to the next hop and toward their intended destinations. The best path is frequently the path with the lowest value of metric or cost to the destination.

IP forwarding involves processing information in the header of an IP packet to determine how to advance it toward the target destination. This includes activities such as looking up the destination address in a forwarding database for the exit interface, reducing the IP time-to-live (TTL) value, calculating the IP checksum value, queuing the packet at the exit interface, and eventually getting the packet out of the router onto the link to the next-hop router. Similar forwarding functions are performed independently on the router at the next hop and at every router in the path, each time getting the packet closer to its destination until it finally arrives there.

Figure 1-1   *Distributed router architecture.*

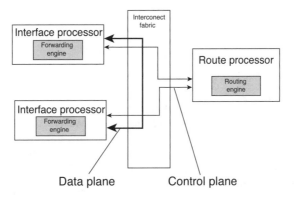

Figure 1-1 illustrates the architecture of a router with distributed forwarding capabilities. In this architecture, each interface processor (or line card) features an independent forwarding engine, which is responsible for IP forwarding. The interface processors directly switch packets between each other. IP forwarding engines are optimized for faster packet processing and switching from the source interface to the destination interface on a router.

The IP routing functionality is performed on the route processor, which has a *routing engine* for calculating routes. The route processor runs a routing protocol that allows it to interact with other routers, gather and process routing information, and build the routing table. The route processor is optimized for gathering routing information, which it eventually shares with the interface processors. The Cisco 12000 Series routers have a fully distributed architecture.

Figure 1-2 shows an alternative router architecture with a dedicated *packet processor* featuring a high-speed forwarding engine designed to provide centralized packet switching for the whole system. Also shown is a separate route processor. As in the distributed architecture, the data and control planes are separated. Interface processors in the centralized architecture do not have forwarding intelligence to exchange packets directly but, instead, direct all packets to the packet processor where actual forwarding is done. This type of router architecture is described as *centralized*.

Figure 1-2   *Centralized router architecture.*

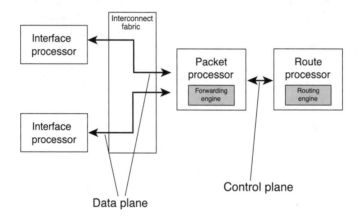

Fully distributed and centralized router designs are the extremes of router architecture options, and there are various hybrid options in between them. One option is to integrate the packet and route processors shown in Figure 1-2 into a single hardware element, commonly referred to as a *route switch processor*. Other options mix centralized and distributed forwarding capabilities in the same router as in the architecture of the Cisco 7500 Series routers. These routers feature hardware modules called *versatile interface processors (VIP)* and *route switch processors (RSP)*. The VIP provides distributed forwarding, whereas the RSP combines routing and centralized packet-processing capabilities.

The routing information collected by a router and shared with other routers in the network consists of IP subnets or address prefixes that are associated with various links in the network. The hosts in a network where most applications reside are typically connected to local-area network (LAN) media. The IP address of a host is based on the subnet assigned to its LAN.

The following section briefly discusses IP addressing in general and provides a refresher for IP subnetting and related subjects, such as *variable-length subnet masking (VLSM)* and *classless interdomain routing (CIDR)*. Later discussions focus on various categories of IP routing protocols and packet-switching mechanisms used for IP forwarding on Cisco routers.

Essentials of IP Addressing

Addressing and routing are inextricably linked. To provide a datagram (packet) delivery service, IP needs to have an addressing scheme to denote the source of a packet and its intended destination. Having a native addressing scheme enables IP, which operates at Layer 3, to be independent of the underlying LAN or wide-area network (WAN) transport medium. The original architects of the IP protocol chose a 32-bit addressing scheme, which in raw value allows 2^{32} (4,294,967,295) unique host addresses to be defined.

Although this number seemed reasonably large at the initial stages of deployment of the Internet, the 32-bit addressing scheme has turned out to be one of the significant shortcomings of IP version 4 (IPv4). This is because of the unexpected large-scale, multinational expansion of the Internet. Various clever schemes, such as *Network Address Translation (NAT)*, have been adopted by the Internet community to slow down the pace of depletion of the IPv4 address space. NAT allows translation between the private address space and public space, making it possible for a large number of hosts using private addresses to share a few public addresses on an as-needed basis. Also building momentum and gaining popularity is a new IP addressing scheme referred to as *IP version 6 (IPv6)*. IPv6 provides a larger address space with 128-bit-wide addresses. With an address size four times longer, IPv6 can support a far larger number of addresses than its predecessor, IPv4.

The following subsections discuss various concepts related to IP addressing, including the following:

- IPv4 address classes
- Private IPv4 address space
- IPv4 subnetting and variable subnet masking
- CIDR

Classful and Classless Addressing

In general, an important aspect of network design involves management of the allocated address space through frugal assignment of groups of addresses of varying sizes. The concept of address classes was introduced into IP networking to assist manageability of the IPv4 address space by carving it into predefined "chunks." Five address classes (A, B, C, D, and E) were defined and distinguished by the setting of the most significant bits of the most significant byte in the IP address. These settings allowed the address space to be carved into groups or classes of addresses, each of which supported a certain number of hosts. IP networks were then allocated a group of addresses from the various address classes to match their current size and future growth potential. Administrators of these networks were, in turn, supposed to assign addresses to the connected hosts, thus facilitating management of the address space. Three of the five address classes (A, B, and C) delineated the associated

32-bit IP addresses into network identifier (network ID) bits and host identifier (host ID) bits as follows:

- **Class A**—8-bit network ID, 24-bit host ID
- **Class B**—16-bit network ID, 16-bit host ID
- **Class C**—24-bit network ID, 8-bit host ID

Class D addresses were set aside for IP multicast, and Class E addresses were for experimental use. Figure 1-3 illustrates the assignment of bits in Class A addresses.

Figure 1-3   *Assignment of Class A address bits.*

The dotted-decimal notation used for representing 32-bit binary IP addresses makes them readable by humans. In the dotted-decimal representation, the bits are grouped into octets and separated by dots. Each octet of binary bits is then converted into the decimal equivalent. Table 1-1 shows the address ranges in dotted decimal for all classes. These reflect only host ranges, and network number ranges are implied. Various rules guide the actual address assignment for network devices.

RFC 1700 provides information on reserved addresses and other Internet-related protocol parameters.

Table 1-1   *IP Address Classes and Representation*

Address Class	Bit Pattern of First Byte	First Byte Decimal Range	Host Assignment Range in Dotted Decimal
A	0xxxxxxx	1–127	1.0.0.1 – 126.255.255.254
B	10xxxxxx	128–191	128.0.0.1 – 191.255.255.255.254
C	110xxxxx	192–223	192.0.0.1 – 223.255.255.254
D	1110xxxx	224–239	224.0.0.1 – 239.255.255.254
E	11110xxx	240–255	240.0.0.1 – 255.255.255.255

The foregoing discussion relates to what is described as *classful addressing*, so called because of the class-related interpretation of the IP address space. The flip side of classful addressing is *classless addressing*.

Classless IP addressing abandons the notion of IP address classes by denoting the "would-be" network number of an IP address as some prefix of a specific length. This method of interpreting IP addresses allows for more flexibility in address allocation and contributes to efficient usage of the IPv4 address space. Classless interpretation of IP addresses allows a large address block (Class A, for example) to be split among multiple organizations instead of being allocated to a single organization that doesn't have enough hosts and growth potential for the whole class. In the reverse direction, classless addressing allows multiple Class C addresses to be aggregated into a larger block and advertised as a single address prefix. Address aggregation using CIDR provides great memory-saving opportunities on routers connected to the Internet, which is necessary for scaling routing on the Internet.

Private Address Space

The private address space was originally set aside for IP networks that are not connected to the public Internet. NAT has emerged as one of the innovative ways to conserve IP addresses by converting between public Internet and private addresses. This procedure allows some networks with private addresses to connect to the public Internet. The following three blocks of addresses are reserved for private Internets by RFC 1918:

- 10.0.0.0 – 10.255.255.255
- 172.16.0.0 – 172.31.255.255
- 192.168.0.0 – 192.168.255.255

Subnetting and Variable-Length Subnet Masks

IP address subnetting existed before the introduction of classless addressing and provided a way to split a classful IP network number into multiple smaller address groups that can be applied to different segments of a network. Subnetting introduced another level of hierarchy into the structure of IP address classes, by taking a couple of bits from the host ID field to extend the network ID, creating *subnetworks* (or simply *subnet*). For example, one octet of the two-octet host bits of a Class B address might be used to create 255 subnets, each with only an octet of host bits (see Figure 1-4).

Figure 1-4   *Class B subnet example.*

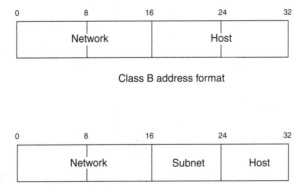

Subnetting an original IP network number into smaller blocks allows efficient assignment of addresses to the smaller segments of a network. An IP subnet mask is used with IP addresses to demarcate the host bits. A subnet mask uses a contiguous string of 1s to represent the network and subnet bits and 0s for the host bits. The subnet mask is also represented in dotted-decimal format. The mask for the subnetted Class B in Figure 1-3 is illustrated in Figure 1-5.

Figure 1-5   *Subnet mask example.*

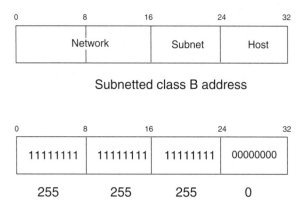

As shown in Figure 1-5, the range of subnets for 172.16.0.0, which has an original mask of 255.255.0.0 when subnetted by 8 bits, is 172.16.1.0, 172.16.2.0, 172.16.3.0,…,172.16.255.0, each with a mask of 255.255.255.0.

A common way to represent an IP address and its mask is by specifying the address and just the number of bits in the mask. For example, 172.16.1.0 255.255.255.0 can be represented as 172.16.1.0/24 and 172.16.0.0 255.255.0.0 as 172.16.0.0/16.

VLSM is an abstraction of subnetting that allows different masks to be applied to one network number, providing more flexibility and efficiency in the use of IP addresses. In essence, VLSM uses multiple subnet masks to subnet an address multiple times and into different sizes as needed. For example, you can take 172.16.0.0/16, subnet it to 8 bits, take one of the subnets (172.16.1.0/24), and subnet it further to another 4 bits to obtain smaller blocks, such as 172.16.1.0/28, 172.16.1.16/28, 172.16.1.32/28, and so on.

Classless Interdomain Routing

As discussed in the previous section, VLSM helps improve efficiency of address usage within a network. Yet another problem, which became apparent in the early 1990s, was the imminent depletion of IPv4 addresses because of an inefficient allocation method, which assigned large classful chunks of the IP address space (typically Class B addresses) to not-large-enough organizations. To alleviate this problem, organizations were instead assigned multiple Class C addresses that would meet their immediate needs. As the Internet grew in size, however, routing software and hardware became strained by the growing size of the Internet routing tables because of the many individual Class C entries. The introduction of CIDR allowed the IP network number in addresses to be any length, obsolescing the notion address classes and paving the way for resource-saving (memory and processing cycles) efficient aggregation of routes in the Internet tables. However, eliminating the strict boundaries enforced by IP address classes allowed splitting of classful network addresses, such as Class A network numbers, over multiple network domains.

With CIDR, a group of Class C address, such as 192.168.0.0 – 192.168.255.0, can be aggregated as 192.168.0.0/16 instead of floating in the routing tables as 256 individual Class C addresses. Such an aggregation (192.168.0.0/16) is frequently referred to as a *CIDR block* or a *supernet*.

Similarly, CIDR allows an address such as 131.108.0.0/16 to be divided and allocated to four different organizations rather than one, as follows: 131.108.0.0/22, 131.108.64.0/22, 131.108.128.0/22, and 131.108.192.0/22 (see Figure 1-6). See the section, "References," for suggested reading on CIDR.

Figure 1-6   *CIDR blocks.*

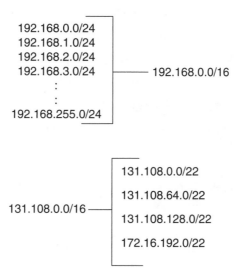

Classification of IP Routing Protocols

Routing between the various segments of a network can be achieved by programming the routers with manual routing information, commonly referred to as *static routes*, or by using a dynamic protocol to automate the collection of routing information and intelligence. The applications or protocols used in the latter case are referred to as *dynamic routing protocols*. In addition, a router can just use a default route for forwarding packets heading to nondirectly connected subnets. The next hop along the default route is referred to as the *default gateway*. Default routes can be generated by either static or dynamic methods. Some common dynamic IP routing protocols in use today are the Routing Information Protocol (RIP) version 1 and version 2, Interior Gateway Routing (IGRP), Enhanced Interior Gateway Protocol (EIGRP), Integrated Intermediate System-to-Intermediate System Routing Protocol (IS-IS), Open Shortest Path Routing Protocol (OSPF), and the Border Gateway Protocol (BGP).

The different breeds of routing protocols have different capabilities related to both architectural design and embedded functionality. The following sections differentiate between commonly used routing protocols. The material covered focuses mostly on unicast routing protocols and distinctions are primarily provided for such protocols.

The following classifications are covered:

- Classful versus classless protocols
- Intradomain versus interdomain protocols
- Distance-vector versus link-state protocols

Classful Versus Classless Protocols

Dynamic IP routing protocols can be categorized into classful and classless protocols, as shown in Table 1-2.

Table 1-2   *Classful and Classless Protocols*

Classful Routing Protocols	Classless Routing Protocol
RIP version 1	RIP version 2
IGRP	EIGRP
	Integrated IS-IS
	OSPF
	BGP

Classful protocols obtain routing information through the exchange of network numbers without mask information and are designed to deal with only classful IP addresses. When IP subnetworks are exchanged, classful protocols arbitrarily apply known masks for matching classful entries that are locally configured. Therefore, such protocols are confused by the notion of a variable prefix length embodied in CIDR. However, classless protocols exchange masking information in addition to network numbers when collecting routing information, allowing them to work flexibly with VLSMs or classless addressing. Table 1-3 summarizes the differences between classful and classless protocols.

Table 1-3   *Attributes of Classful and Classless Protocols*

Classful Routing Protocols	Classless Routing Protocols
Do not support supernets	Support supernets
Do not carry subnet masks in updates	Advertise routes together with subnet masks
Cannot handle VLSMs	Support VLSMs
Do not support discontiguous subnets	Support discontiguous subnets
Mostly periodic updates	Mostly incremental updates
Simple to configure and troubleshoot on Cisco routers	Simple to complex to configure on Cisco routers, and complex to troubleshoot

Intradomain Versus Interdomain Routing

A network of interconnected routers and related systems managed and maintained together by a common administration is often referred to as a *network domain*. A network domain is also sometimes called an *autonomous system*. The Internet consists of several interconnected network domains spanning the whole world. Routing protocols are designed and optimized for use within a domain (intradomain) or between domains (interdomain). Figure 1-7 shows three network domains (AS1, AS2, and AS3) interconnected into a global routing system. Also depicted in the diagram are instances of intradomain and interdomain routing.

Figure 1-7   *Intradomain and interdomain routing.*

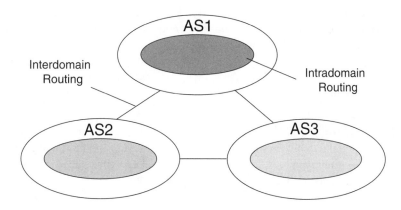

All the routing protocols listed in the preceding section, with the exception of BGP, are optimized for intradomain functionality. Intradomain routing protocols typically do not offer flexibility for policy implementation and also cannot deal with a large number of routes, such as in the global Internet routing table. Obviously, more complex policies will be required to control the exchange of routing information between two separate domains, and this is certainly what BGP is optimized for.

Because of the vastness of the global Internet, the number of routes that need to be handled globally is large. The size of the global Internet routing table is currently in the order of 100,000.00 routes and is slated to grow further. Therefore, an interdomain routing protocol must provide the following basic capabilities:

- Support configuration of complex policies, such as route filtering, tagging, and so on

- Handle a large number of routes under both stable and unstable conditions

- Respond reasonably fast to network changes—that is, sending updates, receiving and processing updates, and selecting alternative routes

An interdomain protocol also must handle multiple peers, with each peer presenting a different view of the same large tables. Currently, only BGP can deliver on all these requirements, and it remains the de facto interdomain routing protocol on the Internet. The current version of BGP for unicast IP routing, version 4, is specified by RFC 1771. BGP is still evolving and has had many enhancements in recent times, including the addition of multiprotocol capabilities in RFC 2858. RFC 2858 specifies multiprotocol extensions to BGP4, providing the architectural framework for multiprotocol label-switching virtual private networks (MPLS VPNs), interdomain multicast routing, and support for IPv6 interdomain routing.

Distance-Vector Versus Link-State Protocols

This chapter discusses the classification of routing protocols based on architectural design (distance-vector and link-state protocols). Essentially, this categorization applies to intra-domain protocols, also known as *Interior Gateway Protocols (IGPs)*. The only surviving interdomain protocol, BGP, was discussed in the preceding section. BGP is normally con-sidered a path-vector protocol because a key attribute it ascribes to routes is a vector of path information known as *AS Path*. An AS Path is a vector of autonomous systems that a route has traversed.

Table 1-4 shows the classification of IGPs into distance-vector and link-state protocols. IGPs are easily placed into these two categories. Distance-vector protocols are simpler in design and tend to be classful. This classful attribute disqualifies them from being viable options for routing in most large modern networks. Distance-vector protocols use periodic update mechanisms that consume a lot of bandwidth resources. Link-state protocols send only incremental updates for any network changes. In general, link-state protocols require a lot more processing and memory resources than distant-vector protocols. They don't have some of the inherent problems associated with distance-vector protocols, however, such as periodic updates, transient loops, count to infinity, and slow convergence issues.

Link-state protocols are more processor-intensive than distance-vector protocols. This is true because a change in the topology of an area would normally trigger a complete SPF run over the entire link-state database, whereas distance-vector protocols perform their computation on the basis of individual routes, requiring less computation for minor topology changes.

A critical advantage of link-state protocols over distance-vector protocols is the capability to support hierarchical network architectures, giving them high potential to scale. Distance-vector protocols work in only flat network architectures and generally have limited scaling capabilities.

Table 1-4   *Distance-Vector and Link-State Protocols*

Protocol	Category	Metric	Algorithm
RIP v1	Distance Vector	Hop count	Bellman-Ford
RIP v2	Distance Vector	Hop count	Bellman-Ford
IGRP	Distance Vector	Composite	Bellman-Ford
EIGRP	Distance Vector	Composite	Diffusing Update Algorithm
OSPF	Link State	Bandwidth-based cost	Shortest Path First
IS-IS	Link State	Manual cost	Shortest Path First

IGRP and EIGRP

IGRP and EIGRP are proprietary protocols developed by Cisco Systems. As indicated by their names, EIGRP is based on IGRP and features critical enhancements, such as support for VLSM, classless routing. EIGRP uses a different algorithm for route computation, as indicated in Table 1-4. Another improvement over IGRP is incremental updates and faster convergence using the concept of feasible successor. EIGRP also features multiprotocol capabilities, supporting routing for IP, Internet Packet Exchange Protocol (IPX), and AppleTalk, whereas IGRP is limited to only IP.

RIP v1 and RIP v2

RIP version 1 and version 2 have origins in the IETF. Version 2 introduces enhancements, such as multicast updates and advertisement of routes, with mask information to support VLSMs and classless addressing.

OSPF

OSPF also originated from the IETF and is probably the most popular and well-understood IGP because of its originality as an IP protocol and extensive coverage in internetworking literature. OSPF has evolved over time into a robust protocol, acquiring the necessary capabilities to build complex routing infrastructures in both enterprise and service provider environments. Although the entirety of the OSPF protocol is complex, its basic concepts and capabilities are not difficult to understand and configure on Cisco routers.

Integrated IS-IS

This book is about the IS-IS protocol and the following chapters provide insights into this protocol's innards and capabilities. IS-IS (ISO 10589) was originally specified by the International Telecommunications Union (ITU), formally the International Organization for Standardization (ISO), as a routing protocol for connectionless network layer protocol (CLNP). IS-IS was first implemented for routing within the DECnet Phase V architecture at Digital Equipment Corporation (DEC). It was later adapted to support IP routing by the IETF in RFC 1195. Despite their different functional designs and origins, IS-IS and OSPF share a lot in common. Both are link-state protocols and use the SPF algorithm for route computation.

Unicast Versus Multicast Routing

IP routing is needed to direct units of data known as *packets* through a network. In a packet-based network, a large file is broken down into packets before it is transmitted from one end of the network to the other. Routing is required in network environments where multiple segments are patched together over a large area. The segments, which can potentially be different transport media, are linked by routers. No routing is required when nodes are connected to the same network segment, such as a LAN or a point-to-point link. The following two kinds of routing are distinguishable by their different approaches to packet forwarding:

- Unicast routing
- Multicast routing

In unicast routing, packets are forwarded toward the single-host addresses in their destination fields. In multicast routing, however, the address in a packet's destination field is a multicast group address. This allows a single packet to be forwarded to multiple receivers in the multicast group, effectively forwarding the same data once to multiple hosts. The discussion so far in this chapter is biased toward unicast protocols because the objective is to provide background material for IS-IS, which is a unicast routing protocol. IP unicast forwarding is designed on a destination-based "forward-to-next- hop" paradigm. This means that each router in the path looks at the destination in a packet and forwards it to the next hop along the best known path the destination. Except in the case of special policy-based forwarding schemes, the source address of a packet is irrelevant in forwarding and exists for the two-way handshake between the origin and destination communication where necessary.

In contrast, multicast forwarding inherently depends on both the source and destination addresses. A method known as *reverse path forwarding (RPF)* is used to check the multicast routing table, for the best path to the source address of a packet through the interface on which the packet was received, before the packet is accepted. The destination address in the multicast packet is a multicast group address. Each multicast group has an associated outgoing interface list (OIF) that determines the location of receivers that have joined the group. After the RPF check is done on the source, copies of the packet are forwarded to the interfaces in the OIF list associated with the group address in the packet. Examples of multicast protocols are Distance-Vector Routing Protocol (DVMRP), Protocol-Independent Multicasting (PIM), Multicast OSPF (MOSPF), and Multicast Source Discovery Protocol. Multicast routing is not further discussed in this section; for more information on multicast routing, read *Developing IP Multicast Networks,* Volume I (Cisco Press, 2000. ISBN: 1-57870-077-9). A recently introduced Cisco IOS security feature known as Unicast Reverse Path Forwarding (Unicast RPF) uses the concept of reverse path checking for controlling unicast forwarding in a manner that successfully addresses Internet Denial of Service (DoS) attacks based on source address spoofing.

Unicast Routing

As mentioned previously, the essence of IP unicast routing is to help routers figure out the next hop to pass on packets, along the best path to a target destination. Choice of the best path is determined by choosing the path with the lowest cost. This best path determination boils down to determination of the data-link or MAC address of the next hop. Each non-directly connected entry in the routing table consists of a prefix, the IP address of the next hop, and the outgoing interface to the next hop.

Actual forwarding may involve extra steps to determine the corresponding data-link address of the next hop from the ARP table or an equivalent address map table for the specific media. If the destination is directly connected, the address resolution retrieves the data-link address of the destination; otherwise, the data-link address of the router at the next hop is obtained.

During forwarding, the original destination IP address of the packet does not change, but the data-link address keeps changing as the packet traverses different links until it arrives at its destination. The data-link information that a router appends to a packet before sending it off to the next hop is referred to as the *Layer 2 rewrite string* (or as just the *MAC rewrite* in the case of LANs).

IP Unicast Forwarding Example

Figure 1-8 shows a simple IP network that consists of three network segments. Each segment is assigned a unique IP subnet. To get to destinations on the segment or same subnet, the ARP protocol is used to resolve the data-link address associated with the destination IP address. To get to a remote segment, however, routing is required. If Host1 needs to forward data to Host2, for example, it relies on ARP to obtain the corresponding MAC address of Host2. If Host1 needs to send data to Host3, which is on another segment, however, it forwards the data first to RT1, which then forwards the data on to RT2, which finally delivers the packets to Host3.

Figure 1-8 *Illustration of IP forwarding.*

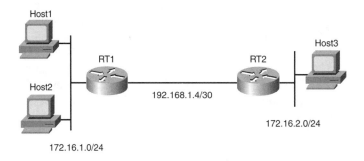

In summary, routing works by finding the corresponding Layer 2 rewrite of the next hop to the destination address in the packet. The IP packet is then encapsulated in a data-link frame with the Layer 2 rewrite and forwarded on to the next hop. The next hop can be the ultimate destination of the packet or a router on the path toward the destination. Figure 1-9 shows a flowchart of IP packet-forwarding process.

Determination of the Layer 2 rewrite string is one of the most important steps in packet forwarding. Other activities related to forwarding include validation of the IP header checksum and reduction of the IP TTL value. IP packet processing also might involve policy enforcement, such as packet filtering, traffic rate limiting, congestion control, latency control through various quality-of-service queuing schemes, and setting of the type of service bits in the IP header. All of this additional packet processing takes time and processing resources, requiring the assistance of various packet-switching optimization schemes in high-speed routers to achieve line-rate forwarding at 10 gigabits per second and beyond. Cisco routers have evolved through various packet-switching mechanisms: Process, Fast, and Cisco Express Forwarding. These switching methods are briefly covered in the section "Cisco Packet-Switching Mechanisms."

Figure 1-9 *IP packet-routing process.*

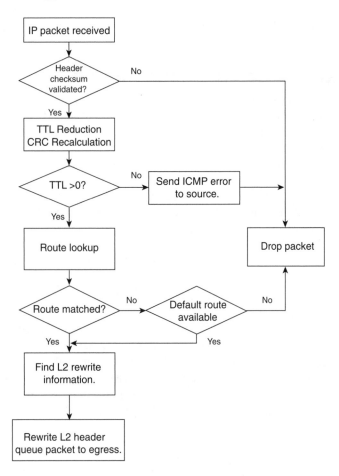

Longest Match Routing

In many cases, before a router selects the best path to a destination, it might run into several similar routes that differ only in their prefix length. Recall from the previous discussion that in today's world of classless routing, routes are no longer differentiated by their classes but by their prefix length, as determined by the subnet masks. For example, the address 192.168.1.1 can match both 192.168.0.0/16 and 192.168.1.0/24 if they are both in the routing table. However, one important rule for matching routes, *longest match routing*, dictates that the matching route with the longest prefix length, 192.168.1.0/24, should be preferred over the less-specific entry, 192.168.0.0/16. This makes sense because the less-specific route is normally a summary route that might have lost specific details during aggregation. Therefore, the more specific entry must be preferred. This basic lookup rule is critical for a router to support VLSMs.

Cisco Packet-Switching Mechanisms

At the beginning of this chapter, the distinction between IP forwarding and IP routing is discussed, and the separation between the forwarding plane and the control plane in modern routers is mentioned. As noted, the control plane is associated with the route processor, which runs the routing protocols. As illustrated in Figure 1-9, actual forwarding of packets is performed by dedicated hardware-based forwarding engines, which are mainly implemented in application-specific integrated circuits (ASICs). ASIC-based forwarding engines are necessary to achieve high forwarding rates. CPU-based forwarding is relatively slow; however, over the years, Cisco has developed various methods for speeding up the lookup process on CPU-based router processors. Fast switching is one such mechanism. Fast switching later evolved into Cisco Express Forwarding (CEF). The predecessor of both fast switching and CEF switching is referred to as *process switching*.

Process Switching

Process switching refers to switching packets by queuing them to the CPU on the route processor at the process level. In this case, every packet-switching request is queued alongside other applications and serviced, in turn, by the CPU on the route processor. The CPU performs route lookup for every packet to determine the Layer 2 rewrite string before the packet is switched to the next hop or destination. Obviously, process switching is slow and can be CPU-intensive. Process switching is illustrated in Figure 1-10.

Figure 1-10 *Illustration of process switching.*

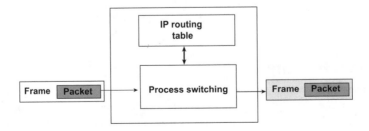

Fast Switching

Fast switching is an enhancement of process switching in which any packet-switching request is first performed at the process level, and the Layer 2 rewrite information obtained is cached for reuse. When fast switching is enabled, the CPU receives an interrupt for any forwarding request to check the IP cache for a matching entry to the destination. If an entry is found, the Layer 2 rewrite is retrieved and the packet is switched immediately. If no entry exists, the packet is queued for process switching. After it is process switched, the Layer 2 rewrite is then cached for reuse. Note that the fast-switching cache is built by process switching the first packet to any destination. Figure 1-11 shows the fast-switching process.

Figure 1-11 *Illustration of fast switching.*

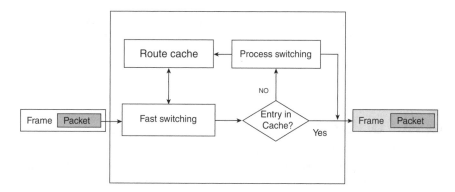

Cisco Express Forwarding

CEF takes fast switching a step further by abandoning the latter's demand-based mechanisms and dependence on process switching to build the fast-switching cache (see Figure 1-12). Instead, CEF predetermines all the Layer 2 rewrite information, where possible, for all known entries in the routing table. This allows CEF to switch at interrupt context for even the first packet to any destination. An exception exists for destinations on connected multipoint media such as LANs, where an ARP process is required for the first packet to any connected host, to obtain Layer 2 rewrite information for the destination. CEF also optimizes storage by using two databases: one for prefixes, called the *forwarding information base (FIB)*; and the other for Layer 2 rewrite information, called the *adjacency database*.

Currently, most Cisco routers have only one active route processor if even more than one are installed; therefore, where process switching is allowed, it is done at only a central location. In routers with distributed architecture, such as the Cisco 7500 Series, however, the fast-switching cache and the CEF tables can be distributed to intelligent interface processors known as *versatile interface processors (VIP)* to enable concurrent distributed forwarding at many locations in the router. The Cisco 12000 Series routers have a fully distributed architecture and also support only distributed CEF switching to achieve high forwarding rates. For more information on packet switching on Cisco routers, read *Inside Cisco IOS Software Architecture* (Cisco Press. 2000. ISBN: 1-57870-181-3) and *Large-Scale IP Network Solutions* (Cisco Press. 2000. ISBN: 1-57870-084-1).

Figure 1-12 *Illustration of CEF switching.*

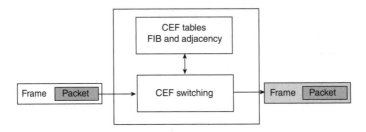

Comments on IPv6

Depletion of the IPv4 address space has been steep with the tremendous growth of the Internet. Efficient and innovative schemes for controlling address usage, such as CIDR, Network Address Translation (NAT), and Dynamic Host Configuration Protocol (DHCP), have helped contain the problem. A limitation of IPv4 is challenges with renumbering, especially in cases where a medium-size network changes service providers. IPv4 addresses are assigned to service providers and portability is an issue. The inability of many sites to renumber as they migrate their networks to new service providers has led to severe fragmentation of the IPv4 address space, exacerbating the already high growth rate of the global Internet routing table. The growth of the Internet routing table and the increasing number of prefixes carried within service provider networks place undue demand for memory and route computation resources on Internet routers. These issues and many other limitations of IPv4 led to several enhancement proposals. These proposals were eventually consolidated into the IETF standard IPv6. In tackling one of the critical limitations of IPv4 (size of the address space), IPv6 proposes a larger 128-bit address size, compared to the 32-bit size of IPv4 addresses. Presumably, the four-times larger address should be large enough to support predicted future growth of the Internet. It might be interesting to note that IPv6 does not completely overhaul the IPv4 architecture but rather improves it in the following key areas:

- Larger address space with flexible renumbering capability
- Simplified header format with improved extensions and options
- Flow labeling for improved quality-of-service handling
- Improved security capabilities for authentication and data-integrity verification

IP mobile networking is one of the key drivers behind IPv6. It is envisaged that rapid evolution of mobile communications and related applications will result in numerous personal communication devices, such as cellular phones and personal digital assistants connecting to the Internet. This, in turn, should drive the need for more IP addresses, differentiated services, and secured data transmission.

An increasing number of data communications equipment vendors are delivering both router and host implementations of IPv6 at the same time as the international IPv6 testbed (6bone) expands to embrace more sites worldwide.

The three important protocols used on the Internet (BGP, IS-IS, and OSPF), as well as RIP, are being enhanced to support IPv6.

IPv6 Addressing

IPv6 retains the IPv4 notions of unicast and multicast addressing but removes the concept of broadcast addressing while introducing another type of address, referred to as *anycast*. The functions of broadcast addresses have been folded into those of multicast addresses. An anycast address represents a group of addresses, where data to the group is delivered to only one of the addresses in the group. Anycast addresses cannot be used as data sources and should be assigned only to routers.

IPv6 employs a constrained hierarchy in assigning addresses to promote efficient aggregation. Concepts such as top-level aggregator (TLA), next-level aggregator (NLA), and site-level aggregator (SLA) have been adopted in the addressing model. The general format of IPv6 addresses is shown in Figure 1-13. The 48 leftmost bits represent a public routing topology (PRT) prefix. A site obtains a PRT from its Internet service provider and uses it as its base prefix to autoconfigure hosts. Renumbering also involves just changing the site's PRT using a newly introduced Router Renumbering (RR) protocol.

To support IPv6, IP protocols originally designed for IPv4 need format changes to modify all occurrences of the 32-bit IPv4 addressing to 128-bit IPv6 fields. In particular, the IS-IS protocol lends itself to carrying additional information because of the flexibility in its packet formats and architectural design.

Figure 1-13 *IPv6 address format.*

TLA – Top level aggregator
NLA – Next level aggregator
SLA – Site Level aggregator
RES – Reserved

Representation of IPv6 addresses is done in hexadecimal because of the address size. Three methods of representation are proposed. The first is preferred for normal representation, another allows for compression of an address when it consists of a continuous string of 0s, and the last enables concatenation of IPv6 and IPv4 addresses in a mixed format. This scheme suggests grouping the bits,16 in a group with a colon separating them. Each 16-bit (2-byte) group is represented in hexadecimal, as follows:

```
FEDC:BA98:7654:3210:FEDC:BA98:7654:3210
```

Because of the length of IPv6 addresses and their encoding in hexadecimal, humans have a greater level of difficulty when handling Ipv6 as compared to the dotted-decimal representation of IPv4. Name-to-address resolution will be key for operator interface requirements. Consequently, work is already in place for extensions to the IPv4 DNS to support IPv6. In an analogy to the IPv4 DNS A record, the new resource record defined for IPv6 is symbolically AAAA (code 28).

Summary

This broad chapter on IP routing concepts provides readers with an overview of IP routing protocols and an understanding of the underlying mechanisms involved in routing packets generally in any IP network and specifically on Cisco routers.

Addressing is a key aspect of routing, and IP addressing bears similar importance in IP routing. Subnetting and classless notions in IP addressing are intended to provide efficient allocation schemes, which effectively result in efficient use of assigned addresses from the public IP address space, as well as conservation of network resources in maintaining IP routing information on routers. Classless addressing provides the framework for prefix-length-based IP addressing schemes, such as CIDR and VLSM. Various types of IP routing protocols exist, differing in protocol design as well as functional capabilities. In general, routing protocols can be classified into various categories, as follows: unicast versus multicast, classful versus classless, intradomain versus interdomain, and distance-vector versus link-state protocols. These classifications provide insights into the capabilities of well-known routing protocols, emphasizing strengths and weaknesses that should be considered when selecting the appropriate routing protocol for a network design project.

The subtle distinction between IP routing and IP forwarding is important for understanding the architecture of modern routers. IP routing extends the notion of IP forwarding to include the process of gathering routing intelligence in a network. The concept of next-hop routing, using the destination address in packets, is the basic forwarding paradigm of IP, even though modern routers can use policy-based mechanisms as well, based on the source address for forwarding. The following three basic IP forwarding methods are supported in Cisco IOS Software: process switching, fast switching, and CEF. Process switching is CPU-based forwarding, and it is much slower than the other switching methods. Fast switching uses a demand-based forwarding cache to speed up the switching process, whereas CEF optimizes further by precomputing the information used for switching packets over the whole of the routing table.

IP networking is still evolving with IPv6 being a fairly recent introduction that is not yet widely accepted. IPv6 provides enhancements to the IPv4 architecture by addressing some of the limitations of the latter, such as the size of the IPv4 address space and problems with renumbering networks. IPv6 addresses are 128 bits long compared to the 32 bits of IPv4 and should provide a large enough address space for further growth of the global Internet.

Review Questions

Complete the following review questions to test your understanding of the concepts covered in this chapter. The answers are listed in Appendix B, "Answers to Review Questions."

1 Name the two planes of operation in a modern router.

2 IP forwarding and IP routing are related concepts. What is the difference between them?

3 Name common classifications of IP routing protocols.

4 Name the three switching mechanisms supported in Cisco IOS Software.

5 What is the critical shortcoming of the IPv4 architecture that IPv6 tries to address and how it is addressed?

References

Bennett, Geoff. *Designing TCP/IP Internetworks*. John Wiley & Sons, 1997. ISBN 0-4712-8643-5.

Bollapragada, V., Murphy C., White R. *Inside Cisco IOS Software Architecture*. Cisco Press, 2000. ISBN 1-57870-181-3.

Christian Huitema. *IPv6, The New Internet Protocol*. Prentice Hall, 1996. ISBN: 0-13-241936-X.

Christian Huitema. *Routing in the Internet. 2nd Edition* Prentice Hall, 2000. ISBN:0-13-022647-5.

Default_XREF_styleREFhttp://www.cisco.com/warp/customer/701/3.html. "Understanding IP Addresses"

Halabi, Bassam. *Internet Routing Architectures*. Cisco Press, 2000. ISBN 157870233x.

Hopps, Christian E. "Routing IPv6 with IS-IS." IETF DRAFT 2001. http://search.ietf.org/internet-drafts/ draft-ietf-isis-ipv6-02.txt.

http://www.cisco.com/warp/public/103/index.shtml

http://www.6bone.net/

IETF RFC 1700, " Assigned Numbers." Raynold J, Postel Jon. 1994.

IETF 1992, RFC 1519, "Classless Inter-Domain Routing (CIDR): An Address Assignment and Aggregation Strategy." Fuller, V., Li, T., Yu, J., Varadhan, K. http://www.ietf.org/rfc/rfc1519.txt?number=1519

IETF RFC 2328, "OSPF version 2," Moy, J. 1998.

IEFT RFC 1800, "Internet Official Protocol Standards," Postel, Jon. 1995.

IETF 1996 RFC 1918, "Address Allocation for Private Internets," Rekhter, Y., Moskowitz, B., Karrenberg, D., de Groot, D. J., Lear, E.

IETF 1999 RFC 2545P, "Use of BGP-4 Multiprotocol Extensions for IPv6 Inter-Domain," Marques, F. Dupont.

ISO 10589, "Intermediate System to Intermediate System Intra-Domain Routing Information Exchange Protocol for Use in Conjunction with the Protocol for Providing the Connectionless-mode Network Service" (ISO 8473).

IETF 1990 RFC 1195, "Use of OSI IS-IS for Routing in TCP/IP and Dual Environments," Callon, R.

IETF RFC 2545, "Use of BGP-4 Multiprotocol Extensions for IPv6 Inter-Domain Routing," Marques, P., Dupont, F.

IETF RFC 2740, "OSPF for IPv6," Coltun, R., Ferguson, D., Moy, J.

IETF RFC 2080, "RIPng for IPv6," Malkin, G., Minnear, R.

Khalid Raza, Mike T. *Large Scale IP Network Solutions*. Cisco Press. 2000. ISBN: 1-57870-084-1.

Miller, Phillip. *TCP/IP Explained*. Digital Press. 1997. ISBN 1-55558-166-8.

Naugle, Mathew. *Network Protocol Handbook*. McGraw Hill. 1994. ISBN 0-07-046461-8.

RFC 1771, "Border Gateway Protocol Version 4 (BGP 4)," Li, Rekhter, 1995.

RFC 2858, "Multi-Protocol Extensions for BGP4," Bates, T., Chandra, R., Rekhter, Y., Katz, D. 2000.

RFC 1058, "Routing Information Protocol, STD 34," Hedrick, C. 1988.

RFC 1723, "RIP v2 carrying Additional Information," Malkin, G. 1994.

RFC 2373, "IP Version 6 Addressing Architecture," Deering, S., Hinden, R. July 1998.

RFC 2546, "6Bone Routing Practice," Durand, A., Buclin, B.

Williamson, Beau. *Developing IP Multicast Networks*. Cisco Press, 2000. ISBN: 1-57870-077-9.

CHAPTER 2

Introduction to the IS-IS Routing Protocol

To understand the innards and underlying operational principles of the Intermediate System-to-Intermediate System (IS-IS) routing protocol, it is important to place it in perspective within the overall scheme of internetworking protocols and related technologies. This chapter provides insight into the roots of the IS-IS protocol and discusses the connectionless networking environment that it was envisioned to support by the International Organization for Standardization (ISO).

The chapter begins with an introduction to the Open System Interconnection (OSI) reference model and then briefly discusses the two types of data communications services specified by ISO within the framework of the OSI reference model: *Connection Network Service (CONS)* and *Connectionless Network Service (CLNS)*. IS-IS was designed as part of the CLNS environment to provide the necessary intelligence for automatic and dynamic routing of data packets in ISO CLNS networking environments. From its inception, the IS-IS protocol has been adapted for IP routing and other capabilities, such as traffic engineering with Multiprotocol Label Switching (MPLS).

ISO Connectionless Network Service

The *International Organization for Standardization (ISO)*, currently known as the *International Telecommunications Union (ITU)*, laid the foundation for standardization of computer networking by defining the seven-layer OSI reference model (see Figure 2-1). The OSI reference model, also known as the OSI stack, is specified in ISO 7498. (The ISO standards documents cited in this chapter can be found at www.itu.org/.)

The OSI reference model is a significant contribution to the foundations and subsequent evolution of data communications and information technology. It provides the architectural framework for developing open standards that allow flexible interconnectivity and interoperability between communications devices from different manufacturers. Although the OSI reference model does not specify the internal details of any communications protocol or system, it provides general guidance regarding design and architecture of such systems. Each of the seven layers in the OSI reference model defines a single service capability and provides a premise for grouping related functional elements into functional layers, thus simplifying and facilitating protocol design. Each functional layer defines specific services provided to the adjacent higher layer. For example, the network layer provides services for the transport layer (see Figure 2-1), whereas the transport layer provides data transport services to the higher layers, thus helping transport user data between communicating devices. Furthermore, data transport services can be either connection-oriented or connectionless. Connection-oriented services require prior setup of a connection along a specific path between communicating nodes before data can be transmitted between them, whereas connectionless services do not.

Figure 2-1   *The OSI reference model.*

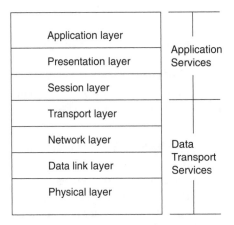

Originally, only connection-oriented communication services (CONS) were specified by the network service definition component in the OSI reference model. CONS was defined by two specifications: X.25 Packet-Level Protocol for Data Terminal Equipment (ISO 8208) and Network Service Definition (ISO 8348).

Later amendments to the network services specification, which appeared in "Network Service Definition, Amendment 1," defined the capabilities for enabling connectionless communication between network devices, referred to as Connectionless Network Services (CLNS). Unlike CONS, CLNS does not require a predefined and presetup of the end-to-end path for forwarding data packets between two communicating devices. Instead, it provides a datagram service in which each data packet is forwarded independently by routers along the currently known best path between the source and destination. The connectionless datagram service defined by CLNS is supported by the following ISO protocols (see Figure 2-2):

- **ISO 8473**—Connectionless Network Protocol (CLNP) for providing the CLNS

- **ISO 9542**—End System-to-Intermediate System (ES-IS) routing exchange protocol for use in conjunction with the protocol for providing the CLNS

- **ISO 10589**—Intermediate System-to-Intermediate System (IS-IS) intradomain routing exchange protocol for use in conjunction with the protocol for providing the connectionless-mode service

CLNP, ES-IS, and IS-IS are specified as separate network layer protocols, coexisting at Layer 3 of the OSI reference model. They are differentiated by the value of the Initial Protocol Identifier (IPI) field in the first octet of their encoded protocol formats, as follows:

CLNP: 10000001 (0x81)
ES-IS: 10000010 (0x82)
IS-IS: 10000011 (0x83)

Figure 2-2   *Diagram of ISO protocols and specifications.*

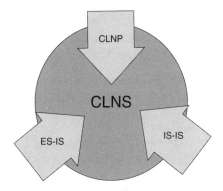

CLNP

The Connectionless Network Protocol is similar to the Internet Protocol (IP), but specified for providing network services for ISO transport protocols rather than the transport protocols in the TCP/IP suite. Like IP, CLNP is defined to rely minimally on the underlying data link layer, which makes it virtually independent of the underlying physical medium. The physical medium can be either point-to-point (as is the case with most wide-area network [WAN] connectivity) or broadcast (as in local-area network [LAN] connectivity). Unlike IP, however, which is the only network layer protocol of TCP/IP and ultimately encapsulates all higher layer protocols, including routing and user applications, CLNP coexists at the network layer, ES-IS and ES-IS, all of which are defined to support the ISO CLNS environment. That is, CLNP, ES-IS, and IS-IS are all network layer protocols and are encapsulated independently in data-link frames. The ISO network layer protocol family is identified at the data-link layer by protocol type 0xFEFE.

This book does not delve into CLNP further, except to the extent that it pertains to the subject matter at hand: the IS-IS routing protocol.

ES-IS

The End System-to-Intermediate System (ES-IS) routing exchange protocol automates information exchange and facilitates adjacency discovery between ISO end systems and routers connected to the same network segment or link. The routers transmit intermediate system hello (ISH) messages and the hosts transmit end system hello (ESH) messages as part of the ES-IS protocol. The hellos, which are transmitted between directly connected nodes, convey network and data-link addresses of the communicating nodes. The hellos are also referred to as configuration information. The end systems forward packets to nonconnected devices through the routers.

Another type of packet used within the ES-IS protocol is called *route redirection (RD)*. A route redirection packet is sent by a router to an end system to inform it of a better path to reach a specific destination of interest. The function of ISO RDs is similar to those of Internet Control Message Protocol (ICMP) redirects used in IP environments. Basically, the operation of the ES-IS protocol between routers and end systems in the ISO environment can be related to the combined operation of the ICMP, Address Resolution Protocol (ARP), and Dynamic Host Configuration Protocol (DHCP) within the IP framework.

ES-IS is not relevant to IP workstations and servers that are involved in processing and transfer of only IP datagrams. For such IP devices, IP ARP provides the necessary network-to-data-link address resolution that might be needed to locate routers and other directly connected hosts. IP hosts also usually use static default routes for their default gateway, even though it is not uncommon for some advanced servers to support simple IP routing protocols, such as the Routing Information Protocol (RIP). Some modern IP servers even support the more sophisticated Open Shortest Path First (OSPF) Protocol for IP routing.

Some aspects of the operation of the IS-IS protocol are dependent on functions provided by the ES-IS protocol; therefore, even in situations where IS-IS is used for routing only IP on Cisco routers, the ES-IS protocol is needed to provide background support. For example, IS-IS point-to-point adjacency formation is preceded by the exchange of ES-IS-related ISHs between the two neighbor routers.

The IS-IS Routing Protocol

Specified in ISO 10589, the IS-IS routing protocol was intended to provide a way to dynamically exchange routing information between routers running CLNP in the ISO CLNS environment. CLNP was designed to use a hop-by-hop route-selection mechanism to move data within a network. The IS-IS protocol was specified to automate the best path calculation and selection process.

The design goals of IS-IS included the following:

- Function as an intradomain routing protocol
- Present a global view of the network for optimal routing decisions
- Provide fast convergence in case of failures
- Provide network stability
- Efficiently use network resources, such as router memory, CPU cycles, and network bandwidth

To achieve these goals, IS-IS was designed as a link-state routing protocol and optimized for use within a single network domain; therefore, it provides Interior Gateway Protocol functionality. IS-IS supports a two-level routing (level 1 and level 2 routing) designed to scale routing over large domains. It also uses the Dijkstra shortest path first (SPF) algorithm to optimize route calculation, path selection, and to achieve fast convergence.

Integrated IS-IS

The Internet Engineering Task Force (IETF) RFC 1195, "Use of OSI IS-IS for Routing in TCP/IP and Dual Environments," specifies the version of the IS-IS protocol, commonly known as *Integrated IS-IS* or *Dual IS-IS*. Integrated IS-IS adapts the original IS-IS protocol that was specified for CLNS environments, for also routing IP. It is interesting to note that Integrated IS-IS is one of few protocols that provides an integrated framework for concurrent processing of more than one network layer protocol; in this case, IP and CLNP. Other routing protocols, such as the OSPF, usually support routing for only one type Layer 3 protocol. OSPF deals only with routing for IP. Integrated IS-IS can be used for routing in CLNP-only or IP-only networks, as well as in dual environments, which have both CLNP and IP traffic.

This book focuses on the use of Integrated IS-IS in IP networks and specifically on the service provider networks that make up the Internet. Even though not inherently designed for routing IP, the successful use of IS-IS for IP routing on the Internet led to development of many proprietary features outside of RFC 1195 to improve usability and to provide flexibility and scalability. The IETF has recently reopened the IS-IS Working Group to explore possibilities of standardizing some of the vendor-specific features of Integrated IS-IS and developing new standards to meet the requirements of emerging applications, such as Multiprotocol Label Switching (MPLS) traffic engineering. Many recently standardized capabilities of IS-IS are documented as RFCs, whereas others are still under review in the IETF standards track. Also, a second version of ISO 10589, which would include most of these new capabilities, is still undergoing review (at the time of writing) and should be published soon. IETF RFCs and draft publications that are relevant to the subject matter of this book are mentioned where necessary.

Chapter Summary

The IS-IS routing protocol is one of three network layer protocols specified by ISO to support the CLNS. The others are CLNP and ES-IS. Even though IS-IS was designed for routing ISO CLNP packets, it has been adapted for use in IP environments as Integrated IS-IS.

Integrated IS-IS has evolved over the years into a scalable, robust, and easy-to-use Interior Gateway Routing Protocol (IGP) that can operate in dual mode to support overlayed IP and ISO CLNS networks. However, IS-IS has probably gained more popularity on the Internet, where its primary application is for intradomain IP routing. As an IGP in an Internet routing domain or autonomous system, Integrated IS-IS plays a critical supportive role for the Border Gateway Protocol (BGP). BGP is designed with more elaborate policy-handling capabilities and can handle a significantly large number of routes of the scale that can be found on the Internet.

IS-IS is a link-state protocol and therefore gathers routing information from adjacent neighbors into a link-state database and uses the SPF algorithm (named after Dijkstra) to determine the best paths to destinations within the network.

In recent years, the Integrated IS-IS has been further enhanced to handle emerging networking technologies, such as Traffic Engineering with Multiprotocol Label Switching (MPLS/TE).

Review Questions

1 Name the three network layer protocols that support the ISO CLNS.

2 In comparing the layers of the TCP/IP protocols suite and the ISO CLNS architecture, describe how the Internet Protocol (IP) differs from the ISO Connectionless Network Protocol (CLNP).

3 What is the use of the Intradomain Routing Protocol Discriminator in the ISO network layer protocol packet headers?

4 What was IS-IS originally designed for?

5 How is IS-IS used in an IP network?

6 Describe any similarities or differences between the ES-IS protocol and IP ARP.

References

Adrian Tang, Sophia Scoggins. *Open Networking with OSI*. Prentice-Hall, 1992. ISBN 0-13-351842-6

James Martin, Joe Leben. *DECnet Phase IV – An OSI Implementation*. Digital Press, 1992. ISBN 1-55558-076-9

ISO 7498 AD1: Information Processing Systems – Open Systems Interconnection – Basic Reference Model – Addendum 1: Connectionless-Mode Transmission

ISO 7498: Information Processing Systems – Open Systems Interconnection – Basic Reference Model

CHAPTER 3

Integrated IS-IS Routing Protocol Concepts

A span of interconnected routers operated and managed by the same administrative group is referred to as an *autonomous system* of routers or a *routing domain*. Such a system of routers allows forwarding of data traffic from one location to the other. The current IS-IS specification, ISO 10589, refers to network nodes as *intermediate systems*, but this book uses the equivalent terminology of *routers* more frequently because it is more popular in current networking literature.

Individual routing domains are interconnected to form larger networks, such as the Internet, allowing transfer of data from one routing domain to the other over a large geographic span. Routers use *routing protocols* to learn about various locations within local or remote network domains. The two basic types of routing protocols follow:

- **Interior Gateway Protocols (IGPs)**—Optimized only for operation within a single network domain. IGPs are also known as intradomain routing protocols.

- **Exterior Gateway Protocols (EGPs)**—Optimized for exchange of routing information between domains. EGPs are also referred to as interdomain routing protocols.

IS-IS is designed and optimized to provide IGP functionality. The Border Gateway Protocol (BGP) is a well-known routing protocol with extensive capabilities for interdomain routing.

Typically, routing protocols support only one network layer protocol (Layer 3 in the OSI reference model). Therefore, when you use routers to provide connectivity for multiple Layer 3 protocols concurrently, they are usually configured with different routing protocols for each type of Layer 3 protocol supported. This approach is referred to as *ships in the night*.

As mentioned in the preceding chapter, Integrated IS-IS supports two network layer protocols: ISO CLNP and IP. Another routing protocol, which supports multiple Layer 3 protocols, is the Cisco proprietary Enhanced Interior Gateway Routing Protocol (EIGRP). EIGRP can be used to route IP, the Internet Packet Exchange Protocol (IPX), and AppleTalk all at the same time. Popular routing protocols that support only one network layer protocol include the NetWare Link Services Protocol (NLSP), which is based on the IS-IS protocol and supports only IPX; the Open Shortest Path First (OSPF) Protocol supports only IP. Versions 1 and 2 of the Routing Information Protocol (RIP) are also IP-only routing protocols. IS-IS and OSPF are similar in many regards and are the two most popular IGPs that are widely deployed in Internet service provider, IP-based enterprise networks.

IS-IS Routing Domain

An IS-IS routing domain is a network in which all the routers run the Integrated IS-IS routing protocol to support intradomain exchange of routing information. The network environment can be IP-only, ISO CLNP-only, or both. The IS-IS protocol was originally intended to support only CLNP. RFC 1195 adapts the original IS-IS specification (ISO 10589) to support IP, in what is referred to as Integrated IS-IS. The following implementation requirements are specified by RFC 1195:

- Pure IP domains route only IP traffic but support forwarding and processing of OSI packets required for IS-IS operation.

- Pure ISO domains carry only ISO traffic including those required for IS-IS operation.

- A dual domain routes both IP and OSI CLNP traffic simultaneously.

It is also possible to design a dual domain so that some areas route IP only, whereas others route CLNP only, and yet others route both IP and CLNP. RFC 1195 imposes restrictions on the manner in which IP and CLNP can be mixed within an area. The underlying goal is to achieve consistent routing information within an area by having identical Level 1 link-state databases on all routers in that area. Hence, all routers in an area are required to be configured in the same way, either for IP-only or CLNP-only or both. To clarify further, a router is not allowed to have a set of links dedicated to IP only and another set to CLNP and yet another set to both protocols. At the domain level, there is no restriction on mixing areas that are uniformly IP-only with other areas that are uniformly CLNP-only or uniformly configured for both IP and CLNP. In order words, all links in an area must be configured the same way, but links in the backbone can have the attached routers configured differently.

IS-IS Areas and Routing Hierarchies

As specified in ISO 10589 and RFC 1195, the IS-IS protocol supports a two-level hierarchy for managing and scaling routing in large networks. A network domain can be carved out in a planned way or arbitrarily by the network designer or architect into small segments known as areas. This allows hierarchical routing to be leveraged for efficient routing within the domain. Integrated IS-IS uses the legacy CLNP node-based addresses to identify routers even in pure IP environments. The CLNP addresses, which are known as Network Service Access Points (NSAPs), are made up of three components: an area identifier (area ID) prefix, followed by a system identifier (SysID), and an N-selector. The N-selector refers to the network service user, such as a transport protocol or the routing layer. It has similar interpretation as the application port number used in the IP Transmission Control Protocol (TCP). The CLNP addressing scheme is introduced later in this chapter (see the section "Addressing Concepts in Integrated IS-IS") and discussed further in detail in Chapter 4, "Addressing in Integrated IS-IS."

For now, just remember that each IS-IS router has a unique SysID, which together with the area ID and an N-selector value of 0x00 forms a special NSAP known as the node's network entity title (NET).

A group of routers belong to the same area if they share a common area ID. Note that all routers in an IS-IS domain must be associated with a single physical area, which is determined by the area ID in the NSAP. In practice, an IS-IS router can be configured with multiple NSAPs all with different area IDs and same SysID in situations where the router is "homed" to multiple areas. As discussed later, however, multihoming merges all the areas involved into a single physical area. Routers belonging to a common area and engaged in Level 1 routing are referred to as Level 1 routers. In CLNP routing, Level 1 routing involves collecting SysID and adjacency information through all routers and hosts in the local area. Routers in different areas exchange routing information through Level 2 routing and are referred to as Level 2 or backbone routers. In CLNP Level 2 routing, routers exchange area prefix information with their peers. For IP routing, however, intra-area IP prefixes are exchanged within the area in Level 1 routing. The IP prefixes originated in the various areas are then exchanged between areas in Level 2 routing by routers connected to the backbone.

In most designs with routing hierarchy, the Level 2 routers are also Level 1 routers by virtue of their identification with a certain area. Therefore, in IS-IS, a router can function as Level 1-only or Level 2-only and possibly as both Level 1 and Level 2 (Level 1-2). Level 1-2 routers act as border routers to their respective areas, providing connectivity to other areas. The Level 2 backbone is essentially a virtual IS-IS area consisting of routers engaged in Level 2 routing (see Figure 3-1). The Level 2 stretch in a network must be contiguous, requiring all routers to be interconnected. Because partition repair is not supported in Cisco IOS and most other implementations, the contiguity requirement also applies to Level 1 areas. In a hierarchical network, some Level 2-only routers could be embedded in the backbone without impacting traffic flow between the respective areas supported by Level 1-2 routers. Existing IS-IS specfications require only Level 2 routers to provide connectivity to external domains; however, Cisco IOS allows redistribution of external routes into Level 1 for historical and practical reasons.

Level 1-only routers are aware of the local area topology only, which involves all the nodes in the area and the next-hop routers to reach them. Level 1 routers depend on Level 2 routers for access to other areas and forward all traffic to destinations outside the area to the closest Level 2 router.

Cisco routers running IS-IS can be configured to be either Level 1-only, Level 2-only, or both. By default, they are both Level 1 and Level 2, and special configuration is required to disable Level 1 or Level 2 capability. Caution must be exercised when disabling either capability because this might introduce disruptive inconsistencies into the routing environment. In Figure 3-1, routers RTA-1, RTA-2, RTA-3, and RTX must be Level 2-capable to participate in routing between the areas. RTX can be in its own dedicated area and because it doesn't connect to any Level 1 routers, it can be configured to be Level 2-only. However, the others must be Level 1-2 and each identified with a specific area for which it provides interarea connectivity. RTB-n, RTC-n (n = 1,2,3) can be configured to be Level 1-only if they don't need to connect to the backbone.

Figure 3-1   *IS-IS areas.*

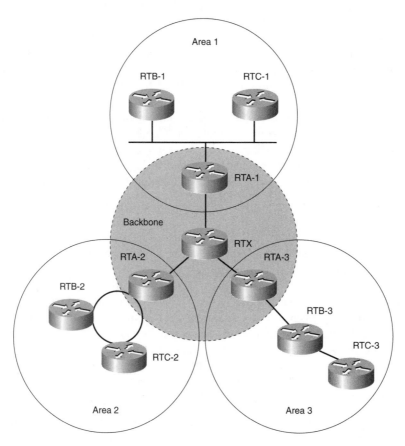

IS-IS Packets

Before delving into other concepts behind the IS-IS protocol, you need to understand the fundamentals of IS-IS packets and packet formats. This knowledge aids in the understanding of the capabilities of the protocol and how it works. Connectionless protocols, such as CLNP and IP, transmit data in little chunks known as packets. In ISO 10589, packets are referred to as *protocol data units (PDU)*. This book refers to them as packets in conformity with IP terminology. Multiple packet types are used in connectionless environments, with data and routing information packets being predominant.

This section briefly reviews the types of packets used in the IS-IS protocol and their general format. IS-IS packets have three categories: hello packets, link-state packets, and sequence number packets. Hello packets are used to establish and maintain adjacencies between IS-IS neighbors. Link-state packets are used to distribute routing information between IS-IS nodes. Sequence number packets are used to control distribution of link-state packets, essentially providing mechanisms for synchronization of the distributed Link-State databases on the routers in an IS-IS routing area.

Hello packets have the following subcategories:

- LAN Level 1 hello packets (PDU Type 15)
- LAN Level 2 hello packets (PDU Type 16)
- Point-to-point hello packets (PDU Type 17)

Link-state packets have the following subcategories:

- Level 1 link-state packets (PDU Type 18)
- Level-2 link-state packets (PDU Type 20)

Finally, sequence number packets have the following subcategories:

- Level 1 complete sequence number packets (PDU Type 24)
- Level 2 complete sequence number packets (PDU Type 25)
- Level 1 partial sequence number packets (PDU Type 26)
- Level 2 partial sequence number packets (PDU Type 27)

IS-IS Packet Formats

Each type of IS-IS packet is made up of a header and a number of optional variable-length fields containing specific routing-related information. Each variable-length field has a 1-byte type label that describes the information it contains. The value of the variable-length field is the specific information it contains. Typically, the value is composed of repeated blocks of similar information, the length of which is specified in a 1-byte length field. Type, length, and value form a *tuple (TLV)*, which has become a synonym for variable-length fields. The types of variable-length fields are actually specified as numeric code values. Both current IS-IS specifications, ISO 10589 and RFC 1195, use *code* in rather than *type*, but TLV has gained more popularity than CLV in current networking literature because it is used in other protocol specifications.

The different types of IS-IS packets have a slightly different composition of the header fields but the first eight fields, each 1-byte long, are repeated in all packets (see Figure 3-2). Each type of packet then has its own set of additional header fields, which are then followed by TLVs. The additional header fields vary in composition, length, and order of the information. Figure 3-2 shows the generic packet format and the common fields shared by all IS-IS packets.

Figure 3-2 *IS-IS header fields.*

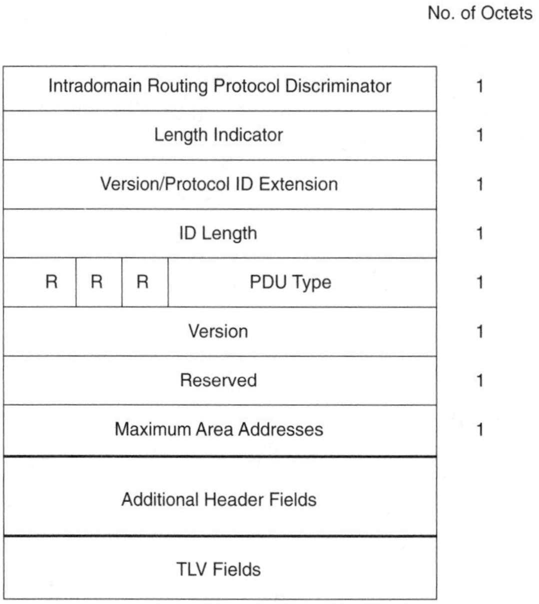

No. of Octets

Field	No. of Octets
Intradomain Routing Protocol Discriminator	1
Length Indicator	1
Version/Protocol ID Extension	1
ID Length	1
R R R PDU Type	1
Version	1
Reserved	1
Maximum Area Addresses	1
Additional Header Fields	
TLV Fields	

- **Intradomain Routing Protocol Discriminator**—This is the network layer identifier assigned to IS-IS, as specified by ISO 9577. Its value is 10000011 (binary), 0x83 (hexadecimal), or 131 (decimal).
- **Length Indicator**—Length of the packet header fields in octets.
- **Version/Protocol ID Extension**—Currently has a value of 1.
- **ID Length**—Indicates length of the source ID (SysID) field. A value of 0 implies a length of 6 bytes; a value of 255 implies 0 length. Other possible values are 1 to 8 for actual length in bytes.
- **PDU Type**—Specifies the type of IS-IS packet. The three types of IS-IS packets are hello packets, link-state packets (LSPs), and sequence number packets (SNPs).
- **Version**—The value is 1.
- **Reserved**—Unused bits. Set to 0s.
- **Maximum Area Addresses**—Values between 1 and 254 for actual number. A value of 0 implies a maximum of three addresses per area.

The Type, Length, and Value attributes of TLV fields have the following meaning:

- **Type**—A number code for a specific TLV. ISO10589 uses the word *code* in place of *type*. However, *type* seems to be preferred in IETF and Cisco literature on IS-IS.
- **Length**—Length specifies the total length of the TLV.
- **Value**—Value indicates the content of the TLV.

All packets in each category of packet type have similar information in the header. The TLV fields are appended to the header to make up the entire packet. Each type of packet supports only specific TLV fields, which might optionally be present in a real packet. This topic is explored further later in this chapter.

Table 3-1 lists TLVs specified in ISO 10589.

Table 3-1   *ISO 10589 TLVs*

TLV	Type	Description
Area Address	1	Area address(es) of source node
Intermediate System Neighbors	2	Neighboring routers and pseudonodes (appended to the link-state packet)
End System Neighbors	3	Connected workstations
Partition Designated Level 2 Intermediate System	4	Level 2 neighbors that interconnect pieces of a partitioned area with a virtual link over the Level 2 area
Prefix Neighbors	5	Reachable NSAP prefixes (not including local area prefixes)
Intermediate System Neighbors	6	LAN-connected routers from which IS-IS hello packets have been received (appended to LAN hello)
Not Specified	7	
Padding	8	Padding for hello packets to maximum transmission unit (MTU)
LSP Entries	9	Link-state information
Authentication Information	10	Information for IS-IS packet authentication

Enhancements to the original IS-IS protocol as specified in ISO 10589 are normally achieved through the introduction of new TLV fields. Enhancements, attained in this manner include TLVs introduced by RF1195 for Integrated IS-IS and recent modifications to support Multiprotocol Label Switching (MPLS) Traffic Engineering. Table 3-2 lists the TLVs introduced by RFC 1195. Note that a key strength of the IS-IS protocol design lies in the ease of extension through the introduction of new TLVs rather than new packet types.

Table 3-2   *RFC 1195 TLVs*

TLV	Type	Description
IP Internal Reachability Information	128	Intradomain IS-IS routes
Protocols Supported	129	Protocol identifiers of supported network layer protocols (for example, IP and CLNP)
IP External Reachability Information	130	Routes external to the IS-IS domain, such as those imported from other sources via redistribution
Interdomain Routing Protocol Information	131	For transparent distribution of interdomain routes
IP Interface Address	132	IP address of the outgoing interface
Authentication Information	133	IS-IS packet authentication (similar to Type 10, but doesn't define authentication Type 255)

IS-IS Protocol Functions

The routing layer functions provided by the IS-IS protocol can be grouped into two main categories: subnetwork-dependent functions and subnetwork-independent functions. In IS-IS, subnetwork refers to the data-link layer. This notion fundamentally differs from IP terminology, in which a subnetwork refers to an IP address subnet. Only two types of IS-IS subnetworks are of practical significance in current applications of the IS-IS protocol: point-to-point and broadcast links.

The subnetwork-dependent functions relate to capabilities for interfacing with the data-link layer and primarily involve operations for detecting, forming, and maintaining routing adjacencies with neighboring routers over various types of interconnecting network media or links. The ES-IS protocol and certain elements of CLNP are key to the operation of the subnetwork-dependent functions.

Subsequent sections explore the subnetwork-dependent functions. In those sections, you will learn about IS-IS links, IS-IS adjacencies, and types of IS-IS systems (nodes).

The subnetwork-independent functions provide the capabilities for exchange and processing of routing information and related control information between adjacent routers as validated by the subnetwork-dependent functions.

The IS-IS routing engine, discussed later in this section, elaborates on the relationship between subsystems (processes and databases) that provide the subnetwork-independent functions within the framework of a conventional router.

Subnetwork-Dependent Functions

The role of the subnetwork-dependent functions of the IS-IS protocol was described in the previous section. Critical component functions are further described within this section. The IS-IS routing protocol distinguishes two main types of subnetworks or links in a network: general topology subnetworks and broadcast subnetworks.

General Topology Subnetworks

General topology subnetworks are permanent or dynamically established point-to-point links. An example of the former is Packet over SONET/SDH. Asynchronous Transfer Mode (ATM) point-to-point switched virtual circuit (SVC) is an example of the latter.

Broadcast Subnetworks

Broadcast subnetworks are multipoint or local-area network (LAN) media with broadcast capabilities, such as Ethernet, Fiber Distributed Data Interface (FDDI), or the Cisco-invented Dynamic Packet Transport Technology (DPT).

NOTE   The Cisco implementation of the IS-IS routing protocol operates in broadcast mode over nonbroadcast multiaccess (NBMA) technologies, such as Frame Relay and ATM, when configured in multipoint mode. This mode of operation requires the use of Layer 3-to-Layer 2 address map statements and assumes a full-mesh permanent virtual circuit (PVC) environment. In certain cases, special workarounds might be required for effective application of IS-IS in such environments. However, for such media, point-to-point configuration is highly recommended.

IS-IS Network Nodes

The ISO Connectionless Network Protocol is specified for transfer of data between two main categories of network devices:

- **End systems**—The analogy for an end system is a workstation or network host with limited routing capability.

- **Intermediate systems**—These are network devices such as routers with extensive packet-forwarding capabilities. The word *intermediate* refers to the capabilities of routers as intermediate forwarding or relay devices. Routers are referred to as *gateways* in some older networking literature.

The IS-IS routing protocol is designed to provide routing intelligence for intermediate systems, whose role in the network is to relay data between user applications running on distantly located end systems. IS-IS allows the gathering and processing of routing information by routers within the same domain. Routers can locate end systems on directly connected segments using ES-IS for CLNP or ARP for IP. Therefore, the combination of ES-IS and IS-IS or ARP allows routers to perform their primary function of helping move data packets from one end system to another within the network domain.

Adjacencies

The subnetwork-dependent functions of the routing layer provided by IS-IS are responsible for discovering, establishing, and maintaining adjacencies between the routers in an IS-IS domain. As stated previously, IS-IS works in conjunction with ES-IS and certain elements of the CLNP protocol to achieve this. No special configuration is required on Cisco routers to enable ES-IS. The ES-IS operation is enabled automatically when IS-IS is configured on Cisco routers, and it runs as a background process to support the operation of IS-IS. The subnetwork-dependent functions of IS-IS work with ES-IS to determine network layer addresses of all adjacent neighbors (both end systems and routers). On multiaccess links, data-link addresses (for example, MAC addresses; also referred to as subnetwork points of attachment [SNPAs]) are obtained for all adjacent neighbors and stored in the adjacency database.

ES-IS Adjacencies

ES-IS is designed for host-to-router communication in a pure ISO environment, such as implemented in Digital's DECnet Phase V networking architecture. In an IP environment, ES-IS is relevant only to the extent that it facilitates router-to-router adjacency formation. IP hosts do not participate in the ES-IS protocol and instead rely on ARP for Layer 3-to-Layer 2 address resolution in determining the Layer 2 addresses of LAN-connected hosts and the IP default gateway. In CLNP environments, end systems and routers use the ES-IS protocol to discover each other by sending ESHs and ISHs to well-known LAN broadcast addresses. End systems send ESHs targeted at the routers to 09-00-2B-00-00-05 (AllIntermediateSystems), and routers send the ISHs to 09-00-2B-00-00-04 (AllEndSystems). ES-IS allows end systems to locate the closest router for access to other nondirectly connected media. Routers, in turn, learn about the location of end systems through the ES-IS adjacency information. Routers also distribute the SysID of known end systems to other routers within the same area by means of Level 1 IS-IS routing. Other ES-IS events, such as redirection, are beyond the scope of this book.

Figure 3-3   *End System Hello (ESH) and Intermediate System Hello (ISH).*

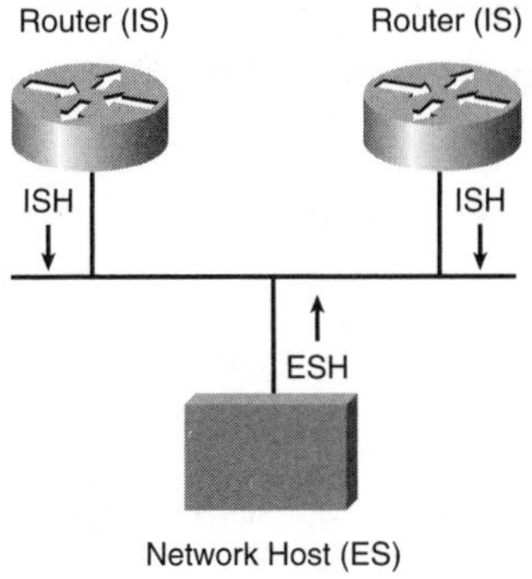

IS-IS Adjacencies

Directly connected routers enabled for IS-IS routing go beyond the ES-IS adjacencies described in the preceding section to form IS-IS adjacencies. The IS-IS adjacencies on point-to-point links are formed and maintained a little differently than on broadcast links. Consequently, different types of IS-IS hellos (IIHs) are used. The three types of IIHs follow:

- **Point-to-point IIH**—Used over point-to-point links
- **Level 1 LAN IIH**—Used over broadcast links, but for Level 1 adjacencies
- **Level 2 LAN IIH**—Used on broadcast links, but for Level 2 adjacencies

Like all IS-IS packets, the IS-IS hello packets are made up of headers and variable-length fields. The point-to-point IIHs and LAN IIHs have slightly varied information in their header area. Mostly, however, similar information is contained in the header area of both packet types except that point-to-point IIHs have a local circuit ID in place of the LAN ID in LAN IIHs. Also, point-to-point IIHs do not have the priority information found in LAN IIHs. As specified in ISO 10589, TLV types used in point-to-point IIHs are limited to the following:

- Area Addresses (Type 1)
- Padding (Type 8)
- Authentication Type (Type 10)

LAN IIHs support the following TLVs fields:

- Area Addresses (Type 1)
- Intermediate System Neighbors (Type 6)
- Padding (Type 8)
- Authentication Information (Type 10)

NOTE   The absence of information on intermediate system neighbors in point-to-point IIHs as specified in the original hello format caused reliability issues in forming point-to-point adjacencies. A recent IEFT draft proposes TLV Type 240 to address this problem. This draft is discussed later in this chapter.

Successful formation of an IS-IS adjacency between two nodes paves the way for the exchange of IS-IS routing information by using special routing information and control packets known as link-state packets (LSP) and sequence number packets (SNP), respectively. LSP and SNP exchange between IS-IS routers is discussed in-depth in Chapter 5, "IS-IS Link-State Database." The type of adjacency formed between neighbor routers determines the type of routing information that is exchanged between them. As mentioned previously, IS-IS routing has a two-level hierarchy, Level 1 and Level 2, and the types of adjacencies that can be formed are consistent with this hierarchy. As specified, routers in the same area must be able to form at least a Level 1 adjacency, regardless of the type of interconnecting links (point-to-point or broadcast). On Cisco routers, the default mode of operation for routers in the same area, is to form both Level 1 and Level 2 adjacencies. Routers that belong to different areas can form only Level 2 adjacencies. Point-to-point and broadcast adjacencies are further covered in detail in later sections of this chapter.

Hello Interval, Hello Multiplier, and Hello Holdtime

Routers periodically send hello packets to adjacent peers, every *hello interval*. The hello interval is jittered, up to about 25 percent, to reduce the likeliness of synchronized IIH transmission over the network. On Cisco routers, the default value of the hello interval is 10 seconds for ordinary routers and 3.3 seconds for the designated intermediate system (DIS) on a multiaccess link. IS-IS uses the concept of hello multiplier to determine how many hello packets can be missed from an adjacent neighbor before declaring it "dead." The maximum time lapse allowed between receipt of two consecutive hello packets received is referred to as the *holdtime*. The holdtime is defined as the product of the hello interval and the hello multiplier. On Cisco routers, the default value of the hello multiplier is 3; therefore, the default hold time is 30 seconds. If a router does not receive a hello from a neighbor before the holdtime expires, the adjacency is torn down. The holdtime is reset anytime a hello is received. Hellos are transmitted periodically by routers to neighbors at the expiration of the hello interval. However, the following conditions will also trigger immediate transmission:

Any change in network conditions causing changes in TLV information advertised in the most recent hello transmitted

Election to or resignation from LAN DIS position

IS-IS Point-to-Point Adjacencies

IS-IS adjacencies on point-to-point links are initialized by receipt of ISHs through the ES-IS protocol. This is followed by the exchange of point-to-point IIHs. The type of adjacency formed will depend on the parameters exchanged in the IIHs. The IIHs also are sent periodically over the link to every hello interval to maintain the adjacency. On Cisco routers, the default hello interval for point-to-point links is 10 seconds. The format of the point-to-point hello packet is shown in Figure 3-4.

Figure 3-4   *Point-to-Point Hello Packet (PDU Type 17).*

No. of Octets

Intradomain Routing Protocol Discriminator		1
Length Indicator		1
Version/Protocol ID Extension		1
ID Length		1
R | R | R | PDU Type		1
Version		1
Reserved		1
Maximum Area Addresses		1
Reserved (6 bits) | Circuit Type		1
Source ID		ID Length
Holding Time		2
PDU Length		2
Local Circuit ID		1
TLV Fields		Variable Length

A router performs checks on a received IIH to confirm various parameters in the hello header, such as SysID length, Maximum Area Addresses, and so on. System capabilities are advertised in the appended TLVs. The TLV fields that might be appended to the point-to-point hello packet are Area Addresses (Type 1), Padding (Type 8), and Authentication (Type 10) information. Padding is applied in increments of 2 bytes up to at least 1 byte short of the physical MTU of the outgoing interface.

The following is a list of packet type-specific fields in the header of a point-to-point hello:

- **Circuit Type**—Level 1, Level 1-2, or Level 2 only
- **Source ID**—System ID of the router that generated the hello packet
- **Holding Time**—Maximum interval between two consecutive hello packets before the router is considered no longer available
- **PDU Length**—Length of the entire PDU, including header
- **Local Circuit ID**—Unique link identifier
- **TLV Fields**—Variable-length fields

When an ISH is received on a newly enabled point-to-point link, the router verifies whether an adjacency already exists with the sender by checking the source SysID in the ISH against its adjacency database. The ISH is ignored if an adjacency exists. If not, the receiving router creates a new adjacency and sets its state to "initializing" and the system type to "unknown." The router then sends the new neighbor an IIH in response. Upon receiving a subsequent IIH from the new neighbor, the router then moves the adjacency to an up state and changes the neighbor's system type to IS. In this process, the local router is unable to determine whether its hellos are reaching the remote end.

As specified in ISO 10589, point-to-point hellos do not include the IS Neighbors TLVs (Type 6); therefore, it is impossible to use a three-way process to confirm whether hellos generated locally are reaching neighbors. This might lead to situations where one end of an adjacency is up but the other end is not. An Internet draft submitted to the IETF proposes a more reliable way to form point-to-point IS-IS adjacencies—by using a three-way handshake process, which is backward-compatible to the ISO 10589 procedure.

In the default mode of operation, IIHs are padded to the MTU size of the outgoing interface. Routers match the size of IIHs received to their local MTUs to ensure that they can handle the largest possible packets from their neighbors before completing an adjacency.

When a router sends out a hello packet, it sets the Circuit Type field in the header to Level 1 only, Level 2 only, or Level 1-2, depending on its configuration, either globally by IS type or on an interface level by circuit type. The default IS type on a Cisco router is to be both a Level 1 and Level 2, but this can be modified to be Level 1 only or Level 2 only. Cisco routers also allow the circuit type of a link to be modified individually and independent of the global IS type. A router assigns a locally unique link identifier to each point-to-point link by using the 8-bit Local Circuit ID field in the hello header. The 8-bit field allows up to 256 unique point-to-point links only to be defined in an IS-IS router. Efforts in the IETF's IS-IS Working Group to remove this limitation is discussed in a later section.

One of the key requirements of IS-IS is that the length of the SysID must be consistent on all routers across the domain. Consequently, if the ID Length field of the hello packet (which indicates the length of the SysID) is set to a different value from what is expected, the receiving router discards the IIH. On Cisco routers, the length of the SysID is fixed at 6 bytes. A value of 0 in the ID field of an IIH indicates support for a 6-byte SysID. This means that all nodes interoperating with Cisco routers in an IS-IS network need to set the value of the ID field to 0, to indicate they also support 6-byte SysIDs. Details of the CLNS addressing scheme used in IS-IS is covered in Chapter 4, "Addressing in Integrated IS-IS."

The maximum number of area addresses supported in a single router configuration must match between adjacent neighbors as well, unless the verifying router supports only a maximum value of 3. By default, Cisco routers support a maximum of three area addresses. This can be changed to 255 in recent IOS releases. Any disagreement in the maximum number of supported areas causes the IIH to be discarded; otherwise, it is accepted for further processing. As previously noted, adjacency information such as SNPAs and corresponding SysIDs are obtained from the ISHs that are exchanged through the ES-IS protocol. A key role of IIHs, however, is to help establish the type of the adjacency to be formed. The receiving router determines the type of adjacency to be formed with the remote router from the IS type and the Area ID advertised in the received hello. Thus, in determining the type of adjacency, a router considers all the addresses defined in the Area Address TLVs present in the IIH received. Because they belong to different areas, two routers with non-matching Area IDs can form only a Level 2 adjacency. If two connected Cisco routers match in Area IDs, they'll form both Level 1 and Level 2 adjacencies according to default behavior.

If authentication is configured, the router appends an Authentication TLV field (Type 10) to the hello packet, which is then checked by the receiving node. ISO 10589 and RFC 1195 specify use of clear-text, simple passwords only. Currently, Cisco routers do not support any other more sophisticated authentication methods. More sophisticated authentication using MD5 message digest might be supported in the future.

If any of the adjacency checks previously described fails, a router will not bring up the new adjacency or will tear down an existing adjacency. When a router tears down an adjacency, it generates a notification message and removes the corresponding entry from its adjacency database. In case of a link failure, the IS-IS process reacts as soon as it obtains appropriate notification from the interface subsystem, by removing any adjacencies associated with the affected interface. The router then generates and floods an updated LSP reflecting the change to other neighbors.

Forming a Reliable Point-to-Point Adjacency

The three-way handshake process for reliably forming point-to-point adjacencies introduces a new type length value field (Type 240), known as Point-to-Point Adjacency State TLV. For backward compatibility, older systems running IS-IS implementations that do not support TLV Type 240 can ignore it, if encountered in an IIH, and follow conventional procedures for forming the adjacency. This is necessary so that newer and older systems can coexist in the same network. The three-way handshake requires a conforming system to move the state of the point-to-point adjacency to up only after confirming that there is bidirectional communication with the remote router and that its hellos are reaching the remote end. Compliant routers include the SysIDs of neighbors from which they have received hellos in TLV 240. A router knows its hellos are reaching a point-to-point neighbor when it receives a hello from that neighbor in which it is listed in this TLV. The TLV Type 240 consists of the following information:

Type: 0xF0 (decimal 240)
Length: 5 to 17 octets
Value (1 octet): Up (0), initializing (1), down (2)
Extended Local Circuit ID: 4 octets
Neighbor System ID: 0 to 8 octets
Neighbor Extended Local Circuit ID: 0 or 4 octets if known

This TLV enhances the IS-IS point-to-point adjacency formation process in two ways. First, a node can confirm three-way communication with its neighbor by confirming the presence of its SysID in a TLV 240 attached to hellos received from the neighbor. The local adjacency state can then be adjusted based on the existing state and the state featured in the Value field of TLV 240 from the hello received. Second, the Extended Local Circuit ID field in TLV 240 can be leveraged to provide unique link IDs for point-to-point links beyond the 256 limit specified in ISO 10589.

IS-IS Adjacencies over Multiaccess Media

The method specified in ISO 10589 for building adjacencies over broadcast media, such as LANs, differs slightly from that used on point-to-point links. Some of the significant differences are as follows:

- The process is not triggered by receipt of ISHs. A router sends IIHs on broadcast interfaces as soon as the interface is enabled.

- The broadcast medium is modeled as a node, called the *pseudonode*. The pseudonode role is played by an elected DIS.

- Depending on the configuration, nodes on the LAN broadcast their hellos to well-known Level 1 and Level 2 broadcast MAC addresses.

- Two-way communication is confirmed between adjacent nodes by using a three-way handshake procedure made possible by the presence of an IS Neighbors field in the LAN (Level 1 or Level 2) hello packets. The reliable point-to-point adjacency formation introduced by TLV Type 240 is similar to this process.

Details of the process for forming LAN adjacencies is discussed later in this chapter. For now, however, take a look at the format of the LAN hello packets, which is the same for both Level 1 and Level 2.

Figure 3-5   *IS-IS LAN Hello (PDU Types 15, 16).*

No. of Octets

Field	Size
Intradomain Routing Protocol Discriminator	1
Length Indicator	1
Version/Protocol ID Extension	1
ID Length	1
R R R PDU Type	1
Version	1
Reserved	1
Maximum Area Addresses	1
Reserved (6 bits) Circuit Type (2 bits)	1
Source ID	ID Length
Holding Time	2
PDU Length	2
R Priority	1
LAN ID	ID Length + 1
TLV Fields	Variable Length

The packet type–specific fields for IS-IS LAN hellos are as follows:

- **Circuit Type**—Tells whether this circuit is Level 1-only, Level 2-only, or both.
- **Source ID**—The SysID of the originator.
- **Holding Time**—Tells how long to wait for hellos from this router before declaring it dead and removing its adjacency.

- **PDU Length**—Length of the entire PDU, fixed header, and TLVs.

- **Priority**—This 7-bit value designates the priority to be the DIS (Level 1 or Level 2) on the LAN.

- **LAN ID**—SysID of the DIS plus an octet-long unique ID for this router assigned by the DIS.

The differences between LAN Level 1 and LAN Level 2 hellos is only in the interpretation of the values in the fields and the broadcast addresses to which they are transmitted. The MAC-level broadcast addresses are as follows:

- 01-80-C2-00-00-15 for Level 2 adjacencies (AllL2ISs)

- 01-80-C2-00-00-14 for Level 1 adjacencies (AllL1ISs)

The IS-IS PDU types for LAN Level 1 and Level 2 packets are 15 and 16, respectively. Example 3-1 shows a sample trace capture of a LAN Level 1 hello frame. The example displays a source address of 0x00D058F78941 and a destination or destination address of 0x0180C2000014. The target address is the AllL1IS address.

Example 3-1 *Trace of IS-IS LAN Level 1 Hello*

```
DLC:  ----- DLC Header -----
      DLC:
      DLC:  Frame 1 arrived at  19:03:01.2025; frame size is 1514 (05EA hex) bytes.
      DLC:  Destination = Multicast 0180C2000014
      DLC:  Source      = Station 00D058F78941
      DLC:  802.3 length = 1500
      DLC:
LLC:  ----- LLC Header -----
      LLC:
      LLC:  DSAP Address = FE, DSAP IG Bit = 00 (Individual Address)
      LLC:  SSAP Address = FE, SSAP CR Bit = 00 (Command)
      LLC:  Unnumbered frame: UI
```

The following TLVs fields can be found in LAN hello packets:

- **Area Addresses (Type 1)**—Contains area addresses configured on the router

- **IS Neighbors (Type 6)**—MAC addresses (SNPAs) of Level 1 (Level 2) neighbors that IIHs received from over the LAN interface in an initializing or up state

- **Padding (Type 8)**—Used to make hello as large as MTU (or at least MTU - 1 octets)

- **Authentication (Type 10)**—Password information

Forming LAN Adjacencies

When a LAN interface is enabled for IS-IS routing, the router immediately sends out IIH packets with a locally defined LAN ID, consisting of its own SysID and a unique local circuit ID. It also begins to listen to ESHs, ISHs, and IIHs to discover any connected adjacencies. It subsequently runs the DIS election process, depending on its configuration, to determine whether it is eligible to be a Level 1 or Level 2 DIS on the LAN.

The manner in which a router processes received IIHs depends on its configuration (IS type and circuit type). As in the case of point-to-point links, all IIHs received are checked for configuration conformity and authentication. The ID Length and Maximum Area Addresses fields in the received IIHs must match local values, and authentication passwords must be confirmed before the adjacency is further processed. Examples of additional information contained in hello packets are the neighbor's SysID, holding timer (holdtime), Level 1 or Level 2 priority, and configured area addresses.

A Level 1 adjacency is formed when the area addresses match unless configured otherwise. A Level 2 adjacency is formed alongside the Level 1 unless the router is configured to be Level 1-only. If no matching areas exist between the configuration of the local router and the area addresses information in the received hello, only a Level 2 adjacency is formed. If the transmitting router is configured for Level 2-only, the receiving router must be capable of forming a Level 2 adjacency; otherwise, no adjacency forms.

When a router receives a hello packet, it checks for an existing adjacency with the transmitter. If an adjacency is known, it resets the holdtime to the value in the hello received. If the neighbor is not known, the receiving router creates one, indicating the type of adjacency (Level 1 or Level 2) and sets its state to initializing until subsequent received hello packets confirm two-way communication. Routers include the MAC addresses of all neighbors on the LAN that they have received hellos from, allowing for a simple mechanism to confirm two-way communication. Two-way communication is confirmed when subsequent hellos received contain the receiving router's MAC address (SNPA) in an IS Neighbors TLV field. Otherwise, communication between the nodes is deemed one-way, and the adjacency stays at the initialized state. An adjacency must be in and up state for a router to send or process received LSPs.

Pseudonodes

As discussed in the preceding section, all IS-IS routers connected over a common LAN multicast hellos to well-known addresses, thereby forming adjacencies with each other.

After adjacency is determined, link-state information is exchanged (also referred to as LSP flooding). LSP flooding is the essence of dynamic routing information exchange between IS-IS routers. The two key requirements for LSP flooding are as follows:

- Accuracy of information and timeliness of the updates
- Minimum bandwidth usage and low processing overhead

Accuracy and timeliness imply spontaneous and frequent updates. This contradicts the need to conserve network resources, as stipulated by the requirement for minimum bandwidth usage and low processing overhead. This section focuses on the adjacency formation process and network resource management on multiaccess media.

To minimize the complexity of managing multiple adjacencies on multiaccess media, such as LANs, while enforcing efficient LSP flooding to minimize bandwidth consumption, IS-IS models multiaccess links as nodes, referred to as pseudonodes (see Figure 3-6). As the name implies, this is a virtual node, whose role is played by an elected DIS for the LAN. Separate DISs are elected for Level 1 and Level 2 routing. In the election process, only routers with adjacencies in an up state are considered. Election of the DIS is based on the highest interface priority, with the highest SNPA address (MAC address) breaking ties. The default interface priority on Cisco routers is 64.

Despite the critical role of the DIS in LSP flooding, no backup DIS is elected for either Level 1 or Level 2. Fortunately, this doesn't turn out to be a contentious problem because of the frequency of periodic database synchronization that occurs on broadcast links. If the current DIS fails, another router is immediately elected to play the role. As mentioned previously, the DIS transmits hello packets three times faster than the interval for other routers on the LAN. The default hello interval for the DIS is 3.3 seconds rather than the 10 seconds specified for other nodes. This allows for quick detection of DIS failure and immediate replacement.

Figure 3-6   *LAN Pseudonode.*

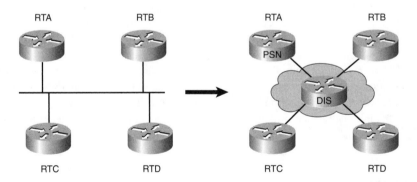

As previously expressed, periodic database synchronization on broadcast links allows preemption of the existing DIS without significant disruption of IS-IS operation on such media. This implies that an elected router is not guaranteed to remain the DIS if a new router with a higher priority shows up on the LAN. Any eligible router at the time of connecting to the LAN immediately takes over the DIS role, assuming the pseudonode functionality. No mechanism is specified for making a router ineligible to be the DIS. However, this is achievable, to some extent, by configuring a router's LAN interface with the lowest priority value relative to the priorities of other nodes on the LAN.

The IS-IS specification (ISO 10589) defines three types of designated intermediate systems, as follows:

- LAN Level 1 DIS
- LAN Level 2 DIS
- Partition-designated Level 2 IS

Election of partition-designated Level 2 ISs is specified in ISO 10589 to provide a means for repairing partitioned Level 1 areas in an IS-IS domain. An IS-IS virtual link is established over the Level 2 backbone between partition-designated Level 2 routers, which are elected from among the Level 2 routers in the partitions. Intra-area traffic is then forwarded between the partitions over the virtual link. IS-IS partition repair is not supported on Cisco routers and, therefore, is not discussed further in this book.

The responsibilities of LAN Level 1 and Level 2 DISs include the following:

- Generating pseudonode link-state packets to report links to all systems on the broadcast subnetwork
- Carrying out flooding over the LAN for the corresponding routing level

The newly elected or resigning DIS is also responsible for purging the old pseudonode LSP from the network. A DIS might resign when preempted or when disconnected from the link either by an interface shutdown or the disabling of the IS-IS process. Because of its critical role, detection of DIS failure is expedited using a shorter hello interval, which is 3.3 seconds rather than the 10 seconds used for ordinary nodes.

The IS-IS Routing Engine

Figure 3-7 shows the IS-IS routing engine, which is adapted from the more elaborate representation of the processes that work together to provide the complex of subnetwork-independent functions defined in ISO 10589. This simplified representation shows only the relevant dependencies between various processes of the IS-IS protocol within the framework of a conventional router's forwarding architecture. The receiving and forwarding processes specified in ISO 10589 are not necessarily applicable to an IP router and are therefore not discussed. Identical but separate routing engine architecture is maintained for each of the two levels of routing.

IP routers using Integrated IS-IS as the routing protocol conform to requirements for IP packet handling as specified by RFC 1812 (Requirements for Internet Gateways). Such IP routers must handle the ISO packets relevant to the operation of IS-IS and also must support other IP router functionality, such as Internet Message Protocol (ICMP) and Address Resolution Protocol (ARP).

Figure 3-7 *IS-IS routing engine.*

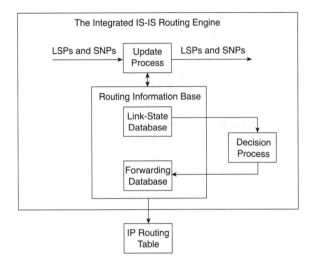

The Routing Information Base

The Routing Information Base is composed of two databases that are central to the operation of IS-IS: the Link-State database and the Forwarding database. The Link-State database is fed with routing information by the update process.

The Update Process

The update process generates local link-state information, based on the adjacency database built by the subnetwork-dependent functions, which the router advertises to all its neighbors in link-state packets. A router also receives similar link-state information from every adjacent neighbor, keeps copies of LSPs received, and re-advertises them to other neighbors. Routers in an area maintain identical Level 1 Link-State databases, which are synchronized using SNPs. This means that routers in an area will have identical views of the area topology, which is necessary for routing consistency within the area. A Level 2 Link-State database contains area prefix information that ties all the areas together for inter-area (Level 2) routing.

The Decision Process

The decision process creates the Forwarding database by running the shortest path first (SPF) algorithm (also referred to as the Dijkstra algorithm) on the Link-State database. A router runs separate SPF processes for Level 1 and Level 2.

Routing Table

The IS-IS Forwarding database, which is made up of only best IS-IS routes, is fed into the Routing Information Base (RIB), essentially the IP routing table of a router to be used in packet-switching decisions. When multiple sources exist for routing information in a router, such as static routes and BGP, a Cisco router uses the concept of administrative distances to prefer one routing source to the others. The protocol with the lowest administrative distance wins. (Table 3-3 lists administrative distances for various routing protocols.) The accepted best route is then installed in the routing table. Routing table information might be processed further into the fast-switching cache or the Cisco Express Forwarding (CEF) Forwarding Information Base (FIB) to speed up switching packets through the router. Typically, IS-IS is used in conjunction with BGP for routing IP packets. BGP brings in external routes, whereas IS-IS, as an IGP, is responsible for internal routes (mostly next-hop information for the BGP routes). Consequently, little overlap occurs in routing information obtained from either source, allowing IS-IS and BGP routes to coexist in the routing table.

Table 3-3   *Administrative Distances of Routing Protocols*

Route Protocol	Administrative Distance
RIP v1 and v2	120
IGRP	100
EIGRP Internal	90
EIGRP External	170
OSPF	110
Integrated ISIS	115
BGP Internal	20
BGP External	200
Static to Next Hop	1
Static to Interface	1
Connected	0

Addressing Concepts in Integrated IS-IS

This section is a short prelude to Chapter 4, "Addressing in Integrated IS-IS," introducing only the key concepts for addressing in the IS-IS environment.

As a protocol originally designed for routing CLNP packets, IS-IS used the node-based addressing scheme of CLNP as its basic addressing premise. Integrated IS-IS, which can be used for routing IP packets, inherits many concepts from the original specification, including the CLNS addressing scheme for identifying network nodes. Therefore, it is a fundamental requirement that even when Integrated IS-IS is used in an IP-only environment, the nodes must have ISO NSAP addresses (referred to as NETs). However, IP requires the links to be addressed with IP subnets. Fortunately, the format for CLNS addresses used on IP routers is simple; most people can deal with the two addressing schemes and solve the single issue of routing IP.

Chapter 4 reviews CLNS addressing and provides practical examples of how they are used on IP routing. IP addressing on the links conforms to basic IP addressing principles and has no relationship with the CLNS addressing scheme. The latter exists solely for use by the IS-IS protocol.

As Integrated IS-IS for IP routing is enabled on the interfaces, the IP subnets are automatically added to the router's LSP by using the IP reachability and related TLVs introduced by RFC 1195. The IP prefixes are then assembled into an IP Link-State database, which is the fed to SPF algorithm to determine the best routes.

Security

IS-IS enforces basic security through packet authentication by using special TLVs. ISO 10589 specifies TLV Type 10, which can be present in all IS-IS packet types. RFC 1195 also specifies TLV Type 133 for authentication, which removes password length restrictions imposed by ISO 10589. Both specifications define only simple passwords transmitted as clear text without encryption.

Simple, clear-text password authentication obviously does not provide enough protection against malicious attacks on the network, even though it can help isolate operator configuration errors related to adjacency setups. TLV Types 10 and 133 both provide accommodation for future TLV field types, which might permit more complex and secured authentication using schemes such as HMAC-MD5. An IETF draft proposal specifies this approach for improved and sophisticated authentication of IS-IS packets.

Only the simple passwords specified in ISO 10589 are supported in available (at the time of writing) Cisco IOS releases.

A unique security advantage of IS-IS compared to other IP routing protocols is that IS-IS packets are directly encapsulated over the data link and are not carried in IP packets or even CLNP packets. Therefore, to maliciously disrupt the IS-IS routing environment, an attacker has to be physically attached to a router in the IS-IS network, a challenging and inconvenient task for most network hackers. Other IP routing protocols, such as RIP, OSPF, and BGP, are susceptible to attacks from remote IP networks through the Internet because routing protocol packets are ultimately embedded in IP packets, which makes them susceptible to remote access by intrusive applications.

Summary

This chapter reviews the basic concepts underlying the design of the IS-IS routing protocol. The chapter also discusses the two-level hierarchy for controlling distribution of routing information within IS-IS areas and between them: Level 1 and Level 2, respectively. You learned that technically all IS-IS routers belong to one physical Level 1 area because of the node-based addressing scheme of CLNP. The related issue of suboptimal interarea routing resulting from the architecture proposed in ISO 10589 and adopted by RFC 1195 is discussed in detail in Chapter 7, "General Network Design Issues." Chapter 7 also discusses workarounds and IS-IS protocol enhancements that address this major limitation of the original IS-IS protocol architecture.

Other characteristics of the IS-IS protocol discussed in this chapter include functional organization into subnetwork-dependent and subnetwork-independent capabilities, IS-IS packet formats, addressing, and security.

Tied into the subnetwork-dependent capabilities are processes that relate to adjacency discovery, formation, and maintenance. On broadcast links, management of the potentially complex database synchronization process between the many possible adjacent routers is achieved by the election of the designated IS to provide the pseudonode functionality.

The section on IS-IS packet formats elaborated on the basic building blocks—namely, the header and the TLV fields. It was noted that a key strength of the IS-IS protocol is the simplicity by which it can be extended through the introduction of new TLVs without major changes to the protocol architecture. Perhaps the most confusing aspect of IS-IS is the need to deal with two addressing schemes when using it for routing IP. Because Integrated IS-IS adapts the original IS-IS to carry IP information, most of the original architecture (including node addressing) is ported. Integrated IS-IS supports dual-mode operation, in which both IP and CLNP packets are routed essentially by the same IS-IS process. The next chapter covers CLNP addressing and helps alleviate some of the challenges in dealing with this dichotomy.

Like most protocols, security is a concern for IS-IS even though neither ISO 10589 nor RFC 1195 specified any strong authentication schemes for dealing with malicious attacks within an internetworking environment. The simple, clear-text passwords specified provide a useful way to control network misconfiguration and to implement configuration policies.

An IETF draft specification (IS-IS HMAC-MD5 Authentication) proposes more secured authentication of IS-IS packets by using HMAC-MD5 authentication schemes.

Review Questions

1 How many levels of hierarchy does the IS-IS routing protocol support and what is their significance?

2 What is the reason for suboptimal interarea routing in the ISO 10589 architecture?

3 Name the two categories of IS-IS protocol functions and describe the services they provide.

4 What is the general layout of IS-IS packet formats?

5 List the TLVs specified by ISO 10589.

6 List the TLVs specified by RFC 1195 and describe their significance.

7 How does the TLV Type 133 specified by RFC 1195 differ from the original authentication TLV Type 10 specified by IS0 10589?

8 Describe any differences between the adjacency formation processes on point-to-point and broadcast links.

9 Describe the three-way adjacency formation process that has been proposed in the IETF to enhance the method for forming adjacencies on point-to-point links.

10 What is the relevance of the pseudonode functionality?

11 Briefly describe the DIS election and replacement process.

12 Explain why no backup DIS exists.

NOTE   RFC drafts are continuously being updated, so their number suffixes might change—at one point, they might cease to exist as drafts as they become RFCs.

References

draft-ietf-isis-3way-02.txt: Three-way Handshake for IS-IS Point-to-Point Adjacencies

draft-ieft-isis-hmac-01.txt: IS-IS HMAC-MD5 Authentication

ISO 9542, "End System to Intermediate System Routing Exchange Protocol." For use in conjunction with ISO 8473. Also published as RFC 995.

ISO/8473/Add.3 Protocol for providing the connectionless-mode network service-Addendum 3: Provision of the underlying service assumed by the ISO 8473 over subnetworks, which provide the OSI data link service.

Addressing in Integrated IS-IS

This chapter focuses on network addressing concepts in Integrated IS-IS and attempts to demystify the seemingly cumbersome CLNP network addressing, which is mandatory on IP routers, even when using Integrated IS-IS in IP-only environments. As discussed in Chapter 3, "Integrated IS-IS Routing Protocol Concepts," Integrated IS-IS retains most of the concepts of the original IS-IS routing protocol, as specified in ISO 10589, and defines new TLVs (RFC 1195) that enable support for IP routing. The CLNP node-based addressing scheme is one of the key concepts retained in Integrated IS-IS. The node-based addressing scheme requires only a single address for the entire node. In contrast however, link-based addressing applies multiple addresses to a node by assigning a unique address to each connecting link. These addresses are applied to the interfaces where network links connect to the router. The IP addressing scheme is link-based, as mentioned in Chapter 1, "Overview of IP Routing." In this scheme, each link is assigned an IP subnetwork number that defines the corresponding interface address. Consequently, an IP node can have many IP addresses assigned to it, depending on the number of enabled interfaces.

In the node-based scheme, IS-IS needs only a single address per IS-IS node. Multiple addresses can be defined on an IS-IS router, but they are not tied to any specific links. This can be done for special reasons discussed later in this chapter. Even when multiple CLNP addresses are defined on an IS-IS router, the same unique System Identifier is retained in all the addresses. CNLP addresses used in IS-IS are called network service access points (NSAP) and are, therefore, frequently referred to as NSAP addresses. Recall from Chapter 2, "Introduction to the IS-IS Routing Protocol," that in the Open System Interconnection (OSI) reference model, each layer provides special services to the next higher layer. The NSAP defines the appropriate service interfaces, similar to the protocol type used by IP routers for TCP and UDP.

An NSAP address consists of several components, including a unique System Identifier that allows it to identify an entire node in a Connectionless Network Protocol (CLNP) network. When using Integrated IS-IS for routing IP, both CLNP and IP addresses are configured on the routers. However, IP hosts not participating in the dynamic routing process don't need to have NSAP addresses. Frequently, the IP hosts do not need to run a dynamic routing protocol and instead rely on IP services, such as ARP, DHCP, and static default routes to communicate with routers and other IP devices. Some IP hosts support dynamic routing protocols, such as the Routing Information Protocol (RIP) or the Open Shortest Path First (OSPF) Protocol. In a pure ISO or dual network, the ISO hosts (end systems) have NSAPs and rely on the ES-IS protocol to communicate with routers and other end systems. To review the introductory IP material, refer to Chapter 1. This chapter introduces and focuses on only ISO addressing concepts for CLNP. Later, insights into requirements, caveats, and suggested best practices for defining and configuring NSAPs on Cisco routers for Integrated IS-IS routing are discussed.

ISO terminology refers to data link (Layer 2) addresses (LAN MAC addresses, Frame Relay DLCIs, and so on) as subnetwork point of attachments (SNPAs). Because a network device might connect to multiple links, it can have multiple SNPA addresses but requires only one OSI network address. ISO protocols providing network layer services can interpret both NSAP and SNPA addresses. As discussed previously, a primary function of the ES-IS protocol is to provide NSAP-to-SNPA mapping for network devices. Figure 4-1 illustrates the application of SNPAs and NSAPs to various nodes in an IS-IS network.

Figure 4-1   *Application of ISO NSAP and SNPAs.*

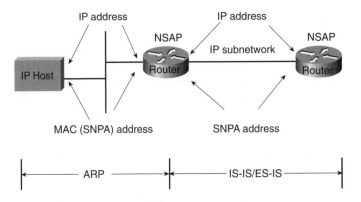

The NSAP addressing scheme, which is a major dependency for IS-IS operation, is specified in ISO 8348/AD2. This specification is also available as RFC 941 from the IETF (www.ietf.org). The parent document, ISO 8348, defines the ISO network layer service requirements for connection-oriented services. ISO 8348/AD1 provides additional specification for connectionless-mode transmission, whereas IS0 8348/AD2 deals with network layer addressing. Subsequent sections of this chapter explain the format of NSAP addresses and how they are configured on Cisco routers to support IS-IS routing. Hopefully, if you feel more comfortable with IP addressing, you will overcome any intimidation that CLNP addressing poses and appreciate its inherent simplicity, especially for IS-IS routing applications in IP environments.

OSI Network Addresses

In the OSI architecture, the network layer provides services to a user in the layer above, such as the transport service element. If you designate the network layer by N, the network user is the N+1 service element (see Figure 4-2). An N+1 entity in Router A that wants to communicate with an N+1 peer in Router B must provide the peer's N service access point (NSAP) as the destination of the service request while providing its own NSAP as the source to facilitate bidirectional communication. In a router, the N+1 entity or the N service user is either a transport layer entity or the routing layer.

Figure 4-2   *Peer-to-peer layer communications.*

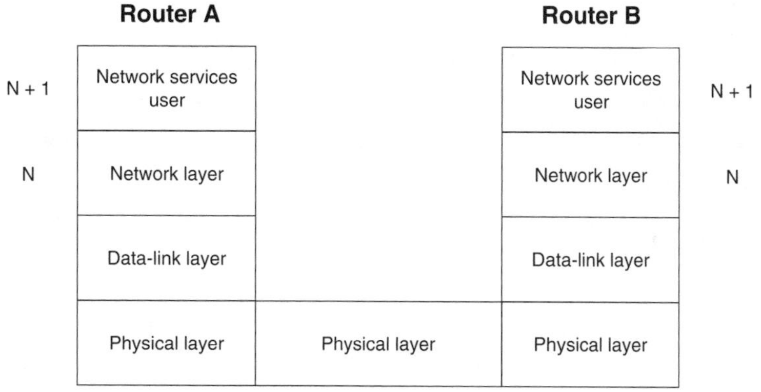

The NSAP address format has a component known as the *NSAP selector* (*NSEL*) for identifying the target network service user. The NSEL is further discussed later in this section. Other components of the NSAP are the *System Identifier* (*SysID*) and the *Area Identifier* (*Area ID*). The SysID uniquely identifies a network node, whereas the Area ID specifies the home area of the node. IS-IS requires all systems to be associated with at least one area in the network domain. In summary, an NSAP address consists of the following three parts: the Area ID, SysID, and NSEL. When the routing layer is specified as the network service user, the value of the NSEL is set to zero, and the NSAP is called the *network entity title (NET)*. In a pure ISO CLNS environment, ordinary data packets have source and destination NSAPs with non-zero NSEL values. Such packets are obviously not meant for the routing layer and might be directed at some transport services element in the router or possibly just traversing the router. On the other hand, in IP-only environments, such as the Internet, there are no CLNP applications, so the routing layer is the only user of CLNP network services. In this case, the only ISO packets in operation are ES-IS and IS-IS routing information and control packets.

The following material focuses only on the ISO CLNS architecture. Refer to Chapter 1 for additional information on IP addressing.

NSAP Format

NSAP addresses are not fixed in length and can be up to 160 bits (20 bytes) long compared to the fixed 32 bits (4 bytes) of IP addresses. ISO 8348/AD2 specifies a hierarchical scheme for defining global and public NSAP addresses. The following are the seven top-level addressing domains:

- **X.121**—International plan for public data networks
- **ISO DCC**—Data Country Code
- **F.69**—Telex
- **E.163**—Public Switched Telephone Network
- **E.164**—ISDN
- **ISO 6523**—International Code Designator (ICD) for organizations
- **Local**—For local use only within network domain

Even though format details differ for each top-level domain, all NSAP addresses conform to the generic format shown in Figure 4-3.

Figure 4-3 *NSAP address format.*

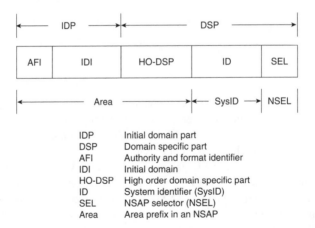

The NSAP format shows two main components: the initial domain part (IDP) and the domain-specific part (DSP). The IDP is further broken down into the authority and format identifier (AFI) and the initial domain identifier (IDI). The DSP consists of the high order DSP, ID, and SEL fields. The ID field is for the SysID of the node and the SEL represents the NSAP selector (NSEL). Both the SysID and NSEL were discussed in the preceding section.

The details of the naming and functions of all various fields in the NSAP are not discussed here because they are irrelevant to the subject matter of this book. However, the AFI and

IDI fields are of great interest, so they are discussed in detail here. The AFI indicates the top-level addressing domain associated with the NSAP and the syntax of the DSP section. Possible values of the AFI range from 0 to 99 decimal values. The top-level address domains sponsor various subdomains, which are assigned a value in the IDI field. Each top-level domain specifies its own format for the IDI field. For example, the ISO 6523 ICD address domain has a four-digit format, whereas the ISO DCC uses a three-digit format for the data country code. Examples of IDI values for ISO 6523 ICD subdomains used by the United States government follow:

- **U.S. government civilian organizations**—0005
- **U.S. Department of Defense**—0006

The IDI value of 0005 refers to U.S. government civilian organizations that conform to the U.S. government standard known as Government Open System Interconnection Profile (GOSIP).

As said before, the value of the AFI also determines the syntax of the DSP. The DSP syntax can be in binary octets, decimal digits, or even characters.

Table 4-1 shows the AFI values for various top-level address domains and DSP syntax types. For example, AFI 47 refers to the ISO 6523 ICD addressing domain and indicates a binary syntax for the DSP. Similarly, AFI 39 refers to the ISO DCC addressing domain and binary syntax for the DSP.

Table 4-1   *AFI Values for Address Domains and DSP Syntax Types*

Address Domain	DSP Syntax		
	Decimal	**Binary**	**Character**
X.121	36	37	
ISO DCC	38	39	
F.69	40	41	
E.163	42	43	
E.164	44	45	
ISO 6523 ICD	46	47	
Local	48	49	50

Example 4-1 shows an ISO 6523 address that conforms to the GOSIP standard.

Example 4-1   *A Complete ISO 6523 NSAP*

```
47. 0005. 80123456000089AB001.AABBCCDDEEFF. 00
^      ^       ^                          ^                    ^            ^
AFI   IDI           AREA                            SYSID        NSEL
```

Example 4-1 shows a complete 20-byte NSAP with key fields in the layout delineated by grouping related characters. The following five major fields can be easily discerned:

- **AFI (47)**—Address domain indicating binary DSP syntax
- **IDI (0005)**—GOSIP IDI
- **Area (80123456000089AB0001)**—Area information with hierarchy details
- **SysID**—6-byte System Identifier
- **NSEL**—NSAP selector specifying routing layer as network service user

Simplified NSAP Format

As shown in Figure 4-4, the various fields in the NSAP format can be grouped into three main sections: Area ID, System ID, and NSEL. This interpretation of the NSAP format reduces its seeming complexity. The resulting structure is referred to as the simplified NSAP format. Future discussions of the NSAP in this chapter are based on the simplified NSAP format.

Figure 4-4   *Simplified NSAP format.*

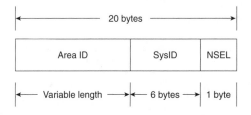

The Area ID field consists of the AFI (first byte) and all subsequent fields up to the beginning of the System ID section. The Area ID field has variable length. The length of the System ID field is specified to be 1 to 8 bytes. The NSEL is the last byte. The maximum size of the NSAP address in the simplified format remains 20 bytes.

NOTE   Most current implementations of IS-IS, including the Cisco implementation, have adopted a fixed-size, 6-byte System ID length in compliance with the U.S. GOSIP version 2.0 standard.

Considering the GOSIP-specified 6-byte length of the System ID field and the 1-byte NSEL field, the Area ID may therefore vary between 1 and 13 bytes. Because only 1 byte is sufficient to define the Area ID, the smallest length of an NSAP on a Cisco router is 8 bytes.

For IP applications, it is sufficient to define NSAPs as simple as possible by allocating 1 byte for the AFI, at least 2 bytes for the actual area information, 6 bytes for the System ID, and 1 byte for the NSEL for a total minimum of 10 bytes. Example 4-2 shows a 10-byte NSAP, based on this recommendation. NSAPs are configured in hexadecimal format from the IOS command-line interface (CLI) with the leading AFI byte (decimal value) and trailing NSEL byte (00) delineated by dots (periods). The remainder of the address between the AFI and NSEL is broken down into 4-digit (2 bytes in Hex) groups and separated by dots. In comparison, IP addressing uses a different format, called *dotted-decimal representation*. See Chapter 1 for a review on IP addressing.

Example 4-2   *Simple NSAP Address*

```
49.0001.0000.0000.0001.00
   ^                         ^              ^
Area ID              SysID          NSEL
```

When using IS-IS for IP routing, you can follow the simplified NSAP format to create a simple Area ID without regard for other details, such as IDI, domain, and details of the area information. In the preceding example, an AFI value of 49 is prefixed to the intended area information (0001) to form the Area ID (49.0001). Recall from Table 4-1 that the AFI value of 49 is designated for local private use similar to the reserved private address space specified in RFC 1618. The next characters after the AFI are in hexadecimal format; the first 12 digits represent the 6-byte SysID and the last 2 digits represent the NSEL byte.

Although 10-byte-long NSAPs are sufficient for IP routing purposes, most service providers using IS-IS still configure 20-byte-long addresses on their routers whether they use conjectured addresses (with AFI 49) or addresses from the public space (obtained from one of the top-level addressing domains). For routing on the Internet, IS-IS (and certainly any other IGP such as OSPF) is confined to the local domain (or autonomous system). The *Border Gateway Protocol (BGP)* is used instead for sharing routing information between autonomous systems. In practice, the NSAPs configured on IP routers for IS-IS routing do not need to be globally unique or even 20 bytes long. This is explained further in the next section.

Obtaining Globally Unique NSAP Addresses

The Internet is composed of many separate IP network domains, which collaborate by sharing routing information to form the Internet's gigantic multinational and intercontinental framework. Each constituent network of the Internet is considered an independent routing domain or an *autonomous system (AS)*.

BGP has stood the test of time to emerge as the only viable protocol for exchanging routing information between the many ASs that form the Internet. In the early days of the Internet, an alternative routing protocol based on CLNP called *Interdomain Routing Protocol (IDRP)* was proposed, but it was not widely adopted because of the ubiquity of IP and its dominance over CLNP. BGP provides flexible routing policies for controlling routing information within an AS, as well as outbound and inbound routing information. IS-IS belongs to the class of routing protocols called *Interior Gateway Protocols (IGPs)*, which work alongside BGP and provide supportive roles for routing in an AS. Typically, all the autonomous systems on the Internet run BGP and an IGP (IS-IS or OSPF). However, all the instances of IGPs running in the different network domains that constitute the Internet are isolated from each other. Only BGP is used for exchanging routing information between ASs. Therefore, a service provider can freely choose any type of IGP to use within its AS. When IS-IS is used as an IGP, the required NSAPs can be based on the simplified format because they do not need to be globally unique—just as private IP addresses can be defined on the internal links in an AS without any significant external implications except breaking Traceroutes and Pings to and from remote networks. Globally unique NSAP addresses do make sense, however, for interconnected telecommunications systems, such as ATM switches, SONET/SDH Add Drop Multiplexers (ADM), and any devices that use CLNP-based applications for global connectivity. Besides OSPF, IS-IS is one of the most widely deployed IGPs in ISP networks. There are many reasons for this: historical reasons based on specific practical experience, troubleshooting simplicity, perceived robustness and fast convergence, or mere subjective convenience. As indicated, even though globally unique NSAP addresses are not required to run IS-IS in an Internet AS for the current application, most service providers have deployed 20-byte globally unique addresses.

ISO NSAP Addressing Authorities

An address registration authority oversees address assignments for each of the top-level addressing domains. For example, ISO 6523 specifies rules for allocation of ICD addresses (AFI 47) by an International Registration Authority (RA). Applications for addresses are processed through a sponsoring authority, such as a country's national standards body. The RA does not process any direct applications from organizations. As indicated in the previous section, IDI 0005 and 0006 are allocated to the U.S. National Institute of Standards (NIST) and subsequently reallocated to institutions and organizations of the U.S. federal government.

The British Standards Institute (BSI), which is the national standards body of the United Kingdom (UK), acts as the UK sponsor for ICD addresses. BSI also runs an independent ICD address allocation scheme through a business development group. The scheme called *Identifiers for Organizations for Telecommunications Addressing (IOTA)* was motivated by demand for *Asynchronous Transfer Mode (ATM) End System Addresses (AESA)* for use on ATM switches in coordination with the ATM forum. The IOTA scheme was introduced with a broader objective to provide ICD format identifiers for organizations, in any part of the world, and to supply globally unique addresses and identifiers for any kind of application. The IOTA IDI value is 0124 and goes with an AFI prefix of 47 at the beginning of the

AESA. An example of an IOTA-based NSAP address is shown in Example 4-3. The reader is referred to the IOTA site listed in the "References" section for more information.

Example 4-3 *IOTA-Based NSAP Address*

```
47. 0124. xxxxxx. yyyyyyyyyyyyyy .  AABBCCDDEEFF .00
--  ----  ------  --------------     ------------ --
 ^    ^     ^           ^                 ^        ^
 |    |     |           |                 |        |
AFI  IDI  OrgID   Org. Assigned        SysID     NSEL
```

As shown in Example 4-3, the first three leftmost bytes of an IOTA-based NSAP are the IOTA organization ID (47.0124). The actual syntax of the DSP is binary, but it is represented in hexadecimal. Counting from left, octets 4 through 6 (Org ID) represent the organization identifier assigned by the IOTA RA. Octets 7–13 are administered and assigned locally by the organization. The last seven octets make up the SysID and NSEL fields.

The ISO DCC NSAP addressing hierarchy is as popular as the ISO 6523 ICD scheme and has been adopted by numerous organizations, primarily for addressing telecommunication systems, devices, and related objects. ISO DCC is specified in ISO 3166 and uses 39 as AFI. Just as in the case of ISO 6523 ICD NSAP addresses, administration of the DCC address space is coordinated through national organizations. In the United States, for example, the American National Standards Institute (ANSI) is the RA. The address allocation procedure is specified in ANSI X3.216 in conformance with ITU X.660/ISO/IEC 9834-1, which describes a hierarchy of RAs. The IDI assigned to ANSI is 840, which is prefixed with AFI 39 and specifies binary encoding of the DSP in accordance with ISO 8348/AD2. The AFI and IDI are decimals but encoded in binary-coded decimal (BCD) format with octet boundaries at 8 bits. Note the leading zero fill in the IDI field in Example 4-4. Refer to the ANSI Web site in the "References" section for additional information.

Example 4-4 *An ANSI ICD NSAP Address*

```
39 0840 xxxxxx yyyyyyyyyyyyyy AABBCCDDEEFF 00
-- ---- ------ -------------- ------------ --
 ^   ^    ^          ^              ^       ^
 |   |    |          |              |       |
AFI IDI OrgID   Org. Assigned     SysID    NSEL
```

Currently, the Cisco IOS CLI does not provide formatting help during entry of the NSAP in a router configuration. Knowledge of field boundaries in the NSAP addressing architecture by network operators is, therefore, critical for configuring NSAPs and enabling IS-IS on Cisco routers.

Defining the System ID

By now, it is clear that the SysID is one of three key components of an NSAP address, which is required to enable IS-IS routing on a router. The other components are the Area ID and the NSEL. According to ISO 10589, the SysID can be of variable length between 1 to 8 bytes. However, Cisco's implementation of IS-IS uses a fixed 6-byte length in conformance with the GOSIP 2.0 standard. It is probably not by coincidence that the 6-byte length specified by GOSIP 2.0 matches the length of a LAN MAC address. Therefore, you can use one of the LAN MAC addresses on a router as its SysID, essentially embedding a MAC address (a Layer 2 address) in the NSAP, which is a Layer 3 address. Of course, on an IP router with many LAN interfaces, you need to decide which MAC address to use as the SysID. However, the SysID doesn't have to be a MAC address.

Although an IP address has no visual relationship with the data-link address, except indirectly through mapping by the Address Resolution Protocol (ARP), a link between the NSAP and the data-link address (SNPA) can be easily established for single-point-attached CLNS hosts by using their MAC addresses at the point of attachment as the SysID. Because a router might have many active LAN interfaces, direct one-to-one LAN address-to-NSAP mapping might not always be possible. Network operators can follow any convenient method to define SysIDs for their routers while conforming to the requirements and caveats listed in the following section.

Requirements and Caveats

The following is a list of requirements and caveats that must be followed to define NSAP for IS-IS routing in general and in particular on Cisco routers:

*   Each node in an IS-IS routing area must have a unique SysID.

*   The SysID of all nodes in an IS-IS routing domain must be of the same length. The length of the SysID is 6 bytes (fixed) on Cisco routers. All routers connecting to the Level 2 backbone must have unique SysIDs relative to each other.

NOTE   SysIDs are required to be unique only within a specific area; therefore, a router in one area can potentially share the same SysID with a router in another area without any conflict unless they are both connected to the backbone for Level 2 routing. In practice, however, most service providers keep SysIDs unique for each router in the entire domain regardless of whether the network is a single-area domain or has multiple areas.

In Chapter 5, "The IS-IS Link-State Database," the IS-IS Link-State database is discussed and it is noted that the identifiers for link-state packets are tied to the SysIDs of the originating routers. This explains the need for unique SysIDs for nodes in the same area (Level 1) or the backbone (Level 2).

One popular way to define unique SysIDs is by padding a dotted-decimal loopback IP address with zeros to transform it into a 12-digit address, which can then be easily rearranged to represent a 6-byte SysID in hexadecimal, by regrouping the digits in fours and separating them with dots. Example 4-5 shows an excerpt from the configuration on a Cisco router. Typically, routers are configured with loopback addresses for other purposes, such as BGP routing or network management. Example 4-5 elaborates the procedure for defining an NSAP based on the loopback address.

Example 4-5 *Example of System ID*

```
Interface Loopback 0
IP address 192.168.1.24


Router isis
Net 49.0001.1921.6800.1024.00
```

In Example 4-5, the loopback address is transformed as follows:

Step 1 Each octet in the dotted-decimal notation of the loopback IP address that is not three digits is prefixed with zeros, padding it to three digits, as follows:

192.168.1.24 ---> 192.168.001.024

Step 2 After Step 1, you have 12 digits, which you can easily rearrange into three groups of 4 digits, as follows:

192.168.001.024 ---> 1921.6800.1024

Step 3 1921.6800.1024 can then be used as the unique SysID of the router. The area prefix and NSEL suffix are added to obtain the complete NSAP address, as shown in Example 4-6.

Example 4-6 *Obtaining the Complete NSAP Address*

```
1921.6800.1024   ---> 49.0001.1921.6800.1024.00
-------  --------------  --
        ^             ^          ^
        |             |          |
      AreaID        SysID      NSEL
```

This method of defining the NSAP or NET is frequently used by Internet service providers that run the IS-IS protocol as IGP. Even though this might not be the only intuitive way, the method offers operational convenience by associating multiple applications to a single loopback address on the router. A single loopback address can be used as the BGP router ID, the basis for the IS-IS SysID, the MPLS/TE router ID, and for network management applications. OSPF also uses a loopback address on a router, when available, as the router ID; in typical situations, however, OSPF and IS-IS are not used together as IGPs in the same network, even though that is possible for merging two originally separate networks or during a routing protocol migration from one to the other. Because the Area ID and the NSEL are the same for all nodes in the same area, it's the unique SysID that provides uniqueness to the NET of a router. An IS-IS router must have at least one NSAP configured, and the SysID must be unique for the area in which it belongs. However, ISO 10589 allows up to three NSAP addresses per node—all of which must have the same unique SysID of the node, differentiated only by the area prefix. The concept of having multiple NSAP addresses on the same router is called *multihoming* in IS-IS. Multihoming is addressed further in the next section. It is important to understand that multihoming does not allow a router to be connected to multiple separate areas. Instead, configuring multiple NSAPs with different area prefixes on a router merges the different areas, and the router continues to belong to a single, but unified, area.

Configuring Multiple NETs for a Single IS-IS Process

Until recently, only a single IS-IS routing process could be enabled on a Cisco router. Even though only a single NET is required for an IS-IS process, multiple NETs can be configured for the same process by defining multiple NSAPs differentiated only by the Area IDs. This allows the router to multihome to the multiple areas defined, effectively merging the areas into a single area. During normal operation, for example, a Level 1 IS-IS router participates in flooding Level 1 LSPs throughout its home area. If this router connects to multiple areas, it also extends the flooding of Level 1 LSPs between those areas, effectively merging them. An example of a multihomed configuration is shown in Example 4-7.

In Example 4-7, 49.0001 and 49.0002 are the two areas to which this router is dual-homed. Notice that it keeps the same system in both NSAP addresses. The NSEL is all zeros in both addresses. Configuring the two addresses allows the router to merge areas 49.0001 and 49.0002 by passing the Level 1 LSPs from each area into the other. This is further illustrated in Figure 4-5.

Example 4-7 *IS-IS Multihoming Configuration*

```
RTA#

Interface Loopback 0
Ip address 192.168.1.24


Router isis
Net 49.0001.1921.6800.1024.00
Net 49.0002.1921.6800.1024.00
```

Figure 4-5   *Multihoming in IS-IS.*

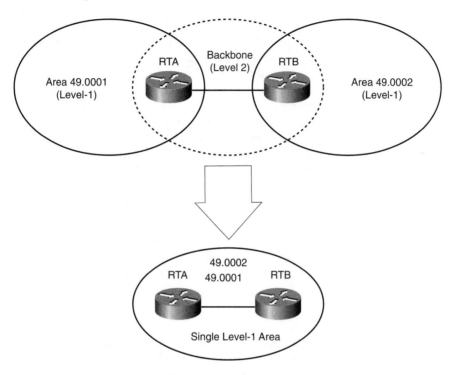

As shown in Figure 4-5, RTA is in Area 49.0001 and RTB is in Area 49.0002. Because they are in different areas, they form Level 2 adjacencies with each other while maintaining Level 1 adjacencies with devices in their local areas. If RTA is configured with a second NET (49.0002.1921.6800.1024.00) (see Example 4-7), the two routers then form a Level 1 adjacency based on the common area prefix (49.0002). RTA continues to maintain its Level 1 adjacencies with devices in 49.0001, and RTB does the same with devices in 49.0002. Because of the newly formed Level 1 adjacency between RTA and RTB, however, the devices begin to exchange all their originally separate Level 1 databases, which are then flooded to the other Level 1 neighbors. This effectively merges the two areas.

Under normal circumstances, operators need to configure routers with only one area prefix. Multihoming is useful for the following purposes, which are further elaborated in subsequent sections:

- Merging areas
- Splitting areas
- Renumbering

Multihoming allows network operators to perform any of these three activities without a major "flag" day (which would require the entire or a major part of the network to go out of service). A recent enhancement in Cisco IOS Software, referred to as *IS-IS multi-area*, enables an IS-IS router to act as an area border router, interconnecting multiple isolated areas to the Level 2 backbone. The essential difference between multi-area support in IS-IS and IS-IS multihoming is that the IS-IS multi-area feature is designed to support multiple, independent Level 1 areas on the same router by using multiple IS-IS processes, whereas multihoming merges multiple areas under a single IS-IS process. In both cases, each area is represented by an NSAP that differs from the others by only the Area ID. In the multi-area configuration, however, each process gets its own NSAP, whereas the NSAPs are grouped under the same process in multihoming configurations. Additional information on multi-area support is available in Chapter 9, "Configuring IS-IS for IP Routing on Cisco Routers."

Merging Areas

The process of merging areas with IS-IS multihoming is illustrated in Figure 4-5, where you start with two distinct areas: 49.0001 and 49.0002 (with RTA in 49.0001). By multihoming RTA, you end up with a unified area and a merged Level 1 Link-State database.

Splitting Areas

The process of splitting areas is, essentially, the reverse of merging. In this case, you start with a common area, 49.0001, dual-home RTB to the new area, 49.0002, and subsequently isolate it from area 49.0001. This results in the formation of a Level 2 backbone for communication between the two separate areas (see Figure 4-6).

Renumbering NSAP Addresses

The process of renumbering is similar to splitting and merging, except that during renumbering, you normally want to eliminate one area prefix and replace it with a newer one on a few or all the routers. As shown in Figure 4-7, you start with 49.0001 as the area prefix and want to renumber to 49.0002. To accomplish this, apply new NSAPs with the new area prefix to both RTA and RTB. In the third step, remove the NSAPs with 49.0001 from one router and then the other. This results in seamless and nonintrusive reconfiguration of the routers with new NSAP addresses, without downtime.

Figure 4-6   *Splitting areas.*

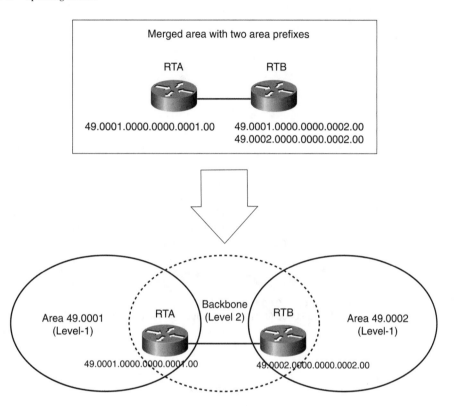

An interesting point to note is that IS-IS multihoming is not analogous to the concept of secondary IP subnets, where multiple isolated logical subnets can be created on the same link.

Another subtle difference is in how the two features are configured. In IS-IS multihoming, the multiple NSAP addresses are configured globally on the entire router, whereas secondary IP subnets are enabled by overlaying separate subnets on a single physical link.

Figure 4-7 *Renumbering NSAP addresses.*

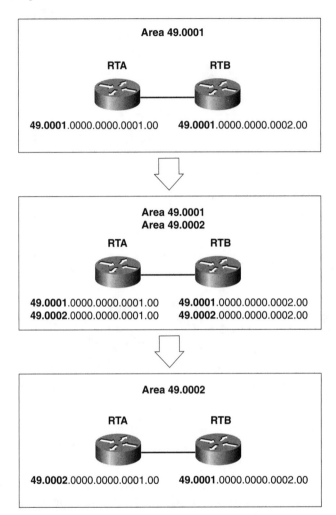

NSAP Selector Values

The NSEL field specifies a user of the network layer service. The routing layer is regarded as a special user of network layer services and is assigned a value of zero for the NSEL. The NSAP configured on IS-IS routers always uses 0x00 for the NSEL; such addresses are also referred to as *network entity titles (NETs)*. NSEL values have the same connotation as the Protocol Identifier in Layer 2 addresses or TCP port numbers. The NSEL value assists the network layer in handing off datagrams to the appropriate application or service user. According to the OSI layering scheme, the basic user of network layer services is the transport layer. CLNP data packets that are not meant for the routing process have target NSAP addresses with non-zero NSEL values to indicate the network service user at the transport layer. This does not apply to IP packets that are routed based on an IP destination address. For example, the NSEL value of 0x21 identifies the transport layer of DECNet Phase IV and a value of 0x22 for OSI Transport Layer TP4. OSI TP4 is implemented in DECNet Phase V (see Table 4-2). The transport layer then ultimately hands off to a higher protocol layer, possibly to the end application.

Table 4-2 *NSAP Selector (NSEL) Values*

NSEL Value	Network Service User
0x00	Routing Layer (for instance, IS-IS)
0x21	DECNet Phase IV Transport Layer
0x22	OSI Transport Layer TP4

NSAP Examples

This section presents concrete examples of CLNP NSAP addresses (see Examples 4-8, 4-9, and 4-10) to help the reader precipitate material covered on CLNP addressing structure.

Example 4-8 *A CLNP Example*

```
47.0001.aaaa.bbbb.cccc.00
Area = 47.0001, SysID = aaaa.bbbb.cccc, NSel = 00
```

Example 4-9 *A CLNP Example*

```
39.0f01.0002.0000.0c00.1111.00
Area = 39.0f01.0002, SysID = 0000.0c00.1111, NSel = 00
```

Example 4-10 *A CLNP Example*

```
49.0002.0000.0000 .0007.00
Area = 49.0002, SysID = 0000.0000.0007, Nsel = 00
```

NSAP Address–to–Host Name Mapping

As discussed in the preceding section, an NSAP can be long (up to 20 bytes, compared to 4 bytes in IP addresses). Also, the hexadecimal representation doesn't provide any operational convenience for router configuration, troubleshooting, or routine operations activities, such as inspection and maintenance of the IS-IS routing environment. Working with long NSAP addresses might be a daunting task, especially in high-pressure troubleshooting situations.

The SysID appears in several attributes, such as adjacency information, identifiers of link-state packets (LSPs) in the IS-IS database, and features in the output of many commands that are used by network operators to gather information about the network. Most people are better at working with symbolic names than with numeric representations. With the great success of the IP Domain Name System (DNS), it is obvious that a similar facility for translating between the hexadecimal representations of NSAP addresses and router host names is a necessary convenience for the network operations staff.

Cisco IOS Software provides two mechanisms for the router host name–to–NSAP address mapping. These mechanisms essentially provide a host name-to-SysID mapping. The first and older method, *static host name mapping*, uses static mapping statements in the router's configuration. The alternative method, *dynamic host name mapping*, was standardized only recently in the IETF. It employs a dynamic mechanism to achieve the same purpose. The following sections review these two methods.

Static Host Name Mapping

The IOS command **clns host <hostname> <nsap>** creates static host name–to–NSAP address (actually SysID) map tables on Cisco routers. This method has been available for a while and, despite its manual approach and usability challenges in large networks, it offers convenience to many network operations engineers who work with IS-IS.

Example 4-11 shows RTA and RTB configured with static CLNP host statements that enable the routers to resolve each other's NSAP (actually the SysID) to the corresponding name. This allows a router's name to be used in place of the SysID component in the Link-State Packet Identifier (LSP ID), providing tremendous convenience when troubleshooting or reviewing entries in the IS-IS Link-State database.

Example 4-11 *Static Host Name–to–NSAP Address Mapping*

```
RTA
Router isis
Net 49.0001.1111.2222.3333.00

CLNS host RTA 49.0001.1111.2222.3333.00
CLNS host RTB 49.0001.4444.4444.6666.00
```

Example 4-11 *Static Host Name–to–NSAP Address Mapping (Continued)*

```
RTB
Router isis
Net 49.0001.4444.5555.6666.00

CLNS host RTA 49.0001.1111.2222.3333.00
CLNS host RTB 49.0001.4444.4444.6666.00
```

Dynamic Host Name Mapping

The challenges involved in maintaining static CLNS host tables in large networks, and the obvious success and convenience of IP DNS, inspired the need for a dynamic approach for mapping and resolving host names to NSAP addresses. RFC 2763 specifies an enhancement to the IS-IS protocol that allows host name–to–NSAP address mapping information to be transported within the IS-IS protocol itself rather than an external DNS-like application. This automatic mechanism for gathering host name–to–NSAP address mapping information between IS-IS routers is significantly more convenient than the cumbersome manual approach that relies on static tables. RFC 2763 introduces an optional TLV (Type 137), which is carried in LSPs of participating routers, providing a simple and reliable mechanism for advertising host name information. Type, Length, and Value (TLV) fields are discussed in detail in Chapter 5.

TLV 137 is used for carrying a 7-bit ASCII representation of a router's host name, 1 byte per character. The length of this TLV ranges from 1 to 255 bytes. Routers running implementations of IS-IS that support optional TLV 137 read and install host names with corresponding SysID information in a host table that is used to resolve the SysID component of IDs of LSPs in the Link-State database. The dynamic host table also allows router host names to be used with the CLNS Traceroute and Ping troubleshooting tools.

Cisco routers running older releases of IOS, and other vendor routers that cannot interpret TLV 137, should just ignore it when encountered in an LSP. Obviously, for such routers, static host name mapping is the only alternative. Static entries must also be configured on all routers in the network for such routers that do not support TLV 137.

Summary

A routing protocol essentially assembles and organizes addressing information according to location within a network. IS-IS was originally designed for routing in ISO CLNS environments where the Layer 3 protocol is CNLP and the network layer addresses are described as NSAPs. Adapting IS-IS to carry IP information didn't eliminate NSAP addressing altogether because of the strong links within the protocol basis. Therefore, using IS-IS on IP routers requires node-based NSAPs to be defined in addition to the link-based IP addresses on the interfaces.

This chapter attempts to demystify NSAP addressing by explaining why it is still featured in Integrated IS-IS, even for IP-only routing, and by discussing the NSAP addressing architecture. The NSAP format is covered and you studied the three major relevant components when using IS-IS for IP routing, namely Area ID, SysID, and NSEL. Even though the IS-IS-related specifications suggest 1 to 8 bytes for the SysID, Cisco routers support a fixed 6-byte length in conformance with the U.S. GOSIP version 2.0 standard. This chapter discusses the significance of the SysID in IS-IS operations and provides guidelines for defining unique NSAPs on routers in an IS-IS area or domain. One method is to base the SysID on a loopback IP address on the router. In general, globally unique NSAPs are not needed for IS-IS routing in the IP domains that form the Internet, even though some service providers obtain and deploy such NSAPs in their networks. The chapter discusses the seven top-level NSAP addressing domains and provides insight into the role of RAs that allocate NSAP addresses to government and private organizations worldwide.

An interesting subject, IS-IS multihoming is discussed and compared with IS-IS multi-area support and IP subnettng. Multihoming configurations are useful for transitions such as merging, splitting, and renumbering of IS-IS areas. Multihoming causes Level 1 LSPs to be exchanged between IS-IS areas instead of using Level 2 routing. However, exchanging Level 1 LSPs between areas effectively merges them. A significant difference between multihoming and the multi-area feature is that the latter uses multiple IS-IS processes to support multiple independent areas, whereas the former merges areas under one process.

An NSAP can be as long as 20 bytes and a greater part of it is represented in hexadecimal, a format with which many people have difficulty working. Network operators who work with IS-IS on a regular basis cherish the convenience of working with symbolic names rather than long NSAP addresses. This chapter discussed the two methods available on Cisco routers for NSAP address–to–symbolic name mapping: static mapping and dynamic mapping. The latter method is specified by the IETF RFC 2763. This chapter concludes with a review of NSAP examples that illustrates how to delineate the three major fields in an NSAP.

Review Questions

1 What does the acronym NSAP represent and what is an NSAP used for?

2 What are the three major components of an NSAP? Describe the significance of each.

3 What is the maximum length of an NSAP and what is the minimum length that can be configured on a Cisco router?

4 What's the AFI field in an NSAP, and what is its significance?

5 How many OSI top-layer address domains exist? List them.

6 Associate the following addresses with one of these top-level address domains:

    1 **39.0005.1100.2200.432A.26CD.00**
    2 **47.0001.2211.3311.5566.ACD7.2351.00AC.210700**

7 How many bytes of the NSAP are allocated to the SysID on a Cisco router? What is the value specified by ISO 10589?

8 IS-IS has two levels of routing, Level 1 and Level 2. Elaborate on the relevance of the major fields of the NSAP to these routing levels in the ISO CLNS environment.

9 List some of the requirements and caveats for defining the system ID on a device.

10 How many NSAPs can you have per router according to ISO 10589? What is the purpose of having more than one NSAP per router?

11 What does SNPA stand for and what is its relevance in the IS-IS routing environment?

12 Identify the area address, SysID, and NSEL values in the following address:

```
47.005.8001.443E.AB11.BD48.0C1F.00
The NSAP address components are as follows:
Area: 47.005.8001.443E
System ID: AB11.BD48.0C1F
N-selector:00
```

References

ANSI Organization Registration Fact Sheet: web.ansi.org/public/services/reg_org.html

Identifiers for Organizations for Telecommunications Addressing IOTA; http://www.bsi-global.com/DISC/index.xhtml

IETF RFC 1237, "Guidelines for OSI NSAP Allocation in the Internet"

IETF RFC 2763, "Dynamic Hostname Exchange Mechanism for IS-IS"

IS0 8348/AD2, "Addendum to the Network Service Definition Covering Network Layer Addressing" (RFC 941)

ISO 8348, "Network Service Definition Standard"

CHAPTER 5

The IS-IS Link-State Database

In Chapter 3, "Integrated IS-IS Routing Protocol Concepts," you read about the two main categories of IS-IS functional capabilities: the subnetwork-dependent and subnetwork-independent functions. As you might recall, the subnetwork-dependent functions are primarily responsible for adjacency formation and management, whereas the subnetwork-independent functions provide capabilities for exchanging and managing routing and related control information. The IS-IS routing engine represented in Figure 3-8 illustrates the functional organization of the key processes and subsystems that are responsible for the subnetwork-independent functions. The IS-IS Link-State database, which is featured prominently in the routing engine, is the bottom line of all the complex operations that work together to achieve the objectives of the IS-IS protocol. Those objectives include the efficient collection and dissemination of routing information and the expedient determination of the most optimal path between any two points in the network.

The significance of the IS-IS routing engine in the overall IS-IS protocol framework underscores the importance of understanding the functions and operation of the IS-IS database for anyone interested in the nuts and bolts of the IS-IS protocol. This chapter focuses primarily on the IS-IS Link-State database and discusses its architectural internals. The discussion covers the role of the database update process, including how it gathers, stores, and disseminates routing information. The objective of the chapter is to provide you with a complete understanding and appreciation of the sophisticated innards of the IS-IS protocol.

The information elements stored in the IS-IS Link-State database are referred to as *link-state packets (LSPs)*. LSPs contain routing information generated by IS-IS routers to describe their immediate surrounding. Recall from Chapter 3 that LSPs are one of three categories of IS-IS packets; hello packets and sequence number packets (SNPs) are the others. LSPs contain information such as the following:

- Area information
- Adjacent routers
- IP subnets
- Metric information
- Authentication information

The information contained in an LSP represents a partial view of the entire topology of the local area. You might recall from previous chapters that the original specifications of IS-IS (ISO 10589 and RFC 1195) require each router in an IS-IS routing domain to be tied to at least one parent area.

NOTE   IS-IS implementation extensions in recent Cisco IOS releases support multi-area configurations in which a single router can connect to multiple independent areas. Multi-area support in IS-IS is intended for use in pure ISO domains and for scaling auxiliary networks for managing telecommunication network elements such as SONET Add Drop Multiplexors.

The routers in an area exchange LSPs by means of a process called *flooding*. The flooding process is discussed in detail later in this chapter.

LSPs learned from neighbors in the same area are stored locally on each router in the Level 1 IS-IS Link-State database. Each area in an IS-IS domain has its own unique Level 1 Link-State database. It is a key requirement of link-state protocols such as IS-IS that all routers in an area receive and assemble all intra-area LSPs into identical Link-State databases that represent the topology of the area. Each router then runs the shortest path first (SPF) algorithm over its database to obtain best paths for destinations within the area.

As discussed in Chapter 2, "Introduction to the IS-IS Routing Protocol," and Chapter 3, IS-IS supports a hierarchical routing architecture with two levels: Level 1 and Level 2. The Level 1 Link-State database supports routing within an area, and the Level 2 Link-State database supports routing between areas. The Level 2 Link-State database is a collection of Level 2 LSPs flooded over the backbone. The Level 2 LSPs contain pieces of information about the Level 2 topology as seen from the perspective of routers attached to the backbone. The complete Level 2 topology is obtained by running the SPF algorithm over the Level 2 database. In a typical network layout, the individual Level 1 areas are interconnected by a backbone formed by Level 2-capable routers, referred to as Level 1-2 routers. Level 1-2 routers maintain two separate Link-State databases for Level 1 and Level 2 routing, respectively. This is illustrated in Figure 5-1, which shows an IS-IS routing domain with two areas, 49.0001 and 49.0002.

Figure 5-1   *Level 1 and Level 2 Link-State databases.*

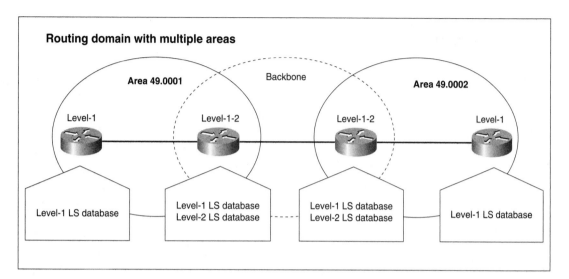

Figure 5-1 also shows routers in each area functioning as Level 1-only and with only a single database. For Cisco routers, the default configuration is both a Level 1 and Level 2 router. However, routing can be turned off for Level 1 or Level 2, if necessary, to conserve memory and processing resources. If a router is not connected to the backbone and it is running low on system resources, for example, it can be configured as Level 1-only so that it builds and maintains only a Level 1 Link-State database. Similarly, a router sitting in the middle of the backbone of the network, without any direct connections to a Level 1 area, can be configured as a Level 2-only router. In this case, the Level 2 configuration is necessary to maintain contiguity of the Level 2 backbone. Chapter 7, "General Network Design Issues," focuses on IS-IS network design issues in service provider environments and elaborates on various design considerations, including scenarios with large flat single Level 1- or Level 2-only architectures without any hierarchy. The purpose of such a design is usually to optimize path selection in the IS-IS routing environment, while at the same time preserving router memory and processor resources. All routers in the single-area domain have the same Level 1 or Level 2 database from which they derive routing information. Figure 5-2 illustrates a nonhierarchical domain spanned by a single Level 1 area.

Figure 5-2 *Single area domain, Level 1-only.*

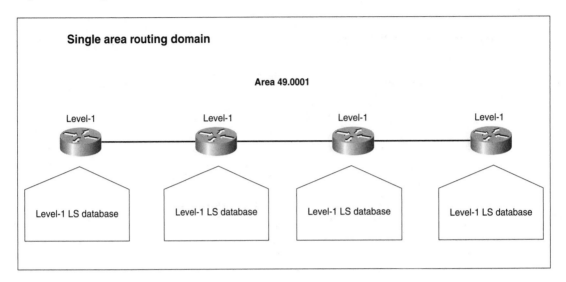

Alternatively, all the routers can be configured as Level 2-only, as shown in Figure 5-3; in which case, they all have identical Level 2 Link-State databases.

Figure 5-3 *Single area domain, Level 2-only.*

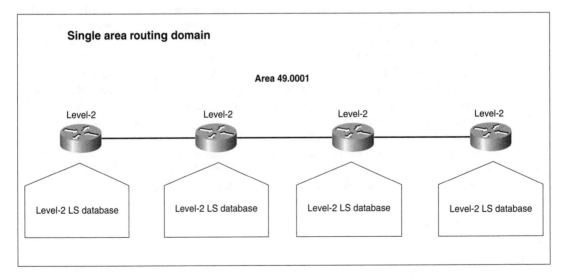

As mentioned earlier, IS-IS packets are categorized as follows:

- Hello packets
- LSPs
- SNPs

Hello packets are central to the operation of the subnetwork-dependent functions, which essentially involve forming and maintaining adjacencies. LSPs relate to the operation of the subnetwork-independent functions, which manage the routing information-gathering process.

SNPs help ensure the reliability of the flooding process, which in turn leads to efficient database synchronization between the Level 1 routers in the various areas and the Level 2 routers in the backbone. Flooding and database synchronization are discussed later in this chapter in the "Flooding and Link-State Database Synchronization" section. That section also discusses the specific roles played by the various types of SNPs in flooding and database synchronization.

The LSPs collected into the various databases together provide the basis for the big picture interpretation of the topology of an area or the backbone. This interpretation is achieved with the help of the SPF algorithm. By piecing together the information contained in the LSPs to determine the topology of the area or the backbone, SPF also helps determine the shortest path between two points in the network. The SPF algorithm is discussed in detail in Chapter 6, "The Shortest Path First Algorithm."

This chapter now turns to issues relevant to the Link-State database, such as security, data integrity, efficiency, and resource conservation. These topics are discussed from both protocol design and implementation perspectives.

IS-IS Link-State Packets

Level 1 and Level 2 LSPs are similar in format even though each type of packet carries information for different levels of the IS-IS routing hierarchy. This section reviews the generic LSP packet format and identifies differences between Level 1 and Level 2 LSPs. It also looks at the TLVs associated with each type of LSP.

Link-State Packet Format

As noted in Chapter 3, all IS-IS packets have a header to which TLV fields are appended (refer to Figure 3-2). A complete layout of the LSP format, including the header and the TLV sections, is shown in Figure 5-4.

Figure 5-4   *LSP format.*

No. of Octets

Field	Octets
Intradomain Routing Protocol Discriminator	1
Length Indicator	1
Version/Protocol ID Extension	1
ID Length	1
R R R PDU Type	1
Version	1
Reserved	1
Maximum Area Addresses	1
PDU Length	2
Remaining Lifetime	2
LSP ID	ID Length +2
Sequence Number	4
Checksum	2
P ATT OL IS Type	1
TLV Fields	

The PDU types for Level 1 and Level 2 LSPs are numbered 18 and 20, respectively. The interpretation of the header fields from the top of the packet up to and including the PDU Length field is the same for all IS-IS packets. The header fields following the PDU Length field are specific to the LSP format and have the following meanings:

- **Remaining Lifetime**—Remaining time for the LSP to expire.
- **LSP Identifier (LSP ID)**—Associates an LSP with its source for identification.
- **Sequence Number**—The sequence number of the LSP.
- **Checksum**—Checksum of the LSP calculated over fields starting from the LSP ID field to the end.
- **Partition**—Bit 8. Set if source of LSP supports partition repair.
- **Attached**—Bits 4–7. Set to indicate attachment to another area with applicable metrics as follows: bit 4 – default, bit 5 – delay, bit 6 – expense, bit 7 – error.

- **Overload**—Bit 3. Set to indicate that the Link-State database of the source is overloaded and that processing and memory resources are limited.

- **IS Type**—Bits 1 and 2. Indicates the type of router; Level 1 (only bit 1 set) or Level 2 (both bits 1 and 2 set). Other combinations are not defined.

Various types of TLV fields can be included in LSPs to propagate different kinds of routing information. Each TLV follows a generic format, which includes fields for the type of TLV, the length of the specific TLV, and the value or contents of the TLV. The section in this chapter titled "Link-State Packet TLVs" provides in-depth coverage of the type of TLVs that might be contained in LSPs.

The LSPs in the Link-State database of a Cisco router can be viewed with the command **show isis database** (see Example 5-1). This command displays two separate Link-State databases: Level 1 and Level 2. A variation of the command can be entered to display only one database by using the Level-1 or Level-2 command options.

Example 5-1 *Output of show isis database Command*

```
RTB# sh isis database
IS-IS Level-1 Link State Database
LSPID                   LSP Seq Num   LSP Checksum LSP Holdtime ATT/P/OL
0000.0000.0005.00-00   0x000007EF    0xDD14       667          0/0/0
0000.0000.0006.00-00   0x000007E7    0x2ECA       1126         0/0/0
0000.0000.0007.00-00*  0x000007FB    0x6FCB       960          1/0/0
0000.0000.0007.01-00*  0x000007E3    0xA91D       782          0/0/0

IS-IS Level-2 Link State Database
LSPID                   LSP Seq Num   LSP Checksum LSP Holdtime ATT/P/OL
0000.0000.0001.00-00   0x000007EB    0x27F        858          0/0/0
0000.0000.0007.00-00*  0x000007EF    0x1637       851          0/0/0
0000.0000.0007.01-00*  0x000007CB    0x2C5F       630          0/0/0
```

Each database contains LSPs for a specific routing level. In Example 5-1, the following information is provided for each LSP: LSP ID, LSP sequence number, LSP checksum, LSP holdtime, remaining lifetime (LSP holdtime), status of attachment (ATT), overload status (OL), and partition support (P).

Depending on the setup of a router, the system ID component in the LSP IDs can be resolved into the corresponding host names of the source routers (see Example 5-2). As you can see, all these elements that describe the LSP in the **show isis database** output are excerpts from the LSP header. The following sections discuss them further.

LSP Remaining Lifetime

The Remaining Lifetime field in an LSP features a timer that tracks the age of an LSP. The ultimate goal for tracking the age of an LSP is to purge the Link-State database of stale information. The two important threshold values associated with the remaining lifetime are LSP maxage and LSP refresh interval.

LSP maxage is the upper bound of the remaining lifetime of an LSP and specifies the maximum life span of an LSP. ISO 10589 specifies a value of 20 minutes (1200 seconds). Recent changes in Cisco IOS Software allow larger values of the LSP lifetime to be configured (up to 653,350 seconds) using the **lsp-max-lifetime** command. When an LSP is created at the originating router, the Remaining Lifetime field is set to the value of LSP maxage and flooded throughout the area through adjacent neighbors. The remaining lifetime of an LSP decreases with time. When an LSP ages up to the refresh interval (that is, the remaining lifetime has decreased by the refresh interval), it is regenerated by the source. Otherwise, the LSP would continue to age until the remaining lifetime reaches zero value; at which point, it would be purged out of the network.

The *refresh interval* is the periodic interval at which LSPs are regenerated or refreshed by the originating routers even if no network changes necessitate that. When the LSP is regenerated, the remaining lifetime is reset to maxage and reflooded into the network. At the refresh time, the value of the Remaining Lifetime is the difference between maxage and the refresh interval. ISO 10589 specifies an LSP refresh interval of 15 minutes, which is 900 seconds. Recent Cisco IOS releases allow higher values of the refresh intervals to be configured using the command **lsp-refresh-interval**. Up to 635,530 seconds of refresh time can be configured in place of the 900-second default. If a router does not refresh its LSP after the refresh interval and the LSP ages on to zero remaining lifetime, all routers that have a copy of this LSP eventually purge it from their databases after a grace period of 60 seconds. The grace period, which is referred to as *ZeroAgeLifetime* is not a configurable parameter in Cisco IOS Software.

Increasing the refresh interval reduces the frequency of periodic refreshing of LSPs. This in turn, reduces the toll on network resources, such as bandwidth and processing costs. Larger refresh intervals than the default are recommended only in stable network environments. If there is a need to adjust the LSP refresh interval, the LSP maxage also must be adjusted accordingly, with maxage being a little higher than the refresh interval.

Link-State Packet Identifier

The Link-State Packet Identifier (LSP ID), as the name implies, is used to distinguish LSPs from each other and to identify the originating routers. The LSP ID consists of the following three components:

- System Identifier (SysID)
- Pseudonode Identifier (PSN ID)
- LSP number

Figure 5-5 shows the LSP structure. The size of the SysID is 6 bytes, with a 1-byte Pseudonode ID and a 1-byte LSP number appended.

Figure 5-5   *Structure of the LSP ID.*

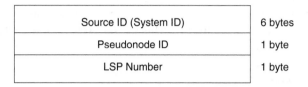

Source ID (System ID)	6 bytes
Pseudonode ID	1 byte
LSP Number	1 byte

The SysID component of the LSP ID refers to the originating router. The non-zero Pseudonode ID identifies special LSPs that are referred to as *pseudonode LSPs*. A pseudonode LSP is associated with a multiaccess link, and it is generated by the designated intermediate system on that link. A router's regular LSP has a Pseudonode ID value of zero. The LSP number refers to fragments of an LSP (regular or pseudonode). The first fragment of an LSP is number zero. When any fragment of a large LSP is lost in transmission, the receiver drops all the other fragments and the whole set must be retransmitted, wasting precious bandwidth.

In contrast to the Open Shortest Path First (OSPF) Protocol, IS-IS does not use many types of LSPs to distribute routing information. All routing information, as for Level 1 routing, is bundled into a single LSP, which can be fragmented as necessary. Because fragmentation on-the-fly has undesirable consequences on processing resources of routers, however, IS-IS mitigates the negative consequences by constraining the maximum size of an LSP unit and proactively fragmenting a large LSP into smaller units, which are independently flooded through the network. The maximum size of an LSP is 1492 bytes. The IS-IS specification, ISO 10589, requires hellos to be padded to the maximum LSP buffer size or the MTU of the outgoing interfaces (MTU usually used), meaning both sides of an adjacency must normally have the same MTU to form an adjacency. Figure 5-6 shows examples of LSP IDs. The third example shows the LSP ID of an LSP fragment.

Figure 5-6   *Figure 5-6 LSP ID examples.*

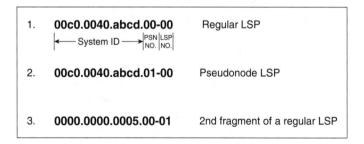

As indicated previously, the numeric SysID in the LSP ID (refer to Example 5-1) is replaced by the host name of the originating router if static host names are in place or dynamic name resolution is in effect. Example 5-2 shows a **show isis database** output in which the LSP IDs feature the host names of the corresponding source routers.

Example 5-2   *Name-Based System IDs*

```
RTB#show isis database

IS-IS Level-1 Link State Database:
LSPID               LSP Seq Num   LSP Checksum LSP Holdtime ATT/P/OL
RTA.00-00           0x00000065    0x1EDF       989          0/0/0
RTA.01-00           0x0000005A    0x370E       744          0/0/0
RTB.00-00          *0x00000067    0x8475       1128         1/0/0

IS-IS Level-2 Link State Database:
LSPID               LSP Seq Num   LSP Checksum LSP Holdtime ATT/P/OL
RTB.00-00          *0x00000070    0x6289       1176         0/0/0
RTC.00-00           0x00000063    0x657A       965          0/0/0
RTC.02-00           0x0000005D    0xB1BE       1088         0/0/0
```

This **show isis database** output contains two LSPs from RTA in the Level 1 database, represented by RTA.00-00 and RTA.01-00, respectively. Even though generated by the same router, each LSP has a different pseudonode number in its LSP ID. RTA.00-00, which has a zero pseudonode number and is RTA's own regular LSP. RTA.01-00 has a non-zero Pseudonode ID, and therefore represents a pseudonode LSP generated for a LAN on which RTA is the DIS. The pseudonode LSP lists all known routers connected to the LAN, whereas a router's own LSP carries information such as adjacent neighbors on all interfaces, IP prefix information, and so on.

Link-State Packet Sequence Number

In the LSP header, 4 bytes are dedicated to the Sequence Number field for numbering LSPs by the update process. The LSP sequence number is specified as a 32-bit unsigned integer and increases in 1 increments from 0 to an upper threshold of 1 less than the number 2 to the power of 32 ($2^{32} - 1$). The value 2^{32} is referred to as *SequenceModulus*. The first LSP generated by a router, when it first connects to a network, has a sequence number of 1. The sequence number is increased by 1 whenever a newer version of the LSP is generated as a result of changes in a router's environment. The sequence number plays a key role in the database synchronization process by helping routers in the same area identify older LSPs from newer versions. Also, when a router crashes and reconnects to the network, it generates a new LSP with a sequence number of 1. If the router's older LSP at the time of crash has a higher sequence number and hasn't been purged from the network, however, one of the other routers in the same area sends a copy of the older LSP to the recovered router.

The router then adjusts its sequence number to be close to the value before it crashed, by generating yet another LSP with current information but with a sequence number that is larger than that of the older LSP by 1.

The size of the Sequence Number field (4 bytes) allows a router to generate new LSPs with incrementing sequence numbers for a long time without running over. The following calculation elaborates on the reasoning behind this claim. First, consider the maximum possible sequence number, account for inherent protocol delays in regenerating LSPs, and then convert the time it takes to attain the maximum sequence number into years.

Step 1   The total number of possible sequence number adjustments, counting from 1, is $2^{32} - 1 = 4,294,967,295$.

Step 2   Using the specified minimum LSP regeneration interval of 30 seconds, the time required to deplete the sequence number space is $(4,294,967,295 \times 30)$ seconds.

Step 3   The resulting value from Step 2 is converted into years, as follows:

$(4,294,967,295 \times 30$ seconds$)/(60$ seconds $\times 60$ minutes $\times 24$ hours $\times 365$ days$) = 4085.77$ years

Even accounting for leap years, it will take more than 4000 years for a router that is continuously generating its LSP (unrealistically) to overrun the Sequence Number field.

Still wondering what might happen if by some magic a router's LSP sequence number were to reach the maximum possible sequence number? Well, ISO 10589 instructs that an event referred to as *AttemptToExceedMaximumSequenceNumber* should be logged and the IS-IS process disabled for the period of maxage + ZeroAgeLifetime to allow the most recent LSP to expire and be purged from the network. The router can then be restarted, enabling it to kick off with a new LSP with a sequence number value of 1.

Link-State Packet Checksum

To guarantee the integrity of the information in an LSP, the originating router computes a checksum on the LSP and enters it into the LSP Checksum field. The checksum value is verified by any router that receives a copy of the LSP. The Checksum field is the third column in the output of the **show isis database** command (refer to Example 5-2). The LSP checksum is calculated over fields starting after the Remaining Lifetime field up to the end of the LSP. The checksum is unmodified as copies of the LSP are propagated through the network from one router to the other. It makes sense to exclude the Remaining Lifetime field because it contains a continuously changing timer value. The checksum helps detect corrupted LSPs or stale LSP duplicates that have not yet been purged from the network.

When a router receives what looks like a copy of its LSP but with corrupted information, it tries to purge it from the network by flooding a newer LSP with current link-state information and a higher sequence number than that of the corrupted LSPs. All other routers in the area then receive and install the newer LSP, thus purging the older LSP from their databases.

In general, any router that detects a corrupted LSP initiates a purge by flooding a copy with the remaining lifetime reset to 0. This action effectively causes other routers in the area also to purge the LSP. Corrupted LSPs are not used in routing calculations or reflooded as is. If the originator is still connected to the area, it originates and refloods a valid copy of the LSP.

If an LSP is continuously being corrupted in transmission, purged from the network by other routers, and then reissued by the source, this results in a situation described as an *LSP corruption storm*. This phenomenon is covered in detail later in this chapter in the section "IS-IS Link-State Database Integrity Issues." An LSP corruption storm is a resource-intensive activity that can potentially result in more complicated network problems and even a network meltdown if pervasive.

Cisco IOS Software allows routers to be configured to ignore corrupted LSPs and to log errors only locally. The router-level IOS command **lsp-ignore-errors** can be used to enable this capability.

Other LSP Header Information: Partition, Attached, Overload, and IS Type Fields

This section looks at the bit fields in the last byte of the LSP header. These fields include the 1-bit Partition field, the 4-bit Attached field, the 1-bit Overload field, and the 2-bit IS Type field.

Partition—The original IS-IS specification, ISO 10589, describes how to repair a partitioned Level 1 area by creating an alternate Level 1 path through the Level 2 backbone. This arrangement takes advantage of the existence of connections from each of the Level 1 partitions to the backbone and the latter's contiguity to establish a repair path by reconnecting the partitions over the backbone. This works by electing a Level 2-capable router in each partition as the partition-designated Level 2 IS and establishing a special adjacency, known as *virtual adjacency* or *virtual link* between them.

The virtual link provides the Level 1 repair path through the backbone. The partition-designated routers advertise the virtual adjacencies by setting the partition bit in their Level 1 LSPs, thus signaling the existence of the virtual link to Level 1 routers for forwarding data between the partitions. Figure 5-7 illustrates area partition repair. Details regarding detection of an area partition, election of partition-designated routers, and establishment of virtual links are beyond the scope of this book. (For more complete coverage, refer to ISO 10589.) Partition repair is an optional capability in IS-IS and is currently not supported in Cisco IOS Software. Cisco routers enabled for IS-IS routing, therefore, always set the partition bit in their LSPs to zero and also ignore the partition bit if it is set in any received LSPs. Consequently, the partition bit has no relevance to the operation of Integrated IS-IS on Cisco routers.

Figure 5-7   *Area partition repair.*

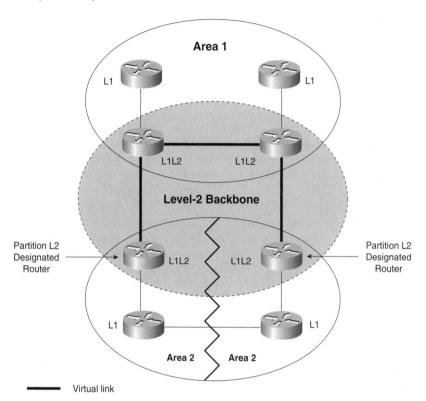

Attached—The 4-bit Attached field is set by Level 2 routers in their Level 1 LSPs to indicate to same-area Level 1 routers that they are connected in other areas. Connectivity to another area in the domain essentially implies attachment to the backbone. IS-IS areas, as specified in ISO 10589, are stubs, and Level 1 routers forward packets to other areas in the domain through the closest Level 2 router. Level 2 routers in an area advertise themselves to the Level 1 routers by setting the attach bits in their Level 1 LSPs. Even though the attached bits are specified in both Level 1 and Level 2 LSPs, they are relevant only in the Level 1 routing framework. The 4 bits also allow an IS-IS router to indicate which of the 4 metric types are supported for attaching to the backbone. Each bit is dedicated to a specific type of metric (see Table 5-1). The four types of metrics supported by the IS-IS protocol (default, delay, expense, and error) is discussed in detail in Chapter 3. These metrics are designed for quality-of-service application. Only the default metric is supported in Cisco IOS Software.

Table 5-1   *Attached Bits Field Settings*

Bit position in Octet	Attached Field Bits	Metric Type
4 (00001000)	0001	Default
5 (00010000)	0010	Delay
6 (00100000)	0100	Expense
7 (01000000)	1000	Error

Overload—Bit 3 in the last byte of the LSP header signals the resource availability state of a router. If this bit is set, it indicates an overload condition at the router. An overload condition indicates the router's performance is inhibited by low memory and processing resources. LSPs with the overload bit set are not reflooded and also are not used in calculating paths through the overloaded router. This means that the overloaded router is circumvented for transit traffic; however, paths in which the overloaded router is the last hop are calculated. The Cisco IOS command **set-overload-bit** allows manual setting of the overload bit. The overload bit can be leveraged to deliberately prevent transit traffic from flowing through a specific router. This is discussed further in Chapter 7.

IS Type—The IS Type bits in the LSP indicate whether the LSP is from a Level 1 or Level 2 router. This essentially indicates the target Link-State database for storing the LSP. The possible bit settings for the IS Type field are shown in Table 5-2.

Table 5-2   *IS Type Field Settings*

Bits Values	Bits in Octet	IS Type
00	00000000	Unused
01	00000001	Level-1
10	00000010	Unused
11	00000011	Level-2

Example 5-3 is a decode of an LSP from a packet analyzer showing the fields in the LSP header section. All the LSP-specific header fields discussed earlier are featured, presenting an interesting view of the structure and format of the LSP header.

Example 5-3   *LSP Header Decode*

```
IS-IS: Protocol ID = 83 (Intermediate System Routing Exchange Protocol)
IS-IS: Header length = 27
IS-IS: Version / Protocol ID Extension = 1
IS-IS: ID Length = 0, Indicate 6 Octets
IS-IS: PDU type = 18  (Link State, Level 1)
IS-IS: Version = 1
IS-IS: Reserved = 0
IS-IS: Maximum Area Addresses = 0
```

Example 5-3   *LSP Header Decode (Continued)*

```
IS-IS: Frame length is 100 byte(s)
IS-IS: Remaining life is 1199 second(s)
IS-IS: Link State Frame ID:
IS-IS:    Source ID      = 000000000001
IS-IS:    Pseudo-node    =      (Not a pseudo-node)
IS-IS:    Link frame no. = 0
IS-IS: Frame Sequence = 6203
IS-IS: Checksum = E6CF
IS-IS: Attributes = 0B
IS-IS: 0...  .... = Partition repair not supported
IS-IS: .0..  .... = Not attached using error metric
IS-IS: ..0.  .... = Not attached using expense metric
IS-IS: ...0  .... = Not attached using delay metric
IS-IS: ....1  ... = Attached using default metric
IS-IS: .... .0.. = No LSP Database Overload
IS-IS: .... ..11   = Level 2 intermediate system
```

Link-State Packet TLVs

The previous sections of this chapter reviewed the LSP packet format and discussed fields in the LSP header. As shown in Figure 5-2, TLV fields are appended to the header of an IS-IS packet, depending on its type and the specifics of the routing environment, to form the complete packet. This section covers the TLVs defined for Level 1 and Level 2 LSPs by ISO 10589 and RFC 1195. Table 5-3 lists the TLVs for Level 1 LSPs defined in both standards, and Table 5-4 lists the TLVs for Level 2 LSPs. Some TLVs are used in both Level 1 and Level 2 LSPs. Those unique to a specific level of LSP are bolded. Some of the recent TLVs defined by the IETF for various extensions to Integrated IS-IS, such as MPLS traffic engineering, are covered in the section "IS-IS Metric Extensions" later in this chapter.

TLVs for Level 1 LSPs

Table 5-3 lists the TLVs specified in ISO 10589 and RFC 1195 to support the IS-IS Level 1 routing environment. TLVs (Type, Length, Value) fields also are referred to as CLV (Code, Length, Value) fields in the previously mentioned standards. TLV is used because it is more common in recent literature and IETF publications. The End System Neighbors information TLV (Type 3) is bolded because it is specific only to the Level 1 routing environment.

Table 5-3   *Level-1 TLVs*

TLV	Type	Source
Area Address	1	ISO 10589
Intermediate System Neighbors	2	ISO 10589

continues

Table 5-3   *Level-1 TLVs (Continued)*

TLV	Type	Source
End System Neighbors	**3**	**ISO 10589**
Authentication Information	10	ISO 10589
IP Internal Reachability Information	128	RFC 1195
Protocols Supported	129	RFC 1195
IP Interface Address	132	RFC 1195

The uses of the various Level 1 TLVs are described here:

- **Area Address TLV**—This TLV lists the set of area addresses configured on the originating router. The TLV features only in nonpseudonode LSPs and is in the first fragment if the LSP is fragmented. The Area Address TLV is made up of the following fields:

  — **Type (1 byte)**—1

  — **Length (1 byte)**—Total length of the Value field

  — **Value**—n × (1-byte address length + variable area address)

- **Intermediate System Neighbors TLV**—This TLV captures the list of adjacent Level 1 routers. It consists of the following fields:

  — **Type (1 byte)**—2

  — **Length (1 byte)**—1 byte + n × (system ID length + 5 in bytes) for n neighbors

  — **Value**—1 byte virtual flag + n multiples of (4-byte neighbor metric information + neighbor SysID + 1 byte Pseudonode ID)

The Intermediate System Neighbors TLV is repeated for each neighbor. The TLV differs from the IS Neighbors TLVs (Type 6) used in LAN hello packets. Specifically, this TLV (Type 2) also carries metric information for each of the neighbors. IS-IS metrics is an interesting topic and is discussed in detail in the sections "IS-IS Metrics Information" and "IS-IS Metric Extensions" later in this chapter.

- **End System Neighbors TLV**—This TLV is available only in Level 1 LSPs. It captures and lists adjacent Level 1 routers as well as end systems, such as ISO CLNP workstations captured through the ES-IS protocol. It has the following structure:

  — **Type (1 byte)**—3

  — **Length (1 byte)**—4 bytes + SysID length of ES neighbor

  — **Value**—Common metric + multiples of SysID of ES neighbors

End systems with the same metric are grouped together in a single TLV.

- **Authentication Information TLV**—This TLV provides for LSP authentication through a simple clear-text password scheme. No other password types for IS-IS packet authentication have been standardized as of this writing. However, the IETF IS-IS Working Group is looking at a more sophisticated MD5-based authentication scheme. Authentication is discussed in further detail in Chapter 9, "Configuring IS-IS for IP Routing on Cisco Routers."

  — **Type (1 byte)**—10

  — **Length (1 byte)**—Specified length of the Value field in bytes within the range of 1–254 bytes

  — **Value**—This field is made up of two components: Type of Authentication and Authentication Password, as follows:

    - Type of authentication (1 byte)
      0 and 2–254 – Reserved
      1 – Clear-text password
      255 – Domainwide authentication

    - Authentication password—For authentication Type 1, this is a variable-length clear-text password up to 254 bytes long.

- **IP Internal Reachability Information TLV**—This TLV stores a list of directly connected IP prefixes. It is used only in nonpseudonode LSPs. Each prefix is assigned a metric value, which corresponds to that of the link over which the IP prefix is configured.

  — **Type (1 byte)**—128

  — **Length (1 byte)**—Multiples of 12 bytes

  — **Value**—Multiple entries, each consisting of the following:

    - 4 bytes for metric information

    - 4 bytes for IP prefix

    - 4 bytes for IP subnet mask

- **Protocols Supported TLV**—This TLV identifies the Layer 3 protocols supported by Integrated IS-IS. It must appear in the first fragment (LSP number 0) if the LSP is fragmented. Currently, the only protocols supported are CLNP (NLPID 0x81) and IP (NLPID 0xCC).

  — **Type (1 byte)**—129

  — **Length (1 byte)**—Total length of the Value field in bytes

  — **Value**—Network layer protocol identifiers (NLPIDs) for supported protocols, 1 byte each

- **IP Interface Address TLV**—This TLV contains one or more of the IP addresses configured on the originator of the LSP. In recent IOS releases, the highest loopback address is entered automatically in this field.

  — **Type (1 byte)**—132

  — **Length (1 byte)**—Total length of the Value field in bytes

  — **Value**—Multiples of 4-byte IP addresses

Example 5-4 shows a Level 1 LSP output from a Cisco router displayed by the command **show isis database**. An LSP ID and the keyword "detail" are entered as arguments to display the details of a specific LSP. The output shows the LSP header and the TLVs in the LSP. The following TLVs are present: Area Address TLV, Protocols Supported TLV, IP Address TLV, Internal IP Reachability TLV, IS Neighbors TLV, and the ES Neighbors TLV. LSP shows that only IP (NLPID 0xCC) is supported. This is because CLNP routing is not enabled and because IS-IS is used for routing only IP on this router.

Example 5-4 *Level-1 LSP from a Cisco Router*

```
RTD#show isis database 0000.0000.0004.00-00 level-1 detail

IS-IS Level-1 LSP 0000.0000.0004.00-00
LSPID               LSP Seq Num  LSP Checksum LSP Holdtime ATT/P/OL
0000.0000.0004.00-00* 0x0000000F    0x6699       1036           1/0/0
 Area Address: 49.0002
 NLPID:    0xCC
IP Address:  11.1.1.4
Metric: 10 IP 10.1.2.0 255.255.255.0
Metric: 10 IP 192.168.2.12 255.255.255.252
Metric: 10 IP 11.1.1.4 255.255.255.255
Metric: 10 IS 0000.0000.0004.02
Metric: 10 IS 0000.0000.0002.01
Metric: 0 ES 0000.0000.0004
```

The following calculation enables you to determine how many IP prefixes can be advertised in an LSP. The following constraints are to be considered in the calculation:

- The maximum size (maxLSPsize) of an LSP is 1492 bytes.

- The LSP header (lspHeadersize) is 27 bytes.

- The maximum length of a TLV (maxTLVlength) is 255 bytes.

- Each TLV 128 consists of type (1 byte), length (1 byte), and IP prefixes ($n \times 12$ bytes) up to total of 255 bytes.

- The maximum number of fragments of an LSP (maxLSPfragments) is 256. The number of fragments is determined from the 1-byte LSP Number field in the LSP identifier.

- The first fragment contains other TLVs, and the remaining 255 fragments are packed with only TLV 128.

The actual calculation is as follows:

1 The total space available for TLVs in an LSP is

   TLVSpace = maxLSPsize - lspHeadersize = 1492 - 27 = 1465 bytes

2 The number of TLVs that can fit into TLVSpace is

   1465/255 = 5.7, approximately 6

   Assuming a 1–byte Type field and 1-byte Length field, overhead for 6 TLVs is

   $6 \times 2 = 12$ bytes.

3 Actual space available for prefixes is

   1465 – 12 bytes overhead = 1453 bytes

4 Number of prefixes, each 12 bytes (address + subnet mask + metric) that can fit into TLVSpace is

   1453/12 = 121.08 (approximately 121 IP prefixes per LSP)

Considering that few other TLVs can be generated by the router, the number of IP prefixes that can be supported per IS-IS router is 256 fragments, each containing 121 prefixes, for a total of 30,976 prefixes.

TLVs for Level 2 LSPs

Table 5-4 lists the Level 2 TLVs, which are the subject of this section. The blocked TLVs are available only in Level 2 LSPs. The others are shared TLVs and can be used in both Level 1 and Level 2 LSPs (refer to Table 5-3). As in Table 5-3, the TLV type and the standard in which a TLV was originally specified are shown in this table.

Table 5-4   *Level-2 TLVs*

TLV	Type	Source
Area Address	1	ISO 10589
Intermediate System Neighbors	2	ISO 10589
Partition-Designated Level 2 Intermediate System	4	ISO 10589
Prefix Neighbors	5	ISO 10589
Authentication Information	10	ISO 10589
IP Internal Reachability Information	128	RFC 1195
Protocols Supported	129	RFC 1195
IP External Reachability Information	130	RFC 1195
Interdomain Routing Protocol Information	131	RFC 1195
IP Interface Address	132	RFC 1195

The uses of the various Level 2 TLVs are as follows:

- **Area Address**—Type 1. Same as defined for Level 1 LSPs.

- **Intermediate System Neighbors**—Type 2. Same as defined for Level 1 LSPs.

- **Partition-Designated Level 2 Intermediate System TLV**—This TLV supports partition repair of a partitioned Level 1 area by creating a virtual path over the backbone between two Level 2 routers in each of the partitions. Partition repair is currently not supported on Cisco routers.

  — **Type (1 byte)**—4

  — **Length (1 byte)**—Length of SysID

  — **Value**—SysID of partition-designated Level 2 IS

- **Prefix Neighbors TLV**—This TLV collects information on reachable NSAP prefixes. The TLV is relevant only for ISO CLNP routing between areas (Level 2 routing). Prefixes with the same metric value are bundled together in the same TLV. There can be multiples of this TLV in an LSP, and it can occur in any fragment of an LSP.

  — **Type (1 byte)**—5.

  — **Length (1 byte)**—Total length of the Value field.

  — **Value**—Each Prefix Neighbor TLV consists of 4 bytes of common metric + multiples of (1-byte address prefix length + address prefix).

  Authentication Information TLV—Type 10. Same as defined for Level 1 LSPs.

- **IP Internal Reachability Information**—Type 128. Same as defined for Level 1 LSPs.

- **Protocols Supported**—Type 129. Same as defined for Level 1 LSPs.

- **IP External Reachability Information**—This TLV collects IP routes obtained from other routing protocol sources by means of redistribution into IS-IS:

  — **Type (1 byte)**—130

  — **Length (1 byte)**—$n \times 12$, where n is the number of external routes

  — **Value**—Multiples of 4-byte metric information + (4-byte IP prefix and 4-byte prefix mask)

Only the IS-IS default metric type is supported on Cisco routers. When configuring redistribution on a Cisco router, two choices of metric labels for external routes apply: internal or external. The actual value applied to external routes depend on the label selected in the configuration. Redistribution is covered in detail in Chapter 9.

- **Interdomain Routing Protocol Information (IDRPI) TLV**—This TLV is specified in RFC 1195 to support interaction of the IS-IS protocol with any Interdomain Routing Protocol running on the boundary of the IS-IS domain. It is currently not supported in Cisco IOS Software:

    — **Type (1 byte)**—131.

    — **Length (1 byte)**—Total length of the Value field.

    — **Value**—This field is made up of two components.

  A byte specifies the type of Interdomain Information field as follows:

    0 – Reserved.

    1 – External Information field has special format.

    2 – External Information field contains a single 2-byte autonomous system (AS) number. The AS number is to be used for tagging all subsequent IP external reachability information in the LSP up to the occurrence of another IDRPI TLV.

  External Information field, which depends on the type of the Interdomain Information field.

- **IP Interface Address TLV**—Type 132. Same as defined for Level 1 LSPs. The TLV can occur multiple times and in any LSP fragment. The same addresses must be in both Level 1 and Level 2 LSPs if the router is Level 1-2.

Example 5-5 shows a Level 2 LSP from a Cisco router. Some of the information in this LSP is also present in the Level 1 LSP displayed from the same router (refer to Example 5-4). Information specific to the Level 2 LSP is the IP External Reachability Information TLV. The ES Neighbors TLV is present in only the Level 1 LSP and the two LSP share a common IP address in the IP Interface TLV (11.1.1.4).

Example 5-5 *Level-2 LSP from a Cisco Router*

```
RTD#show isis database 0000.0000.0004.00-00 level-2 detail

IS-IS Level-2 LSP 0000.0000.0004.00-00
LSPID                   LSP Seq Num  LSP Checksum LSP Holdtime ATT/P/OL
0000.0000.0004.00-00* 0x00000012    0xC837       389          0/0/0
 Area Address: 49.0002
 NLPID:    0xCC
IP Address:   11.1.1.4
Metric: 10 IS 0000.0000.0004.02
Metric: 10 IS 0000.0000.0003.00
Metric: 10 IS 0000.0000.0002.01
Metric: 128 IP-External 172.16.0.0 255.255.0.0
Metric: 10 IP 10.1.2.0 255.255.255.0
Metric: 20 IP 11.1.1.2.255.255.255.255
Metric: 10 IP 11.1.1.4 255.255.255.255
Metric: 10 IP 192.168.2.12 255.255.255.252
```

IS-IS Metrics Information

TLVs specified by ISO 10589 contain metric information:

- ES Neighbors TLV (Type 2)
- IS Neighbors TLV (Type 3)
- Prefix Neighbors TLV (Type 5)

The overall formats of these TLVs exhibit minor differences; however, the format of the metric fields is the same in all of them. Figure 5-8 shows the metric fields in the IS Neighbors TLV. Of the following four types of metric specified, only the default is currently supported on Cisco routers:

- **Default metric**—Must be supported by all routers in the domain. Frequently interpreted as a measure that is inversely proportional to bandwidth. Therefore, lower values imply high bandwidth and are better.
- **Delay metric**—Optional. Measures the transit delay of a link.
- **Expense metric**—Optional. Measures the financial-related costs of using a link.
- **Error metric**—Optional. Measures the residual error probability of a link.

Figure 5-8   *IS Neighbors TLV metric fields.*

0	I/E	Default Metric
S	I/E	Delay Metric
S	I/E	Expense Metric
S	I/E	Error Metric
Neighbor ID		

Bit 8 (the S bit) of each metric byte indicates support for the specific metric. For the default metric, this bit is reserved and is always set to 0. In the case of the other metric types, if bit 8 is set, the metric is unsupported. Bit 7 is this internal/external bit. It is set to 0 to indicate that the specific metric is an internal type and to 1 to indicate external type.

The following IP information TLVs specified by RFC 1195 also contain metric information:

- IP Internal Reachability TLV (Type 128)
- IP External Reachability TLV (Type 130)

Figure 5-9 shows the layout of the metric fields in the IP Internal Reachability TLV, which is quite similar to the format of the IS Neighbors TLV, as shown in Figure 5-8. Obviously, RFC 1195 borrows directly from the metric definitions of ISO 10589. Notice that, in Figure 5-9, only the default metric has the I/E field. The setting for the default metric (internal or external) applies to all the other metrics. The I/E bit fields in the other bytes are reserved.

Figure 5-9   *IP Internal Reachability metric fields (TLV 128/ TLV 130).*

1	1	6 bits
0	I/E	Default Metric
S	R	Delay Metric
S	R	Expense Metric
S	R	Error Metric
IP Address (4 bytes)		
Subnet Mask (4 bytes)		

The default metric must be supported on all nodes in the routing domain. The delay, expense, and error metrics are optional and are specified to support quality-of-service routing. The delay, expense, and error metrics are relevant to path selection criteria defined by the Globally Unique Quality of Service parameters that can be set in the Quality of Service (QoS) Maintenance field of a CLNP packet header. The QoS Maintenance field specifies optional path selection criteria by the network services user.

Each type of metric is independent of the other, and their consideration in path selection relative to each other depends on various bit settings of the QoS Maintenance field in conjunction with selection of a globally unique QoS criterion. Each type of metric is allocated a byte in the TLV. Setting bit 8 (S) of a QoS metric indicates that it is not supported. Because the default metric must be supported, its bit value 8 is specified as 0. As indicated previously, currently none of the optional QoS-related metrics are supported in Cisco IOS. Only the default metric is available as path selection criteria. The default metric is a scalar parameter referred to as *cost*. In most current applications, it is given an inverse bandwidth connotation. It is essentially a numeric representation of the traffic-handling capacity of a link.

In subsequent text, any reference to a metric implies the default metric, which is the only type IS-IS metric supported on Cisco routers. As discussed previously, bit 7 of the metric field is used to classify the metric as internal or external. *Internal metrics* refer to routes generated within the IS-IS domain, whereas *external metrics* refer to routes originating outside the local domain or from another routing protocol source. With bit 8 reserved and bit 7 for internal or external classification, only the remaining 6 bits of the metric byte are available for the metric value. Using 6 bits for the metric value gives a maximum value of 63 per link.

On Cisco routers, metric values are configured on interfaces and apply to the outgoing link. IOS does not automatically assign the link metric based on bandwidth. The default value for IS-IS metrics on all interfaces, regardless of connecting link speed, is 10. Link metric can be modified by configuration. For computational purposes, the metric must be a positive value, and 1 is recommended as the minimum. The total metric for a path is the sum metric on the outgoing interfaces of all links between source and destination. ISO 10589 specifies the maximum metric value for a complete path to be only 1023. Therefore, it is important for operators to plan link metric assignments to achieve the desired path differentiation.

The next section discusses recent IETF extensions to the IS-IS protocol that increase the maximum values of the default metric. The extension introduces more flexibility in metric assignment and facilitates the designing of IS-IS networks. It also provides support for recent innovations in IP routing, such as IS-IS-based MPLS traffic engineering.

IS-IS Metric Extensions

Two newly proposed LSP TLVs specify wider fields for the default metric, allowing larger interface metric values than the previous 63 maximum. This enhancement can be leveraged for basic IP routing, as well as MPLS-based traffic engineering applications. These new TLVs are as follows:

- Extended Intermediate System Reachability TLV (Type 22)
- Extended IP Reachability TLV (Type 135)

The Extended IS Reachability TLV is an extension of the Intermediate System Neighbors TLV (Type 2), and the Extended IP Reachability TLV extends the IP Internal Reachability TLV (Type 128). These TLVs take advantage of the fact that current and most widely deployed implementations of the IS-IS protocol do not support the QoS metric types, namely delay, expense, and error metrics. The fields reserved for these metrics are, therefore, wasted. These TLVs are designed to reassign the QoS metric fields to the default metric. TLV Type 22 dedicates 24 bits for metric, and TLV Type 135 dedicates 32 bits compared to the 6 bits originally specified.

Another new TLV is the Traffic Engineering Router ID TLV (Type 134), which is used to designate the address on a stable interface, such as a loopback interface, for configuring various capabilities of the router. The Router ID TLV contains the 4-octet Router ID of the router originating the LSP, and it is essentially relevant only for MPLS traffic engineering. This TLV is not discussed further because MPLS is beyond the scope of this book.

Extended IS Reachability TLV (Type 22)

The Extended IS Reachability TLV is intended to replace the IS Neighbors TLV (Type 2) with a primary objective to provide support for larger metric values, in general, and also to support IS-IS-dependent MPLS traffic engineering. The proposed format for this TLV is as follows:

- **Type (1 byte)**—22
- **Length (1 byte)**—Total length of the Value field
- **Value**—3 bytes of default metric
    - 1 byte of length of sub-TLVs
    - 6 bytes of system ID + 1-byte pseudonode number
    - 0–244 bytes of sub-TLVs

The 3 bytes of the metric field are used to encode the metric as a 24-bit unsigned integer. For practical purposes, a maximum path value (0xFE000000) is specified to prevent computation overflows by existing implementations of the SPF algorithm. Also links with the maximum possible metric of $2^{24} - 1$ are to be ignored in path calculations.

Sub-TLVs are used for MPLS traffic engineering purposes.

Extended IP Reachability TLV (Type 135)

The Extended IP Reachability TLV embodies the same ideas behind the Extended IS Reachability TLV and is designed to replace TLV 128. Its primary goal is to utilize the QoS metric fields to support large metric values for IP prefixes while using sub-TLVs for distributing MPLS traffic engineering resource information. The format of this TLV is as follows:

- **Type (1 byte)**—135
- **Length (1 byte)**—Total length of the Value field
- **Value**—4 bytes of metric information
    - 1 byte of control information, composed of the following:
        1 bit of up/down status

        1 bit of sub-TLV presence bit

        6 bits of prefix length
    - 0–4 bytes of IPv4 prefix
    - 0–249 bytes of optional sub-TLVs made up of:
        1 byte of length of sub-TLVs

        0–250 bytes of sub-TLVs

The up/down status bit is intended to prevent routing loops, and it is set when a route is advertised from Level 2 into Level 1. This prevents such routes from being re-advertised back into Level 2. Sub-TLVs specify MPLS traffic engineering attributes. The 4-byte (32-bit) metric field permits large metric values limited to a maximum of **MAX_PATH_METRIC** (0xFE000000). Prefixes with metrics larger than **MAX_PATH_METRIC** are ignored in SPF computations. Figure 5-10 shows a side-by-side comparison of graphical representations of TLV Types 128/130 and TLV Type 135.

Figure 5-10 *Comparison of TLV 128/130 and TLV 135.*

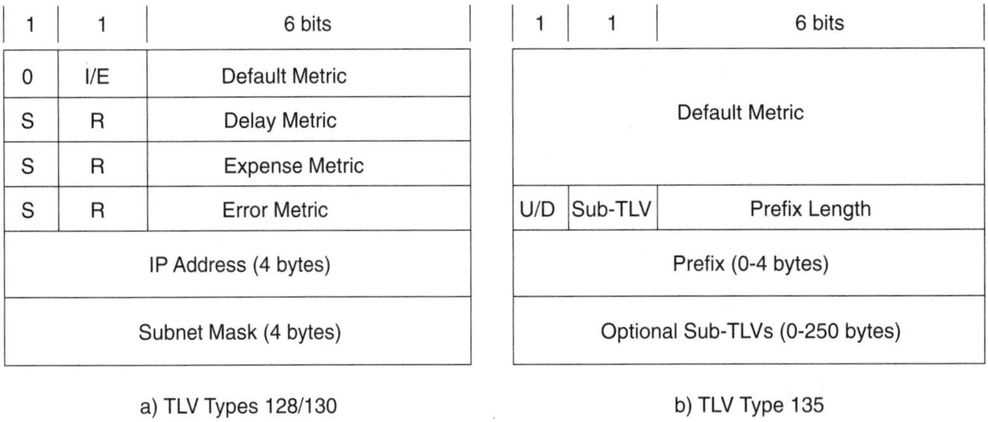

1	1	6 bits
0	I/E	Default Metric
S	R	Delay Metric
S	R	Expense Metric
S	R	Error Metric
IP Address (4 bytes)		
Subnet Mask (4 bytes)		

a) TLV Types 128/130

1	1	6 bits
Default Metric		
U/D	Sub-TLV	Prefix Length
Prefix (0-4 bytes)		
Optional Sub-TLVs (0-250 bytes)		

b) TLV Type 135

Example 5-6 shows an LSP with entries for TLV 22 and TLV 135 in italics captured on a Cisco router with the **show isis database detail** command.

Example 5-6 *LSP with Extended TLVs*

```
RTX#show isis database RTB.00-00 level-1 detail

IS-IS Level-1 LSP RTB.00-00
LSPID LSP Seq Num    LSP Checksum  LSP Holdtime ATT/P/OL
RTB.00-00 0x000000FE 0x59C3        1185         1/0/0
  Area Address: 49.0001
  NLPID:        0xCC
  Hostname: RTB
  IP Address:   11.1.1.2
  Metric: 10    IP 10.1.1.0/24
  Metric: 10    IP 192.168.2.0/30
  Metric: 100   IP 11.1.1.2/32
  Metric: 100   IS-Extended RTB.02
  Metric: 10    IS-Extended RTA.01
Metric: 0     ES RTB
```

Support for TLV Types 22 and 135 (IS-IS wide metrics) is available in recent Cisco IOS releases of the 12.0S and 12.0T trains. The router-level command **metric-style wide** enables a Cisco router running the appropriate IOS release to send LSPs with wide metrics and to receive and correctly interpret LSPs with TLV Types 22 and 135. The command **metric-style transition** allows smooth migration from old narrow metrics to the new wider metrics. This option works by allowing a router to send and receive both narrow and wide metrics. In particular, MPLS traffic engineering configuration requires use of the new wide metric option. The command **metric-style narrow** reinstates original and default behavior. Metric configuration and use of the **metric-style** command are discussed in more detail in Chapter 8, "Network Design Scenarios" and Chapter 9, "Configuring IS-IS for IP Routing on Cisco Routers."

Sequence Number Packets

Link-state packets and their relevance to the process of gathering and disseminating routing information within the IS-IS protocol is covered, in detail, in the preceding section. This section discusses SNPs, which are used in auxiliary mechanisms that ensure integrity of the LSP-based routing information distribution process. You might recollect that hello packets establish and maintain adjacencies between neighbor routers, whereas LSPs are the vehicles for sharing routing information. In a link-state routing environment, routers in an area receive the LSPs from all other routers in the area through their directly connected neighbors in a process called *flooding*. Through flooding, routers in an area build identical (synchronized) Level 1 Link-State databases. The Level 1 Link-State databases on the routers in an area are synchronized by means of explicit mechanisms in which SNPs play a key role as control packets. The two kinds of SNPs follow:

- Complete sequence number packets (CSNP)
- Partial sequence number packets (PSNP)

CSNPs and PSNPs share the same packet format and each carries a collection of LSP summaries. The basic difference between them is that a CSNP advertised by a router contains summaries of all the known LSPs in its database, whereas the PSNP contains only a subset. Separate Level 1 and Level 2 CSNPs and PSNPs are generated to support the Level 1 and Level 2 Link-State databases, respectively. For example, a Level 1 CSNP contains summaries of all the LSPs in the Level 1 Link-State database.

Each of the LSP summaries packed into CSNPs and PSNPs consists of four key pieces of information extracted from the LSP header adequate for unique LSP identification. The following are contained in an LSP summary:

- Link-State Packet Identifier (LSPID)
- Sequence number
- Checksum
- Remaining lifetime

Complete Sequence Number Packets

IS-IS provides mechanisms that allow routers to use CSNP on both point-to-point and broadcast links to check consistency of their Link-State databases. This way, they can determine whether they have current copies of all LSPs generated by the other routers in the local area or in the backbone. As you might recall, intra-area routing is Level 1 and interarea routing is Level 2. Routers that discover they do not have current copies are missing some LSPs, a result of the CSNP exchange (on point-to-point links) or broadcast (on LANs), use PSNPs to request current copies. This process is referred to as *Link-State database synchronization*. The database synchronization process over point-to-point links differs a little from how it is performed over broadcast links. In the case of point-to-point links, CSNPs are sent only once when the IS-IS adjacency is initialized, preceding the exchange of LSPs over the link. LSPs are exchanged reliably over point-to-point links in a way that ensures all LSPs sent over the link from one end are received at the other end.

On broadcast links, CSNPs are broadcast periodically by the DIS to compensate for an LSP exchange process that is not inherently reliable. As explained in Chapter 2, the DIS plays the role of pseudonode, which is an abstraction for representing broadcast links as network nodes. This reduces the number of one-to-one communications in a broadcast environment and, consequently, reduces the amount of information that is exchanged when many nodes interconnect in such environments.

Routers connecting to the same broadcast link form and maintain Level 1 and Level 2 adjacencies with each other by periodically sending hellos to the multicast addresses known as AllL1IS and AllL2IS, respectively. Adjacency maintenance and database synchronization on broadcast links are independent processes. On broadcast links, LSPs are also broadcast to the same broadcast address mentioned before: AllL1IS for Level 1 LSPs and AllL2IS for Level 2 LSPs. The Level 1- and Level 2-designated routers coordinate Link-State database sychronization by also periodically multicasting Level 1 and Level 2 CSNPs to these same broadcast addresses.

In conformity to the generic IS-IS packet format, CSNPs consist of headers and variable-length fields (TLVs). Figure 5-11 shows the CSNP packet format.

Most of the fields in the CSNP header are discussed in Chapter 2. The following fields are of interest:

- **Source ID**—The Source ID refers to the SysID of the router that generated the CSNP. On a point-to-point link, it is the SysID of the nodes on either side of the link. On a broadcast link, it is the SysID of the designated router.

- **Start LSP ID**—The start LSP ID is the LSP ID of the first LSP in the LSP Entries TLV attached to the header.

- **End LSP ID**—This is the LSP ID of the last LSP in the LSP Entries TLV field.

Figure 5-11 *CSNP format.*

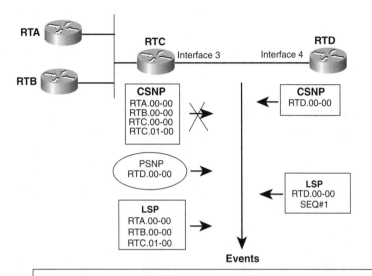

CSNP
RTA.00-00
RTB.00-00
RTC.00-00
RTC.01-00

CSNP
RTD.00-00

PSNP
RTD.00-00

LSP
RTD.00-00
SEQ#1

LSP
RTA.00-00
RTB.00-00
RTC.01-00

Events

• After adjacency is established, RTC and RTD both exchange CSNPs.
• RTC receives CSNP from RTD and sends PSNP requesting LSP, RTD.00-00.
• CSNP from RTC is lost in flight; however, RTD notices from RTC's CSNP that
  RTD doesn't have any of the LSPs in its local LS database, and proactively sends
  copies of RTA.00-00, RTB.00-00, RTC.00-00, and REC.01-00 to RTD.
• If both CSNPs are lost, synchronization will be delayed much longer.

Table 5-5 lists the types of TLVs in CSNPs: the LSP Entries TLV and a TLV for authentication of the CSNP packet.

Table 5-5   *TLVs Supported in CSNPs*

TLV	Type	Source
LSP Entries	9	ISO 10589
Authentication Information	10	ISO 10589

- **LSP Entries**—This is collection of LSP summaries of all known LSPs in the corresponding Level 1 or Level 2 Link-State databases of the advertising router, sorted in order of ascending LSP ID.

    — **Type (1 byte)**—9

— **Length (1 byte)**—Total length of the Value field

— **Value**—Multiples of LSP summaries, each consisting of the remaining lifetime (2 bytes), LSP ID (ID length + 2 bytes), LSP sequence number (4 bytes), and LSP checksum (2 bytes)

- **Authentication Information**—TLV Type 10. As defined for Level 1 and Level 2 LSPs (see Tables 5-3 and 5-4).

Partial Sequence Number Packets

As indicated in the preceding section, PSNPs normally do not contain summaries of all the LSPs in the originating router's database. Instead, PNSPs complement CSNPs in the database synchronization process and perform the following two key functions:

- Routers use PSNPs to acknowledge receipt of one of more LSPs over point-to-point links.

- Routers request transmission of current or missing LSPs by using PSNPs. This applies to both point-to-point and broadcast links.

Because the list of LSP summaries entered into a PSNP is not consistent as in the case of CSNPs, which list summaries of all known LSPs, the Start LSP ID and End LSP ID fields are irrelevant to the application and purpose of PSNPs. These fields are therefore not present in the PSNP header (see Figure 5-12).

Table 5-6 lists the TLVs that can be found in PSNP. These are the same as those supported by CSNPs.

Table 5-6   *TLVs Supported in PSNPs*

TLV	Type	Source
LSP Entries	9	ISO 10589
Authentication Information	10	ISO 10589

Figure 5-12 *PSNP format.*

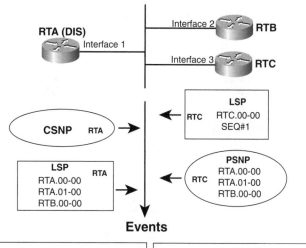

Events

RTA	RTC
• Receives RTC.00-00, SEQ#1 from RTC. • Later advertises CSNP with summaries of all known LSPs RTA.00-00, RTB.00, RTC.00-00 and Pseudonode LSP RTA.00-01. • Receives PSNP from RTC requesting missing LSPs. • Floods RTA.00-00, RTA.00-01, and RTB.00-00. • Continues to advertise CSNP periodically.	• Only connects to LAN, RTA, and RTB already there. • Floods RTC.00-00, SEQ#1 on interface 3. • Later receives CSNP from RTA (DIS). • Verifies contents of CSNP with LS database and determines following LSPs are missing: RTA.00-00, RTA.01-00, and RTB.00-00. • Sends PSNP request for missing LSPs. • Receives complete LSPs from RTA.

Flooding and Link-State Database Synchronization

Link-state routing protocols, such as IS-IS and the OSPF Protocol, operate on the premise that all nodes in an area obtain the same description or view of the area through the exchange of link-state information (LSPs in the case of IS-IS). The LSPs, which are stored in the Link-State database, are then fed as input to the route calculation algorithm (SPF algorithm), to determine the shortest path to any node in the area. A consistent view of the area's topology allows all routers in the area to independently calculate optimal and loop-free routes to all destinations within the area. Each IS-IS router assembles information about its immediate surrounding, such as its own SysID and those of neighbors, directly connect IP subnets, and so on, into an LSP. The LSP is then advertised to directly connected neighbors and eventually reaches all nodes in the area by means of a mechanism known as flooding. Under stable conditions, the Level 1 Link-State database is identical on all routers in the area. The local route calculation algorithm at each node sews the LSPs together into the topology of the entire area, just like putting the pieces of a jigsaw puzzle together. Figure 5-13 shows how a router assembles the LSPs from every node in the area to represent the area's topology.

It is necessary for all routers in the area to obtain the same and consistent view of the area's physical and addressing layout to achieve efficient and loop-free forwarding within the area. The flooding process is complemented with auxiliary mechanisms, referred to as *database synchronization*, to guarantee exact replication of the area database at every node.

Figure 5-13 *LSPs in an area Link-State database.*

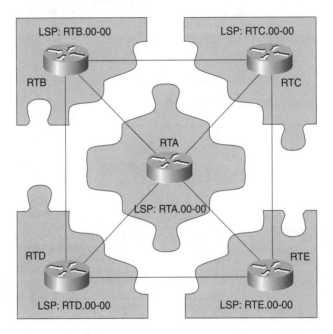

Chapter 2 discussed the key processes underlying the IS-IS protocol (receive, update, decision, and forward processes). The update process is responsible for flooding. The individual update processes running on the IS-IS routers in an area work collaboratively to achieve the same Link-State databases on all the routers in the area. The interrelated processes—flooding and database synchronization—are the subject matter of the subsequent sections in this chapter.

When fed with the Link-State database, the SPF algorithm organizes the various network destinations in the LSPs into the shortest-path tree with the calculating router at the root. This is achieved by using available metric information to compute the paths with the lowest cumulative metric to all known destinations. These best routes are then fed into the forwarding database. The SPF algorithm is discussed in detail in Chapter 6.

Even though Level 1 routing within an area is mainly cited to explain flooding and database synchronization, similar and independent flooding also occurs within the backbone between the Level 2 routers that interconnect areas. When routing converges, the Level 1 routers attain a complete topological view of their respective areas, whereas Level 2 routers attain a complete map of the topological relationship between areas.

Like all link-state routing protocols, IS-IS uses a suite of timers and flags to manage processes, such as flooding and operation of the SPF algorithm. The timers and flags provide control and event management that ensure stability in the routing environment. The timers help optimize use of system resources, such as processing capacity, memory, and link bandwidth. Timers are also a major factor in achieving optimal routing convergence during significant changes in the network. The following section discusses two important flags: the Send Routing Message (SRM) flag and the Send Sequence Number (SSN) flag. Database maintenance-related timers, such as maxage, regeneration, and retransmission timers, are then discussed.

SRM and SSN Flags

SRM and SSN flags play important roles in flooding and database synchronization. The update process uses the SRM flag to control delivery of LSPs to adjacent neighbors. The SSN flag is used in the following two ways:

- To acknowledge LSPs received in reliable flooding over point-to-point links
- To request complete LSP information during database synchronization over broadcast links

The SRM and SSN flags essentially provide a means to enforce efficient queuing of LSPs and PSNPs by decoupling LSP forwarding and acknowledgment to achieve optimized utilization of processing and link bandwidth resources. The relevance of these flags is discussed further in the following sections.

Flooding

Flooding is the vehicle for replication and distribution of the Link-State databases within a network, a phenomenon that is critical to the operation of link-state routing protocols. An IS-IS router generates an LSP, which it floods out to all adjacent neighbors over its IS-IS-enabled interfaces. The IS-IS router also receives and processes LSPs flooded by other neighbors. When a router receives an LSP from a neighbor, it keeps a copy in the corresponding local Link-State database (Level 1 or Level 2) and also floods copies over all IS-IS interfaces other than the one on which the LSP was received. To flood out an LSP, the router first sets the SRM flag individually for target interfaces and clears the flags when the specific LSP has been successfully transmitted. On point-to-point links, successful transmission is confirmed by receipt of a PSNP acknowledgment. No acknowledgment is required on broadcast links. When LSPs that are duplicates of already known versions are received, they are dropped.

Flooding over point-to-point links is described as reliable because LSPs transmitted over such links must be acknowledged with a PSNP by the router at the receiving end. On broadcast media, CSNPs are periodically transmitted by the Level 1- and Level 2-designated routers to assist other routers in synchronizing their databases. Any router on the medium that does not have all or current copies of the LSPs summarized in the CSNP uses a PSNP to request what it needs. Database synchronization is a dynamic activity in a network. Routers generate new LSPs when changes occur in their immediate routing environment. New LSPs are flooded with higher sequence numbers and new checksum values, and the SRM and SSN flags are used to effectively coordinate flooding and synchronization.

The command **show isis database private** can be used to check the status of SRM and SSN flags on Cisco routers (see Example 5-7).

Example 5-7 *Status SSN and SRM Flags*

```
RB#show isis database private

IS-IS Level-1 Link State Database:
LSPID           LSP Seq Num  LSP Checksum  LSP Holdtime   ATT/P/OL
RTA.00.00       0x00000068   0x18E2          909            0/0/0
 Address 0x614846DC,length 360,max_length 360,on_paths
 Root distance 10,index 13,parent index 1,parent count 1
 RTA    Sc0/0    *HDLC*         Up   28   L1   IS-IS
SRM bits set on no interfaces
SSN bits set on no interfaces

RTB.00-00       0x000007DF   0x1A73          721            0/0/0
 Address 0x1391B),length 415,max)length 415,on_paths
 Root distance 10,index 3,parent index 2,parent count 1
 RTB    Sc0/0    *HDLC*         Up   27   L1   IS-IS
 SRM bits set on no interfaces
 SSN bits set on no interfaces
```

Example 5-7 shows that no SRM and SSN flags have been set for any LSPs, meaning that there are no LSPs that are pending to be flooded or that need to be acknowledged for any interface. This command can be useful in troubleshooting situations of congestion resulting from relatively large volumes of traffic or lack of processing and bandwidth resources on routers in the network.

Flooding over Point-to-Point Links

As mentioned in the preceding section, IS-IS uses a reliable flooding mechanism on point-to-point links. This seems reasonable because on a point-to-point link, only one neighbor is on the other end, and it should be fairly straightforward to track explicit acknowledgment of LSPs from that single neighbor at almost insignificant bandwidth cost.

CSNPs simplify the synchronization process. They contain a summary of the router's Link-State database. CSNPs are exchanged only once on a point-to-point link, when adjacency is first established between the two connected routers. CSNPs provide a quick way to review and match the LSPs in each neighbor's database with the contents of the local database to determine missing or outdated copies of LSPs. The currency of LSPs is determined by sequence number comparison. PSNPs request current or missing copies of LSPs. A router also can proactively flood out LSPs that it determines the neighbor does not have. As indicated previously, SRM and SSN flags are at the heart of the reliable flooding process. Whereas the SRM flag is set on any links over which copies of a specific LSP need to be flooded out, the SSN flag is set on only point-to-point links over which LSPs have been received and flag the need to send out a PSNP acknowledgment. The flags are cleared after appropriate actions have occurred.

When a router transmits an LSP over a point-to-point link, it expects to have a PSNP acknowledgment back from the neighbor. If the acknowledgment is not received within a specified period, referred to as the *retransmission interval*, the LSP is assumed lost during transmission and is retransmitted. An LSP is continually retransmitted on a point-to-point link until it is acknowledged with a PSNP by the neighbor.

Figure 5-14 illustrates the flooding process on a point-to-point link. RTB has a point-to-point connection to RTA and RTC. In this example, RTB receives an LSP from RTA with LSPID RTA.00-00 and sequence number (SEQ#) 100. It installs a copy of RTA.00-00 in the LS database, sets SSN on interface 2, and sets SRM on interface 3. RTB then forwards a copy of RTA.00-00 to RTC and a PSNP acknowledgment to RTA. Then RTA immediately clears the SSN flag on interface 2 but leaves the SRM flag on interface 3. RTC receives RTA.00-00 from RTB, installs it in the LS database, and sets an SSN flag on interface 4. RTC then sends a PSNP acknowledgment to RTB and clears the SSN flag on interface 4. When RTB receives the PSNP acknowledging RTA.00-00 from RTC, it then clears the SRM flag on interface 3.

Initial CSNP exchange over point-to-point links helps speed up the synchronization process. Losing any of these CSNPs undoubtedly drags out the synchronization process. Figure 5-15 illustrates a scenario in which an initial CSNP is lost. RTC is already adjacent and synchronized to RTA and RTB. RTC, therefore, has its own LSP and those of RTA and RTB in its database. If the CSNP from RTC is lost in the process of synchronizing with the newly adjacent RTD on the point-to-point connection, RTD will not immediately know about LSPs from RTA and RTB. When RTC receives RTD's CSNP, however, it detects that RTD doesn't yet know about LSPs from RTA and RTB. Therefore, it proactively floods them out. This prolongs the time it takes RTD to know about all LSPs.

Figure 5-14 *Flooding over point-to-point links.*

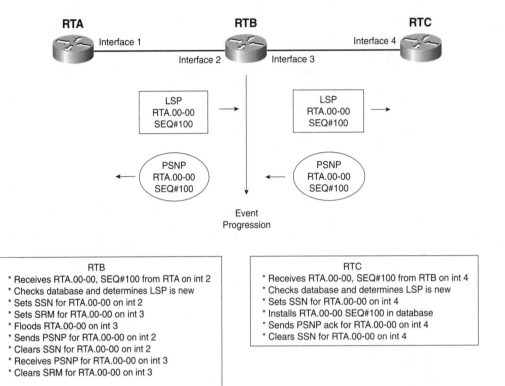

Flooding on Broadcast Links

On broadcast links, LSPs are flooded to Level 1 or Level 2 neighbors by using the applicable multicast address, allL1IS (01-80-C2-00-00-14) or allL2IS (01-80-C2-00-00-15), respectively. The flooding operation does not employ acknowledgment routines that guarantee reliable delivery of LSPs, as in the point-to-point case. Flooding on broadcast links is, therefore, described as *best effort*.

Reliable flooding simplifies the database synchronization process, removing any clear delineation between the flooding and synchronization processes. On the contrary, unreliable flooding requires a distinct mechanism to ensure database synchronization. To synchronize databases over broadcast links, IS-IS routers rely on periodic multicast of CSNPs from the DIS. Separate CSNPs for Level 1 and Level 2 that exist are advertised to allL1IS and allL2IS multicast addresses, respectively.

Figure 5-15 *Loss of initial CSNP on a point-to-point link.*

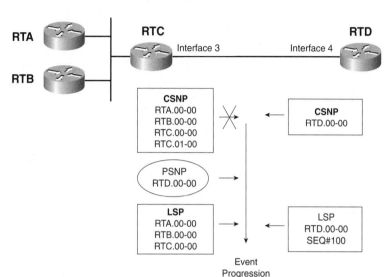

* After adjacency is established, RTC and RTD both exchange CSNPs.
* RTC receives CSNP from RTD and sends PSNP requesting LSP RTD.00-00.
* CSNP from RTC is lost in flight; however RTC notices from RTC's CSNP that it doesn't have any of the LSPs in the local LS database, and so proactively sends copies of RTA.00-00, RTB.00-00, RTC.00-00 and RTC.01-00 to RTD.
* If both CSNPs are lost, synchronization will be delayed much longer and incrementally as newer refreshed LSPs are received and reflooded to each other.

As discussed in Chapter 3, IS-IS models broadcast links, such as LANs, as pseudonodes, which are represented by DISs. The DIS controls only flooding and database synchronization on broadcast links. IS-IS routers on a broadcast link are not restricted to forming adjacencies with only the DIS. Hello packets are multicast out and routers become adjacent to each other after a three-way handshake, which essentially means each router has reported seeing the other. The CSNPs sent out by the DIS are not acknowledged either, and periodic flooding ensures that all routers receive copies, which they check against the contents of their Link-State database. By looking at the contents of CSNPs, LAN routers can identify missing or newer LSPs and subsequently request copies with a PSNP. The PSNP sent out is packed with summaries of requested LSPs. The requester then receives the complete LSPs from the DIS or other peers on the link. SRM flags also are set on broadcast links; however, they are immediately cleared after the corresponding LSPs are transmitted because no acknowledgment is expected. CSNPs are periodically advertised on broadcast links every CSNP interval, which is 10 seconds by default. Periodic CSNP advertisement can be expensive with regard to bandwidth consumption. This is, however, the tradeoff for a simpler scheme to achieve reliability on broadcast links. Such links were traditionally thought to be less expensive than point-to-point wide-area links, and this might have influenced the protocol design in this regard. Cisco IOS provides a command that allows the periodic interval for transmitting CSNPs to be modified to reduce transmission frequency.

Figure 5-16 is a simplified illustration of flooding on a broadcast link. In the scenario shown, RTC is the last to connect to the link. RTA and RTB are already connected, and RTA is the designated router (DIS). After forming adjacencies with RTA and RTB, RTC builds an LSP, RTC.00-00, stores a copy in its Link-State database, and floods another copy out of interface 3 onto the link. Later RTA, the DIS, advertises a CSNP by multicast over the link. RTC receives a copy of the CSNP, checks it against the local Link-State database, and notices three missing LSPs: RTA.00-00, RTA.01-00, and RTB.00-00. At this time, RTC has only its own LSP, RTC.00-00, in the local Link-State database. RTC then sends out a PSNP onto the link to obtain the complete copies of RTA.00-00, RTA.01-00, and RTB.00. RTA floods RTA.00-00, RTB.00-00, and the pseudo LSP RTA.01-00 through multicast, and RTC receives copies.

Figure 5-16 *Flooding over broadcast links.*

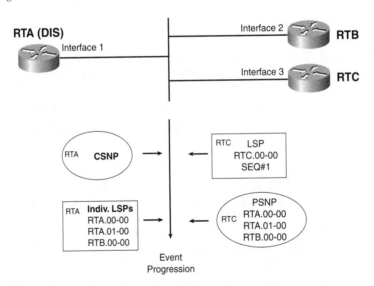

RTA
* Receives RTA.00-00, SEQ#1 from RTC on int 1 and adds to local LS database
* Advertises CSNP with summaries of LSPs RTA.00-00, RTB.00, RTC.00-00 and Pseudonode LSP RTA.01-00
* Receives PSNP from RTC requesting RTA.00-00, RTA.01-00 and RTB.00-00
* RTA floods LSPs requested by RTC through multicast
* Advertises CSNP periodically

RTC
* Connects to LAN, RTA, and RTB already connected
* Floods RTC.00-00, SEQ#1 on int 3
* Receives CSNP from RTA (DIS)
* Checks contents of CSNP against local LS database and determines LSPs, RTA.00-00, RTA.01-00, RTB.00-00 are missing
* Sends PSNP to request for missing LSPs
* Receives all requested LSPs
* Continues to receive periodic CSNPs from DIS

Flooding over NBMA Transport Media

In IS-IS, network links are either point-to-point or multipoint broadcast and no special provisions are made for nonbroadcast multiaccess (NMBA) media, such as Asynchronous Transfer Mode (ATM), Frame Relay, and Integrated Services Digital Network (ISDN). Although it is frequently recommended to use point-to-point subinterfaces for NBMA links, some practical situations might not lend themselves to this type of design. In this case, such NBMA links must be configured as broadcast multipoint links. However, this configuration requires all nodes connecting over the NBMA cloud to be fully meshed. In most cases, the virtual circuits in the NBMA cloud are not fully meshed, therefore, the most suited approach (adopted by most network operators) is to configure the ATM or Frame Relay permanent virtual circuits (PVCs) as point-to-point subinterfaces. Because an NBMA interface can have a large number of PVCs, an ATM or Frame Relay cloud can have a potentially high degree of meshed PVCs, leading to extreme levels of LSP flooding activity. This, in turn, can adversely impact network stability and scalability. You can limit excessive flooding over highly redundant NBMA PVC meshes by grouping a subset of subinterfaces into IS-IS mesh groups.

IS-IS Mesh Groups

IS-IS mesh groups help limit excessive and redundant flooding over NBMA clouds. During normal operations, IS-IS routers reflood any new LSPs over all other interfaces except the one on which the LSP was received. The concept of IS-IS mesh groups allows grouping of router interfaces, typically NBMA subinterfaces, together so that when an LSP is received from one of the subinterfaces in the group, it is not reflooded over other subinterfaces in the same group. The trick about mesh groups is that they assume a full mesh between all routers in the mesh and that every member router gets a copy of the original LSP that is not flooded to the group. Although this solves the problem of redundant flooding, some routers might not receive their copies of LSPs that are not to be flooded to the group if the full mesh is broken. Therefore, you might need alternative unrestricted flooding paths within the network to guarantee that all flooded LSPs reach every target node in the network. The concept of IS-IS mesh groups is elaborated in Figure 5-17, which shows a group of routers connected over an NBMA cloud with a partial PVC mesh.

A subset of the routers in Figure 5-17 (RTA, RTC, RTD, and RTF) form a fully meshed subcloud. RTB and RTE connect only to two neighbors each.

In this scenario, it is desirable to use point-to-point subinterfaces to interconnect the routers; however, the relatively high level of interconnectivity implies a lot of redundant flooding over this cloud. If RTA floods an LSP, for example, all the other routers in the fully meshed subcloud (RTC, RTD, RTF) receive copies of the original and subsequently reflood it to each other, even though they all received copies already. This evidently results in redundant flooding.

Figure 5-17 *IS-IS mesh groups.*

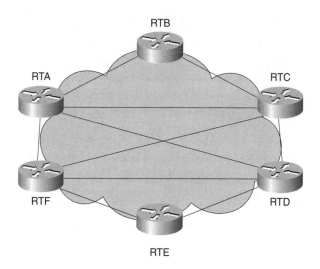

In a full mesh of *n* number of routers, a single LSP transmitted to (*n* – 1) nodes results in (*n* – 2) unnecessary transmissions of the same LSP at the expense of critical processing and bandwidth resources. Initially, one of the routers in the mesh floods an LSP to (*n* – 1) adjacent neighbors. Then the remaining (*n* – 2) neighbors flood copies of this LSP to each other, with copies on the same link crossing each other. After a specific LSP is received from a neighbor, the same LSP received secondhand from another neighbor is not flooded to the first neighbor. This is why the number of redundant transmissions is limited to (*n* – 2). If all *n* nodes transmitted LSPs, there would be a total of *n*(*n* – 1) original LSP transmissions and (*n* – 1)(*n* – 2) redundant transmissions.

Mesh groups can be used to limit the waste in bandwidth and processing resources resulting from redundant flooding. Because the operation of mesh groups assumes a full mesh of routers in the group, the likely candidates in Figure 5-17 for a mesh group setup are RTA, RTC, RTD, and RTF. RTB and RTE are left out of the mesh group and flooding is not restricted over their interfaces. In this scenario, RTB and RTE provide redundant paths for guaranteeing delivery of any LSP to every router in the network if any of the links in the mesh group fail. In this arrangement, any new LSP that RTA receives from a member of the mesh group is flooded to only nonmembers (RTB and RTE). If an LSP is received on a subinterface that is not in the mesh group, it is flooded over all other interfaces as usual.

The Cisco IOS interface command **isis mesh-group** [*num* | *blocked*] configures mesh groups. You can use the optional keyword *blocked* to completely disable flooding on an interface or subinterface. Even though the IS-IS mesh group feature has been supported in Cisco IOS for a while, a draft proposal describing the mechanism was submitted only recently to the IETF IS-IS Working Group for consideration and adoption as a standard feature of Integrated IS-IS.

Protocol Timers and Other IS-IS Database Parameters

IS-IS uses a suite of timers to control various events and to ensure routing stability without compromising the capability to converge fast enough in case of significant changes in the network. Various timers are used to ensure integrity of the Link-State database by enforcing periodic refresh of individual LSPs and aging out of stale information. This section discusses relevant timers for network operation purposes and provides insight into associated IOS commands that allow timer adjustments where possible.

Maxage

Maxage refers to the maximum life span of an LSP from the time it is generated by the source. ISO 10589 specifies maxage as a protocol constant with a value of 1200 seconds (20 minutes). The time lapse until expiration of an LSP is indicated in the Remaining Lifetime field of the LSP on Cisco routers. Cisco IOS adheres to the maxage specification in ISO 10589 by setting the Remaining Lifetime field of an LSP to 1200 seconds when it is first generated. Actually, the remaining lifetime is referred to as LSP holdtime on a Cisco router (**show isis database detail** command). Usually, an LSP is refreshed by its source before its remaining lifetime reaches zero (see the next section, "LSP Generation Interval"). If a router is removed from the network, however, it is not available to refresh its LSP, and the LSP ages until it expires at a remaining lifetime value of zero.

Occasionally, another router in the network initiates a purge of a corrupted LSP from the network by setting the remaining lifetime of the LSP to zero and reflooding the LSP to its neighbors. The ZeroAgeLifetime is the time an LSP is retained after it expires, before it is purged from the database. Its value is specified as 60 seconds by ISO 10589.

You can use the IOS command **max-lsp-lifetime** to modify the default value of maxage, which is specified as 1200 seconds. All of the 2 bytes of the Remaining Lifetime field are leveraged by Cisco IOS to allow a much higher value (up to 65,535 seconds) to be configurable on Cisco routers; 65,535 ($2^{16} - 1$) seconds is approximately 18.2 hours.

Maxage is considered a protocol constant and must have a consistent value on all IS-IS routers in the network. Therefore, if a router receives an LSP with a remaining lifetime higher than the expected value of maxage, the LSP is considered corrupted and is therefore discarded.

LSP Generation Interval

This timer has two varieties:

- **The maximum LSP generation interval**—This interval is known also as the LSP refresh interval. It refers to the periodic replacement of an LSP by the originating routers before the LSP expires; 900 seconds (15 minutes) is specified (compared to 1200 seconds of maxage).

- **The minimum LSP generation interval**—This interval defines the minimum interval between consecutive generations of an LSP by a router. A value of 30 seconds is specified for this parameter.

The LSP refresh interval needs to be less than maxage to require a router to periodically generate a newer copy of its LSP into the network, even when there are no changes to report, before the LSP expires. This procedure helps ensure the continued integrity of the LSP throughout the network. You can use the IOS command **lsp-refresh-interval** to modify the refresh interval. Setting this timer reasonably high helps cut down on bandwidth overhead and saves processing resources. Exercise caution when setting the refresh interval. If set too high, you might significantly inhibit expedient removal of incorrect link-state information from the network.

Minimum LSP Transmission Interval

The minimum LSP transmission interval specifies the minimum interval between consecutive transmissions of two LSPs. The default is 33 milliseconds. The related IOS command for modifying the set value is **isis lsp-interval**.

As discussed in the section on point-to-point flooding, the reliable flooding mechanism requires a router to retransmit LSPs onto point-to-point links until it receives an acknowledgment from the neighbor. The interval between retransmissions is the retransmission interval and is set at a default value of 5 seconds. You can use the IOS command **isis retransmit-interval** to modify the LSP retransmission interval to a more desirable value.

CSNP Interval

The CSNP interval relates to the periodic transmission of CSNPs by the DIS on a broadcast medium. The default value is 10 seconds. The IOS command **isis csnp-interval** enables you to modify this default. If the routers on a broadcast link are fairly stable, an operator might decide to increase the CSNP interval so that CSNPs are advertised less frequently, thereby conserving link bandwidth.

Table 5-7 lists the timers discussed in this section, providing default values and the relevant Cisco IOS commands for modifying them.

Table 5-7   *IS-IS Database Timers*

Timer	Default Value	IOS Command
Maxage	1200 seconds	**isis max-lsp-interval**
LSP refresh interval	900 seconds	**isis lsp-refresh-interval**
LSP transmission interval	33 milliseconds	**isis lsp-interval**
LSP retransmit interval	5 seconds	**isis retransmit-interval**
CSNP interval	10 seconds	**isis csnp-interval**

More About the IS-IS Link-State Database

The previous sections review components of the IS-IS Link-State database and discuss flooding mechanisms designed to optimize Link-State database synchronization on various media. In a stable IS-IS network, usual routing-related activities include sending and receiving hello packets to maintain adjacencies, periodic advertising of CSNPs on broadcast links, and the refreshing of LSPs. Network instabilities trigger dynamic disruptions, which when extensive result in a depletion of processing and bandwidth resources and ultimately meltdown of the network. This section looks at the operation and maintenance of the IS-IS database and discusses some stability and performance-related issues pertaining to these activities.

IS-IS Link-State Database and Network Stability

After initial flooding and synchronization of the Link-State database, the network becomes relatively quiet. LSPs are generated and flooded only when a change occurs in a router's environment, which creates corresponding changes in the TLVs contained in its LSP. IS-IS routers use only a single LSP to represent the router's immediate environment, and the LSP can be fragmented if necessary. A TLV content change results in generation and flooding of the entire LSP with appropriate modifications. The following events can trigger regeneration of a new LSP:

- IS-IS adjacency flap
- IP interface flap
- Change in interface metric
- Changes interarea routes
- Changes in redistributed (external) routes

Any occurrence of the listed events compromises the previously issued LSP and requires a new LSP to be generated to replace the old one.

IS-IS Link-State Database Integrity Issues

The integrity of the Link-State database is critical to the operation of the IS-IS protocol in general and specifically for calculating accurate routing information to prevent costly routing loops. Database synchronization and periodic LSP refresh are key mechanisms for ensuring the integrity of the Link-State database. This section discusses other auxiliary mechanisms that directly or indirectly help guarantee the reliability of the information in the database. It also covers the mechanisms for discovering duplicate SysIDs and details the use of the Sequence Number and Checksum fields.

LSP Checksum

The IS-IS protocol does not rely on the data-link cyclic redundancy check (CRC) to guarantee the LSP integrity. Instead, IS-IS routers use a checksum value calculated over a greater part of the LSP to ensure the integrity of the contents of any LSP. The checksum is calculated from the SysID field to the end of the LSP and is inserted into the header by the originator of the LSP. The LSPs might be corrupted while sitting in memory; therefore, it is necessary to check the validity of LSPs before flooding them during refresh. When a node receives an LSP, it checks to make sure that the LSP was not corrupted in transmission before it installs a copy in the local database and refloods copies to other neighbors.

It is common knowledge that in certain networking environments, typically where Frame Relay to ATM conversion switches are used, LSPs are easily corrupted when flooded from one end of the network to the other. The standard procedure for handling a corrupted LSP at a receiving node is to not only discard it but also to attempt to purge it from the entire network.

To initiate a purge, a router sets the Remaining Lifetime field of the LSP to zero and floods it to into the network. Eventually, the owner or original source of the LSP receives a copy of the LSP being purged. The owner then reissues a newer copy back into the network. If the media problem remains, a situation of continuous flooding and purging of many LSPs in the network occurs, a network situation referred to as an *LSP corruption storm.*

LSP corruption storms consume network resources, cause tremendous network problems, and can potentially disrupt network services. In general, routers receive copies of an LSP over multiple links; therefore, although a corrupted copy might come in over one link, a good copy might make it over another link. It might be possible to obtain accurate network information by ignoring bad LSPs obtained over a specific path in the network, instead of creating a situation that can deteriorate the network.

Cisco IOS provides a command for configuring IS-IS routers in environments prone to LSP corruption storms to ignore LSP checksum errors. The router-level command **ignore-LSP-errors** enables Cisco routers to silently discard corrupted LSPs and to log the event. On a point-to-point link, if an LSP is discarded, it is not acknowledged and the source retransmits it. On broadcast links, no retransmission occurs; however, routers eventually discover missing LSPs from CSNPs advertised by the DIS and can subsequently request full copies with PSNPs.

LSP Sequence Number

As mentioned previously, the primary role of the Sequence Number field is to help identify newer LSPs from older versions. Any time that a router regenerates its LSP, either because of a refresh (normally every 15 minutes) or a change in the network, it increases the sequence number by 1.

An interesting phenomenon occurs when a router crashes and reloads. The router's neighbors drop their adjacencies, but they do not remove the LSP of the crashed router from their databases until the remaining lifetime reaches a zero value and the ZeroAgeLifetime passes. When the router recovers, it generates and floods its LSP with an initial sequence number of 1. The neighbors that have the same LSP with a higher sequence number then flood their copies to the rebooted router, thinking their LSPs are newer because of the higher sequence number. Upon detecting a sequence number mismatch of its own LSP, the reloaded router issues yet another copy of the LSP with a sequence number greater by 1 than the highest sequence number value in the LSPs received from neighbors. This process restores the router close to its sequence number value before the reboot.

Duplicate System IDs

The fundamental objective of addressing is to achieve unique identification of the addressed elements. In conformance with this ideal, IS-IS does not tolerate duplicate addresses. In discussing IS-IS addressing concepts, Chapter 4, "Addressing in Integrated IS-IS," notes that both IP addresses and ISO NSAP addresses need to be configured on IS-IS routers even in IP-only environments. As discussed in the section on IP addressing in Chapter 1, "Overview of IP Routing," IP addresses are made unique by defining unique IP subnets for the links in the network and assigning unique host addresses to the interfaces of devices that connect to links. However, the node-based addressing scheme used in ISO CLNP and adopted by Integrated IS-IS assigns a globally unique address to each network device in a domain. Within an area, a node's NSAP is made unique by its unique SysID component of the NSAP. The unique SysID also forms part of the LSP ID, providing a means to differentiate between LSPs in the Link-State database.

To simplify operations, service providers use domainwide unique SysIDs—even though in a two-level network with many areas, it is possible to have Level 1 nodes in separate areas share the same SysID provided they do not connect to the IS-IS backbone (Level 2). A unique SysID is, however, required for each node in single-level (Level 1-only or Level 2-only) routing domains and is highly recommended for hierarchical domains with many areas. You can easily achieve this by using unique IP loopback addresses on the routers to create SysIDs (as discussed in Chapter 4). Using domainwide unique SysIDs in multi-area networks provides advantages in network operations involving device management, troubleshooting, and maintenance.

Obviously, IS-IS operations are seriously impacted in scenarios in which two or more routers in the same area or connected to the backbone share the same SysID. First, this means assigning the same NSAP or NET to them if they are in the same area; second, this means mixing up their LSPs, regardless of whether they are in the same area or connected to the backbone. Each router encloses information specific to its routing environment into its LSP—that is, it calculates and enters a checksum on information in the LSP header. When the LSPs are mixed up, the sources see a different checksum than expected on what looks like their LSPs. Suspecting a corrupted LSP, each router issues another copy with a higher sequence number and floods it out into the rest of the network.

Similar activity occurring on other routers with duplicate addresses creates a situation of continuous regeneration and purging of the LSPs with duplicate IDs. This situation undoubtedly results in network instability. If a router detects that another device might be sharing its SysID, it generates an error similar to the following:

```
%CLNS-4-DUPSYSTEM: ISIS: possible duplicate system ID 0000.0000.0002 detected
```

Summary

This chapter covers one of the key underlying concepts of the IS-IS routing protocol: the IS-IS Link-State database. First, the functional organization of the IS-IS Link-State database is discussed. In support of the two-level routing hierarchy, each router supports a Level 1 and a Level 2 database for Level 1 and Level 2 routing, respectively. Subsequent discussions in the chapter focus on elements stored in the database (LSPs) and the associated control processes and elements that help in building and maintenance of the distributed Link-State database. Sequence number packets (CSNP and PSNP) and various timers used in related control processes ensure the integrity and consistency of the LSPs stored in the Level 1 and Level 2 Link-State databases across multiple routers.

Each Level 1 database describes the topological organization of the corresponding area in the domain, whereas a single Level 2 database captures the overall layout of the Level 1 areas in relation to each other. Consequently, all the routers in an area build the same Level 1 database for the area and attain a consistent view of the intra-area topology. In a similar manner, Level 2 routers connecting to the backbone build identical Level 2 databases. This is a critical requirement for each router to calculate loop-free paths to all known destinations in the network. Each router feeds the information in the Link-State database as input to the SPF algorithm for computation of best paths. Chapter 6 provides detailed coverage of the SPF algorithm.

LSP copies are distributed in the Level 1 areas and the backbone by a mechanism referred to as flooding. Control mechanisms involving CSNPs, PSNPs, SRM and SSN flags, and various timers are employed to assist flooding of LSPs and synchronization of the Link-State database between routers.

This chapter covers packet formats of LSPs, CSNPs, and PSNPs, providing details about fields in the headers, as well as the TLVs supported by these packets. Flooding operations are discussed and elaborated on for point-to-point and broadcast links and recommendations are made for dealing with NBMA links. Mesh groups provide an alternative for handling excessive and redundant flooding in highly meshed NBMA environments.

This chapter also covers IS-IS metrics, noting that metric information is carried in specific LSP TLVs. The IS-IS protocol supports four types of metrics, of which only the default metric is implemented by most router vendors, including Cisco Systems. The metrics discussion reviews recent extensions to the IS-IS protocol within the IETF to support larger metric values. These metric-related enhancements are designed to overcome limitations of the default metric, which was originally specified to have a maximum of only 63 per interface and 1023 for an entire path. The Extended IS Reachability and Extended IP Reachability TLVs, which were recently proposed in the IETF, are designed to address these limitations.

In general, operation of routing protocols is automated and guided by many protocol timers. The IS-IS protocol has its fair share of timers (as indicated previously in relation to the Link-State database). This chapter concludes with an overview of various critical timers, which are key to the operation of IS-IS and are ultimately responsible for routing stability.

Review Questions

1 What type of information is stored in an Link-State database, and how is this information collected?

2 Describe the use of the Link-State database in IS-IS.

3 What is the difference between Level 1 and Level 2 Link-State databases?

4 What is the meaning of Link-State database synchronization?

5 Describe the general format of a link-state packet.

6 List the four fields in the LSP header that adequately describe the LSP.

7 What are TLVs?

8 List five TLVs that carry metric information and where they are originally specified.

9 What is the format of the LSP Identifier (LSPID)? Give an example.

10 Name the types of metric information specified by ISO 10589.

11 What are the limitations of the default metric specified by ISO 10589?

12 How are the metric limitations of ISO 10589 addressed by TLVs Type 22 and Type 135 recently proposed in the IETF IS-IS Working Group?

13 What are sequence number packets? List all types.

14 What are IS-IS mesh groups?

15 What is maxage and maximum LSP regeneration interval? List the Cisco IOS commands that can be used to change their values.

16 Can two routers in the same area have the same system ID? Briefly describe what happens when two routers in the same area are configured with the same system ID.

References

draft-ietf-isis-hmac-00.txt: IS-IS HMAC-MD5 Authentication

http://search.ietf.org/internet-drafts/draft-ietf-isis-traffic-02.txt

IETF RFC 2763, "Dynamic Hostname Exchange Mechanism for IS-IS." N. Shen, H. Smit. 2000. http:// www.ietf.org/rfc/rfc2763.txt?number=2763

IETF RFC 2973, "IS-IS Mesh Groups." R. Balay, D. Katz, J. Parker. 2000. http://www.ietf.org/rfc/ rfc2973.txt?number=2973

ISO 10589, "Intermediate System to Intermediate System Intra-domain Routing Exchange Protocol" for use in conjunction with the protocol for providing the connectionless-mode network service (ISO 8473). ISO/IEC. 1992. Also reprinted as RFC 1142, "OSI IS-IS Intra-domain Routing Protocol." Editor D. Oran. 1990.

Perlman, Radia. *Interconnections, Second Edition: Bridges, Routers, Switches and Internetworking Protocols*. Addison-Wesley, 1991. ISBN 020-1634481

RFC 1195, "Use of OSI IS-IS for Routing in TCP/IP and Dual Environments." Ross Callon. 1990.

CHAPTER 6

The Shortest Path First Algorithm

The essence of a routing protocol is to collect routing information about the networking environment and to determine the best paths to all known destinations. As discussed in Chapter 2, "Introduction to the IS-IS Routing Protocol," these functions are performed by two processes within the architecture of the IS-IS protocol: the update process and the decision process. The update process is responsible for building the IS-IS database and ensuring its integrity. The decision process uses the shortest path first (SPF) algorithm to calculate the best paths to all known destinations based on the information in the Link-State database. The SPF algorithm works by computing the shortest path tree from a specific node to all other nodes in the area, thereby, yielding the best routes to every known destination from that particular source.

The SPF algorithm is named after the Dutch mathematician, Edsger Wybe Dijkstra and is also known as *Dijkstra's algorithm*. E. W. Dijkstra was born in Rotterdam, Netherlands in 1930, where he studied physics and mathematics and later became a renowned computer scientist. Dijkstra discovered the SPF algorithm in 1956, while researching an algorithm to assist in finding the best way to travel between two points. Referring to it as the *shortest subspanning tree algorithm*, Dijkstra used his discovery to solve the problem of distributing electric current to all essential circuits of an early computer design, in a manner that optimized usage of expensive copper wire. This chapter focuses on the IS-IS route calculation process and operation of the SPF algorithm. The material in this chapter is organized into the following sections:

- Overview of the SPF algorithm
- Calculating IS-IS routes with the SPF algorithm
- IS-IS SPF operation on Cisco routers

NOTE   The Open Shortest Path First (OSPF) protocol is another routing protocol that utilizes the Dijkstra algorithm for route calculation. OSPF is similar to IS-IS in many regards, even though they fundamentally differ in design and architecture.

Overview of the SPF Algorithm

The SPF algorithm is one of two popular algorithms employed by routing protocols for best path determination. The other is the Bellman-Ford algorithm, which is more frequently used in distance-vector routing protocols. A basic difference between the Bellman-Ford algorithm and the SPF algorithm is that in the former, each node bases it path calculation on knowledge of the cost to all directly connected neighbors plus the advertised costs for routes heard from these neighbors. In contrast, the SPF algorithm requires each node to have complete information about the entire topology. All nodes inside an area, therefore, obtain an identical Link-State database for the area. The Link-State database contains the link-state information of all nodes within the area (that is, the link-state packets from each node in the area).

An advantage of routing protocols based on the SPF algorithm over those based on the Bellman-Ford algorithm is that they are less susceptible to routing loops. Protocols based on the Bellman-Ford algorithm are easily susceptible to loops because the routers depend on information from neighbors, which might no longer be useful after a failure. Such protocols, therefore, use elaborate hold-down mechanisms, and other procedures, such as split-horizon, poison reverse, and count-to-infinity, to prevent loops. The hold-downs result in the long convergence times associated with Bellman-Ford based protocols, which are typically distance-vector routing protocols. Link-state routing protocols converge faster because each node recalculates routing information based on receipt of changed link-state packets (LSPs), and LSPs are immediately generated and flooded out when changes occur. However, SPF-based protocols are more resource-intensive, with each router requiring more memory to hold the Link-State database and more processing capacity to run the SPF algorithm.

Basics of Graph Theory

Dijkstra's algorithm provides a generic solution that is applicable to any problem that can be modeled as a directed graph (digraph). A directed graph consists of a set of vertices (nodes) interconnected by a set of directed edges or arcs (links). In the sample graph shown in Figure 6-1, vertices are the numbered circles and can be represented by the set {1, 2, 3, 4, 5}. An arc is an ordered pair of vertices. For example, the arc between vertex 1 and 2 is the arrow pointing from vertex 1 to vertex 2, which is represented as (1, 2). Two arcs between vertices 2 and 3 point in opposite directions. These are represented as (2, 3) and (3, 2) and correspond to the direction of the links between vertex 2 and 3.

Figure 6-1   *A directed graph.*

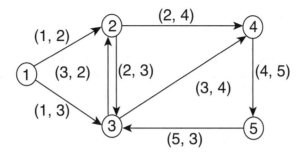

The set of arcs in Figure 6-1 can therefore be represented as {(1, 2), (1, 3), (2, 3), (2, 4), (3, 2), (3, 4), (4, 5), (5, 3)}. The set of vertices and set of arcs can be assigned lettered names as follows:

N = {1, 2, 3, 4, 5}, for the set of vertices
L = {(1, 2), (1, 3), (2, 3), (2, 4), (3, 2), (3, 4) (4, 5), (5, 3)}, for the set of arcs

The graph can be named G and represented as G = (N, L), where N is the set of vertices and L is the set of arcs.

A path is a sequence of similarly directed arcs between any two vertices in a graph. In Figure 6-1, for example, the path from vertex 1 to vertex 4 can be either the sequence (1, 2), (2, 4), or (1, 3), (3, 2), (2, 4). The objective of the SPF algorithm is to determine the shortest path from any reference vertex, s, to all other vertices in the graph. The SPF algorithm uses an iterative mechanism to solve the problem.

The next section shows the operation of the SPF algorithm for a directed graph represented by G = (N, L), given a fixed vertex, s, in the set N where

- **N**—Set of vertices
- **L**—Set of arcs
- **d(i, j)**—Distance from vertex i to j, where
    - d(i, j) = infinity, if vertices i and j are not directly connected
- **P**—Set of vertices whose shortest paths from the reference vertex have already been determined
- **L(n)**—Current least cost from vertex s to vertex n

The algorithm determines the shortest path from reference vertex s to each vertex n in the graph. In general, three main steps are involved in the process:

1 Initialization

2 Selection of the next vertex

3 Update of least cost paths

Operation of the SPF Algorithm

The three primary steps in the operation of the SPF algorithm are elaborated as follows:

Step 1   Set i = 0,P0 = {v0 = s}, L(s) = 0.

L(n) = d(s, n) if n is directly connected to s. L(n) = infinity for n not directly connected to s. Label each node n with [L(n),s]. set i = 1.

Step 2   Find the next vertex vi not in P, which has L(vi) = min L(n), for all vi}. Move vi to P. New vertex is vi.

Step 3   Update least cost paths of vertices not in P:

L(n) = min{L(n), L(vi)+d(vi,n)}.

If L(n) is replaced, update label on n to [L(n), NH(vi)], where NH(vi) is the next hop to vi from S.

Replace i by i+l, (i = i+l).

If i = N-i, stop; otherwise go to Step 2.

Step 1 is the initialization stage. Because the algorithm is iterative, it proceeds in stages, with each stage denoted by the value of i. At the initialization stage, i is set to 0. The computation is performed relative to a reference vertex, s. The reference vertex is also known as the source. Three separate lists are used in the operation of the algorithm:

Unknown (U)—Set of vertices that haven't been considered yet
Tentative (T)—Set of vertices under consideration
Paths (P)—Set of vertices to which the shortest path has been computed

At initialization (i = 0), the reference vertex, v0 = s, is selected and placed in the set of known closest vertices (P)—that is, P0 = {v0 = s}. The rest of the vertices in the graph are placed in set U. The cost of s to itself, L(s), is 0. The costs from s to directly connected vertices are set to their known values, whereas costs for vertices that are not directly known are considered unknown and, therefore, set to infinity.

In Step 2, the algorithm determines the next closest vertex to s from the set T, notes the associated cost and its next hop, and then promotes it to the set P. Initially, only the vertices directly connected to s are moved from the U set to T for consideration. The vertex with the lowest cost is promoted to the set P. When a vertex is promoted from T to P, all nodes directly connected to it are then placed in T for consideration, if they are not already there.

In the final step, the least cost associated with every node in T is updated relative to the most recent vertex promoted to P and the next hop is also changed to that of the promoted vertex. An existing least cost value is replaced only if the new valve is lower.

The algorithm then proceeds to the next iteration by going to Step 2 and continues through Step 3 again, until every node has been moved to the set P. For a graph with N vertices, including the reference vertex at which the calculation is centered, N-1 iterations exist starting at 0. At the end of the (N-1) iteration, the computation provides the shortest distance from the reference to all other vertices in the graph.

The determination of the shortest path between any two vertices in a digraph is analogous to finding the shortest path between any two nodes in a data communications network. As noted earlier, the function of routing protocols is to determine the shortest path between nodes in a network by some optimality criteria, frequently the least cost or lowest metric. In a perfect analogy, the routers in a communications network correspond to the vertices of a digraph, and the links or adjacencies correspond to the arcs. Because the traffic flow between network nodes is bidirectional, each network link corresponds to a pair of parallel arcs facing opposite directions. The links in a network are typically assigned weighted values referred to as costs or metrics. Most real networks apply scalar link costs, which are inversely proportional to bandwidth. Therefore, the fastest links are assigned smaller cost values. Finding the shortest path between nodes in a network, therefore, implies determining the least cost path between them. Other possible metric options are hop count and composite metrics. Composite metrics are based on the combined evaluation of bandwidth, delay, reliability, load, maximum transmission unit (MTU), and other link characteristics.

Computational Cost of the SPF Algorithm

The previous sections describe how the SPF algorithm works and indicate that the computational cost associated with the algorithm depend on the number of nodes and links involved. The SPF algorithm can be resource-intensive for large networks with the computation time required reaching an order of N^2, where N is the number of nodes. This order of complexity can be discerned intuitively considering that, for a total of N nodes, N-1 iterations are required to determine all the least cost paths from a reference node to all other nodes in the graph. At each iteration, the number of operations required to determine the vertex with the least cost is proportional to N.

If N nodes are in a graph and the total number of links in the graph is L, it can be shown that, in general, the SPF computation time is proportional to the number of links—L times the log of the number of links, L in the network. That is the computational cost of the SPF of the order, O(LlogL).

In nonhighly meshed networks—for example, where all nodes are interconnected with the fewest possible links in a linear arrangement, L equals to N-1. LlogL can be expressed as Llog(N-1), which is equivalent to LlogN. In summary, you can estimate the order of computational complexity of Dijkstra's SPF algorithm to be O(LlogN), where L is the total number of links and N is the number of nodes in the network. The computational complexity is directly related to the processing time required for execution to completion of the algorithm.

Another element of interest in the operation of the Dijkstra algorithm is storage or memory requirements.

Memory Requirements

Each router in the graph stores N LSPs, one from each node in the area. Because each LSP contains information about connected links and adjacent neighbors, the size of each LSP is proportional to K, the number of connected links. Therefore, each node needs storage space proportional to N*K links. That is, memory requirements at each node is of the order O(N*K) or O(L), where L is the total number of links. In a nonhighly meshed environments, where L is of the same order as the number of nodes (N), the memory requirements can be estimated to be of the order O(N).

Excessive memory requirements and the corresponding high processing time of the SPF algorithm for large numbers of nodes are the primary drivers for introducing hierarchy into the network design. IS-IS provides a two-level hierarchy that allows area explosion to be contained by building multiple reasonably sized Level 1 areas and gluing them together with a Level 2 backbone.

SPF Calculation Example

Table 6-1 illustrates the operation of the Dijkstra algorithm based on the graph in Figure 6-2. An animation that also illustrates in step-through manner the operation of the Dijkstra algorithm is at the following referenced Web site: http://ciips.ee.uwa.edu.au/~morris/Year2/PLDS210/dijkstra.html.

In Figure 6-2, bidirectional arrowed links are used for arcs and to imply same cost between adjacent nodes in either direction. This might not be the case in real networks. Specifically, IS-IS does not require matching metric values in both directions for the same link. The topology shown in Figure 6-2 has five nodes and seven links. The algorithm is performed using node 1 as the reference node. In a real network, each node performs a similar calculation by using itself as the reference. The goal is to obtain the least cost (best) path from the source of the calculation to all other nodes in the topology.

Figure 6-2   *Topology for illustration of Dijkstra algorithm.*

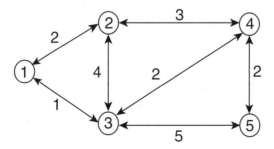

The algorithm is initialized at i = 0. Column i represents the iterations. L(n) is the value of the current total cost from s to node n for a specific iteration. "next hop" is the directly connected next hop to get to a specific node. Other abbreviations in the table are as follows:

- **P**—The set of entries in the Paths set or list

- **(value)**—Directly connect next hop from S

Table 6-1 *Example of Dijkstra's Calculation (s = 1)*

		Node 1	Node 2	Node 3	Node 4	Node 5
i	P	L(1), next hop	L(2),next hop	L(3),next hop	L(4),next hop	L(5), next hop
0	{1}	**0 (1)**	2 (2)	1 (3)	Infinity	Infinity
1	{1, 3}	-	2 (2)	1 (3)	-	-
2	{1, 3, 2}	-	**2 (2)**	-	3 (3)	6 (3)
3	{1, 3, 2, 4}	-	-	-	**3 (3)**	6 (3)
4	{1, 3, 2, 4, 5}	-	-	-	-	**5 (3)**

Table 6-1 shows the paths that are selected from the Tentative set at every iteration in boldface. Only Nodes 2 and 3 are moved to the Tentative set in iteration i = 1. Each path shows the metric to the destination and the next hop. The next hops from node 1 to nodes 2 and 3 are nodes 2 and 3 themselves because they are directly connected.

Nodes that are not directly connected to s inherit the next hop of their parents. For example, the best path to get to node 4 is through node 3 with a cost of 3. The best path to node 5 is through node 4; however, the parent of node 4 is node 3. Therefore, node 3 becomes the next hop to get to node 5 from node 1. Note that the next-hop computation expresses the datagram forwarding paradigm, in which each node is interested only in the next hop as it forwards a packet toward the destination along the optimum path.

Explanation of Table 6-1 (SPF Calculation Example)

The steps in the operation of the SPF algorithm illustrated in Table 6-1 are explained here. The explanations follow the iterations in the example.

1 = 0   In the first iteration, node 1 is selected as the source, and corresponding L(1) = 0 and NH = 1 are entered under node 1 to indicate the next hop from the source to node 1 is itself, and the cost is 0. No action is taken for the other nodes.

i = 1   In iteration 1, nodes directly connected to node 1, which are nodes 2 and 3, are put into the T set. The next hop from node 1 to node 2 is node 2, and the cost is 2. The next hop from node 1 to node 3 is node 3 itself, and the cost is 1. Nodes 4 and 5 remain in the Unknown set and are assigned costs of infinity. Node 3 is promoted from T to P because it has the lowest cost.

i = 2 After node 3 is promoted from T to P, its directly connected neighbors that are not yet in P, nodes 4 and 5, are entered into T. Note that node 2 is already there with a cost of 2. The path from the source to node 2 through 3 has a cost of 5, so the original entry is retained because it has a lower cost. Nodes 4 and 5 use node 3 as next hop from the source. The total cost from node 1 to node 4 is 3, and the corresponding cost to node 5 is 6. Node 2 is, therefore, promoted from T to P because it has the lowest cost.

i = 3 After node 2 is promoted to P, its directly connected neighbors that are not yet in P are considered. This happens to be only node 4, which is already in T. The total cost from node 1 to 4 through node 2 is 5, so the previous path with lower cost is retained. Node 4 is promoted to P because it has a lower associated cost than node 5.

i = 5 After node 4 is promoted to P, its directly connected neighbors that are not yet in P are considered. This happens to be only node 5. Node 5 is currently in T. However, the cost from node 1 to node 5 through 4 is lower than the previous cost of 6. Therefore, node 4 replaces node 3 as the parent of node 5. Also, node 5 inherits the next hop associated with node 4, which is coincidentally node 3. The next hop from node 1 to node 5 remains node 3, but the cost is reduced to 5. Because node 5 is the only node in T, it is promoted to P.

Figure 6-3 shows the resulting least cost topology, at the end of the algorithm, as seen from the perspective of node 1. Nodes 2 and 3 are directly connected, but the best path to node 4 is through node 3, and the best path to node 5 is through node 3 and then node 4.

Figure 6-3 *Least-cost topology from node 1.*

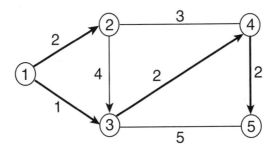

Calculating IS-IS Routes with the SPF Algorithm

Annex C2 of ISO 10589 specifies use of the SPF algorithm for route calculation within the IS-IS protocol. Annex C of RFC 1195 specifies modifications of the SPF algorithm for supporting IP routing within the IS-IS protocol. Dijkstra's algorithm creates a shortest path tree of the network topology, from which the shortest (best) paths to various destinations in the network are determined and entered into the IP routing table. To obtain best paths for IP routes, IP subnets are considered as leaves in the shortest path tree. Therefore, network events resulting in changes in only IP reachability entries contained in link-state packets do not require computation of the entire shortest path tree. In such cases, the IS-IS protocol performs partial route calculation (PRC) rather than a full run of the SPF algorithm. The pervasiveness of PRC in IS-IS route computations optimizes performance for IP routing convergence in most situations.

The preceding section indicates that the computation time of the SPF algorithm is of the order $O(L\log N)$, where L is the number of links and N is the number of nodes. The logN factor results from Step 2 in the operation of Dijkstra's algorithm (refer to Figure 6-2). The elements in the set T are presorted by cost to avoid the need for a linear search in selecting the element with the lowest cost. The processing time required by the binary search mechanism used in sorting T while inserting new entries introduces the logN factor. By using a finite path cost based on a 6-bit field (as specified by ISO 10589), it is possible to further optimize and reduce the order of complexity to just $O(N)$, eliminating the logN factor. This is achieved using quick array sort data structures, which sort nodes by hashing them according to path cost rather than logical distance. Unfortunately, over time, the 6-bit metric field has proved insufficient for providing flexibility in designing IS-IS networks, as well as in other applications of IS-IS routing, such as MPLS traffic engineering. The adoption of larger path costs (wide metrics) in IS-IS (see Chapter 5, "The IS-IS Link-State Database") obviously takes away the optimization opportunity with small finite path costs (narrow metrics).

The modifications to the SPF algorithm introduced by RFC 1195 for use in IS-IS routing allows load balancing over multiple equal-cost paths. In general, however, the Dijkstra algorithm works as described in the preceding section. The operation of the SPF algorithm is described well in Annex C of RFC 1195. The following three lists are used in building the shortest path tree: Unknown or candidate list (UNK), Tentative (TENT) list, and known Paths (PATHS) list. At the start of the SPF process, all nodes are placed in the Unknown list. The source node is then moved to PATHS at initialization. Nodes examined for candidacy to the PATHS list are placed in the TENT list with their next-hop and metric information adjusted accordingly. IS-IS maintains an adjacency database for all neighbors, which feeds the SPF process with next-hop information for directly connected neighbors in the TENT list. For nondirectly connected hosts, the first hop is obtained from the parent in PATHS. Entries are stored in TENT and PATHS as triple sets, $\{n, d(n), Adj(n)\}$, where

- **n** = System ID
- **d**(n) = Distance of n from the root system, s
- **Adj(n)** = Set of valid adjacencies for n known by s

At each step of the algorithm, the TENT list is examined, and the node with the least cost from the source is moved into PATHS. When a node is placed in PATHS, all IP prefixes advertised by it are installed in the IS-IS Routing Information Base (RIB) with the corresponding metric and next hop. The directly connected neighbors of the node that just made it into PATHS are then added to TENT if they are not already there and their associated costs adjusted accordingly, for the next selection.

Note that IP internal and external prefixes are stored as 8 bytes consisting of the address and mask and are always leaves.

IS-IS SPF Operation on Cisco Routers

The actual implementation of a protocol on a specific router platform is mostly transparent to the network operator, and interoperability between products from different vendors is guided by compliance to standards. The details of a specific vendor implementation and software coding also are frequently proprietary information. However, a network engineer seeking a better understanding of IS-IS and the mechanics of operation on a specific platform might benefit significantly from studying various parameters, such as default timers, flags, and other default constants, and how they are configured. Additionally, specifications such as ISO 10589 and RFC 1195 provide useful guidance. This section provides some insights into the operation of IS-IS, and specifically the operation of the SPF algorithm, on Cisco routers.

The SPF process works on Cisco routers as described in the preceding section. Three separate lists (UNK, TENT, and PATH) are used in the algorithm for calculating the shortest path tree for an area. The computation is based on the contents of the Link-State database and the configuration of the routers. The SPF algorithm is executed on the route processor by the SPF process, which is controlled by the IS-IS decision process from an architectural standpoint of IS-IS. The decision process liaises with the update process, which manages the Link-State database. Any changes in the Link-State database triggers the SPF process and can result in a full run of the SPF algorithm or a PRC. As specified by ISO 10589, the SPF process runs no more frequently than every 10 seconds by default. Events that trigger the SPF process can be viewed with the command **show isis spf-log** (see Example 6-1). In a dynamic environment, a sequence of consecutive events can take place within the 10 seconds between runs of the SPF process. Only the first trigger is stored in the SPF event log in current releases of IOS. Some older IOS releases store the last trigger.

Example 6-1   **show isis spf-log** *command*

```
#show isis spf-log
Level 2 SPF log
When      Duration    Nodes    Count    First trigger    LSP Triggers
08:52:29  4           72       4        RTA.00           TLVCONTENT
```

On a Cisco 7500 router, with the RSP4 processor, the duration of the SPF process is normally less than 1 second for a network with fewer than 1000 nodes. A 200 MHz processor, executing one instruction per cycle, performs 200 million instructions per second. Considering that an average of approximately 100,000 instructions are expended per node to calculate the SPF tree, this translates into computing the shortest path tree for 2000 nodes in a second. Therefore, for a reasonably large network of about 500 nodes in a single all Level 1 IS-IS area, it takes about 250 milliseconds to compute the shortest path tree. Note that this number is not a hard figure, and several factors, such as the following, can influence the outcome:

- Actual topology of the network (highly meshed or not).
- Type of operating systems (preemptive or nonpreemptive processing).
- The actual number of instructions executed per cycle. (Some processors can perform two instructions per cycle.)
- Inherent optimizations in the code.

As previously noted, the processing time required by the SPF algorithm is of the order $O(L\log N)$, where L is the number of links, and N is the number of nodes. The logN factor exists because of the sorting of the TENT list during each iteration in the SPF algorithm. In addition, the complexity of the sorting process depends on the extent of interconnectivity between nodes. Note that when a node moves from the TENT list into the PATHS list, all directly connected nodes still in the UNK list move into the TENT list, where sorting is performed during insertion.

The entries on the PATHS lists at the end of each run of the SPF process are only candidates for the routing table on the router. The route processor expends some more cycles comparing the IS-IS routes with similar routes (same prefixes) from other sources, such as BGP, static routes, OSPF, and so on, and installs the prefixes from the source with lowest administrative distance in the routing table. The SPF tree computed by the Dijkstra algorithm considers the routers as vertices with IP addresses advertised by the routers as leaves. As a result, the entire shortest path tree for network changes related only to IP prefixes does not need to be recalculated. Instead, the router runs a partial computation to find an alternative IP prefix if one exists. Also, when best paths are selected, two or more similar routes with worse metrics are kept as backup elements for use as alternative routes in case the selected primary goes away. This allows Cisco IOS to quickly find an alternative path when any route change occurs. Because the topology of the network is determined by the adjacencies advertised in the LSPs, the loss of an adjacency implies a change in topology and, therefore, subsequent scheduling of a complete SPF run. When a point-to-point link goes down, for example, a router loses the adjacency to the neighbor at the other end. This signals a change in topology and, therefore, scheduling of a full SPF. However, a broadcast interface, such as Ethernet, might have only an IP subnet connecting to IP workstations, so losing that interface can imply losing only the IP subnet and not necessarily an adjacency because there might not be another IS-IS router on the link. Because the IP subnet is only a leaf of the SPF tree, this does not flag a change in network topology, and, therefore, only PRC is run to find an alternative path.

The three costly activities for the route processor of an IS-IS router are SPF, PRC, and LSP generation. Delays are employed between successive occurrences of any of these activities to help control processor utilization. The initial wait and minimum interval between successive runs of the SPF and PRC process and consecutive LSP transmissions over the same link are shown in Table 6-2.

Table 6-2   *Delays Between Processing-Intensive IS-IS Events*

Process	Initial Wait (seconds)	Interval (seconds)
SPF	5.5	10
PRC	2	5
LSP generation	0	5

An LSP is generated and flooded as soon as possible without any delay. However, an interval of at least 5 seconds occurs between two consecutive LSPs. When a router receives an LSP, which indicates an adjacency change, a 5.5-second delay is imposed before running the SPF process. Periodic SPF runs are scheduled at least 10 seconds apart. Running of the SPF process stalls transmission, as well as processing of LSPs received from neighbors. Because PRC runs are involved only with calculating leaf information, they are held up when a full SPF is scheduled. This is because a new topology might emerge after running the full SPF process, which might impact the IP path resolution. Cisco IOS provides commands to modify the default intervals, shown in Table 6-2. You can use the following commands to modify the SPF interval, PRC interval, and LSP generation interval, respectively:

- **isis spf-interval**
- **isis prc-interval**
- **isis lsp-gen-interval**

Chapter 7, "General Network Design Issues," discusses network design recommendations for the IS-IS protocol and covers in-depth adjustment of these timers to provide optimal performance of the IS-IS protocol. Also, a recent IETF draft studies convergence characteristics of IS-IS implementations and recommends changes in the current specifications and implementation approaches to attain convergence times in the order of milliseconds rather than the order of seconds achievable today.

Summary

This chapter introduces the reader to the theoretical foundations of the SPF algorithm. It explains how the SPF algorithm calculates routes in IS-IS and provides an overview of how SPF operates on Cisco routers running IS-IS.

The SPF algorithm is named after its inventor, Dutch mathematician and computer scientist Edsger W. Dijkstra. SPF is used in conjunction with the graph theory to find the shortest path between two points. This innovation is used with numerous applications, and certainly use in data communications networks for path determination is one of them. The routers and links (adjacencies) in a communications network can be modeled as the vertices and arcs of a directed graph, and the Dijkstra algorithm can be used to calculate the best paths between nodes in this model. The IS-IS protocol uses the Dijkstra algorithm in this manner to determine the best routes in a network.

Within the IS-IS architecture, the update process is responsible for the building and maintenance of the Link-State database whereas the decision process uses the information in the database to calculate routes. The SPF algorithm is at the core of the operation of the decision process. On Cisco routers, the IS-IS SPF process runs the SPF algorithm to calculate IS-IS routes. The processing time associated with the SPF algorithm depends on the number of nodes and links in the network; generally, it is of the order $O(L\log N)$, where L is the number of links, and N is the number of nodes. The Dijkstra algorithm builds a shortest path tree of the routers in the network based on adjacency information advertised in IS-IS link-state packets. IP prefixes advertised by routers are grafted into the SPF tree as leaves. Any adjacency changes trigger a complete recalculation of the shortest path tree (that is, a full run of the SPF process). Only a partial route calculation is performed for changes in only IP information.

Review Questions

1 What is the basic application of the SPF algorithm?

2 What is a directed graph, and how is an internetwork modeled as a directed graph?

3 Name the three lists used in the operation of the Dijkstra algorithm for computing IS-IS routes.

4 What is the estimated processing cost of the Dijkstra algorithm?

5 What is the difference between a full SPF and a partial route calculation (PRC)?

References

Alaettinoglu, et al. "Towards Millisecond IETF Convergence." Draft-alaettinoglu-isis-convergence-00.txt. IETF INTERNET DRAFT. 2000.

Chartrand, Gary. *Introduction to Graph Theory*. Dover Publications, 1977. ISBN 0-486-2475-9. pp. 10–24.

Cormen, Thomas H. H., Ronald L. Rivest, and Charles E. Leiserson. *Introduction to Algorithms*. MIT Press, 1990.

Edsger Wybe Dijkstra: http://www.cs.utexas.edu/users/UTCS/report/1997/dijkstra.html.

John Morris: http://ciips.ee.uwa.edu.au/~morris/Year2/PLDS210/dijkstra.html.

Perlman, Radia. *Interconnections, Second Edition: Bridges, Routers, Switches and Internetworking Protocols*. Addison-Wesley, 1999. ISBN 0201634481. pp. 317–322.

Profile page of E. W. Dijkstra: http://kzoo.edu/~k98mn01/dijkstra.html.

RFC 1195, "Use of OSI IS-IS for Routing in TCP/IP and Dual Environments." Ross Callon. 1990. pp. 51–57.

Stallings, William. *High-Speed Networks, TCP/IP and ATM Design Principles*. Prentice Hall, 1998. ISBN 0-13-525965-7. Chapter 12, pp. 384–397.

PART II

Integrated IS-IS Network Design for IP Internets

CHAPTER 7

General Network Design Issues

Significant issues that deserve consideration in general network design mostly relate to scalability, stability, and convergence. This applies to the design of the physical layout of the network, as well as routing and traffic management. Scalability, stability, and convergence are relevant to both interdomain and intradomain routing. For intradomain routing, these issues deserve careful consideration, regardless of the IGP selected; and in all cases, only a systematic, well-structured approach will lead to the desired objectives of the design.

The following elements of network design directly impact network scalability, stability, and convergence and are certainly important considerations when designing Integrated IS-IS networks:

- **Hierarchy**—The network architect must decide to deploy IS-IS in flat architecture or with a two-level hierarchy. This also means deciding whether to run the whole domain logically flat (Level 1-only or Level 2-only) or to use hierarchy with multiple Level 1 areas with a Level 2 backbone. If deploying a hierarchy, when and where to create area boundaries become important considerations.

- **Addressing**—Both IP and CLNP (NSAP) addresses are needed in the IS-IS network, and assignment of both types of addresses should be well planned.

- **Summarization**—This is a key consideration, both from the standpoint of constraining routing instabilities as well as reducing the amount of routing information that is advertised in the network. Selection of the points in the network at which to summarize routing information is usually influenced by the location of area boundaries. Summarization points are not always obvious and related decisions are, therefore, important early in the design process.

Each of these factors needs to be thoroughly explored in the planning stages of the network and re-evaluated during the deployment stages to test viability of any assumptions made earlier. This is important to successfully achieve the ultimate design objectives of the network. Each of these factors is further discussed in detail in this chapter.

IP Network Design Principles

The basic principles of good network design apply to all IGPs including IS-IS. The classic design methodology of layering the network into three main components (core, distribution, and access) needs to be applied as much as possible. The following sections discuss these three components.

Core

The core is the network backbone and its primary function is to switch packets as fast as possible. As the core is the heart of the network, it must be redundant, reliable, and have full reachability to every destination in the network.

Because packet switching in the core must be fast, filtering and policy implementations in this part of the network must be limited and, if possible, avoided because, in general, these features slow down the rate of packet processing and adversely impact performance of the core routers. Backbone routers need full routing information so that they can optimally forward packets to any other device in the network without relying on a default-route.

Distribution

The distribution layer is normally the aggregation point of traffic upstream from the edge to the core or downstream traffic in the opposite direction. It can also control and isolate instabilities on the edge from the core.

The distribution routers are the points at which route summarization should take place. This reduces the size of the routing tables and also aids in preventing instabilities on the edge or access layer from disrupting the core. The smaller the number of routes that a backbone router has to deal with, the faster it can make switching decisions, which in turn helps reduce switching latency in the core.

Packet filtering and policy implementation can also be performed at the distribution layer or further out at the access layer as discussed in the next section. By using packet filtering, you can protect the core from uninteresting or unwanted traffic.

Policy routing can be used to forward traffic based on other criteria, such as packet type or source address, instead of the usual destination address.

Access

The access layer is normally the point at which customers connect to the service provider network. Access routers provide the interconnection between customer premise equipment (CPE) and the distribution layer (see Figure 7-1).

Because the access layer is the connection to the exterior of the service provider network, appropriate security measures must be enforced to prevent unauthorized access and any security holes that might be used to launch denial of service attacks of any form. Therefore, filtering and security policies must be applied to access devices to ensure that all devices within the network are protected from external attacks and also customer devices are protected from attacks originating from within the network or its other peripheries.

You can apply a number of basic common access filters to protect from spoofing, broadcast, and directed broadcast sources. RFC 2827, "Network Ingress Filtering: Defeating Denial of Service Attacks which employ IP Source Address Spoofing," provides guidance for implementing such security filters.

Figure 7-1   *Classic three-layer model.*

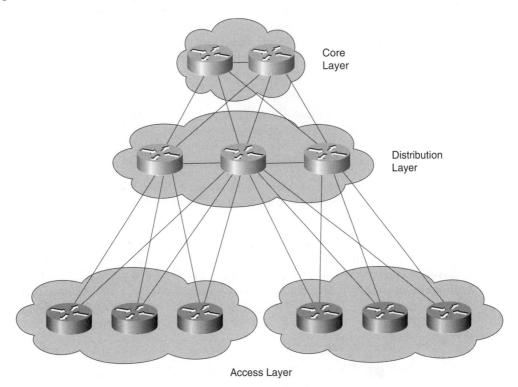

This section briefly discussed the importance of a layered methodology as the basic underlying principle for designing scalable networks. The three-layered approach is recommended as the basis for architecting networks that can grow to a significantly large number of nodes. For completeness, however, the following two design issues also need to be considered: A hierarchical routing topology and a well-laid-out IP addressing scheme.

Hierarchical Topology and Routing

Hierarchy is ultimately the key to successfully scale a network. If you design a network with hierarchy in mind from the start, the network can be extended in size with only trivial adjustments. If you leave hierarchy out, the network will likely encounter problems as it grows and ultimately will compromise performance and reliability.

Why must you always design with hierarchy in mind? The main reason is that, ultimately, a flat network does not scale. For example, in the case of IS-IS, as the network grows, increasing the number of nodes increases the number of LSPs flooded, which in turn increases the complexity and time taken for the SPF computation.

The more nodes within the network, the more links there are, the more LSPs that are flooded, the more information that SPF has to deal with, the more CPU cycles required for route computation, and so on. The most expensive part of the route computation (SPF) is over the intra-area topology—therefore, it makes sense to segment the network into smaller manageable sections or areas. If this is done, there will be fewer nodes and links in each area, and fewer LSPs will be flooded. Consequently, the SPF process will have less information to deal with during route computation, saving valuable CPU cycles for other critical functions of the router.

Another sound reason for using a hierarchical design with areas is to hide instabilities within a problematic region from the rest of the network. IS-IS currently supports two levels of hierarchy. By adopting a hierarchical design, you can use summarization to reduce the amount of information transferred between areas and also at redistribution points.

Layering the network into core, distribution, and access gives you more control and, therefore, makes the network more manageable. This approach is beneficial in IS-IS network design scenarios.

A small and simple IS-IS network can be initially deployed as a flat network. However, you need to determine up-front when it might be necessary to migrate to a hierarchical topology. It is difficult to say exactly how many nodes justify moving to a hierarchical model. Certainly, this depends on many factors and requires keeping the final goal in mind when making such a call. The following factors need to be considered when designing an IS-IS network to scale into the future:

- How many nodes are there currently?
- How many nodes are expected in the future?
- How is the network split in terms of geography?
- What media technology is used to interconnect the nodes? What are the link speeds and how stable are they?

Other factors that need to be considered are interdomain reachability and default route origination and propagation. Each of these factors influences the network design. Obviously, some have a stronger influence than others.

You might start with a simple network of 10 nodes, for example. With only 10 nodes, do you have an immediate need for hierarchy? Perhaps not. Suppose, however, that 1 or 2 of these nodes are in a region that experiences constant flapping, which is uncontrollable because of operating conditions; one approach to contain the problem is to introduce hierarchy into the network. Having the flapping links in one area constrains the instabilities to only the affected region.

As shown in Figure 7-2, when a link goes down, a new router LSP is generated and flooded. The LSP is then flooded further through the network so that all routers become aware of the event and make adjustments as necessary.

Figure 7-2   *LSP flooding.*

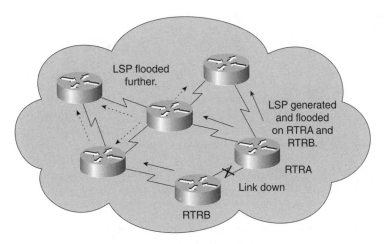

By moving to a hierarchical topology with multiple areas, you can contain the flooding of LSPs within the area. Where possible, you can also configure the routers for only a single level of routing (Level 1-only or Level 2-only instead of Level 1-2). This saves on memory and CPU processing because route calculations will be performed on only one Link-State database instead of two. By default, a Cisco router behaves as Level 1 and Level 2 (that is, Level 1-2). Additional configuration is required to reduce it to a single level capability.

The most logical place to start when designing an IS-IS network is the backbone. As previously discussed, IS-IS currently supports two levels of hierarchy: the backbone, where Level 2 routing is performed, and the areas where Level 1 routing occurs. (see Figure 7-3). Therefore, it makes sense to start with a contiguous Level 2 backbone. This way, as the network grows, you can add in the Level 1 areas and migrate to a full hierarchical model for scaling purposes, if necessary.

Figure 7-3   *IS-IS hierarchical areas.*

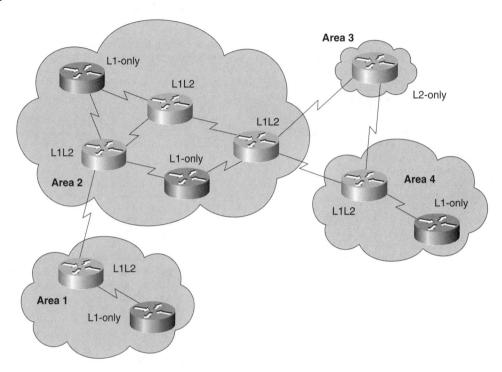

In the past, Internet service providers avoided building hierarchical IS-IS domains because the stubby areas specified in ISO 10589 and ported into RFC 1195 did not provide the necessary intelligence for Level 1-only routers to determine the best exit point from the area. In this framework, Level 1 routers follow a default route to the closest Level 1-2 router. Level 2 routers flag connectivity to the backbone to Level 1 routers by setting the attached bit in their Level 1 LSP, which is flooded throughout the area. Even though the selected default router might be the closest in the area, it might not be the best exit out of the area when the overall cost to the destination is considered. This possibility of suboptimal path selection was the main reason why most service providers built flat IS-IS topologies. Figure 7-4 shows that to send traffic from RTA to RTB, you need to traverse a number of links—the closest exit point for RTA is through the link with a metric of 40. This leads to the nearest Level 1-2 in the direction of the final destination. However, the total path cost of 150 is worse when compared to the alternate path, which has a better total path cost of 120, even though the cost of 50 to the Level 1-2 router on that path is worse.

Figure 7-4   *Suboptimal routing.*

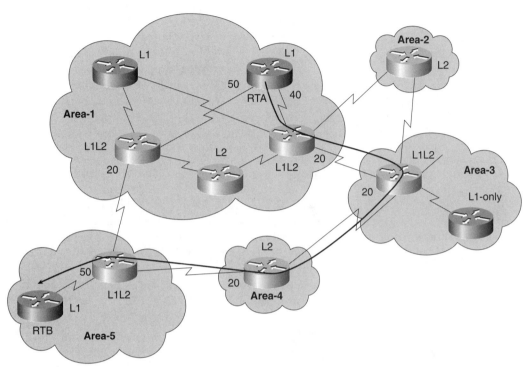

Because interarea routes are not available to Level 1-only routers, they are unaware of the end-to-end metric information associated with such routes. Therefore, this model does not facilitate BGP shortest path selection, making it generally unsuitable for use in ISP networks. Building a flat network provides a workaround. Additionally, you might also argue that building a flat network is much less complex than building a hierarchical one. After all, in ISP networks, the IGP is primarily used for determination of the BGP next-hop and local routes, so why make the topology more complex than it needs to be?

A recent enhancement in Cisco IOS Software, known as Interarea Route Leaking, removes the suboptimal routing limitation in IS-IS Level 1 routing. When enabled, this feature allows a Level 1-2 router to inject IP prefix information from the Level 2 database into the Level 1 database of its local area through its Level 1 LSP, thereby "leaking" interarea routes into Level 1.

When designing IS-IS networks, always remember that the backbone must be contiguous. In other words, a Level 1-only router should never be inserted between any two Level 2 routers (Level 2-only or Level 1-2).

In general, the design of the network topology needs to start from the core. As discussed previously, the core aligns with the IS-IS Level 2 backbone when considering a hierarchical topology. Proper layout of the core provides more flexibility for future growth. If the initial size of the network is not large, the backbone can be deployed as a flat topology without multiple areas. In this case, the backone is configured as Level 2-only. As the nextwork grows, it might get to a point where hierarchy must be introduced to scale further. This means deploying Level 1 areas in addition to the existing Level 2 backbone to accommodate growth. Depending on the design and growth objectives of the network, the Level 1 areas can be added in a manner that reflects the hierarchy of physical topology. A key design consideration at this juncture is the demarcation of the Level 1 areas from the backbone.

As noted previously, the core routers ideally should not perform any functions that place additional load on the CPU because the primary function of the core is to switch IP packets as fast as possible. Within an IS-IS network, however, you can summarize IP subnets from Level 1 areas into the Level 2 backbone, and also when leaking routes, from Level 2 into Level 1. One of the goals of good network design is to reduce the amount of routing information that is transferred to and from the core. Therefore, it might be beneficial to configure the core routers as Level 1-2 and then push the Level 1-only routing out to the distribution layer. However, this design also has some drawbacks. Many access routers might be attached to the distribution routers, which can result in too many routers in a single area. In such cases, network instabilities might be unmanageable, imposing limitations on scaling and future growth potential. A possible solution is to make the core routers pure Level 2; then configure the distribution routers as Level 1-2, and finally the access routers as Level 1-only. As the distribution routers take over the dual Level 1-2 function, suboptimal routing is eliminated by using Route Leaking. Finally, with the access routers being Level 1-only, any instabilities are not passed back up into the core.

As obvious from the preceding discussion, tradeoffs must be made in the design process. The perfect network is not always realizable. A successful IS-IS networks is one that is stable and scalable and converges reasonably fast when there are changes.

A definitive maximum number of routers that can be supported within a single IS-IS area is hard to determine. Currently (at the time of writing), there are some reasonably large-sized networks with close to a 1000 routers in a single area, operating successfully without any significant issues. However, 1000 nodes per area is not an absolute number. The number of nodes that can be crammed into a single area depends mainly on the design of the physical topology, stability of the links, the number of IP subnets, and the memory and CPU capacities of the routers. What works for one network might not necessarily work for another network; and therefore, each design must be evaluated individually on its own merits.

Figure 7-5 shows how you can combine hierarchy and area routing over the core, distribution, and access layers. Only Level 2 LSPs are flooded between the core and distribution layers. The access layer devices in the same area as the distribution routers receive and exchange only Level 1 LSPs with the distribution routers. Designing the network this way protects the core layer from instabilities within the access layer.

Figure 7-5   *IS-IS hierarchy using area routing.*

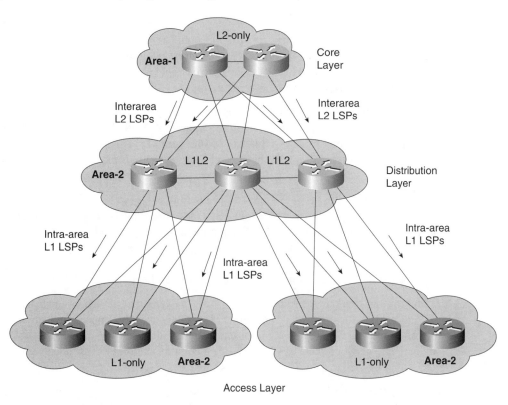

IP Addressing Layout

One of the main factors that determines how well an IGP scales is the addressing layout planned into the network architecture. This applies to any routing protocol regardless of whether it is link-state or distance vector, intradomain or interdomain. If an incorrect addressing scheme is used in the design and deployed in the earlier phases of the implementation, there might be challenges in the future to scale further. This section briefly examines and highlights some of the issues that should be considered when designing an IP addressing layout for use with IS-IS.

Perhaps Integrated IS-IS lends itself a little more toward a less-stringent IP addressing structure than other link-state IGPs, especially in single area deployments. This is because it can handle a large number of nodes in an area. This is particularly advantageous for existing IP networks that have poor, discontiguous addressing layouts, which are difficult or nearly impossible to summarize. However, this is not a good reason for not following good design practices and principles when laying out an IP addressing structure for use with IS-IS.

Improper addressing assignment can significantly impede successful operation of a network. Poor IP addressing makes a good level of summarization difficult to achieve. Networks that run without decent levels of summarization are prone to stability problems because they cannot take advantage of summarization to help contain instabilities and route flaps, as well as reduce the load on routers. Without summarization, the number of routes propagated throughout the network could be larger. This, in turn, requires more processing and places more demands on the CPU during network churns.

IP address assignment is often seen as a laborious task by most network operators, being a mundane administrative chore. It is, therefore, often implemented without due care and consideration of the pitfalls that poor planning brings. After IP addresses have been allocated and assigned, it is often difficult to change and reassign them. If reassignment is possible, downtime is involved; therefore, service is interrupted. Of course, the changes are implemented during a maintenance window.

When designing an IP addressing structure, also ensure that the chosen address range of any subnet is large enough to allow for additional growth. It would be a great waste of effort to meticulously plan the address assignment scheme, only to later run out of addresses on some segments. Always keep summarization in mind when designing the IP addressing scheme because it will help control the number of routes that populate the IP routing table.

You learned that summarization is important when designing an IP addressing scheme—but you might be wondering what summarization actually does. In simple terms, summarization enables more detailed topology information to be hidden and sets a boundary limit for containing any network changes. This reduces the number of routers that are affected by any such changes.

By reducing the number of routers affected by a change, you effectively reduce the number of routers that are involved in convergence calculations that shield the network from a potential meltdown. Now that you have seen the huge benefits to be gained from using a well-planned IP addressing scheme (with good summary capability), it is time to consider which parts of the network to apply summarization to. The most logical places to configure summarization are on routers at the distribution layer between the core and access layers (when dealing with the classical three-layer hierarchical model). This ensures that you allow full topology information to be leaked only where required.

Summarize from the access layer toward the core, by having the distribution routers summarize each block of access layer prefixes into shorter prefixes that are advertised into the core. At the distribution router, you can summarize the four advertisements coming from the access routers into a single prefix (refer to Figure 7-6). The four access prefixes are hidden from the core router, protecting the core router from any instabilities that might arise on the access routers.

Figure 7-6   *Summarizing from distribution to core.*

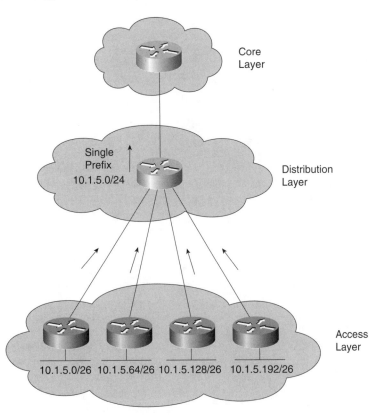

You can also summarize at the distribution layer from the core downstream toward the access layer. Typically, access devices that attach to a distribution layer (or directly to the core) require only a default route. In other scenarios, such as dual homing, it may be necessary to take appropriate measures to avoid any potential for suboptimal path selection. In Figure 7-7, you can see that practically all core prefixes are summarized into one advertisement—the default route. This is shown as a prefix of all 0s—0.0.0.0/0.

The primary objective of IP route summarization is to limit the size of the routing table, which assists in scaling the network in a stable manner. Designing an IP addressing scheme to be used with Integrated IS-IS is no different from designing for any other IGP. In summary, to achieve the objective of a successful, scalable network, apply the design practices and principles elaborated here. and plan carefully for future growth.

Figure 7-7 *Summarizing from distribution to access.*

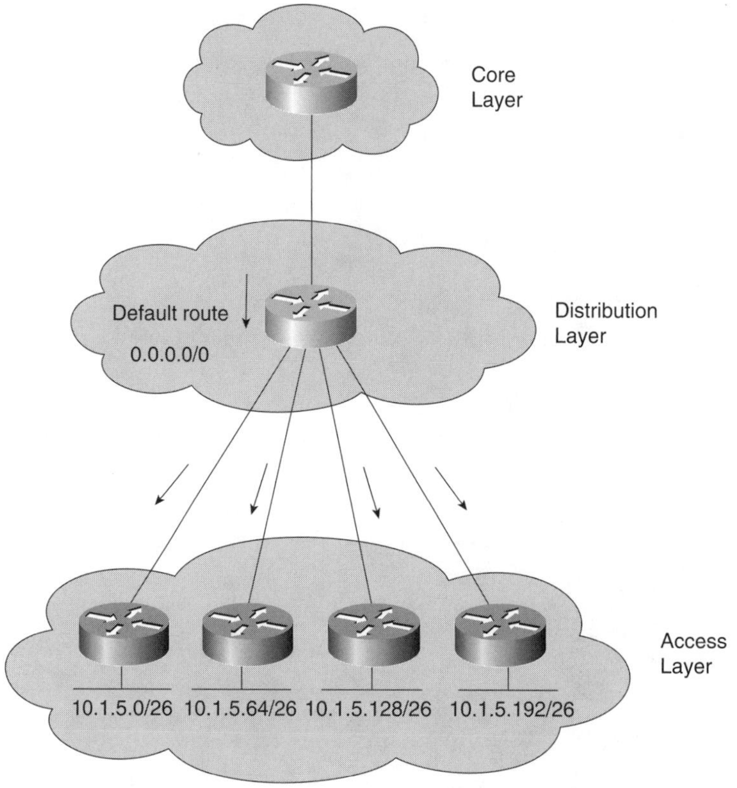

Using IS-IS as an IGP

Over the past few years, IS-IS has become increasingly more popular for use as an IGP. Previously, IS-IS was more prevalent in government and academic networks, the majority of which were pure CLNS environments that did not carry IP prefix information.

The IS-IS protocol seems to be widely perceived as difficult to understand and to configure. One of probable reasons for this is the additional requirement for CLNP (or NSAP) addresses. The node-based NSAP addresses differ vastly from IP addresses (see Chapter 4, "Addressing in Integrated IS-IS") and require familiarity to work with comfortably. However, the comparable routing protocol, such as the Open Shortest Path First (OSPF) Protocol, works with only IP addresses. Even though OSPF is similar in many regards to IS-IS, differences in the CLNP and IP addressing schemes (node-based versus link-based, respectively) result in OSPF defining its area boundaries on the router itself, whereas IS-IS defines its boundaries on the network links between routers in different areas.

Also, because an NSAP can potentially be up to 20 bytes in length, it adds to the complexity of the protocol. Another reason many people did not adopt the protocol earlier was that there was inadequate information regarding design and configuration guidelines. This is now improving and certainly a major factor in the growing popularity of the protocol.

Many major service providers run IS-IS in some of the largest IP networks in the world. Inherently, the IS-IS protocol tends to be very scalable and can accommodate large areas. Being pure link-state, it can react quickly to changes and thus attain fast convergence. Also, because IS-IS uses TLVs to encode information in all packets, it can be easily extended. IS-IS has many configurable timers that you can tune to enhance its operation, such as reducing convergence time, increasing stability, and controlling flooding—to name but a few. Although these timers might be more challenging to tune effectively, they make the protocol more flexible, scalable, and robust. This is a definite plus because you can literally tailor the protocol by using the timers to meet your specific network requirements.

One of the reasons that IS-IS is such a flexible and relatively simple protocol is that not many rigid standards exist for it to adhere to—especially when compared to OSPF. Some might be disappointed about the lack of rigorous standards that cover some the more recently added capabilities, yet other might see it as an advantage.

Protocol Limitations to Consider

Like any IGP, Integrated IS-IS has some limitations. Many of the previous protocol limitations have been removed as a result of recent IETF drafts and RFCs and corresponding enhancements in Cisco IOS Software. The following sections examine these limitations in more detail.

Metric Limitation

Before the introduction of new TLVs that support larger metrics, Integrated IS-IS was limited to a 6-bit interface metric and a 10-bit path metric. This gave a range of 1 to 63 for the interface metric and a value of 1023 for the total path metric. If implementations that do not support the new TLVs are used, the interface and maximum path metric limitation still applies.

Area Limitation

Before the introduction of route leaking, IS-IS areas resembled the model of an OSPF "stub area," with the exception that external information could be redistributed into the Level 1 areas on Cisco routers. As a result, the only way to exit an area was to forward packets to the closest Level 1-2 router, increasing the potential for suboptimal forwarding.

Route leaking eliminated this problem by providing a means to "leak" routes present in the Level 2 database to the Level 1 areas. As a result of this new capability, a Level 1 router can make a much better decision regarding the best point to exit the area to reach the final destination. This is particularly useful for shortest exit routing when coexisting with BGP, and also for optimal reachability to the loopback address of the provider edge (PE) router when using Integrated IS-IS in Multiprotocol Label Switching-based Virtual Private Networks (MPLS-VPN) applications.

MPLS is a mechanism used to forward packets across a network from an ingress router toward an egress router without the need to analyze network layer destination IP addresses. MPLS assigns labels to packets and utilizes label swapping to forward the packets through the network. Each packet carries a short, fixed-length label that informs switching nodes along the path how to process and forward the data.

Virtual private networks (VPNs) can be defined as networks in which connectivity between multiple customer sites is deployed on a shared infrastructure with the same access or security policies as a private network infrastructure. A detailed description of the concepts and architectures of MPLS-VPN is beyond the scope of this book.

Maximum Number of Advertised IP Prefixes

A major limitation to consider is the maximum number of routes an IS-IS router can support, which is limited to approximately 30,000 routes. This limitation exists because of a maximum of 256 LSP fragments per router, each of which will not take more than 121 IP prefixes. This is essentially a technical limitation of the protocol and should not be considered for practical purposes because in most applications, the IGP does not carry this many routes. The majority of the routes are carried in BGP, which relies on the IGP to help resolve next hop information. Therefore, the IGP tracks subnets assigned to links in the networks, and the order of IGP routes is normally significantly far less than 30,000.

A recently published IETF draft, draft-hermelin-ext-lsp-frags-00.txt, proposes increasing the maximum number of LSP fragments beyond the 256 current limit by using multiple system IDs on the same intermediate system. However, as mentioned previously, a currently deployed network that carries anywhere close to the 30,000 IP prefixes per router in its IGP is open to serious scrutiny. Existing IGPs were never designed to carry this number of routes and might experience operational problems if they are pushed to these limits.

Metrics, Nonhierarchical Design

As previously mentioned, by default, all IS-IS interface metrics are set to 10. Therefore, all the interface metrics might need to be redefined and configured depending on the required traffic flow.

Two main styles of metrics exist: narrow and wide. Narrow metrics are commonly called old-style TLVs and wide metrics are referred to as new-style TLVs. The following sections look at how the metrics are used and assigned.

Using Narrow Metrics

If using older implementations that do not support the new TLV types (which allow interface metric values larger than 63), you must take care when deciding which value to apply to each interface. All interface metrics must be configured manually because autoconfiguration does not exist based on parameters, such as bandwidth, as in OSPF.

Also, with bandwidth capacity of media types increasing to extremely high values, such as OC-192, there is a huge range of bandwidth to fit into the small range of narrow metrics—especially if there are small bandwidth interfaces to consider in the network.

Metrics are an important consideration when designing any network, and IS-IS is no exception. The interface and path metrics influence the way the traffic flows around the network, and, therefore, you must carefully plan metric assignments to achieve the desired results.

As with most routing protocols, in IS-IS, a lower metric is preferred over a larger value. Therefore, when using narrow metrics, which allows an interface metric range from 1 to 63, 1 is the best and 63 is the worst that can be assigned. If you have no other alternative than to use the old-style TLVs and, therefore, "narrow" metrics, you need to make an informed decision about which metric values to assign to the lowest and highest bandwidth interfaces in the network. When deciding which values to assign, it is prudent to take into consideration additional interfaces of higher bandwidth that might be used in the near future.

There is little benefit to designing a metric scheme that requires major modifications when new interfaces are added. So, plan ahead and be proactive. Investigate which interface speeds might be added in the future and leave room for growth. If future interfaces are known in advance, you can easily accommodate them.

Using Wide Metrics

Wide metrics provide a much larger range for both interface and total path metrics. Wide metrics use 24 bits for interface metrics and 32 bits for path metrics compared to 6 bits and 10 bits, respectively, for narrow metrics. This provides a huge range to design with and effectively removes the limitations associated with narrow metrics.

Some recent applications, such as MPLS traffic engineering, are supported using only wide metrics. Therefore, all routers that are required to run MPLS traffic engineering must support the new-style TLVs (Types 22 and 135).

Again, a structured approach must be taken when deciding on a metric assignment using wide metrics. Although the previous issues have been removed, it would be difficult and time consuming to enter large metric values on each router interface. This calls for a simple and practical metric assignment scheme.

Assigning Metric Values

In the vast majority of cases, you initially need to assign a lower metric value to a higher bandwidth interface to ensure that the traffic is forwarded along the path with the lowest delay. Because a high price tag is associated with high bandwidth interfaces and corresponding circuits, it seems logical to use the large capacity links as much as possible. Also, the less-congested path should be the one that has the least delay—although this is not always the case.

NOTE   Although bandwidth is the term that is perhaps most commonly used when choosing the best path, the most important factor to consider is delay.

Of course, this might not be applicable to all design scenarios. In a number of valid cases, you might want traffic to follow along the path with the least number of hops, which might not be the same high-bandwidth path (again, seeking the lowest delay, or possibly the highest reliability). Because Integrated IS-IS uses only interface cost as a valid metric, you can rely only on manual configuration to achieve the desired traffic-flow.

When designing traffic flow within and between points of presence using Integrated IS-IS, you might want traffic to flow across the shortest path possible with the least number of hops to reach the destination, instead of taking the route with the highest bandwidth. Consider Figure 7-8, for example, which shows a higher metric assigned to the 155 Mbps interfaces than the other lower bandwidth interfaces. This ensures that the traffic takes the path with the least number of hops to get from source X to destination Y.

Usually, Internet service providers try to keep the number of hops that traffic traverses in their networks to a minimum. Therefore, in some cases, assigning a lower cost to a lower bandwidth link might be preferred to reduce the hop count, provided there is enough capacity on the path to handle available traffic.

Using Both Narrow and Wide Metrics Together

You can use either narrow or wide metrics when using a nonhierarchical design. The type of metric that can actually be configured depends on the IOS version in use.

NOTE   Cisco IOS Software defaults to narrow metrics. If wide metrics is desired, it must be enabled with the command **metric-style wide** under **router isis**. The additional keywords **level-1**, **level-2**, or **level-1-2** should be appended depending on the mode of operation of the router. All nodes should be configured with the same metric style.

Figure 7-8   *IS-IS Interface metric assignment.*

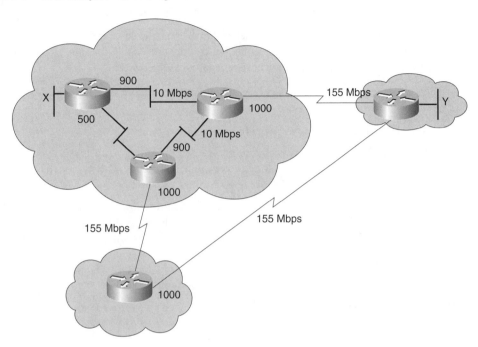

Narrow and wide metrics can coexist. The predominant reason to configure wide metrics, in addition to the existing narrow metrics, is to provide a required transition from one metric style to the other. Routing issues might occur when some nodes use the old-style TLVs and others use the new-style TLVs.

In such circumstances, the information on which the SPF calculation is based might vary significantly from node to node. This can cause routing loops; and therefore, network administrators need to ensure that all nodes are configured similarly.

Migration from Narrow to Wide Metrics

Cisco IOS Software provides a third metric style command to support transition during metric migration. The command **metric-style transition** is hidden in IOS.

If a migration from old-style to new-style metrics is required, the easiest and most pain-free method is to introduce a *flag day*, when availability of network services is completely disrupted while the changes are being implemented. The downside of this is that service interruption might not be acceptable because of operations charter. Another approach to metric migration is to use both the new-style and old-style TLVs together with the **metric-style transition** command. Doing this, forces each router to advertise and process routes with old and new metric information, which even though implies redundancy, ensures that all routers in the network understand all the advertised information.

One requirement for using this approach is that the configured metric limits for the old-style and new-style TLVs need to be the same. By keeping both values the same, the computation of the SPT is not affected and is consistent across the network.

Beware, however, that this particular method does have some short-term disadvantages, such as the following:

- All interface metrics are limited to a maximum value of 63.

- The size of the LSPs increases because more information must be contained within them. Therefore, the originating router might fragment the LSPs more frequently than before, which might lead to some performance issues.

- There might be some instability experienced during the transition period because of the possibility of increased fragmentation and flooding of more LSPs throughout the network. This might consume additional network bandwidth and also require additional buffering and processing.

NOTE   If different interface metrics are used and an adjacency is advertised more than once by both TLV types, the interface and adjacency with the lowest metric is used.

Because the use of both metric-styles is only recommended in transition, the duration of this period must not be excessive; and therefore, the disadvantages hold true only over the short term. Chapter 8, "Network Design Scenarios," provides practical examples for transitioning between narrow and wide metrics.

Nonhierarchical Design

When designing a nonhierarchical Integrated IS-IS network, you use the same area prefix in the NSAP for all routers in the domain. The area is normally run as a flat Level 1 or Level 2 network. In this scenario, each router maintains a single database, and there is no need for summarization or route leaking within the area. A nonhierarchical design has scaling limitations and ultimately requires some form of redesign into a hierarchical topology if the network is to grow successfully to a large number of nodes.

As discussed previously, the main driver for using a nonhierarchical design in the past was that it helped avoid suboptimal interarea routing in Level-1 areas. This limitation no longer exists in recent IOS software.

A nonhierarchical single area design might potentially have more routers per area than a hierarchical design using a number of areas. This might make the SPF computation more complex and require a longer run time to completion. As discussed previously, only a partial SPF (PRC) needs to be run when changes are external to the area or only IP prefixes are affected by the changes. Instabilities in one part of the network are not masked from other parts within a single area.

The benefits of running a router as both Level 1 and Level 2 within a single area are reduced in a nonhierarchical design. Such a scenario is certainly possible; although in practice, it makes little sense. Consider the design in Figure 7-9. The design has a core of routers running as both Level 1 and Level 2, with leaf routers running as Level 1-only and connected redundantly (dual-homed) to the core. Assume only Level 2 adjacencies are enabled between the core routers so that they do not exchange Level 1 LSPs—meaning Level 1 LSPs will not traverse the core between Level 1 routers. Level 1 routers have to depend on default routes to reach remote segments; however, because all routers are in the same area and the core routers are not attached to routers in different areas, they will not set the "attached bit" in their Level 1 LSPs. Therefore, the Level 1-only routers hanging off the core will not set defaults to nearby Level 1-2 routers, making end-to-end reachability impossible. Route leaking could be used to advertise routes from the Level 2 database into Level 1 routers, but there would be little point in doing this because route leaking is meant for advertising inter-area routes into Level 1 in a multi-area hierarchical network.

A way around this is to enable Level 1 routing over all routers. However, this defeats the purpose of running Level 2 additionally on the core routers because this transforms the whole domain into a flat Level 1 area with redundant Level 2 routing. If no connections to external areas exist, no interarea routing is required and, therefore, you can make all routers Level 1- or Level 2-only to optimize use of network resources.

If an area is designed as Level 1-2 and one or more of the core routers are connected to other areas, the attached bit is set in the Level 1 LSPs of Level 1-2 routers, providing an exit point for Level 1 only routers.

In this scenario, you can also selectively leak interarea prefixes Level 2 into Level 1. This avoids the possibility of suboptimal routing and ensures that the Level 1 routers pick the best point for exiting the area. Figure 7-10 shows this type of design.

A design without hierarchy is certainly much simpler than one with hierarchy. As you have just seen, however, a design can sometimes be a little more challenging when mixing both Level 1 and Level 2 routing.

Figure 7-9 *Nonhierarchical areas.*

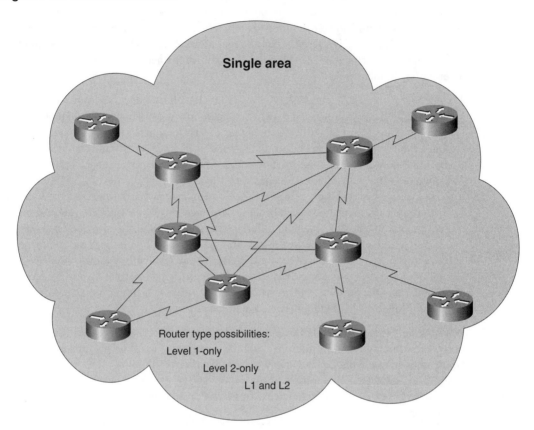

Interaction with BGP

Integrated IS-IS coexists with BGP, predominantly within Internet service provider networks. Understanding the interaction between IS-IS and BGP is paramount when designing such networks. Sometimes, this interaction can be complex.

Within such environments, Integrated IS-IS, being an Interior Gateway Protocol, is used to carry the BGP next-hop and local routes. This is the main function when using Integrated IS-IS as an IGP in such environments. As discussed later, however, Integrated IS-IS interacts in other ways with BGP.

Figure 7-10 *Running an IS as Level 1 to Level 2 in a single area.*

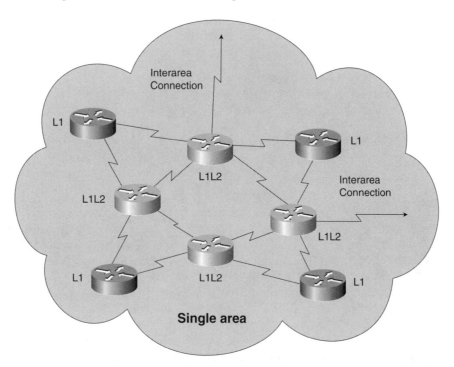

The next hop addresses associated with BGP routes must be known for the BGP routes to be useful for forwarding traffic. A process within IOS scans the IP routing table to ensure that the next hop of BGP learned prefixes is valid and reachable. If a next hop is found to be invalid or unreachable, an alternate path is selected. Synchronization is a BGP capability that controls how BGP interacts with the IGP. The synchronization feature is enabled by default when running BGP, and its purpose is to ensure that all Internal BGP (iBGP) learned routes are known also within the IGP and, therefore, available at all other routers in the autonomous system before advertising such routes to external destinations. This avoids traffic black-holing, where traffic is attracted from remote ASs, only to be dropped because some router in the path doesn't know how to route to the target address.

The synchronization requirement can be disabled with the "no synchronization" command under the BGP process. In this scenario, routes will be advertised, irrespective of the existence of an IGP route. However, synchronization needs to be turned off only when all transit routers within the AS are running BGP or when the AS is not a transit AS. In Figure 7-11, AS2 is shown as a transit, forwarding traffic between AS1 and AS3.

Figure 7-11 *Interaction with BGP: iBGP synchronization.*

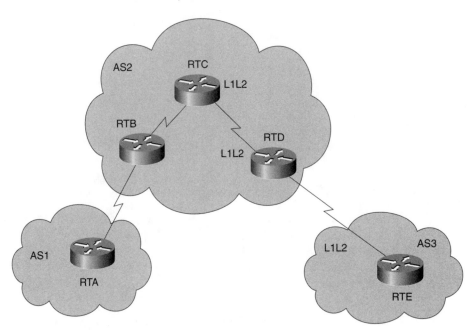

RTA and RTB are external BGP peers (eBGP) and so are RTD and RTE. RTB and RTD are internal BGP peers (iBGP). If RTC in AS2 were to run IS-IS only and not participate in the iBGP with RTB and RTD, you would need to redistribute eBGP routes into IS-IS to ensure that RTC has full information to forward packets between AS1 and AS3. However, redistributing BGP into IGP should be avoided at all costs. One simple reason for this is that there might be more routes carried in BGP than IS-IS can support. You might recall that currently IS-IS is limited to about 30,000 routes, whereas the Internet BGP table is currently (at the time of writing) holding over 100,000 routes.

Synchronization ensures that traffic is not routed between AS1 and AS3 through RTC, which has no knowledge about the external routes exchanged between RTB and RTD through BGP. The best aproach to solve this is to enable BGP peering on RTC. In that case, synchronization can be turned off on all BGP routers in AS2.

Use of the Overload Bit with BGP

Another situation where Integrated IS-IS interacts with BGP is when using a feature of the IS-IS protocol to avoid black-holing traffic at initial power-on or during reload of a router.

Normally, the router sets the overload-bit in its LSP to warn all other routers of an overload condition that would make it potentially unreliable as transit. The capability is defined in the original IS-IS specification but was never leveraged in actual implementations. A recently introduced application of the overload bit is for controlling interaction of IS-IS and BGP in potential service-impacting situations.

When a router running both Integrated IS-IS and BGP reloads, it might not have had enough time to receive the full BGP table before it starts participating in forwarding traffic, even though it might advertise reachability to IGP next hop of a BGP route. In such a situation, traffic can be dropped if the router is used as transit for destinations it does not yet know. To avoid this situation, you can use a protection mechanism within IS-IS that sets the overload bit in the router's LSP to tell all other routers not to include this particular router when calculating the shortest path tree. The router then waits for a signal from the BGP process after a reasonable interval when all BGP prefixes are expected to have been received. Because BGP has many more prefixes to receive and deal with than an IGP, such as IS-IS, it typically takes much longer to converge. After BGP convergence is flagged, the router can then flood out another LSP with the overload bit turned off. The following command can be used to set the overload bit on start up until BGP signals that it has finished converging:

```
router isis
set-overload-bit on-startup wait-for-bgp
```

Figure 7-12 illustrates the use of the overload bit. There is a default delay of two minutes (within which BGP is expected to update IS-IS with its state). However, this update delay parameter is configurable under the BGP router process as shown here:

```
router bgp 100
    bgp update-delay <sec>
```

In most current Internet domains, BGP typically converges in less than 5 minutes depending, of course, on a number of factors, such as the number of routes, number of peers, type of routers, bandwidth capacity, and so on. Should it take longer than expected for BGP to converge and the BGP notification is delayed significantly longer than expected, IOS clears the overload bit after 10 minutes.

Another scenario in which the use of the overload bit provides a similar advantage as in the interaction with BGP is when running Integrated IS-IS as the IGP for MPLS networks. During boot up, an MPLS router might not yet have received all labels; therefore, it would be wise not to use this router for a period of time, to allow it to fully receive all labels. In this situation, the IS-IS overload bit can again be set on start up of the router. A typical value in this case would be approximately 2 minutes.

The additional commands that allow the overload bit to interact with BGP are available in recent releases of Cisco IOS Software. The IETF draft draft-mcpherson-isis-transient-00.txt explains and formalizes the use of the overload bit in IS-IS to avoid black-holing traffic.

Figure 7-12 *Interaction with BGP: overload bit.*

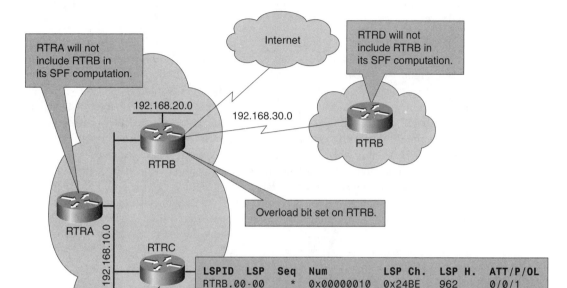

IS-IS Scaling Issues—Network Stability and Convergence

As with any protocol, the capability to scale is important because it allows a network to grow in a controlled and stable manner. Many factors determine whether a network will *successfully scale*. If a network is inherently unstable, it will be difficult to scale. The instabilities might be because of flapping links, which frequently are not under the control of the network operator. However, the network operator can impose certain changes to contain the instabilities.

Scalability

The main factors that contribute to network scalability are as follows:

- Number of routers
- Number of links
- Number of internal and external routes
- Stability of links
- Flooding
- Memory
- Processing capacity (CPU)

The flooding of LSPs is probably the most influential of these factors when looking at scaling. The less information that routers in the network have to handle, the more the network can scale. In other words, you can scale by controlling the amount of flooding throughout the network. This also profoundly affects the amount of processing that the routers have to perform. The route processors in the routers don't need to work as hard when there are only few LSPs and not much routing information in each LSP to work with. Therefore, the amount of background flooding can be significantly reduced to enhance scalability. The two main flooding-related timers—Maxage and LSP refresh interval—can be increased to the region of their maximum values, approximately 18.7 hours, to help reduce the frequency of periodic flooding.

The LSP refresh interval and Maxage can be adjusted, as shown in the following configuration

```
snippet:router isis
    lsp-refresh-interval 65000
    max-lsp-lifetime 65535
```

IOS jitters these timers within some limits from the configured values to ensure that routers do not refresh their LSPs at the same time to prevent overloading the routers.

NOTE   The **lsp-refresh-interval** is always configured with a value less than the **max-lsp-lifetime** to ensure that existing LSPs are refreshed before they reach maxage and expire.

Other timers can be modified to reduce the amount of flooding and increase scalability. For example, because excessive flooding over low-bandwidth links might cause problems, Cisco IOS Software uses a pacing mechanism that allows flooding to consume only 50 percent of the configured bandwidth, on low-bandwidth links at T1 rates and below. The interface command **isis lsp-interval** also can be used in conjunction with this to control the interval between successive LSP retransmissions.

Another scenario in which flooding needs to be controlled to assist scalability is when running Integrated IS-IS over NBMA networks. IS-IS does not support the point-to-multipoint network type, and, therefore, it is recommended to use point-to-point subinterfaces for NBMA media. For highly meshed NBMA environments, mesh groups can be used to control the flooding over the point-to-point links. Mesh groups selectively block flooding on a per-subinterface basis. Flooding must be facilitated over the best- and most-robust paths only. The mesh-group feature must be used with care because misconfiguration coupled with link failures can result in partitioned flooding. See Chapter 8 for further discussions on IS-IS mesh-group applications. The operation of IS-IS mesh groups has been recently standardized in the IEFT and published in RFC 2973.

Stability

By using a hierarchical network design with multiple areas, you can control the amount of flooding in the network. Also, by implementing a structured IP addressing scheme and taking advantage of summarization, you can reduce the amount of IP information that the routers have to cope with. So, by using a combination of areas, sound IP addressing, and summarization, the network can be optimized to scale to a large number of nodes.

This combination of areas, well-planned IP addressing scheme, and summarization also contributes largely to the stability of the network. As discussed previously, by using summarization, instabilities can be hidden from the rest of the network. This contributes to the overall stability of the network and must be implemented where possible.

A stable network provides an excellent base for growth and needs to be considered with equal or greater importance than the introduction of new features. It is extremely difficult to introduce new features if the network is not stable; therefore, stability must be given priority attention.

Processing Resources

You might recall from Chapter 6, "The Shortest Path First Algorithm," that the amount of routing information carried in the network has direct bearing on the load placed on the route processors in routers during routing churns. Until recently, the computational toll of the SPF Algorithm posed a significant challenge to IP routers.

Fortunately, the architecture of modern routers provides a clean separation between the data forwarding plane and the control plane. Therefore, route processors in most modern routers are hardly involved in heavy-duty packet forwarding. In such routers, the route processor dedicates most of its processing recources to control plane activities, including route computation. Also, the faster CPUs used in current route processor designs alleviate most computational challenges.

The architecture of the IS-IS protocol also provides unique opportunities to place less stress on the route processor, specifically for IP routing applications. For example, IP prefixes are entered on the shortest path tree as leaves; therefore, any changes in IP-only information results in the less processing-intensive Partial Route Calculations (PRC) instead of the more processor-intensive full run of the SPF algorithm.

The IS-IS process responsible for SPF and PRC computations is the decision process. The update process is responsible for flooding LSPs. The extent of CPU utilization is certainly of much less concern these days because of the availability of fast and capable processors. On RSP4/RSP8-based and the 12000 Internet Router series, the IS-IS SPF process normally consumes less than one percent of the route processor's CPU resources. This provides network operators with greater confidence in running the IS-IS protocol as an IGP. Also, IS-IS can survive substantial instabilities in networks of the scale of hundreds of routers and thousands of routes, with CPU utilization spiking only temporarily to reasonable nonthreatening levels.

Improving Convergence

Convergence has always been an important topic for many network operators because it defines network availability in the face of disruptive instabilities. The time taken for an IGP to converge depends on a number of factors, including the size of the network, stability, and available bandwidth on the links in the network; the processing capacity of the routers; and so on. From a protocol perspective, Dijkstra's shortest path first algorithm is central to IS-IS-related routing convergence issues. Although the base SPF algorithm has essentially remained unchanged in most IS-IS implementations, there has been significant effort in the Cisco implementation to provide various enhancements toward speeding up convergence.

Recent developments led to the emergence of OC-192 interfaces, providing speeds in the 10 Gbps range. There have also been several enhancements to restoration and protection mechanisms at Layer 2, resulting in restoration of link failure within the sub 100-millisecond range. IOS enhancements to Integrated IS-IS include new capabilities, such as being designed to speed up Layer 3 convergence: Fast hellos, capability to disable hello padding, 1-second hello holdtimes, and so on. These features, together with several enhancements to the SPF Algorithm, help achieve better convergence times than before.

A basic definition of convergence is the time it takes for the network to reestablish connectivity between two points after a failure event occurs. This also implies that there is an alternative path between the two points, that traffic is rerouted to after the failure. This is a simple definition of convergence, and often it can be much more complex when applied to a large ISP environment.

The convergence time predominantly depends on the following:

- Link failure detection
- Change propagation
- Initial wait before SPF computation

- SPF computation time
- Routing table update
- Forwarding information base update

Link Failure Detection

Link failures can be detected in a number of ways. Each router keeps track of the state of its interfaces by looking at the physical state. For example, routers with connecting serial lines keep track of an electrical signal from the CSU/DSU. Optical interfaces track incoming light signals. Failures of these signals can be detected within milliseconds.

The detection and reception of an electrical or optical signal is not enough to judge the end-to-end integrity of a link. To ensure full connectivity over a link between end devices, some form of keepalive protocol is used within the framework of a Layer 2 protocol. HDLC and PPP are examples of Layer 2 protocols with keepalive mechanisms. These Layer 2 keepalives are similar to the Layer 3 hellos used in Integrated IS-IS and OSPF. Typical time-out before a failure is established occurs after loss of three keepalives. Keepalives are normally sent every 10 seconds by default, giving a 30-second interval of no keepalives before loss of connectivity is declared. When the use of Layer 2 keepalives does not sufficiently indicate the end-to-end state, other methods must be used; and it is often the routing protocol itself that is relied on to keep track of the state through the hello protocol. As discussed in previous chapters, Integrated IS-IS uses IIHs between routers, and each IIH carries a hold-time field. The holdtime indicates how long a router must wait for a neighbor's hello before tearing down the adjacency. The minimum holdtime that can be advertised in an IIH is 1 second. The default IIH holdtime in IOS is 30 seconds. When an interface or link goes down, Layer 2 keepalives are lost. In this situation, you do not always have to wait for the IS-IS holdtime to expire because the interface is immediately removed from the Layer 2 adjacency table, and the neighbor relationship is torn down. This Layer 2/Layer 3 interaction mechanism assists greatly in detecting link failure and reducing the overall convergence time.

As you can see, the holdtime is an important factor that must be taken into consideration and its value must be chosen with great care when designing or configuring a network to achieve fast convergence. Many ISPs have configured conservative holdtimes of approximately 60 seconds to maintain stability within their networks. By configuring such conservative holdtimes, the network might take longer to converge than necessary, and this is a tradeoff decision that must be made by the network administrator.

In recent IOS releases, you have the option to set the holdtime to a minimum value of 1 second. The following configuration shows how to do this:

```
interface pos0/0
    isis hello-interval minimal
```

With the hold time fixed at 1 second, the **hello-interval** depends on the value of the configured **hello-multiplier**. If you maintain the default **hello-multiplier** of 3, IIHs are then advertised every 333 milliseconds, which is extremely fast and can increase bandwidth, buffer, and CPU usage. When using the minimum holdtime value, it may be necessary to remove the additional padding from the hello packets. You can do so as follows:

```
router isis
   no hello-padding
```

The **no hello-padding** command removes padding from all IIHs on all interfaces that run IS-IS. By removing the hello padding and also setting the hello interval to the minimum, link failures can be quickly detected. Keep in mind, however, that this might cause instability within the network if unstable links exist. Therefore, a tradeoff must be made depending on the required outcome.

LSP Generation and Change Propagation

The preceding section discusses the methods of link failure detection and how you can lessen the time necessary to detect link failures. This section examines how new LSPs that reflect network changes are issued and propagated throughout the network. This action is often referred to as *LSP generation* and *flooding*.

When a change occurs, a router generates a new LSP to reflect the current state of its immediate environment. The following are examples of events that cause new LSPs to be generated:

- Adjacency flap interface or IP address change in redistributed IP routes
- Change in interarea IP routes.
- Assignment of a new interface metric

An IS-IS router also regenerates its LSP periodically at the expiration of the refresh interval or when the LSP is purged by another router because of packet corruption. Both of these situations are not directly related to any changes in the state of the network.

NOTE   In addition to adjacencies and directly connected IP prefixes, other types of routing information are also carried in LSPs. This additional information might include IP prefixes redistributed from other IGPs and interarea IP routes. Any changes in these types of information would also cause a new LSP to be issued to replace the existing LSP.

In the event of constant changes, it might be problematic if the router sends out a constant stream of new versions of the same LSP. To prevent such a situation, a default minimum interval of 5 seconds exists between regeneration of an LSP. Additional changes cannot be advertised in a new LSP until after the 5-second lapse.

The LSP generation itself does not normally take more than a few milliseconds. However, this also depends on the event for which the new LSP is being generated.

After the new LSP is generated, it is flooded to all other routers in the area. As discussed in previous chapters, IS-IS uses a reliable flooding mechanism on point-to-point links and a best effort mechanism supported by periodic synchronization on broadcast media (see Figure 7-13).

Figure 7-13 *Link failure and flooding.*

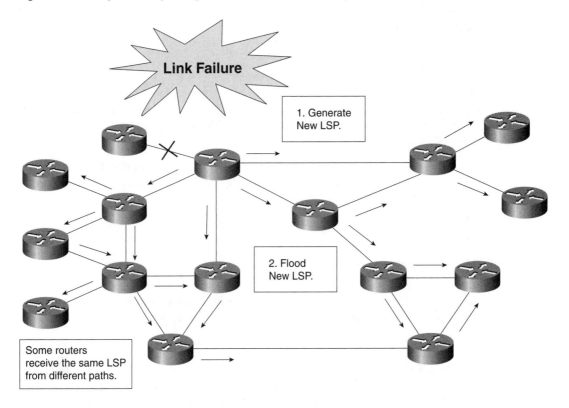

The speed of propagating an LSP throughout the network is an important consideration and depends on a number of factors. The first factor is the available network bandwidth, and the second is the diameter of the network. Each hop that the LSP must traverse can take approximately 15 to 20 milliseconds to process. If multiple LSPs are flooded throughout the network simultaneously, the delay at each hop can increase. On a point-to-point link, if a neighbor does not acknowledge receipt of an LSP, it is retransmitted every 5 seconds by default, until a corresponding acknowledgment is received. If LSPs are dropped, they are likely to be received through different paths. So, as you can see, further exploration is required to fully understand the effect of LSP propagation with respect to overall convergence.

Flooding is stalled during the SPF computation as all processing recources are dedicated to the SPF computation to speed up execution. This also prevents possible race conditions when the link-state database (LSDB) changes during the SPF computation.

Initial database synchronization is another factor that might influence overall convergence. If the **lsp-interval** is 33 milliseconds, for example, and the LSDB is holding 600 LSPs, it might take approximately 20 seconds to flood out the full LSDB. On LANs, a router that has just been brought up can synchronize its LSDB only after it receives CSNPs. On the average, this might take 10 seconds because by default, CSNPs are transmitted by the DIS every 10 seconds. On point-to-point links, the LSDBs are synchronized after adjacency establishment.

Recent IOS releases allow the **lsp-interval** to be reduced, which can speed up database synchronization and, therefore, help decrease the overall convergence time.

Initial Wait Before SPF Computation

Changes to the Link-State database trigger SPF and PRC computations. If a router receives a new LSP, it is probable that it will receive more LSPs in the following seconds. Specifically, any change in the topology can impact many routers.

Therefore, if a router runs SPF immediately when it detects a change, it probably might need to run a second SPF right after the first. Because of this, triggering an immediate SPF can cause slower convergence than instead of waiting a short time to capture multiple events before running SPF.

Cisco IOS Software has a delay mechanism to assist in such situations. An intentional delay of 5.5 seconds occurs between LSDB change detection and running the SPF computation. This value is chosen to be a little higher than the default LSP generation interval of 5 seconds to take DIS changes into consideration. Sometimes, changes in the DIS can cause routers to generate a new LSP twice, where the second LSP generation is deferred for 5 seconds.

OSPF Computation Time

The duration of the SPF computation over an area depends on many factors, including the following:

- Size of the area (number of nodes and links)
- Number of IP prefixes (Internal and External)
- CPU speed
- System capacity of route processor (memory bandwidth, etc.)

The SPF runtime also includes the inserting of best routes into the IP routing table. Note that packet forwarding continues during SPF computation, based on the current contents of the routing table.

Generally, when using a high-speed CPU in the 200 MHz range, SPF runtimes for an average-sized area about 400 nodes should take significantly less than 5 seconds. In Chapter 6, section "IS-IS SPF Operation on Cisco Routers," it was estimated that it would take approximately one second to compute the SPF tree for 1000 nodes by such a processor. If the SPF computation takes longer than 5 seconds, routers that have sent LSPs might start to retransmit them if the LSPs have not been acknowledged yet. Under such circumstances, a higher LSP retransmit value can be used as a workaround; however, a long SPF runtime implies there are underlying issues that need to be further investigated.

Similar to the initial delay between detecting the event and running the first SPF, an intentional delay is also enforced between consecutive SPF runs. This delay is set to a minimum of 10 seconds by default, and it is intended to prevent running excessive SPF computations in rapid succession. The command **spf-interval** can be used to modify the default minimum delay value. In any case, a smaller value than the default does not necessarily reduce the overall convergence time because there might be other factors in play within the specific environment.

Exponential Backoff

The IS-IS Exponential backoff feature was only recently introduced into Cisco IOS Software. The goal of this feature is to expedite convergence by providing fast, appropriate responses to network events, yet slow down responsiveness in the face of consistent churn to regain stability. The slowdown delays convergence but removes the potential for severe and prolonged disruption of network availability. The exponential backoff algorithm is essentially an intelligent throttling algorithm that controls LSP generation, SPF, and PRC computations in response to network events. The algorithm uses the following three parameters and two constants:

- Initial wait period
- Secondary wait period
- Maximum interval
- Increase factor (constant)
- Stable period factor (constant)

The algorithm works as follows. When the first occurrence of a particular network event triggers a response or action, the initial wait timer is started. The appropriate action is taken at the expiration of this timer. If, shortly after this first event, the same event reoccurs, the timer is fired again toward an appropriate response. However, for this event, the timer is set so that the interval between the previous action and the next is at least the secondary wait period. For any subsequent occurrence of the same event, the timer is reset so that the next action occurs after an interval of the secondary wait period times the increase factor. The increase factor is a fixed constant of value two, and it is used to double the wait interval between successive responses to the same network event after the third occurrence. So, the interval between responses to the second and third events is twice the secondary wait period, and the interval between the third and the fourth responses is at least four times the secondary wait period. The interval between response doubles again to at least eight times the secondary wait period after the next event and so on. The interval between two successive responses is allowed to increase only up to the maximum interval. From there on, it is fixed. The algorithm is initialized back to use of the initial wait period only after the same response is not triggered over an interval longer than the stable period factor times the maximum interval. The stable period factor is also a fixed constant of value 2. The increase factor and the stable period factor are currently not configurable.

Exponential Backoff Parameters

The **lsp-gen-interval** command controls how often a router is allowed to generate and flood out a new LSP. Note that except during LSP refresh, no new LSPs are sent out when the network is stable. While the comand **lsp-refresh-interval** (default – 15 minutes) controls periodic resfresh, the **lsp-gen-interval** command controls the frequency of issuing LSPs when triggered by network events. The default is to send out LSPs not more than once every 5 seconds. The command is configured as shown in the following example:

```
router isis
lsp-gen-interval <x> <y> <z>, where x = maximum interval,  y = initial wait
    period,  and z = secondary wait period.
```

The $<y>$ parameter is the number of milliseconds delay between the first trigger and the first LSP generation action. The $<z>$ parameter is the number of milliseconds waited between the first and the second LSP generation actions. From then on, the wait between the second and the third action is 2z, the wait between third and the fourth is 4z, and so on, doubling every time sequentially.

After the wait interval grows to x seconds, it remains fixed until there are no longer any triggers for at least twice the maximum interval (that is, 2x). Then, the wait after a trigger is reverted to the initial wait period.

The **spf-interval** command controls how often a full SPF computation is allowed. This parameter can be adjusted to prevent the router from performing SPF computations too frequently. The default is to run SPF no frequent than once every 10 seconds. The command is applied with the exponential backoff parameters as follows:

```
router isis
spf-interval <x> <y> <z>,  where x = maximum interval,  y =initial wait
    period,  and z = secondary wait period.
```

The parameter $<y>$ is the number of milliseconds wait between the first trigger and the first SPF. The parameter $<z>$ is the number of milliseconds wait between the first and the second SPF. From then on, the wait between successive SPF runs doubles relative to the previous period. After the interval between consecutive SPF runs grows to the maximum interval (x), this delay is retained for all subsequent runs. The wait interval reverts to the intial wait period only when the lapse between to two consecutive trigger is at least twice the maximum interval.

The **prc-interval** command controls how often you are allowed to run a PRC (partial route computation). This is essentially a cut-down version of the SPF computation invoked only when IP prefix information changes. The parameters described for SPF are similarly applied to PRC triggers. The following shows how to configure exponential backoff for PRC:

```
router isis
  prc-interval <x> <y> <z>
```

where x = maximum interval, y = initial wait period, and z = secondary wait period.

Exponential Backoff Example

Suppose you modify the SPF intervals and configure an initial wait of 1 second, a secondary wait of 5 seconds, and a maximum interval of 30 seconds. Suppose, further, that there is a constant stream of SPF triggers. The first SPF run takes place 1 second after the first trigger occurs. The second SPF then takes place 5 seconds later after the first SPF. The third SPF occurs 10 seconds later after the second. The fourth SPF occurs 20 seconds after the third. The fifth SPF takes place 30 seconds after the fourth because the maximum interval between two actions is set to 30 seconds. The sixth SPF happens 30 seconds later, and so on. If the stream of SPF triggers stops for 60 seconds after the last SPF, the initial wait period can be applied again as the interval between the next trigger to the subsequent run of SPF. Suppose that you adjust the LSP-generation interval and configure an initial wait of 10 milliseconds, a secondary wait of 2.5 seconds, and a maximum interval of 10 seconds. Under constant change, an LSP will be created 10 milliseconds after the first change. Thereafter, the intervals between consecutive LSP generations will be 2.5, 5, 10, 10, 10. . . seconds. After 20 seconds of no changes, this series can start over again.

As demonstrated, the exponential backoff algorithm provides a mechanism to aggressively achieve fast convergence while retaining the capability to be more conservative toward achieving stability when flux in the network is prolonged.

Although this feature has been available in Cisco IOS Software for a while now, it has not yet been widely used. Therefore, network operators should exercise caution when deploying it in production networks. Familiarity with the network and a clear sense of objectives and expectations are essential for successful deployment. It is difficult to specify any absolute recommendations for values of the parameters used in the backoff algorithm because effective values depend on the environment and desired results. When choosing parameter values, it might be useful to experiment in a test environment prior to production deployment.

Fast Convergence at Adjacency Setup

Packets sent to a router right after it has completed boot up might be lost. This is possible because IS-IS routers are allowed to be adjacent before their link-state databases are completely synchronized.

Consider Figure 7-14. In the event of RTB reloading, there could be a small window during which it might not have synchronized its database with all neighbors and doesn't know the complete topology. LSPs might flood between neighbors potentially attracting traffic to destinations not yet resolved. This means RTB may black-hole transit traffic that could have been routed by neighbors over alternate paths available.

Figure 7-14 *Fast convergence at adjacency setup.*

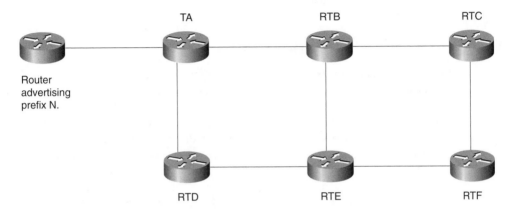

Assume that the shortest path from RTC to network *N* is through RTB and RTA. RTB reloads, and the network reconverges. The new pth from RTC to network *N* is through RTF -> RTE -> RTD -> RTA. However, the LSP originated from RTB does not expire immediately from the LSDBs on all routers (except RTB itself). After RTB has completed the reload and backup running, adjacencies with RTC, RTE, and RTA are re-established. Before databases are synchronized however, RTC runs SPF and uses the old version of RTB's LSP in view of the new valid adjacency and, therefore, rediscovers the old route to prefix *N*.

The LSP of a router is not immediately purged from the Link-State database by neighbors when its adjacency is invalidated, even though related routes are cleaned up from the routing table.

Having discovered the old route from the old LSP of RTB, RTC begins forwarding traffic to RTN through RTB, even though the latter is yet to fully discover the entire topology and compute routes. Traffic forwarded by RTC to RTB in these early stages might be dropped, and RTC would have been better off using the alternate path.

A recent enhancement to the IS-IS implementation in Cisco IOS Software allows a router to immediately flood its own LSP even before sending CSNP packets. This does not eliminate the black-holing problem. However, the overload bit can be set in the early LSP transmitted to notify other routers not to calculate transit paths through the reloaded router for a while. The router can be configured to advertise its LSP with the overload bit for a specific amount of time after reload, as follows:

```
set-overload-bit on-startup <sec>
```

By the end of the interval when the router is expected to be fully operational, a normal LSP with the overload bit cleared is then flooded into the network. A typical setting for the waiting period until the router is fully operational is 120 seconds.

Comparing Integrated IS-IS and OSPF

The increasing popularity of IS-IS has drawn significant attention to its relative merits in camparison with OSPF. The IP networking community has frequently expressed interest in an elaborate comparison between the two protocols, mostly from a practical standpoint. However, very frequently, the IS-IS versus OSPF debate ends up with an academic slant— if not religious. Of interest are the similarities and differences between these protocols, as well as any advantages and disadvantages of using one versus the other. The bottom line, however, is that two protocols are so similar, in terms of basic functionality and operation, such that it is really difficult, if not impossible to say, if one is generally better or more efficient than the other. There are many differences, both significant and trivial, that tend to slant advantages toward one over the other for specific applications or in deployment-specific environments.

This section compares Integrated IS-IS and OSPF, identifies major similarities and critical differences as objectively as possible, and tries to refrain from biased comments, such as those frequently witnessed in similar comparisons. The advantages and disadvantages of either protocol are mentioned where possible. The overall goal of this section is to present you with objective facts about each protocol without making any judgments. Network operators seeking to choose IS-IS or OSPF as an IGP should benefit from the following discussions, which should also help clarify any misconceptions or unfounded bias toward either protocol.

A Brief Historical Tour

A brief historical review of each protocol might be appropriate here to set the stage for the following discussions. Both Integrated IS-IS and OSPF were specified in the latter part of the 1980s. Around 1988, the United States National Science Foundation Network (NSFnet) deployed an interior gateway protocol based on an early IS-IS draft. Around the same time, development work on OSPF was started. OSPF actually evolved from this early version of IS-IS but with IP as its basic premise. OSPF core concepts, such as the flooding of link-state information, the shortest path first algorithm (SPF) for calculating best paths, use of designated router on broadcast links, and so on were all borrowed from this earlier version of IS-IS.

Version 1 of the OSPF protocol was published as RFC 1131 in October 1989. Near the same time (December 1990), Integrated IS-IS featuring extensions for IP routing was also published as RFC 1195. The IS-IS protocol was originally specifed in ISO 10589 for dynamic routing of CLNP datagrams in the ISO CLNS environment.

Cisco's implementation of Integrated IS-IS was first released in the 1991/1992 time frame. Significant enhancements to the Cisco IOS implementation of IS-IS were introduced in 1994 in conjunction with support for Netware Link Service Protocol (NLSP), which was designed for routing Novell's IPX Protocol. These enhancements improved resilience and robustness of the Cisco implementation and introduced new capabilites that attracted the interest of network architects in the Internet community looking at migrating their networks from the Routing Information Protocol (RIP) to a more robust IGP. Large scale deployment of the IS-IS protocol in major ISPs began in 1995. Another issue that potentionally played into this was the U.S. government interest in the ISO CLNS suite, which was reflected in a requirement for CLNP routing support in the NSFNet project by the National Science Foundation (NSF).

With its dual routing capabilities, IS-IS seemed to be the best choice of IGP to support integrated routing of both IP and CLNP. With a fast growing deployed base, the Cisco implementation quickly matured, becoming stable and robust for use in large networks. It is interesting to note that most of the largest ISP networks today run IS-IS for routing IP only. IS-IS still remains popular for ISO routing applications in telecommunication management networks.

Unlike IS-IS, which started life as an ISO protocol, OSPF was inherently designed to support only IP and was promoted in the IETF as the preferred IGP for IP networks—or at least it appeared so. Because IS-IS support was not available on many routers (noticeably Bay and 3Com routers), OSPF automatically became the routing glue for reasonably large networks with multivendor router platforms. An active Working Group in the IETF and evolving specifications also went a long way to help promote OSPF; and so OSPF became more popular and more widely adopted compared to IS-IS.

Interest in Integrated IS-IS for IP routing continued to grow, and most ISPs that sprung up in Europe elected to deploy the ISO standards based on IS-IS instead of OSPF, which is an IETF standard. Some U.S.-based ISPs even migrated from OSPF to Integrated IS-IS. In the later part of the 90s, many new ISPs adopted the business models, network architecture, and protocols of the established large providers and thus went with IS-IS for IGP, further increasing the deployed base. OSPF also continued to flourish and continued to be adopted by many ISPs.

In summary, both IS-IS and OSPF have prevailed through the test of time and have established themselves as the IGPs of choice for service provider netoworks. New extensions to both protocols, such as MPLS traffic engineering, have been developed over the past two years, and with active working groups for either protocol in the IETF, they continue to evolve, essentially in lock-step fashion. OSPF has been updated by many RFCs since RFC1131, including a major revision. Version 2 of the OSPF protocol was first published in July 1991 as RFC1247. The most current IEFT standard for version 2 of the OSPF protocol was published as RFC 2328 in April 1998. All the OSPF RFCs mentioned so far address IPv4. RFC 2740 standardizes OSPF for IPv6.

Most of the original work on the OSPF protocol was done and documented by John Moy, who was then at Proteon, Inc. Moy was chairman of IETF OSPF Working Group for many years. Obviously, the many dedicated participants in the OSPF working group meetings also contributed to the shaping of the protocol in diverse ways.

IS-IS was seemingly abandoned in the IETF after the release of RFC1195 in 1990. Also, there was no major standardization effort in the ITU for a while, so ISO 10589 and RFC1195 remain the authoritative complete standards for IS-IS version 1 and Integrated IS-IS, respectively. However, the IETF IS-IS working group has been re-opened over the last couple of years to standardize various new appliciations of IS-IS, such as MPLS Traffic Engineering, IPv6, and many others. Also, a second version of the IS-IS protocol is currently being worked on with plans to capture most of the enhancements over the years in a single place. It should be noted that the memberships of both relevant ITU and IETF working groups are contributing to this effort.

This section closes with an interesting observation that OSPF seems to be more documented than IS-IS, and a large collection of technical textbooks are readily available in bookstores. There is also a larger collection of OSPF design guides, white papers, and application notes at various vendor web sites, including Cisco Connection Online (cco.cisco.com or www.cisco.com). This obvious disparity in coverage between IS-IS and OSPF is intended to be addressed by this book.

Terminology

The next section continues the discussions by looking at specific commonalities and differences between IS-IS and OSPF. The most obvious place to continue is to consider the similarities. However, before that, take a quick look at terminologies associated with each protocol. As previously indicated, these protocols originated in different standard bodies, IS-IS in ISO (now the ITU) and OSPF in the IETF, and therefore, each is associated largely with different terminologies. Table 7-1 lists the terminology associated with each protocol and attempts to march them with equivalents in other protocol.

Table 7-1   *IS-IS Versus OSPF Terminology*

IS-IS	OSPF	Comments
End System	Host	
Intermediate System (IS)	Router	
Circuit	Link	
Subnetwork Point of Attachment (SNPA)	Datalink Address	
Protocol Data Unit (PDU)	Packet	
Designated Intermediate System	Designated Router (DR)	
Not Applicable	Backup Designated Router (BDR)	
Intermediate System to Intermediate System Hello PDU (IIH)	Hello packet	
Link-State Packet (LSP)	Link-State Advertisement (LSA)	IS-IS routing information is stored in TLVs, which are part of LSPs. LSAs are actually comparable to TLVs used in LSPs, however, each LSA has its own header, whereas TLVs share a common header.
Link-State Packet	Link-State Update	OSPF link-state update is a vehicle for flooding LSAs. LSPs are advertised individually.
Complete Sequence Number Packet (CSNP)	Database Description Packet (DBD)	
Partial Sequence Number Packet (PSNP)	Link-State Acknowledgment or Request Packet	
Routing Domain	Autonomous System	
Level 2 Subdomain	Backbone area	
Level 1 Area	Area (non-backbone)	

continues

Table 7-1   *IS-IS Versus OSPF Terminology (Continued)*

IS-IS	OSPF	Comments
Virtual Link	Virtual Link	Designed in OSPF for connecting a partitioned backbone or connecting an area that is not directly connected to the backbone over another area.
		In IS-IS, virtual links are used to connect a partitioned Level 1 area over Level 2.
Any Level 2 router	AS boundary Router (ASBR)	In OSPF, the ASBR redistributes external routes into the OSPF domain.
		Any Level 2 router can distribute externals into the domain. No special name.
		Note: Cisco IOS Software allows Level 1 routers to redistribute external routes into the IS-IS domain.
System ID	Router ID	The system ID is the key for SPF calculations. An IP address is symbolically carried in LSPs.
		A recent IETF enhancement of the IS-IS protocol introduces a Router ID TLV (Type 134) for MPLS traffic engineering applications.
Link-State Packet ID (LSPID)	Link-State ID	In IS-IS, the LSP ID is consistent and contains the system ID of the originator, the Pseudonode number, and the LSP fragment number.
		In OSPF, the contents of the LS ID field depends on the LS type.
No equivalent in IS-IS	Advertising Router	

Common Grounds

As previously mentioned, there is a lot of similarity between IS-IS and OSPF. The commonalities are strong from a functional perspective, even though there are also significant architectural differences between them, which will be covered in later sections. Some of the high-level similarities are the following:

- Both protocols are link-state protocols, requiring routers in an area to exchange routing or link-state information. The link-state information is gathered in a Link-State database and provides an abstraction of an area's topology.

- Both protocols use a similar mechanism, known as flooding, for exchanging routing information.

- Both protocols use the concept of designated router on broadcast links to control flooding and constrain resource requirements for many-to-many adjacencies over such media.

- Both protocols use practically the same algorithm, the shortest path first algorithm (Dijkstra's Algorithm) for computing best paths based on information in the Link-State database.

- Both protocols support a two-level routing hierarchy.

- Both protocols support classless routing of IP prefixes.

Highlights of Differences

There are several technical differences between the architectures of the IS-IS and the OSPF protocols and their historical background. This section is intended to highlight some of the major technical differences, as shown in Table 7-2.

Table 7-2   *Major Differences Between IS-IS and OSPF*

	IS-IS	OSPF
1	IS-IS is an integrated protocol that supports routing of both ISO CLNP and IP Packets.	Designed to route only IP packets.
2	IS-IS encoding requires transimission of IS-IS packets on the data link.	OSPF packets are encapsulated in IP packets and, therefore, are transmitted over the network layer.
3	IS-IS is designed as one of three network layer protocols that supports the ISO connectionless networking environment. Recognized at the data link as an ISO Family Protocol (data-link type FEFE on Ethernet), IS-IS has Network Layer protocol ID 0x83 within the ISO family.	OSPF is not a network layer protocol and runs over IP as protocol type 89.

continues

Table 7-2 *Major Differences Between IS-IS and OSPF (Continued)*

	IS-IS	OSPF
4	IS-IS routers advertise LSPs containing TLVs with routing information directly to adjacent neighbors.	OSPF uses different LSA types to carry different kinds of routing information. LSAs are packed in update packets for advertising to neighbors.
5	IS-IS packets use TLVs for carrying information allowing easy extensibility of all PDU.	In OSPF, only LSA are extensible.
6	An IS-IS router can skip a TLV type if the implementation does not support it.	All OSPF routers in a network must recognize all enabled extensions or LSA options for proper operation.
7	Multiple TLVs can be nested in an IS-IS Packet with a single header resulting in bandwith efficient transport.	All OSPF LSAs have their own header, such as sequence number, age, and ID of router that generated the information. Only type 1 and 2 LS allow multiple prefixes in each LSA. Because each type 3, 4, and 5 LSAs can hold only a single IP prefix, every destination outside an area will require its own LSA and independent header information.
8	IS-IS supports only broadcast and point-to-point links for all practical purposes and does not support NBMA links, which can be configured as point-to-point or as broadcast if fully meshed.	OSPF supports many link types, such as the following: Point-to-point Broadcast Nonbroadcast multiacess Point-to-multipoint Demand circuits
9	A 3-way adjacency formation is standardized for only broadcast links. Effort is underway in the IETF to standardize a 3-way process on point-to-point links.	OSPF adjacency formation involves a more elaborate multistage process.
10	Initial database synchronization occurs after adjacencies are formed.	Initial database synchronization precedes adjacency formation.
11	IS-IS routers are assocated with a single area. The whole router belongs to the area.	OSPF routers can be attached to multiple areas. Interfaces are assigned to areas.
12	Area boundaries intersect links.	Areas intersect on routers.
13	IS-IS areas are stubs by default. The recently published RFC 2966 standardizes leaking of interarea routes from Level 2 into Level 1.	By default, OSPF areas are not stubs but can be configured as such if necessary.

Table 7-2   *Major Differences Between IS-IS and OSPF (Continued)*

	IS-IS	OSPF
14	IS-IS supports only reliable flooding on point-to-point links. Flooding on broadcast links is not reliable; however, reliability is achieved by periodic synchronization with the help of the DIS.	OSPF ensures reliable flooding on all links.
15	DIS can be replaced pre-emptively. There is no backup DIS.	The designated router (DR) cannot be preempted. There is a backup DR.
16	Partial route calculation (Partial SPF) is more prevalent in an IS-IS area because IP prefixes are leaves in the SPF tree. In general, this implies less load on the route processor on the average and a plus for large areas.	Partial SPF is limited to interarea and external routes. Any interarea link flap will result in full SPF requiring smaller areas and hierarchical topologies to scale.
17	No native support for IP Multicast routing.	MOSPF extensions provide support for native IP Multicast routing.

IS-IS Versus OSPF—A Closer Look

Table 7-2 provides concise point-by-point highlights of the differences between Integrated IS-IS and OSPF. The following section discusses in detail these differences and their relative merits between the two protocols. Where necessary, achitectural details are provided to elaborate the discussions. The discussions are organized in the following topics:

- Encapsulation
- Packet Formats and Encoding Issues
- Neighbor Discovery and Adjacency Maintenance
- Distribution of Routing Information
- Route Characteristics and Metric Information
- Robustness and Reliability Issues
- Network Architecture
- Stability, Convergence, and Scalability
- Security
- Operations: Maintenance and Troubleshooting
- Conclusions: Which Protocol Is Better?

Encapsulation

Integrated IS-IS runs directly over the data link alongside IP as a network layer (Layer 3) protocol. ISIS packets are recognized at the data-link layer as belonging to the ISO network layer protocol family and on Ethernet by the protocol type 0xFEFE. The corresponding protocol type for IP is 0x0800. Even though IS-IS is a network layer protocol, it is essentially a routing application and does not provide complete datagram transmission services as in the case of IP, CLNP, or Novell's Internet Packet Exchange (IPX).

One benefit of running IS-IS over the data link is that it is shielded from IP packet spoofing and similar denial of service (DoS) attacks. The downside, however, is that IS-IS cannot be used over ATM virtual circuits (VC) with the type of encapsulation known as VC Multi-plexing (AAL5MUX). This is because this method of encapsulation supports only one Layer 3 protocol per VC. For most practical purposes, however, when IS-IS is used for IP routing, IS-IS packets must be sent over the same ATM VC. This, therefore, restricts use of IS-IS for IP routing in ATM environments to only alternate ATM encapsulation methods, such as LLC/SNAP (also referred to as AAL5SNAP) or AAL5NLPID encapsulation, where the ATM layer can distinguish between multiple Layer 3 protocols over the same VC. An IETF draft proposes a workaround to this issue in which both IS-IS and IP packets can be sent over an ATM VC with AAL5MUX encapsulation but the ATM layer is not relied on to demultiplex the IS-IS and IP streams. This workaround suggests routers should read into the first byte of the Layer 3 header to distinguish between IP and ISO family packets, such as IS-IS, CLNP, and ES-IS packets. Another issue associated with the Layer 2 encapsulation of IS-IS is that some operating systems that support IP networking have been implemented to differentiate Layer 3 packets in the kernel, requiring arduous kernel modifications to support IS-IS for IP routing in these operating systems.

OSPF runs over IP as protocol number 89. TCP and UDP are similarly encapsulated in IP, with protocol numbers 6 and 17, respectively. Encapsulating OSPF in IP means OSPF packets are transmitted with additional IP header information, thereby increasing packet overhead. This also subjects OSPF packets to IP packet spoofing and denial of service attacks. However, because OSPF is encapsulated in IP, there are no issues with using it for IP routing over ATM VCs with AAL5MUX encapsulation. Also, if an operating system already supports IP, no changes are necessary to support OSPF.

Packets Types and Encoding Issues

Table 7-3 lists IS-IS packet types and their corresponding analogies in the OSPF world. There is striking similarity—even each protocol uses a significantly different encoding schemes.

Table 7-3   *IS-IS and OSPF Packet Types*

IS-IS	OSPF	Comments
Hello packets	Hello packets	
Link-State packets (LSPs)	Link-State Update packets	IS-IS carries routing information in TLVs within LSP.
		OSPF uses LSAs that are transmitted in Link-State Update packets. LSAs also have headers.
Complete Sequence Number packets	Database Description packets	
Partial Sequence Number packets	Link-State Request packets	
	Link-State Acknowledgment packets	

Variable Length Fields

IS-IS uses variable length packets extensively to advertise information about the routing environment. TLVs are used in all IS-IS packets making each of the IS-IS packet types extensible. IS-IS routers are supposed to ignore unsupported TLVs. LSPs are flooded intact with unsupported TLV information. This provides flexibility for extending the entire protocol with new capabilities, such as MPLS Traffic Engineering, IPv6. TLVs can be nested as sub-TLVs, providing even more flexibility for current and potential future extensions. IS-IS does not require any particular alignment of packet fields.

OSPF uses fixed format packets with fields aligned in 32-bit boundaries. This efficient encoding makes it easier for routers to parse OSPF packets. The disadvantage to this, though, is that the packet formats are not extensible. OSPF uses various types of link-state advertisements (LSAs) for advertising routing information. LSAs are advertised to neighbors in link-state update packets. LSAs are however extensible. OSPF uses opaque LSAs for protocol extensions. For example, LSA types 9, 10, and 11 are used for advertising application-specific information, such as MPLS Traffic Engineering attributes. Unlike IS-IS, LSA types that are not recognized on receipt are not flooded to neighbors. This means that all OSPF routers must recognize extensions network-wide for that new capability to work. However, IS-IS allows routers to ignore unrecognized TLVs.

MTU Matching

Both OSPF and IS-IS require communicating routers to have matching maximum transmission unit (MTU) sizes in order to form adjacencies. This is needed so that routers will not advertise packets larger than a neighbor can receive and process. However, each protocol uses a different mechanism to check against MTU mismatch. IS-IS pads hellos to the MTU size while OSPF advertises the interface MTU in database description packets. Recent enhancements to the IS-IS protocol allow hello-padding to be disabled to save link bandwidth. The rational behind this is that most media have consistent default MTUs that are matched on all connected devices. Another reason is that network operators have control over the MTU setting and can ensure matching configurations on all connected interfaces during physical set up of the link.

Fragmentation

Because of the obvious toll of fragmentation and reassembly on routers, both IS-IS and OSPF employ various mechanisms to avoid hop-by-hop conventional fragmentation and reassembly of large packets. The method used by either protocol involves sending small self-contained independent LS packet fragments that are transmitted faster and more efficiently. For example, only a fragment that is lost needs to be retransmitted out of the set representing the original information. The difference in the approach to handling fragmentation between the two protocols is that an IS-IS router fragments a large LSP to the MTU or LSP buffersize at the source. The maximum size of an LSP is 1492 bytes. A set of TLVs are appended to a header that has an LSP ID that differs from that of the other fragments by the LSP fragment number. Also, all the LSP fragments have different sequence numbers and checksum numbers that make them independent units and are flooded independently. A list of TLVs are provided in Chapter 3, "Integrated IS-IS Routing Protocol Concepts," (Table 3-1 and Table 3-2). Chapter 5, "The IS-IS Link-State Database," features additional recently specified TLVs.

In contrast, OSPF controls fragmentation by using different types of self-contained LSAs for advertising different kinds of information. Five LSA types are defined by the base OSPF specification, and additional specifications (Opaque LSAs, and so on) are specified for extensions (see Table 7-4). This approach is equally effective, except that it has the potential of introducing overhead that would adversely impact available network resources, such as bandwidth and memory. Each LSA has its own header containing information such as source router ID, sequence number, checksum, and age. In addition, LSA types 3, 4, and 5 hold only a single prefix per LSA, the overhead can be substantial. Type 1, 2 LSAs can hold multiple prefixes per LSA, however, because there are no size limits for these LSA conventional hop-by-hop fragmentations, and reassembly will be used if they grow large. Table 7-4 lists currently defined OSPF LSA types.

The many different LSAs supported by OSPF have good design protocol intentions, such as limiting fragmentation and reducing bandwidth consumption by providing granular link-state information. This means that potential small-size packets and only the specific information would be advertised in response to any event. However, this undoubtedly introduces complexity into the management of link-state information. On the contrary, IS-IS LSPs are larger and fewer in a network of comparable size. This implies less complexity in managing the IS-IS LS database; however, a lot of redundant information is retransmitted with a regenerated LSP in response to network events wasting bandwidth.

Table 7-4   *OSPF LSA Types*

Type	Name	Description
1	Router	Originated by a router to describe its set of active interfaces and neighbors. It lists the IP prefixes associated with each of the attached links and the state and cost associated with each neighbor.
2	Network	Generated by the Designated Router on a broadcast link and lists all attached routers. It also describes the link type, broadcast, NBMA, and so on.
3	IP Network Summary	Generated by the area border routers (ABRs) in hierachical topologies. Used for reporting interarea routes within the same AS.
4	AS Border Router (ASBR) Summary	Generated by the ABR to provide information about known ASBRs, which import external routes into the AS.
5	AS External	Generated by ASBRs to describe known destinations outside of the AS.
6	Group Membership	Supports multicast extensions to OSPF (MOSPF). Not supported in Cisco IOS Software.
7	NSSA	Used to inject external routes from a stub area into the OSPF domain. Generated by the Not-So-Stubby Area (NSSA) ASBR. Converted into type 5 LSAs by the ABR when exporting to the rest of the OSPF domain.
8	External-attributes	Proposed for interaction with BGP.
9-11	Opaque	Used for extended capabilities such as MPLS Traffic Engineering.

Neighbor Discovery and Adjacency Maintenance

Neighbor discovery and adjacency maintenance are performed by means of periodic transmission and reception of hellos in both IS-IS and OSPF. In both cases, hello packets also serve as vehicles for detecting and negotiating common and extended capabilities.

Because IS-IS runs over the data link, IS-IS hellos are advertised to Layer 2 broadcast addresses (allL1ISs and allL2ISs). On multipoint links such as Ethernet, the corresponding broadcast addresses are 0180.C200.0014 and 0180.C200.0015. Because of their encapsulation in IP packets, OSPF hellos are advertised to Layer 3 multicast addresses AllSPFRouters (224.0.0.5) and AllDRouters (224.0.0.6).

Table 7-5, shows the default values of corresponding hello-related timers in IS-IS and OSPF. An interesting difference between IS-IS and OSPF regarding hello-related timers is that IS-IS does not require the hello interval and holdtime to match between adjacent neighbors. Rather, each hello packet contains a hold-time value that is used to reset the hold timer at the receiver. In contrast, OSPF requires all hello-related timer values (Hello interval, Dead timer) to match on all routers on the same subnet. The downside of this requirement for OSPF is that modifying the hello timers is intrusive, whereas in IS-IS this is not.

The following subsections highlight significant differences in adjacency formation processes between the two protocols.

Table 7-5   *Default Values of Hello-Related Timers*

Type of Interface	IS-IS	OSPF	Comments
Point-to-point	Hello – 10s	Hello – 10s	Wait timer specifies how long to wait if DR fails before starting DR election process.
	Holdtime – 30s	Dead – 40s	
		Wait – 40s	
Broadcast	Hello – 10s	Hello – 10s	
	Holdtime – 30s	Dead – 40s	
		Wait – 40s	
NBMA	N/A	Hello – 30s	
		Dead – 120s	
		Wait – 120s	

Link Types

IS-IS and OSPF support multiacess broadcast media, such as Ethernet or similar media, in the same way. The same goes for point-to-point links. OSPF additionally supports non-broadcast multiaccess (NBMA) media, such as ATM and Frame Relay. OSPF can also model NBMA media as point-to-multipoint. Table 7-6 shows a comparison of the link types supported by the two protocols. IS-IS does not provide direct support for NBMA media. When used in IS-IS networks, NBMA media must be configured as Broadcast media if all nodes are fully meshed. Alternatively, the individual PVCs can be configured as point-to-point links. If the NBMA cloud is highly meshed, IS-IS meshed groups can be used in conjunction with point-to-point configuration to control excessive flooding.

Table 7-6   *IS-IS and OSPF Network Link Types*

IS-IS	OSPF	Comments
Broadcast	Broadcast	
N/A	nonbroadcast multiaccess	NBMA links can be configured as broadcast media, or pvcs can be configured as point-to-point links in IS-IS environments.
Point-to-point	Point-to-point	
N/A	Point-to-multipoint	
N/A	Demand Circuits	

Forming Adjacencies

The essence of forming adjacencies with regards to link-state protocols is to build a stateful relationship that is leveraged by other protocol mechanisms to ensure consistency of relevant link-state information between communicating neighbor routers. The process of exchanging link-state information is also known as *database synchronization*. There are significant differences between IS-IS and OSPF in how routers form adjacencies. IS-IS adjacencies are formed after 2-way (point-to-point links) or 3-way (broadcast links) communication has been established through the exchange of hellos. A recently published IETF draft proposes a mechanism for 3-way handshake over point-to-point links. A 3-way adjacency handshake is available in Cisco IOS 12.0 S and other releases. IS-IS routers proceed to synchronize their LS databases after they have become adjacent. The potential for transient routing problems when adjacency formation precedes database synchronization can be resolved through the use of the IS-IS overload bit.

OSPF follows a complex multistage progressive process that requires routers to synchronize their databases before establishing adjacencies. This is intended to prevent transient routing problems that occur when adjacent routers not having complete forwarding intelligence attract transit traffic. One of the early stages in the OSPF adjacency process involves establishing 2-way communication between neighbors.

Designated Routers

The designated router concept is used by both IS-IS and IS-IS on broadcast media to limit the magnitude of LS state information exchanged between routers on such media. The DR concept helps reduces the number of adjacencies formed on broadcast media to order N instead of order NxN, where N is the number of nodes. Each protocol uses different mechanisms to realize this concept.

For example, IS-IS elects only one designated router (Designated IS) without a backup. The IS-IS DIS can be preempted at any time by a router with a higher priority. A new DIS must be elected when the current DIS is lost. Because the DIS advertises hellos faster (three times faster by default) than other nodes on the LAN, DIS failure detection is fast, so the potential for disruption is minimized. In the DIS election process, IS-IS uses the highest data-link address (MAC) as tie breaker when interface priorities are the same. The priority field available in LAN hello packets is 6 bits, so the range of interface priority for IS-IS routers is 0–127 with 64 as default on Cisco routers. Also on LANs, all IS-IS nodes become adjacent to each other by broadcasting hellos and going through the 3-way handshake. The many-to-many adjacencies through hello broadcast are straightforward because reliable database synchronization is not required to complete adjacency establishment. LSPs are also broadcast to everyone, and the DIS assists with database synchronization by periodically broadcasting CSNPs that contain summaries off all known LSPs.

In contrast, OSPF elects DR and a backup DR (BDR) to conduct flooding on a LAN. The DR cannot be preempted and the BDR takes over the DR; the first active router on the LAN segment usually assumes the DR role. The availability of a BDR makes replacement of the DR transparent in case of a failure. All other nodes on the LAN can be adjacent to only the DR and BDR. This is necessary because OSPF requires databases to be reliably synchronized before adjacencies are established. Forming adjacencies with only the DR and BDR is designed to reduce complexity of data exchange and mininize flooding.

In summary, IS-IS solves the NxN adjacency problem by choosing a simple process that uses periodic sychronization to achieve reliability and a deterministic DIS election process in which the DIS is preemptible. OSPF solves the same problem but uses a slightly more complex process that makes DR election nondeterministic but guarantees reliable flooding on broadcast media.

Distribution of Routing Information

IS-IS and OSPF are link-state routing protocols and, therefore, require routers to obtain accurate information about the network topology that is subsequently used to calculate the best paths to all known destinations in the network at each router. The topology information is also referred to as link-state information, and it is spread from router to router by a mechanism known as flooding.

IS-IS routers use link-state packets to organize a variety of link-state information. LSPs constitute the units of information stored in IS-IS LS database. An LSP is flooded from one node to the next intact. The maximum size of an LSP (LSP Maximum Transmission Unit) is specified as 1492 bytes and should be supported by all links in the IS-IS network. When there is any topology change, a router floods a new copy of its entire LSP with the updated information.

OSPF uses link-state advertisements (LSAs) for distributing routing information. LSAs are the smallest units of information stored in the OSPF LS database. LSAs are generally small fixed-size packets. Type 1 and Type 2 LSAs can have many prefixes per LSA. Other LSAs do not. LSAs are grouped and advertised in LS Update packets. Because LS updates are generated locally at any router, they do not carry a consistent set of LSAs. In contrast, IS-IS link-state packets are always flooded intact as originated at the source.

Flooding

Flooding is the method used by link-state protocols to distribute link-state information in a network. Sharing link-state information in this manner allows routers to have consistent views of the network's topology and, therefore, calculate loop free optimal paths to destinations in the network. Link-state protocols use various mechanisms to compare their databases to ensure consistency. The process of exchanging link-state information to ensure consistent views of the network across routers is known as *database synchronization*. To support synchronization, routers compare their databases by exchanging summary headers of all known LSPs or LSAs.

IS-IS performs reliable flooding on only point-to-point links where explicit acknowledgment of received LSPs is required. On LANs, IS-IS nodes broadcast their LSPs to all attached devices. The DIS then periodically multicasts a CSNP that contains a summary of every known LSP in the LS database to help synchronize databases between routers connected to the LAN.

OSPF performs reliable flooding on both point-to-point links and LANs and, therefore, requires acknowledgment of all LSAs flooded out. On LANs, ordinary routers pass on their LSAs to the DR and BDR. The DR then refloods the LSAs to all other nodes on the LAN and receives acknowledgment from them.

Because in OSPF every destination outside an area (interarea and external) is stored in individual LSAs (Type 3 and Type 5), summarizing the LS database might require a packets larger than the MTU of the outgoing interface. In such cases, OSPF uses IP fragmentation and reassembly. Each of the resulting fragments is assigned a sequence number and advertised sequentially after each fragment is acknowleged by the receiving end.

One advantage of IS-IS that has already been mentioned is that individual interarea and external routes do not need their own LSP headers, and multiple prefixes are packed into TLVs (types 128, 130, and 135), which share the same LSP header. In general, there are fewer LSPs in an IS-IS environment than there are in a comparable OSPF network. Therefore, a change in topology might trigger an update of many different OSPF LSAs, whereas a similar event in IS-IS might trigger fewer LSPs to be flooded.

IS-IS LSP and OSPF LSA Aging

Link-state routing protocols provide mechanisms to remove stale information from the Link-State database. Both IS-IS and OSPF provide aging timers in link-state packets for this purpose. The Remaining Lifetime field (LSP Holdtime on Cisco routers) in IS-IS is a down-counting timer that starts from 1200 seconds (default) and indicates how many more seconds before the LSP will expire. OSPF uses an up-counting counter that indicates the number of seconds since the LSA was originated. The maximum time an LSP/LSA can exist before it expires is known as maxage. For IS-IS, the default is 1200 seconds (20 minutes). For OSPF, the default is 60 minutes. IS-IS allows Maxage to be configurable up to a maximum of 18.7 hours. The OSPF Maxage is fixed at 1 hour.

To purge an LSP from the network before it expires, an IS-IS router sets the remaining lifetime field to 0 and then floods it. IS-IS allows any router to purge corrupted LSPs from the network. This could lead to LSP corruption storms, where one router purges an LSP and the originator reissues the LSP, and it is again corrupted by some intervening device. The router level command **ignore-lsp-errors** prevents a router from purging a corrupted LSP. OSPF allows routers to prematurely purge only unexpired LSAs that they originated. This prevents situations similar to LSP corruption storms that can occur in IS-IS environments.

To ensure continuity of operation, IS-IS and OSPF routers regenerate new copies of their LSPs to refresh existing copies periodically even before they expire. For IS-IS, this occurs every 15 minutes. OSPF routers refresh their LSAs every 30 minutes. OSPF LSAs with the DoNotAge bit set are not aged while stored in a router's Link-State database. Therefore, they do not need to be refreshed every 30 minutes. However, such LSAs will be eventually purged from the LS database if they become stale after being held for at least 60 minutes and the originator not reachable for the same period.

The periodic interval at which LSPs/LSAs are regenerated is known as the Refresh Interval. Table 7-6 lists related timers for IS-IS and OSPF and their default values.

Table 7-7   *IS-IS and OSPF Maxage and Refresh Timers*

Timer	IS-IS	OSPF	Comments
Maxage	20 minutes (default)	60 minutes	Configurable 16-bit field in IS-IS allows up to 18.7 hours.
			The OSPF value is fixed.
Refresh Interval	15 minutes (default)	30 minutes	Configurable up to 18.7 hours for IS-IS.

Route Characteristics and Metric Information

Various types of routes are recognized by both IS-IS and OSPF. In IS-IS, there are Internal routes (TLV type 128 and 135) and External routes (TLV type 130). Internal routes are further categorized into intra-area (Level 1) and interarea (Level 2). By specification, external routes can be introduced into the IS-IS domain only through Level 1-2 routers by redistributing from an external routing source. Cisco IOS Software, however, provides a software knob that allows redistribution of external routes by Level 1-only routers. This is allowed for operation convenience.

Similarly, OSPF supports intra-area routes (Type 1 and Type 2 LSAs) and interarea routes (Type 3 LSAs and external routes (Type 5 LSAs). External routes are not advertised into OSPF stub areas. Not-So-Stubby Areas (NSSA) allow limited introduction of external routes into the rest of the OSPF domain by means of Type 7 LSAs, which are converted to Type 5 by the NSSA. IS-IS routes carry metric information. Out of the four types of metrics specified, only the default type is supported in Cisco IOS Software. IS-IS metrics have an inverse bandwidth intepretation, with smaller values associated with bigger bandwidth. The 7 bits used for narrow metrics allow only values between 0 and 63 per interface and up to 1023 per path. Wide metrics allow larger and flexible metric values, 32 bits in TLV type 135 for extended IP reachability information and 24 bits in TLV type 22 for extended IS reachability information. Cisco IOS Software does not automatically assign metrics on interfaces based on the bandwidth. A default value of 10 is assigned on all interfaces, even though different values can be manually assigned. IS-IS metrics can be tagged as Internal or External based on the setting of the I/E bit. When the I/E bit is set (External), 64 is added to the advertised value of the metric. (Some Cisco IOS releases add 128 instead.)

OSPF also uses a metric (cost) that is inversely proportional to bandwidth. The cost on an interface is automatically assigned based on a default reference bandwidth of 100Mb/s. The cost is calcuated as (Reference Bandwidth)/(Interface Bandwidth). A cost of 1 is assigned if the calculated value is more than 1. The reference bandwidth is configurable. Also, interface cost can be manually assigned. OSPF allows assignment of large costs because of the wide metric fields in LSAs. The metric field is 16 bits in Type 1 LSAs and 24 bits in Types 3, 4, 5, and 7 LSAs. OSPF also recognizes two types of metrics for external routes: Type 1 (E1) and Type 2 (E2). Type 1 considers the cost to the ASBR in addition to the advertised cost of the route. Type 2 uses only the advertised cost.

Robustness and Reliability Issues

Robustness and reliability are introduced in IS-IS and OSPF in various forms. For example, either protocol uses age timers in LSPs/LSAs so that they can be periodically refreshed to ensure their integrity. The age timers also allow stale link-state information to eventually expire so that they can be purged from the network. Flooding loops are prevented by decrementing the Remaining Lifetime in IS-IS LSP at each flooding hop. OSPF also enforces similar robustness by increasing the LS age field. The use of checksums also helps ensure the entegrity of LSPs and LSAs.

IS-IS enforces reliable flooding on point-to-point links requiring every LSP flooded to be acknowledged. LSPs flooded on broadcast media are not acknowledged, but the DIS, which simplifies flooding on an IS-IS LAN, periodically broadcasts CSNPs with summaries of known LSPs to ensure consistency of link-state information across routers. Reliable flooding is achieved through simple periodic updates. Routers that are missing LSPs or have stale information after comparing their databases with contents of the CNSPs can request complete copies with PSNPs.

OSPF requires flooded LSP to be acknowledged on all links. Also, OSPF has a DR and a BDR to ensure the undisruptive operation of the LAN in case the DR fails.

Network Architecture

This section discusses contraints imposed by IS-IS and OSPF on network topologies and explains any differences between the two protocols in this regard.

Hierarchy

Hierarchy is required primarily for the network to contain the perils of growth and expansion while scaling to larger number of nodes. Hierarchy allows the network to be divided into smaller sections. Each section can then operate independently at one level and yet be linked together at a higher level. This type of organization of the network allows routing information to be manageable at the lower level. It also helps by constraining regional problems, thereby hiding instabilities from the rest of the network. Both IS-IS and OSPF support two levels of hierarchy.

IS-IS uses a logical hierarchy based on routing levels, referred to as Level 1 and Level 2. Level 1 routing occurs within a physical area. Level 2 routing occurs between the border routers from the respective areas in the IS-IS domain. All IS-IS routers must belong to a single physical area as defined by the area ID in the NSAP address. The border routers, which are also known as Level 1-2 routers, glue the areas together by exhanging routing information from their respective areas. The collection of Level 1-2 routers is also known as the IS-IS backbone. The IS-IS backbone consists of interconnected Level 2 capable routers, some of which may be Level 1-2 routers. The IS-IS backbone must be contiguous. For IS-IS, this also means that the Level 2 routers must be interconnected through other Level 2 routers. Because IS-IS is designed around a node-based addressing scheme and each router must belong to a single area even though it may be a Level 1-2 router, IS-IS areas, therefore, form boundaries on links as shown in Figure 7-15.

Figure 7-15   *Area topology in Integrated IS-IS.*

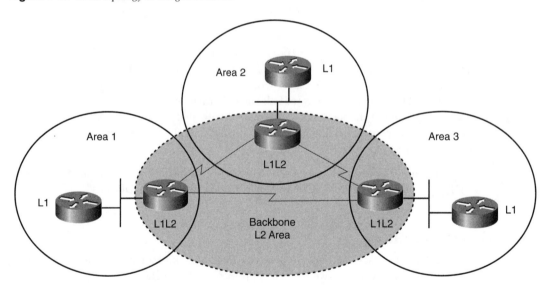

OSPF also supports a two-level hierarchy—regular areas and a backbone area that is designated as area 0 in the Cisco implementation. Because OSPF is designed around links and the link-based IP addressing scheme, area assignment is by links and, therefore, router interfaces. This means that OSPF areas form boundaries on the routers themselves and not the links as in IS-IS. Figure 7-16 shows how OSPF areas are carved out. The backbone glues ordinary areas together. OSPF routers that interconnect more than one area are referred to as area border routers (ABRs). In the Cisco implementation, one of these areas must be area 0 for exchange of interarea information. OSPF also requires the backbone to be contiguous and that all areas connect to the backbone through an ABR. OSPF allows use of virtual links to connect remote areas to the backbone through other areas if direct physical connectivity is not possible. OSPF also allows a virtual link to connect physically separate area 0s to maintain contiguity of the backbone. In contrast, IS-IS virtual links are specified for connecting partitions of a Level 1 area over the Level 2 backbone. Cisco implementation of IS-IS does not support virtual links.

Figure 7-16 *Area topology in OSPF.*

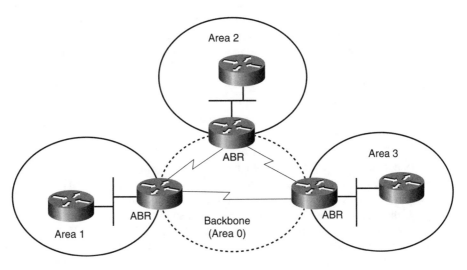

IS-IS and OSPF Areas

OSPF areas can be one of several types, such as ordinary, stub, totally stubby, not-so-stubby, and totally-not-so-stubby. However, IS-IS areas were originally designed to be stubs with the Level 1 areas relying on a default to forward traffic out of the area. According to the original specification, ISO 10589, IS-IS areas are similar to OSPF totally stubby areas (no interarea routes, no externals). However, Cisco IOS Software allows redistribution of external routes into Level 1, making IS-IS areas behave like OSPF totally-not-so-stubby areas (externals allowed, no interarea routes). Recent enhancements published in RFC 2966 and supported in Cisco IOS additionally allow interarea routes to be advertised into IS-IS Level 1, making IS-IS areas look more like ordinary OSPF areas, whereby both externals and interarea routes are broadly allowed.

An interesting difference between IS-IS and OSPF is that IS-IS requires routers on the same segment with mismatched area IDs to form only Level 2 adjacencies, making them Level 1-2 routers connected to the backbone while still identified with their respective areas. Two IS-IS routers in the same area can also form both Level 2 adjacencies, even though they are not required to as in the previous case. If such routers are directly connected, the interconnecting link will be in both the Level 1 area as well as the Level 2 backbone. In contrast, an OSPF link can be associated with only one area, and routers on the same link segment must agree on a common area ID to be adjacent.

This section discussed basic IS-IS functionality and did not consider the IS-IS multiarea feature supported in IOS. IS-IS multiarea functionality enables IS-IS routers to assign interfaces to mutiple Level 1 areas and the backbone, making them behave in the same way as OSPF routers. IS-IS multi-area support is currently not standardized and was designed for ISO CLNS environments to optimize routers usage in such environments. This feature requires running multiple IS-IS processes on the Cisco routers and defining a unique area ID for each process. One of the processes must be Level 1-2 to interconnect the Level 1 areas. The processes can then be applied to interfaces as necessary.

Area ID and Router ID

IS-IS defines the area ID as part of a router's NSAP, which is also known as the Network Entity Title (NET). Integrated IS-IS distinguishes three components in an NSAP: area ID, system ID, and N-Selector (see Chapter 4, for further details). The system ID component plays the role of a unique router ID. LSPs are also differentiated by the system ID component in the LSPID. This is true for both IP and ISO routing. RFC 1195 defines TLV Type 132 for specifying an associated IP interface address when IS-IS is used for IP routing, but this is only for informational purposes and has only operational significance in maintenance and troubleshooting situations. If available, the highest loopback address is entered into the IP Interface Address TLV. An IP Router ID TLV (Type 134) has been specified for MPLS TE applications of IS-IS. Only the area ID and the system ID are relevant for basic routing functionality and both are defined in the NSAP.

OSPF version 2 for IPv4 routing explicitly defines two separate 32-bit numbers for area ID and router ID. In Cisco IOS Software, the area ID is configured as part of network statements. The router ID is usually the highest loopback address or the highest IP address on any interface on the router.

Stability, Convergence, and Scalability

In general, IS-IS and OSPF have comparable stability and convergence characteristics. Apart from the architectural differences discussed in the preceding sections, the two protocols are functionally the same and have few advantages over each other when configured and used properly. Often, stability and fast convergence are opposing virtues. Hello packets are used to detect adjacency failures in situations where the failure is not detected at the lower layers. Because the actual time required for protocol mechanisms to select an alternate path and route-around failures is generally small, the time taken to detect failures becomes critical for fast might result in network instabilities, impacting network resources, such as bandwith, processing capacity, and memory. Adjustable timers, such as the hello-interval, IS-IS holdtime, and OSPF Dead interval, provides trade-offs between stability, fast convergence, and conservation of network resources. In summary, important factors that affect network stability and convergence are the speed at which failures are detected and propagated throughout the network, the size of the network, and the processing capabilities of the routers.

Route Calculation

Both IS-IS and OSPF use the same SPF algorithm for route computation, so they should have comparable convergence times, everything being equal. However, because IS-IS propagates IP routes within an architectural framework designed for the ISO node-based addressing scheme, IP prefixes end up as leaf nodes in the SPF tree. This provides greater opportunities for IS-IS to perform only the less CPU-intensive partial route calculation when network events do not affect the basic topology but only IP prefixes. OSPF is built around links, and any IP prefix change in an area will trigger a full SPF. With OSPF, only changes in interarea and external routes result in partial SPF calculations. Consequently, IS-IS PRC is more pervasive than OSPFs partial SPF runs. This difference allows IS-IS to be more tolerant of larger single area domains whereas OSPF forces hierarchical designs for relatively smaller networks. This seeming advantage allowed ISP network operators to deploy large single IS-IS domains to overcome problems with suboptimal routing with hierarchical designs. Of course, use of areas and hierarchy in networks is good design practice that prepares the network for future growth and helps prevent problems associated with large flat topologies. While areas and hierarchy are good for scalabilty, on the downside, they also add complexity.

Managing Stability and Convergence

Even though not widely deployed, Cisco offers IS-IS exponential back-off mechanisms in recent IOS releases; see the section on "Improving Convergence" earlier in this chapter. These mechanisms allow aggressive timer values to be configured for LSP generation; the SPF and PRC processes in order to achieve responsive reaction to network changes but backs off to less aggressive parameters when the churn persists. Currently, OSPF allows only pacing of flooding and SPF calculations to maintain stability of the network. In the future, IOS will support exponential back-off algorithms for OSPF, as well as other intelligent event dampening capabilities for link flaps and LSA generation.

Cisco's implementations of IS-IS and OSPF are both sensitive to bandwidth consumption and use pacing mechanisms to enforce this bandwidth conservation. For example, IS-IS throttles updates on interfaces with low bandwidths in the T1 range to only a maximun of 50 percent of the bandwidth, and OSPF uses the LSA group pacing feature to ensure that routers do not periodically refresh their LSAs at the same time.

A current IOS implementation advantage of IS-IS over OSPF is the use of the overload bit to prevent undue loss of traffic during BGP convergence. OSPF doesn't support the concept of overload bit that enables a router to signal memory overload, real or fictitiously, in order to deflect potential transit packets before the router is ready to forward them. However, a feature that allows OSPF link-cost manipulation during BGP convergence should provide simlilar functionality, preventing unnecessary blackholing of traffic in certain transient situations. In this application, a router advertises Router LSAs with large cost values so that it is not preferred for transit traffic until it is ready.

Scaling in NBMA Environments

IS-IS can use mesh groups (RFC 2973) to control redundant LSP flooding in highly meshed NBMA environments when PVCs are configured as point-to-point links. OSPF doesn't have an exactly comparable feature but can use per interface LSA blocking to prevent LSA transmission over a link.

Size Limitations of IS-IS LSPs and OSPF LSAs

In IS-IS, an LSP ID contains an 8-bit fragment number field. Therefore, an IS-IS router can allow up to 256 fragments of its LSP. The maximum size of an LSP is 1492 bytes. Taking out header bytes of 27 bytes leaves 1465 bytes for TLVs. This means that an IS-IS router has theoretically up to 256*1465 of space to pack IP reachability TLVs. A couple of other TLVs will be stored in the first fragment. In Chapter 5, a theoretical estimate indicated that the maximum number of IP routes IS-IS can support is approximately 31,000 prefixes. Another issue is that IS-IS uses an 8-bit field for point-to-point circuit IDs limiting the number of point-to-point adjacencies to 256 for each router. Also, 8 bits are used for defining a pseudonode number in the LSPID, which means a router can be DIS for only 256 LANs. There is also a limit to the number of routers that can be advertised in pseudonode LSP by the DIS. Most of these limitations are being addressed by various IETF draft proposals. For example, the RFC draft "draft-ietf-isis-3way-01.txt" proposes a method for new TLV hello packets that increase the maximum number of point-to-point adjacencies.

OSPF has similar limits imposed by the maximum 64K bytes size of Router and Network LSAs. This figure allows approximately 5000 Links for Type 1 and Type 2 LSAs. Consider, for example, Type 1 LSAs. Using 24 bytes for fixed fields, 12 bytes results in a little more than 5400 Entries, as this figure is close to the 65535 maximum number of links that is supported by the 16-bit link field specified in the Router LSA. Note also that all other LSAs apart from Types 1 and 2 hold single prefixes. Because there is no limit to the number of such LSAs, a large number of interarea routes or externals will be demanding on the memory resources of a router. This a good reason why BGP routes held in the Internet route tables should not be distributed into any IGP. There are also practical limitations on how many routes a router can effectively support in an efficient manner.

How Large Can IS-IS and OSPF Areas Be?

How large an area a specific routing protocol can support has always been an intriguing question for many network architects and operators. This issue was discussed earlier in the chapter for IS-IS in the "IS-IS Scaling Issues" section. The size of an area is a function of many factors, including available network resources, such as memory, CPU speed of the routers, bandwidth, and so on, and stability of the links. The larger the area, the more resource required to support it. Also, unstable areas place undue processing burden on the routers. Continuous flooding of link-state information chews up network bandwidth, ultimately leading to network congestion, which makes the network unusable. It is speculated that some IS-IS domains have deployed approximately 1000 routers with any significant problems. This might seem to be true because most of the tier 1 ISPs that use IS-IS currently deploy on single area domains with more than 500 routers.

Approximately, 350 OSPF routers have also been reported in some networks. There are various vendor recommendation regarding maximum tested area sizes. Some vendors recommend 50 routers per area and a maximum of 3 areas per ABR. In reality, numbers are not absolutes. What matters most is network stability and available resources. IS-IS tends to support larger networks mainly because the IP prefixes are leaves in the SPF tree, meaning full SPF is not run in most cases where a link failure does not impact the core nodal topology. In OSPF, all IP link failures in an area trigger LSA updates, which, in turn, cause full SPF runs. Therefore, a large OSPF area would be more demanding on processing resources on the average than an IS-IS network of comparable size.

Security

Integrated IS-IS standards, ISO 10589 and RFC 1195, specifiy only plain-text passwords for authentication of IS-IS packets. Current releases of IOS support only simple passwords IOS. MD5 authentication for IS-IS packets has been proposed in the IETF for standardization and will soon be available in Cisco IOS Software. Because IS-IS packets are not encapsuated in IP packets but rather over the data link, they are harder to spoof and, therefore, less susceptible to common denial of service attacks. OSPF supports plain-text, as well as MD5 authentication. As discussed previously, OSPF packets are encapsulated over IP and are, therefore, subject to spoofing and other denial of service attacks. Use of MD5 authentication is, therefore, strongly advised for OSPF deployments.

Operations: Configuring, Maintenance, and Troubleshooting

Both the Integrated IS-IS and OSPF protocols have been widely deployed and have been in use for some time for most implementations to be matured and well hardened. However, for a long time, only Cisco seemed to have a usable implementation of IS-IS. Currently, there are IS-IS implementations from other router vendors that are interoperable with the Cisco implementation. Of the two protocols, OSPF has evolved the most since inception, under the auspices of IETF OSPF Working Group. It is, therefore, not by coincidence that OSPF is also the most complex of the two protocols from both protocol design and operations perpective. However, Integrated IS-IS hasn't seen much standardization since ISO10589 and RFC 1195 were published. Most of IS-IS implementation experience and feature evolution were developed by Cisco Systems. IS-IS was first implemented as an ISO only protocol at Cisco before later enhanced with IP capabilities. IS-IS's ties with ISO CLNP is obvious from its nonconventional configuration for IP routing, which requires ISO NSAP to be configured in place of IP network statements as found in RIP, OSPF, and EIGRP/IP.

OSPF has a MIB that consists of over 100 management variables. The OSPF MIB is available in Cisco IOS Software and presents itself as a convenient resource for OSPF configuration and general protocol maintenance. A significant number of the OSPF MIB variables are designed for monitoring puposes. IS-IS MIB is still an IETF draft, and it is currently not supported in IOS even though support is imminent.

Conclusion: Which Protocol Is Better?

IS-IS and OSPF have been established as practical IGPs for deployment in large scale IP networks. They are both effective and, for the most part, are functionally identical. The original design of IS-IS was optimized for large LANs (periodic synchronization, simple LAN flooding) and SPF computation performance (small metrics). OSPF was optimized for efficient bandwidth utilization and reliability. High-speed routing technology has significantly evolved since inception of these protocols, obsoleting most of these original design criteria; yet, both protocols have withstood the tests of time and have emerged as the only viable IGP options for large scale routing.

Both protocols have been widely deployed. OSPF is more widespread from medium to large networks. IS-IS is used in most Tier 1 ISP networks and in single area configurations proving itself as very scalable.

It is widely speculated that most of the large ISPs adopted IS-IS because at one time it had the most stable implementation coupled with a U.S. government mandate to support ISO CLNS alongside IP. Having had a lot of success with IS-IS, these large ISPs haven't seen any good reason to switch to OSPF.

OSPF has a larger number of vendor implementations but there are few matured and stable IS-IS implementations. IS-IS is more extensible, even though OSPF can also be extended by using opaque LSAs. OSPF is more of a full Internet standard, better documented and more widely understood. Most IP-based enterprise networks have deployed OSPF whereas IS-IS remains largely deployed in the service provider space. That OSPF is a full Internet standard might explain its complexity. With the exception of the arcane language used in current IS-IS standards and ties to ISO and NSAP addressing, IS-IS is a fairly simple protocol. IS-IS has recently attracted a lot of interest in the IEFT, and there is considerable ongoing effort for its advancement. Many vendors and large ISPs are backing IS-IS efforts in the IETF.

Both protocols continue to evolve and currently provide support for IPv6. IS-IS supports IPv6 through extensions to the original protocol whereas OSPF provides support by means of a new protocol, OSPF version 3. Both protocols continue to cross features and capabilities and seem to be advancing in lock-step. With route-leaking available in IS-IS, any architectural gap between IS-IS and OSPF has further been bridged.

It is completely unrealistic to say one protocol is better than the other. They are both the best in their class to do the job. Consider factors such as the following to help you select one over the other:

- Dual IP and CLNS support requirement
- Technical familiarity of the network engineering and operations staff
- Technical knowledge of vendor support staff
- Coherent standards and maturity
- Maturity of vendor implementation
- Multivendor interoperability requirements
- Need to build flat network or large areas

Summary

The beginning of this chapter examines the fundamentals of network design and discusses basic design principles, such as hierarchy, scalability, and convergence. Addressing, summarization, and redistribution are noted as critical factors in designing a scalable network. Then, the chapter discusses and evaluates various design principles from the standpoint of IS-IS. The use of Integrated IS-IS as an IGP is covered in detail. This discussion considers the limitations and strengths of the IS-IS protocol and interaction with BGP.

Scaling issues are presented and the issues of network stability and convergence are discussed in relation to IS-IS. The size of a network is isolated as a key contributor to network performance. The effect of the number of nodes and number of links are discussed. The chapter also points out that stability of the links also contributes to the overall stability of the network. Various design options are discussed for IS-IS applications, including hierarchical designs with multiple areas, and flat single-area designs are also covered. Hierarchy is discussed as a good approach for constraining network instabilities and for network growth and expansion. The chapter defines design trade-offs between network stability and fast convergence and indicates that, overall, a fast route processor is a key asset for achieving fast convergence.

A key theme of the chapter is that design objectives and expectations should always be clearly stated as a philosophy behind any build out. The later sections of the chapter review the exponential back-off feature, which can be used to mitigate a good compromise between the conflicting design goals of fast convergence and stability. Exponential backoff allows for quick reponse to network changes while retaining the capability to slow down actions to contain massive instabilities during persistent changes in the network.

A considerable amount of space in the chapter is dedicated to comparative analysis of IS-IS versus OSPF. The comparison takes off with a brief historical review of the origins of both protocols. Some time is spent on similarities between the two protocols, and highlights of the differences between them is presented in table format. The rest of the chapter discusses in-depth both architectural and implementation differences. A final conclusion is drawn that the two protocols are similar, for the most part, in functionality and have proven themselves in real-world deployments and either can do the job. Some guidelines are provided to assist network operators in making the difficult choice between the two.

CHAPTER 8

Network Design Scenarios

This chapter looks at deploying Integrated IS-IS in various networking environments from a design perspective. IP-only networks are examined, based on Internet service provider (ISP) deployments. The discussions focus on using Integrated IS-IS in point-to-point and multipoint design scenarios. Packet over SONET (PoS), a common high-speed-to-point transport technology is used as the premise for exploring IS-IS configuration over point-to-point links. The multipoint section looks at Frame Relay, Asynchronous Transfer Mode (ATM), and, in general, mesh transport environments, all of which are currently deployed on a large scale in real networks. The chapter then considers strategies for migrating from other protocols, both classful and classless, to Integrated IS-IS. Examples are provided to demonstrate how to carry out such migrations successfully. The coexistence of Integrated IS-IS with other Interior Gateway Protocols is discussed. In some cases, IS-IS must run alongside another IGP, usually on temporary during migration, yet sometimes, even permanently. Finally, this chapter covers how both IP and CLNP coexist in dual environments. Issues that might exist in dual deployments are highlighted.

Case Study: Migration of Areas

Although Integrated IS-IS requires each router to be in only one area, multiple NSAPs addresses (each with a different area ID) can be used simultaneously for the purpose of renumbering, splitting, or merging of areas. Using multiple NSAPs on an IS-IS router is also known as *multihoming*. In the default mode of operation, Cisco IOS allows up to three NSAP addresses, each with a different area ID but the same system ID. It should be stressed that configuring a router with more than one area address must be for only transitional situations. Multihoming is covered in detail in Chapter 4, "Addressing in Integrated IS-IS," in the "Configuring Multiple Nets for a Single IS-IS Process" section.

As you learned in the previous chapters, for IS-IS routers to form a Level 1 adjacency, they must have at least one area common address.

Figure 8-1 shows the migration of the four routers in area 49.0001 to area 49.0002.

Figure 8-1 *Area migration.*

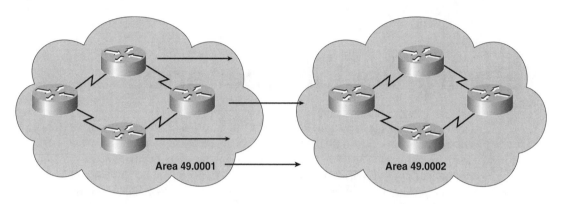

The following elaborates how each of the routers can be migrated. We start with a simplified sample configuration as follows:

```
router isis
  net 49.0001.0000.0000.0001.00
```

The first step is to apply the second NSAP address with the new area prefix 49.0002 to each of the routers as shown here. Each router has its own system ID, which does not change in the new address:

```
router isis
  net 49.0001.0000.0000.0001.00    net 49.0002.0000.0000.0001.00
```

During the migration, multiple adjacencies are not created. However, each router is aware that it has a number of NSAP addresses, placing it in multiple areas.

The final step is to remove the NSAP with the old area ID, 49.0001, from all the routers, leaving the NSAP with the new area ID as shown here:

```
router isis
  net 49.0002.0000.0000.0001.00
```

This completes the migration process. During the migration, no loss of adjacency occurs, and, therefore, there is no loss of connectivity or service disruption.

Case Study: Migration from Narrow to Wide Metrics

With the availability of IS-IS wide metrics support in IOS, operators of many existing networks have been considering migrating their configurations from narrow metrics to take advantage of the flexibility and convenience larger metric values provide. As discussed in the previous chapter, the easiest and least painful way to do this migration is by calling a flag day, shutting down the network, making appropriate changes, and turning the routers back up. However, stringent service level agreements (SLAs) in some environments prevent this approach. Fortunately, there are other options. There are actually two other approaches that are discussed in the following sections. Narrow metrics that allow metric values up to 63 are supported by TLVs that allocate only 6 bits for the metric field. These TLVs are commonly referred to as old style TLVs. Support for new wide metrics is provided by new style TLVs that allocate 24 or 32 bits for metric. See Chapter 5, "IS-IS Link-State Database," section "IS-IS Metric Extensions," for more details.

Method 1

The first method involves advertising the same information twice each time with a different metric format: once with old-style TLVs and once with new-style TLVs. This ensures that all routers understand the advertised information.

The advantages and disadvantages of using this method is covered in Chapter 6, "The Shortest Path First Algorithm." This section focuses on the actual transition steps that need to be followed when using this method:

Step 1   All routers are presumably running old software or new software in default mode so they advertise and use only the old-style TLVs.

Step 2   Make sure the routers are running software that supports new-style TLVs and configure them to advertise both old-style and new-style metrics. Routers that have not yet been upgraded continue advertising and processing only old-style TLVs. Reconfigured routers with new software will receive both types of TLVs and process both. The configuration is shown as follows:

```
router isis
    metric-style transition
```

Step 3   When all the routers have been upgraded as described in Step 2, configure them as follows to advertise and accept only new-style TLVs:

```
router isis
    metric-style wide
```

Step 4   Finally, metric values greater than 63 can now be configured because all the routers can now send and interpret routing received with new-style TLVs.

Method 2

In this method, routers advertise only one style of TLV at the same time but can understand both styles of TLV during the migration.

The benefit of this method is that LSPs remain approximately the same size during migration. Also, no ambiguity exists because the same information is not advertised twice inside a single LSP.

The disadvantage is that all routers must understand the new-style TLVs before any router can start advertising them. Therefore, this transition scheme is useful when transitioning the complete network (or area) to use wide metrics. This method also involves more steps.

This method requires the following transition steps:

Step 1   All routers are running older software or new software but in default mode, so they can advertise and use only old-style TLVs. Upgrade each router to new software that supports new-style TLVs and configure it to advertise old-style TLVs but also accept both TLV styles as follows:

```
router isis
    metric-style narrow transition
```

Step 2   Reconfigure each router in turn to advertise only new-style TLVs but also to accept both styles of TLVs:

```
router isis
    metric-style wide transition
```

Step 3   In this step, all the routers are configured for the last time to advertise and accept only new-style TLVs as follows:

```
router isis
        metric-style wide
```

The migration is over and metrics greater than 63 can be configured as desired.

NOTE

Summary of Cisco IOS Configuration Commands

The following subcommands are available under router isis:

- **metric-style narrow (default)**—Enables the router to advertise and accept only old-style TLVs

- **metric-style wide**—Enables the router to advertise and accept only new-style TLVs

- **metric-style transition**—Enables the router to advertise and accept both styles

- **metric-style narrow transition**—Enables the router to advertise old-style TLVs and accept both styles

- **metric-style wide transition**—Enables the router to advertise new-style TLVs and accept both styles

---

The following is a summary, of the steps used in two metric transition schemes:

Method 1: Narrow, to transition, to wide
Method 2: Narrow, to narrow transition, to wide transition, to wide

Using IS-IS in ISP Networks

As discussed in the previous chapters, Integrated IS-IS has only two types of network models: point-to-point and broadcast. IS-IS does not support the point-to-multipoint model as in OSPF. You can, however, design and configure IS-IS routers with a workaround to support NBMA transport if necessary.

This section reviews the different connection models: point-to-point and multipoint. It also examines typical problem scenarios with running IS-IS over NBMA networks and looks at how you can overcome these issues. The last part of this section discusses scaling in NBMA environments, examines typical problems, and provides various ways to solve them.

Point-to-Point Connections: PoS

The simplest network model is point-to-point connectivity. Running IS-IS over point-to-point links, such as PoS, is straightforward.

PoS is most commonly used in ISP backbones as a high-speed interconnect. There are various types of PoS interfaces, currently reaching speeds of 10 gigabits per second (OC192/STM-16) and deployed in high-speed routers.

Only a single type of hello packet is used when running Integrated IS-IS over point-to-point links, regardless of whether the adjacency is Level 1, Level 2, or Level 1 and Level 2. This differs significantly from running Integrated IS-IS over LANs, where separate hello packets are sent for Level 1 and Level 2. A number of special purpose commands can be applied to point-to-point links, such as commands for adjusting the retransmission interval. In general, configuring point-to-point links for IS-IS is trivial and thoroughly covered in Chapter 9, "Configuring IS-IS for IP Routing on Cisco Routers."

Multipoint environments pose interesting challenges when enabled for IS-IS routing. Some of the issues are discussed in the following section.

Multipoint Connections: Frame Relay, ATM, and IS-IS Mesh Solutions

IS-IS does not directly support NBMA transport and certainly does make provisions for point-to-multipoint network model. This raises an intriguing question: How do you model nonbroadcast multiaccess (NBMA) networks, such as Frame Relay and ATM? The answer is that you can use a broadcast or point-to-point model.

In order to model an NBMA network as a multipoint broadcast LAN, you need full connectivity between all nodes and, therefore, full mesh of permanent virtual circuits between all routers connected to the medium. This is not always possible because most NBMA environments are designed as a hub and spoke architecture, or the NBMA cloud is simply not fully meshed for economic or feasibility reasons.

Even in a full mesh environment, if any of the virtual circuits is lost, you might have a situation in which flooding is broken and the Link-State database is no longer synchronized across all routers, leading to problems such as routing loops. The following sections discuss some possible problem scenarios that might be encountered when designing Integrated IS-IS for an NBMA environment.

Problem Scenarios with NBMA

As pointed out previously, when running IS-IS in a point-to-point environment over serial links, IS-IS generates and sends only a single hello packet, regardless of the type of adjacency, Level 1, Level 2 , or both. In a point-to-multipoint broadcast environment, such as a LAN, Integrated IS-IS generates and sends a different hello packet, Level 1 and Level 2 adjacencies. Cisco IOS considers a serial interface with Frame Relay encapsulation as a multipoint interface, and, therefore, LAN hellos are advertised over such interfaces. With this in mind, consider the scenario shown in Figure 8-2.

Figure 8-2 *Problems forming neighbors over Frame Relay.*

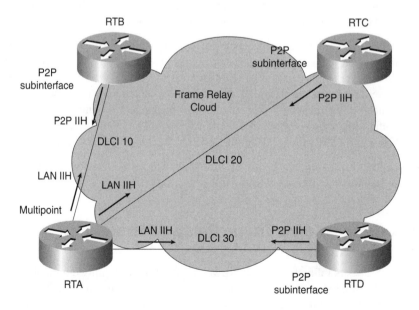

The Frame Relay cloud is shown as a mixed configuration of point-to-point and multipoint interfaces. This results in a connectivity problem. As you can see, RTA is configured as a multipoint broadcast interface and is, therefore, generating and sending LAN hellos. The other routers within the cloud (routers RTB, RTC, and RTD) have single point-to-point subinterface connection to RTA and, therefore, generate and send out point-to-point hello packets to RTA. Consequently, RTA never forms adjacencies with any of them.

The output of the **show clns neighbor** command from RTA shown in Example 8-1 confirms that the adjacencies with all the other routers are in "init" state, meaning the adjacency are stuck in "Initialization". They should be "Up" if completed.

Example 8-1   **show clns neighbor** *command Output on RTA*

```
RT1#show clns neighbors

System Id      Interface    SNPA       State    Holdtime   Type Protocol
RTB            Se0/0.1      DLCI 10    Init     L1L2       IS-IS
RTC            Se0/0.2      DLCI 20    Init     L1L2       IS-IS
RTD            Se0/0.3      DLCI 30    Init     L1L2       IS-IS
```

If all the routers within the Frame Relay cloud are not reconfigured to have the same interface type, point-to-point or multipoint, no adjacency will be completed. Therefore, LSPs are not exchanged over these interfaces. To fix this problem, RTA needs to be reconfigured as a point-to-point subinterface, with each PVC in a different IP subnet.

Figure 8-3 shows a second problem scenario that might occur when running Integrated IS-IS over an NBMA ATM cloud.

Figure 8-3   *Nonfully meshed NBMA cloud with Multipoint configuration.*

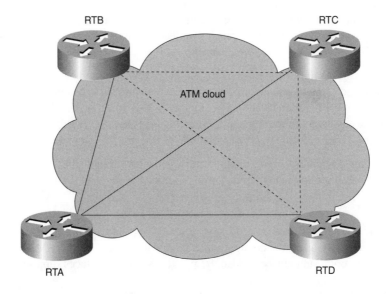

Figure 8-3 shows an ATM cloud in which all routers are fully meshed with virtual circuits and both the solid and dotted lines are active. The full mesh allows the cloud to be modeled as a broadcast link and configured as such to work with IS-IS. The problem with this model is that the full mesh ATM cloud does not have the complete broadcast capabilities of a multipoint broadcast technology, such as Ethernet. When any of the VCs fails (consider the dotted lines as failed circuits), the any-to-any connectivity is lost, breaking the flooding model. Individual VCs are not tracked in the IS-IS adjacency database for multipoint interfaces, so any failures are not dectected in the IS-IS environment.

Although modeling an NBMA cloud as a broadcast LAN is supported, it works only as long as all the VCs of the fully meshed topology are up. The operation of routing and forwarding might break when one or more virtual circuits go down.

The following section covers the preferred solution when running Integrated IS-IS over NBMA.

NBMA Solution: Point-to-Point Subinterfaces

The previous section considered problems associated with NBMA clouds when they are either modeled as broadcast multipoint links or when multipoint interfaces are connected to point-to-point interfaces. In both cases, the associated problems were obvious. Trying to simulate point-to-multipoint connectivity did not work, and modeling as broadcast required all VC to be up all the time or flooding stops working properly and the LS databases will be unsynchronized between routers. The third option is to model the VCs as point-to-point links by using point-to-point subinterfaces. The point-to-point model is more robust and provides a viable alternate. It allows tracking of the individual VCs, and each adjacency is monitored and considered in the LS database. A full mesh of PVCs is not required, making it economically feasible. As viable as this approach is, it presents scaling challenges in environments with highly meshed virtual circuits. These environments might experience redundant flooding problems, placing undue burden on network resources, such as band-width, memory, and processing capacity.

When using point-to-point subinterfaces in NBMA environments, IP addresses can be conserved using IP unnumbered interfaces which are tied to loopback addresses. If distinct addresses are required for the links, IP subnets with 30-bit masks (/30 subnets) can be used. This keeps the minimum number of required hosts to two per subnet. Also, recent releases of Cisco IOS Software support 31-bit masks that provide more address savings.

To address scaling issues resulting from redundant flooding in highly meshed environments, IS-IS mesh groups can be used. This is discussed in the next section.

NBMA Scaling

Most network operators configure their Frame Relay and ATM NBMA networks using point-to-point subinterfaces. Also, frequently, NBMA interfaces support a large number of

PVCs. A full mesh, although, provides convenient redundancy and might result in a potentially high number of LSPs being flooded out of the subinterfaces—across the mesh, resulting in scaling issues.

The higher the extent of the mesh, the larger the number of adjacencies. With a large number of adjacencies to support, a router's LSP might grow more than the maximum LSP size, requiring fragmentation. This can have adverse effects on the network because the number of LSPs is more of a concern than the actual size of the LSPs in such environments. In essence, larger number of LSPs requires more SPF computation time. In summary, a large NBMA full mesh can result in potential performance and scalability issues.

Excessive flooding in such environments can be limited by grouping subinterfaces into *mesh groups*. Mesh groups are designed for optimizing flooding over large NBMA clouds with many point-to-point connections.

The basic idea behind mesh groups is that each member of the mesh group does not reflood LSPs received from another member of the group to other members of the same group because they would have already received copies. However, LSPs received from nonmember routers are flooded to all members of the mesh group, as well as other adjacent nonmembers. Figures 8-4 and 8-5 show the flooding operation of members and nonmembers of a mesh group. Mesh-groups are enabled on Cisco routers as shown in Example 8-2.

Example 8-2 *Mesh-Group Configuration*

```
interface ATM2/0.1 point-to-point
ip address 182.168.200.9 255.255.255.252
ip router isis
isis mesh-group 10
```

All interfaces that belong to the same mesh group are identified with the same mesh group number. For example, the interface shown Example 8-2 is identified with mesh-group number 10. Also, the mesh group syntax allows you to selectively configure full blocking on individual interfaces instead of placing them in a group. Mesh groups need to be used with care. To ensure flooding is not disrupted, select the most reliable PVCs to flood over. Failure to do so might compromise flooding and result in unsynchronized databases when critical VC connections fail.

Figure 8-4 illustrates mesh group operation. As shown, an LSP received from another member is not forwarded to other members of the same group, but forwarded to nonmembers. Figure 8-5 shows that an LSP received from a nonmember of the mesh group is forwarded to both members and nonmembers.

Figure 8-4 *Mesh group example: member flooding.*

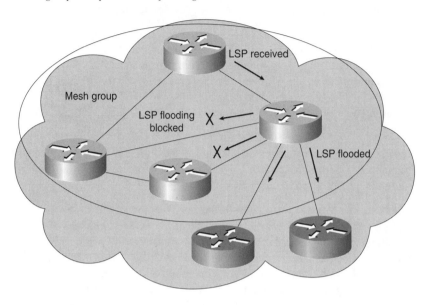

Figure 8-5 *Mesh group example: nonmember flooding.*

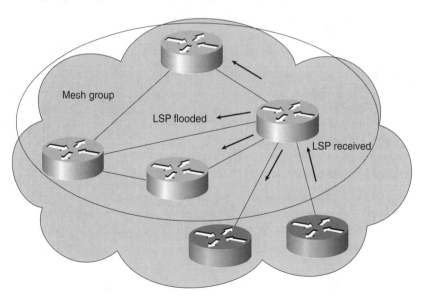

As mentioned previously, the alternative to grouping subinterfaces into a mesh group is to block flooding individually on each subinterface. If full LSP blocking on selected subinterfaces is enabled, no flooding occurs at all over those interfaces. Problems might arise if a large number of subinterfaces are put into blocking mode, and some of the few that are allowed to flood fail. The following configuration (Example 8-3) enables selective interface blocking on an individual subinterface.

Example 8-3 *Blocking LSP Flooding on Individual Interfaces*

```
int ATM2/0.1 point-to-point
ip address 192.168.200.9 255.255.255.252
ip router isis
isis mesh-group blocked
```

When using selective interface blocking, more robust flooding can be achieved by allowing advertisement of CSNPs on those subinterfaces that are otherwise blocked from flooding LSPs. This is configured as shown in Example 8-4.

Example 8-4 *LSP Blocking with CSNP Flooding*

```
int ATM2/0.1 point-to-point
ip address 192.168.200.9 255.255.255.252
ip router isis
isis mesh-group blocked
isis csnp-interval <secs>
```

Of the two methods—selective LSP blocking on individual interfaces and mesh-groups— the preferred approach is selective blocking. This method is preferred mainly because it is more straightforward and easier to configure and monitor. Also, it can be used to generally flood fewer LSPs. Use of mesh groups is a more sophisticated approach and requires more planning to be effective and efficient. Also, troubleshooting problems might be more complicated.

LSP Timers in NBMA Networks

To alleviate some of the load on network resources caused by flooding many LSPs, you can modify a number of LSP timers to restrict the forwarding of LSPs over point-to-point interfaces. The following are relevant commands.

The **isis lsp-interval** command controls the interval between successive LSP transmissions. The value is specified in milliseconds. By default and in line with the standard, Cisco IOS Software maintains a delay of at least 33 milliseconds between consecutive LSP transmissions. On low-speed lines, this might still be too fast and might consume too much of the limited bandwidth available. Recent IOS releases restrict bandwidth used for LSP transmission on links with T1 capacity and less to no more than 50 percent of the configured bandwidth.

The **isis retransmit-interval** command specifies the time between retransmissions of a single LSP on a point-to-point link and has a 5-second default. The command is not applicable to broadcast media. To reduce the number of retransmissions on a link, the configured value needs to be conservatively higher.

Retransmissions occur only when LSPs are dropped; so configuring a higher value will have minimal effect on convergence. In a network with many redundant paths, a higher value is easily justified because the possibility of a router not receiving an LSP in timely fashion is less. The **isis retransmit-throttle-interval** command specifies the minimum delay in milliseconds between retransmissions of LSPs on an interface. In a large network with many nodes, it might be useful to control the rate at which LSPs are resent out of an interface. By default, a 33-millisecond gap exists between consecutive LSPs conformance with an ISO 10589 specification of 30 LSP transmissions per second. All the three commands discussed in this section control LSP flooding and can be used together with mesh-groups in the group mode for maximum effect.

Migrating from Other IGPs to Integrated IS-IS

With the increasing popularity of Integrated IS-IS, a number of ISPs have migrated IGPs from other protocols, whereas others are still weighing the benefits. The main rational behind the migrations is to deploy a scalable and robust protocol that converges fast. Ease of troubleshooting and maintenance are also key factors. Yet, others might have a need to deploy a link-state protocol that supports advanced applications, such as MPLS traffic engineering.

This section discusses basic migration techniques that have been used with a lot of success. There might be several other approaches to IGP migration, and the network operator is advised to chose the most convenient method based on the circumstances.

The migration procedure differs depending on the type of the existing IGP. If the existing IGP is a classful distance-vector protocol, such as the Routing Information Protocol (RIP), or Interior Gateway Routing Protocol (IGRP), for example, the procedure requires different considerations than if migrating from a classless protocol, such as Open Shortest Path First (OSPF).

Migrating from a Classless IGP to Integrated IS-IS

This section covers techniques and strategies for migrating from classless IGPs, such as the Enhanced Interior Gateway Protocol and OSPF, to Integrated IS-IS, which is itself another classless protocol.

The next section elaborates on the methodology for migrating from EIGRP. The entire migration process is presented in detail, and relevant IOS show and debugging commands for verifying and troubleshooting any potential problems are also provided.

Scenario: Migrating from EIGRP to Integrated IS-IS

The scenario considered is migration from a flat EIGRP network to a single (Level 2) Integrated IS-IS network.

EIGRP is actually an intelligent distance-vector protocol. It is classless and supports variable-length subnet masks (VLSMs). EIGRP uses hellos just as IS-IS and OSPF to discover and maintain neighbors. It builds a topology table, based on routing updates exchanged between neighbors. The migration from EIGRP to Integrated IS-IS is not too complex, although a migration from a pure link-state protocol might be simpler because of similar characteristics, such as flooding not being directly tied to the set of routes entered into the routing. A number of methods can be used to achieve a successful migration. Two specific approaches are outlined in the following text. The first approach is the Redistribution method, and the second is the Background method.

- **Redistribution method**—This approach involves configuring Integrated IS-IS at the edge of the network in addition to EIGRP and then redistributing the protocols into each other, while gradually extending the process into the core. This method is complex because configuring mutual redistribution at multiple points in a network can create routing loops if appropriate filters are not carefully applied to stop route feedback. However, if planned and executed carefully, this approach allows graceful migration that does not significantly impact availability of the network.

- **Background method**—The second approach, and possibly the better, involves running both protocols in parallel and making use of administrative distances to make EIGRP routes preferred initially and reversing that later so that IS-IS routes are preferred. This can be achieved by setting the administrative distance of all IS-IS routes to 255 with the **distance** command under the IS-IS routing process. This ensures that Integrated IS-IS routes are never used in preference of EIGRP routes for similar routes with the same prefix length. IS-IS routes have an administrative distance of 115, and EIGRP uses 90 by default. Configuring explicit administrative distance for IS-IS might not be required initially because for similar internal routes, EIGRP routes will be preferred over IS-IS routes. However, care needs to be taken if there are EIGRP summary and external routes in the network. These routes have administrative distances of 5 and 170, respectively. Using explicit distances is, therefore, better and safer.

After IS-IS has been enabled on the whole network and adjacencies and LS databases verified, EIGRP routers can then be made less preferable by moving the administrative distance of 255 from the IS-IS process to the EIGRP process in each router. It is recommended to keep the EIGRP process in the background to expedite restoration to the old setup if there are any issues. The final step involves removing EIGRP from the network altogether.

Both the Distribution and the Background methods require running the two protocols together to some extent and, therefore, can place resource demands on the routers. If running both protocols at the same time is not suitable for the specific environment, an intrusive approach that requires tearing down EIGRP before enabling IS-IS can be employed. This would, however, require network downtime.

Table 8-1 lists *default* administrative distances in Cisco IOS Software for various routing protocols.

Table 8-1   *Default Administrative Distances*

Cisco IOS Routing Protocol	Default Administrative Distance
Connected interface	0
Static route	1
EIGRP summary route	5
eBGP	20
EIGRP (internal)	90
IGRP	100
OSPF	110
IS-IS	115
RIP	120
EGP	140
EIGRP (external)	170
iBGP	200

Software and Hardware Audit

Before enabling Integrated IS-IS to run in parallel with EIGRP, it is essential to understand the capabilites of each router, from both hardware and software standpoints, by carrying out a complete audit of the network.

With regard to hardware, this ensures that no major issues relating to CPU and memory requirements would arise in the middle of the migration. Also, it might be useful to make sure each router is running an IOS release that not only supports IS-IS but also all the capabilities and services required for normal operation of the network.

The network architects and operations staff involved in the migration should jointly plan the entire operation. Some guidance on the phases involved is provided later in this chapter. The migration activities need to also be prudently documented for post mortem evaluation of successful migration or any challenges encountered during the process. This might provide opportunities for enhancing certain aspects of the network.

Integrated IS-IS Configurations

Example 8-5 shows a typical Integrated IS-IS configuration that might be used for the migration. This configuration specifies each router as Level 2-only and includes an administrative distance of 255. This will configure the entire network to run a single flat Level 2 IS-IS area. IS-IS must be enabled on the appropriate interfaces of each router by applying the **ip router isis** command.

Both the **lsp-refresh-interval** and **max-lsp-lifetime** values are increased to their maximum to reduce periodic LSP flooding. Wide metrics are configured to allow greater interface and path metric values to be used. Wide metrics are required when configuring IS-IS to support MPLS traffic engineering.

Example 8-5 *IS-IS Process Configuration*

```
!
router isis
net 49.0001.1234.5678.9abc.00
passive-interface loopback0
lsp-refresh-interval 65000
max-lsp-lifetime 65535
is-type level-2-only
distance 255 ip
log-adjacency-changes
ignore-lsp-errors
metric-style wide level-2
!
```

Other Integrated IS-IS timers might be modified to support the specific network environment after the migration. Some of the timers of interest are listed here.

IS-IS routing-process level command:

- **spf-interval**
- **prc-interval**
- **lsp-gen-interval**

Interface level commands:

- **csnp-interval**
- **hello-interval**
- **hello-multiplier**
- **retransmit-interval**

Chapter 9 covers steps for enabling IS-IS and explains in detail the timer for the preceding commands.

Configuring Integrated IS-IS in Parallel with EIGRP

When enabling IS-IS to run in parallel with EIGRP, attention must be paid to LSP flooding and the frequency of SPF/PRC calculations because they might place heavy demands on network resources, such as memory, CPU, and bandwidth. The following needs to be verified when the two protocols are running simultaneously:

- IP addressing
- Summarization
- Default routing (if required)
- Appropriate interface metrics to direct traffic flow
- Consistent collection of LSP in the Link-State database across all routers
- IS-IS adjacencies formed
- Frequency of SPF and PRC calculations

After the preceding checks have been completed with satisfaction and it has been confirmed that there are no imminent problems, a maintenance period can be scheduled for the final cutover from EIGRP to IS-IS. It is always safe to have a minimal downtime for the cutover, even though it might not be required.

Downtime is a term used when the network is not available to users. This means that part of the network or its entirety will be unavailable. The actual time required might depend on the size and the complexity of the network and also the number and experience of support staff involved in the process. Migration of 500 nodes, for example, might call for several hours of downtime.

After completing all planned verifications, the distance can be reversed, by applying a value of 255 to EIGRP routes or lowering the distance of IS-IS routes so that they would be preferred over EIGRP routes. Usually, a **clear ip route *** command might be required to help flush out the old EIGRP routes and repopulate the IP routing table with the preferred IS-IS routes.

Migration Phases: Example EIGRP to IS-IS Migration

Figure 8-6 depicts a simple network running EIGRP as the IGP. IS-IS is configured to run alongside EIGRP and later to take preference over EIGRP.

Figure 8-6   *Simple EIGRP network to migrate to IS-IS.*

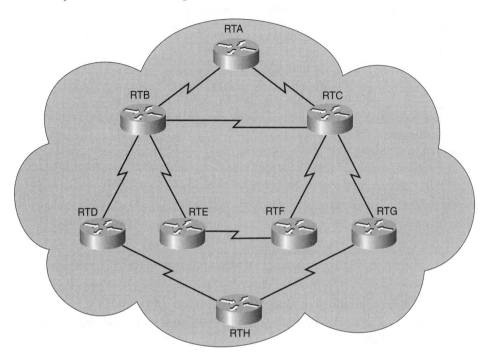

Migration Phases

This section identifies the different migration phases and discusses what occurs in each phase.

Phase 1: The network is running EIGRP in a flat network. Hardware and software audits performed and software and hardware upgraded are needed to support the migration.

Phase 2: Integrated IS-IS is configured to run in parallel and in the background with a higher administrative distance. This allows creation of the IS-IS Link-State database in all the routers but the routing and forwarding tables remain unaltered. This phase is probably the most critical because normal operation of IS-IS must be carefully verified. The good news here is that the operator can troubleshoot any Integrated IS-IS problems without disrupting network service; however, additional memory requirements and an increase in CPU utilization might pose some challenges. This phase can be considered complete only after the IS-IS database has been fully populated in each router with all expected LSPs and the potential for generating IS-IS routes that reflect the EIGRP routes in the current routing table has been confirmed.

Phase 3: Cut-over of the whole network to Integrated IS-IS as the primary IGP by transferring the high administrative distance command to the EIGRP process.

Phase 4: EIGRP is completely removed from the network after normal operation after forwarding under IS-IS is confirmed to be flawless.

Phase 1—Configurations and Other Status Information

Example 8-6 shows a typical EIGRP configuration that might be present on the routers prior to migration.

Example 8-6 *Typical EIGRP Configuration*

```
!
router eigrp 10
 network 192.168.10.0
 network 192.168.20.0
 no auto-summary
!
```

Phase 2—Configurations and Other Status Information

At this point, Integrated IS-IS needs to be configured in the background for every router, as shown in Example 8-7.

Example 8-7 *Enabling IS-IS in the Background*

```
!
hostname RTA
!
clns routing
!
interface Serial1/0:1
 ip address 192.168.20.5 255.255.255.252
 ip router isis
 isis metric 500 level-2
!
router eigrp 10
 network 192.168.10.0
 network 192.168.20.0
 no auto-summary
!
router isis
 passive-interface Loopback0
 distance 255 ip
 net 49.0001.1921.6810.0001.00
 is-type level-2-only
 metric-style wide level-2
```

Example 8-7 *Enabling IS-IS in the Background (Continued)*

```
max-lsp-lifetime 65535
lsp-refresh-interval 65000
log-adjacency-changes
!
```

Because an administrative distance of 255 is configured for Integrated IS-IS, EIGRP external routes with an administrative distance of 170 will not be preempted in the IP routing table. Various **show** commands can be used to monitor and verify normal operation of IS-IS. As mentioned previously, this stage is critical because IS-IS must be tuned and verified to be fully operational. The subsequent stages of the migration should be smooth if this phase goes well.

The following examples show essential information needed to verify the correct configuration and operation of Integrated IS-IS. The **show** commands in Example 8-8 capture the status and operating parameters for IS-IS. Important lines are highlighted.

Example 8-8 *Verifying IS-IS Configuration*

```
RTD#show clns
Global CLNS Information:
  3 Interfaces Enabled for CLNS
  NET: 49.0001.1921.6810.0001.00
  Configuration Timer: 60, Default Holding Timer: 300, Packet Lifetime 64
  ERPDUs requested on locally generated packets
  Intermediate system operation enabled (forwarding allowed)
  IS-IS level-2-only Router:
    Routing for Area: 49.0001

RTD#show clns protocol
IS-IS Router: <Null Tag>
  System Id: 1921.6810.0001.00  IS-Type: level-2-only
  Manual area address(es):
    49.0001
  Routing for area address(es):
    49.0001
  Interfaces supported by IS-IS:
    Serial1/0:1 - IP
    FastEthernet5/0 - IP
    FastEthernet2/0 - IP
  Redistributing:
    static
  Distance: 110  (Comment: This distance is for ISO routing)
  RRR level: none
  Generate narrow metrics: level-1
  Accept narrow metrics:   level-1
  Generate wide metrics:   level-2
  Accept wide metrics:     level-2
```

The command **show clns protocol** is particularly useful because it helps verify the the configuration by displaying a single output that shows the system ID, area address, IS type, IS-IS-enabled interfaces, and wide metric support.

Example 8-9   *Verifying Adjacencies Formed*

```
RTD#show clns neighbor

System Id      Interface  SNPA            State  Holdtime  Type Protocol
RTH             Se1/0:1    *HDLC*          Up     24        L2   IS-IS
RTB             Fa5/0      0003.fec9.cc54  Up     24        L2   IS-IS
```

Use the **show clns neighbor** command to verify that the right adjacencies have been formed. An adjacency matrix, showing which neighbors are expected in the adjacency table, must be prepared ahead to facilitate this verification. Example 8-10 shows how to obtain more information about each neighbor.

Example 8-10 *Obtaining More Information About Neighbors*

```
RTD#show clns neighbor detail

System Id      Interface  SNPA            State  Holdtime  Type   Protocol
RTH             SE1/0:1    *HDLC*          Up     25        L2     IS-IS
  Area Address(es): 49.0001
  IP Address(es):  192.168.20.38*
  Uptime: 00:37:01
RTB             Fa5/0      0003.fec9.cc54  Up     25        L2     IS-IS
  Area Address(es): 49.0001
  IP Address(es):  192.168.10.161*
  Uptime: 01:54:16
```

IS-IS needs to be monitored for stability after it is deployed across the network and prior to promoting it above EIGRP. Typical vital statistics to monitor include incrementing LSP sequence numbers, high numbers of SPF computations, checksum errors, and retransmissions. The output of the **show clns traffic** command provides statistics for IS-IS-related traffic. Excerpts of this command output are shown in Example 8-11. This information is also useful for troubleshooting potential problems. Some of the interesting lines in the output are highlighted.

Example 8-11 *Monitoring IS-IS Traffic Statistics*

```
RTD#show clns traffic
[snip]
IS-IS: Level-2 Hellos (sent/rcvd): 13465/2568
IS-IS: PTP Hellos    (sent/rcvd): 2035/489
IS-IS: Level-2 LSPs sourced (new/refresh): 57/3
IS-IS: Level-2 LSPs flooded (sent/rcvd): 146/399.
IS-IS: LSP Retransmissions: 1
```

Example 8-11 *Monitoring IS-IS Traffic Statistics (Continued)*

```
IS-IS: Level-2 CSNPs (sent/rcvd): 2356/5
IS-IS: Level-2 PSNPs (sent/rcvd): 123/14
IS-IS: Level-2 DR Elections: 15
IS-IS: Level-2 SPF Calculations: 67
IS-IS: Level-2 Partial Route Calculations: 38
IS-IS: LSP checksum errors received: 0
IS-IS: Update process queue depth: 0/200
IS-IS: Update process packets dropped: 0
```

The following text provides guidelines for interpreting the information in Example 8-11.

- LSPs sourced indicate stability of the IS.
- LSP retransmissions need to stay low.
- PRCs cannot be checked elsewhere. Partial route calculations are used when a change that does not affect the topology is reported through an LSP; typical examples are the addition or removal of an IP prefix or metric changes, changes related to externals routes or passive interfaces.
- LSP checksum errors indicate problems and possible packet corruption. This information reflects corrupted LSPs were received on this router. LSPs might be corrupted during transit or when stored in memory. You can track down the cause by moving from one router to the other along the path to the originator and checking which intermediate routers also are seeing the same errors. The IS-IS process also periodically scans the LS database and generates an error log for any corrupted LSPs found.
- LSP corruption storms (purging and reflooding) lead to frequent SPF runs and high CPU. The command **ignore-lsp-error** can be configured under the IS-IS routing process to stabilize the situation if necessary.
- The update queue should not stay full.
- The update queue should not drop much.

After the IS-IS operation is verified across the routers, the Link-State database needs to be scanned for the presence of LSPs from all the routers running IS-IS. Example 8-12 shows how to list LSP entries in the LS database.

Example 8-12 *Listing LSPs in the Link-State Database*

```
RTD#sh isis database

IS-IS Level-2 Link State Database
LSPID            LSP Seq Num  LSP Checksum  LSP Holdtime   ATT/P/OL
RTA.00-00        0x00000006   0xB0CB        62058          0/0/0
RTH.00-00        0x00000016   0xE873        58673          0/0/0
RTC.00-00        0x00000017   0x6A3C        65031          0/0/0
RTB.00-00        0x000000E4   0x5568        62068          0/0/0
```

continues

Example 8-12 *Listing LSPs in the Link-State Database (Continued)*

```
RTG.00-00            0x0000001B   0xFD58      63197      0/0/0
RTG.02-00            0x00000001   0x6C24      56073      0/0/0
RTG.03-00            0x00000006   0x9C28      61399      0/0/0
RTD.00-00          * 0x00000025   0x9BEE      63197      0/0/0
RTD.02-00          * 0x00000004   0xBEF8      61506      0/0/0
RTD.03-00          * 0x00000006   0x3A41      54372      0/0/0
```

Example 8-13 shows how to view the information carried in an LSP. The LSPs are flooded intact, and the same information needs to be present in each LSP when viewed on any of the area routers. During the migration, every LSP needs to be checked to make sure it carries accurate information about the originator's environment. The collection of information in all the LSPs needs to accurately reflect the network's topology.

Example 8-13 *Viewing the Information Carried in a LSP*

```
RTD#show isis database RTA.00-00 detail

IS-IS Level-2 LSP RTA.00-00
LSPID                  LSP Seq Num   LSP Checksum   LSP Holdtime      ATT/P/OL
RTA.00-00              0x0000000D    0xA461         60837             0/0/0
  Area Address: 49.0001
  NLPID:        0xCC
  Hostname: RTA
  IP Address:   192.168.10.8
  Metric: 10        IS-Extended RTA.02
  Metric: 100       IS-Extended RTB.00
  Metric: 100       IP 192.168.20.216/30
  Metric: 0         IP 192.168.10.12/32
  Metric: 10        IP 192.168.10.32/32
  Metric: 100       IP 192.168.10.24/30
```

Broadcast segments, such as Ethernet, should have a consistent DIS for each level of routing. In this migration, IS-IS is being deployed as a single Level 2 domain; therefore, the Level 2 DIS on all broadcast links must be verified, as shown in Example 8-14, to be the same. Any inconsistency will hinder database synchronisation over the segment. If there are any anomalies, the root cause needs to be investigated and corrected before moving on to the next phase of the migration. Example 8-14 shows the output of the **show clns interface** command with the DIS information highlighted. The circuit ID of a broadcast link is associated with the system ID or the host name of the DIS. In this case, RTD is shown to be the DIS. The 02 suffix in RTD.02 indicates this is the second broadcast segment on which RTD is playing the role of DIS. The other interesting information in this output is the number of Level 2 adjacencies on the segment. This does not include the virtual Pseudonode, and the count should reflect other actual adjacent routers directly connected to the segment.

You can read more about DIS and pseudonode functionality in Chapter 4 in the "Forming LAN Adjacencies"section.

Example 8-14 *Confirming DIS Consistency on Broadcast Links*

```
RTD#show clns int fasteth5/0
FastEthernet5/0 is up, line protocol is up
  Checksums enabled, MTU 1497, Encapsulation SAP
  ERPDUs enabled, min. interval 10 msec.
  RDPDUs enabled, min. interval 100 msec., Addr Mask enabled
  Congestion Experienced bit set at 4 packets
  CLNS fast switching enabled
  CLNS SSE switching disabled
  DEC compatibility mode OFF for this interface
  Next ESH/ISH in 33 seconds
  Routing Protocol: IS-IS
    Circuit Type: level-2-only
    Interface number 0x1, local circuit ID 0x2
    Level-2 Metric: 6000, Priority: 127, Circuit ID: RTD.02
    Number of active level-2 adjacencies: 2
    Next IS-IS LAN Level-2 Hello in 2 seconds
```

By default, IS-IS sets the metric to 10 on all interfaces, regardless of bandwidth. Therefore, path selection would be essentially based on hop count if the metric is not adjusted to reflect bandwidth of the various links or to influence traffic flow along the preferred path. In contrast, EIGRP, by default, automatically takes into consideration the characteristics of links, including bandwidth to assign metrics, with the lower metric generally implying better bandwidth. The metric assigned to a route is the total of the metric on all outgoing interfaces on a specific path to that destination. Again, the lower value is better. Therefore, to ensure traffic flow under IS-IS is consistent with the existing traffic flow under EIGRP, the metric on all active IS-IS interfaces needs to be manually adjusted on every router to correspond to EIGRP values or similar, according to a layout that is planned in advance.

Enabling IS-IS on all routers with a distance of 255 should not change the existing traffic flow under EIGRP because EIGRP routes have a better administrative distance and are still preferred over similar IS-IS routes.

At this point, the network has two fully functional routing protocols, with one as the primary source of routes. Vigilant monitoring of the network needs to continue with prying into each router's configuration, checking IS-IS adjacencies, verifying consistency of the IS-IS LS database on all routers, verifying consistency of LSP information, checking the IP routing tables, and forwarding tables (FIB and Adjacency Databases—See Chapter 1, "Overview of IP Routing" section). It would be useful also to take note of the number of routes in the routing table before going on to the next phase. The show **ip routes summary** and show **ip cef summary** commands should provide this information.

Phase 3—Configurations and Other Status Information

The third phase is to transfer the administrative distance of 255 from the IS-IS routing process, the EIGRP routing process, making the latter the less preferred source of routes. This ensures that Integrated IS-IS becomes the primary source of routing information that feeds routes into the routing table, and then makes it into the forwarding tables (CEF, and so on). Example 8-15 shows how the **distance** command is removed from the IS-IS process and a similar command is placed in the EIGRP process. This might require downtime to be scheduled for final clean up.

Example 8-15 *Reversing Priorities with the* **Distance** *Command*

```
RTD(config)#router isis
RTD(config-router)#no distance 255 ip
RTD(config-router)#

RTD(config)#router eigrp 10
RTD(config-router)#distance 255
RTD(config-router)#
```

The routing table might need to be cleared to force routes sourced from IS-IS to take precedence. The **clear ip route *** command does just this. After the routing table is populated with IS-IS routes, a quick **show ip route summary** command entry should provide route statistics that can be compared with similar information gathered from the previous phase. The **show ip route** command should be used to scrutinize the routing table further to make sure all prefixes are available and, most importantly, that they are from the IS-IS process and not EIGRP. The **show ip route isis** and **show ip route eigrp** commands need to be used to check subsets routes for IS-IS and EIGRP, respectively. The **show ip route eigrp** command should not display any EIGRP entries in the routing table. The **show ip cef** and related commands should be used to confirm that all routes are available in the forwarding table. Example 8-16 shows a sample output of IS-IS Level 2 routes for the IP routing table. Also, the **ping** and **traceroute** commands can be used to test reachability and path selection to various destinations in the network to confirm normal routing is restored.

Example 8-16 *Verifying the Routes in the IP Routing Table*

```
RTD#show ip route isis
i L2 196.172.60.0/24 [80/17846] via 192.168.10.161, FastEthernet5/0
       192.28.235.0/28 is subnetted, 1 subnets
i L2    192.28.235.0 [80/17846] via 192.168.10.161, FastEthernet5/0
       192.168.20.0/24 is variably subnetted, 3 subnets, 2 masks
i L2    192.168.20.138/32 [80/17846] via 192.168.10.161, FastEthernet5/0
i L2    192.168.20.216/30 [80/17846] via 192.168.10.161, FastEthernet5/0
i L2    192.168.20.192/30 [80/17846] via 192.168.10.161, FastEthernet5/
       192.168.10.0/24 is variably subnetted, 9 subnets, 3 masks
i L2    192.168.10.8/32 [80/17846] via 192.168.10.161, FastEthernet5/0
i L2    192.168.10.9/32 [80/6000] via 192.168.10.161, FastEthernet5/0
i L2    192.168.10.12/32 [80/17846] via 192.168.10.161, FastEthernet5/0
```

Example 8-16 *Verifying the Routes in the IP Routing Table (Continued)*

```
 i L2    192.168.10.22/32 [80/17846] via 192.168.10.161, FastEthernet5/0
 i L2    192.168.10.23/32 [80/6000] via 192.168.10.161, FastEthernet5/0
 i L2    192.168.10.20/32 [80/17846] via 192.168.10.161, FastEthernet5/0
 i L2    192.168.10.128/30 [80/23458] via 192.168.10.161, FastEthernet5/0
 i L2    192.168.10.104/30 [80/17846] via 192.168.10.161, FastEthernet5/0
 i L2    192.168.10.112/28 [80/14462] via 192.168.10.161, FastEthernet5/0
```

Phase 4—Configuration and Other Status Information

By the end of Phase 4, it should be completely confirmed that all forwarding is restored and IS-IS routes are able to completely support routing in the network. EIGRP is no longer required for primary routing or even for fallback. Disabling of EIGRP routing from the network can, therefore, proceed. The EIGRP configuration is removed with the following line of configuration from each router:

```
RTD(config)#no router eigrp 10
```

This concludes the migration process. The network should continue being monitored for proper forwarding and optimization opportunities, such as summarization, metric adjustments of optimal path selection, and so on in the new routing environment.

The record of events during the migration needs to be consulted for post mortem evaluation. This information can provide the basis for any recommendations on future growth, changes, and management of the network.

Migrating from OSPF to Integrated IS-IS

Both OSPF and Integrated IS-IS are pure link-state protocols and, therefore, use similar mechanisms for flooding and route computation. Migrating from a single area OSPF domain to a single level IS-IS routing domain should be straightforward; there should be no change in the characteristics of routing in any significant manner, as compared to the migration from traditional distance-vector protocols. If OSPF is deployed with hierarchy, the hierarchy can be maintained with IS-IS route leaking. However, if a hierarchical OSPF domain is not large and the simplicity associated with troubleshooting and maintenance of a flat IS-IS domain is of interest, this is also possible, even though more careful planning will be required.

Migration Phases

The same migration principles and phases that were elaborated for EIGRP migration in the previous section can be applied. In particular, the background method can be effectively used. OSPF has a better administrative distance of 110 compared to 115 for IS-IS, so technically in phase 2, the administrative distance for IS-IS does not need to be changed to 255. However, a higher administrative distance must be applied to OSPF in phase 3.

Metrics

In the default mode of operation, OSPF transforms interface bandwidth into metric information. Unlike EIGRP, however, only bandwidth information is used and other link characteristics, such as delay, reliability, and MTU, are not used to compute composite metrics. OSPF metric or cost values are inversely proportional to bandwidth. The cost on an interface is assigned based on a default reference bandwidth of 100Mb/s and calcuated by dividing the reference bandwidth by the interface bandwidth. A value 1 is applied for all results greater than one. The reference bandwidth is configurable. Also, if necessary, the interface metric can also be manually assigned.

For the purpose of migrating to IS-IS, the OSPF costs can be noted for all interfaces and directly ported manually into the IS-IS configuration for corresponding interfaces. The output of the **show ip ospf interface** provides the cost associated with an interface. The OSPF costs should be obtained in advance for each router and entered into a migration planning spreadsheet or table for later use. Because OSPF allows cost values larger than 63 per interface, this approach might require IS-IS wide metrics to support any large values.

Using the same metric values on corresponding OSPF and IS-IS interfaces would guarantee the new IS-IS paths to be identical to the previous OSPF paths. It would make the migration practically loop free as IS-IS is made primary from router to router. Routes intalled from either OSPF or IS-IS would have practically identical characteristics. The network can actually remain fully functional as a higher distance is applied to OSPF in each router and different routers independently choose IS-IS or OSPF as the source of routes based on current configuration.

Monitoring Network Resources

Probably the single most important issue in migrating from OSPF to IS-IS is availability of enough network resources, such as bandwidth, router memory, and CPU capacity, to handle two resource demanding protocols running independently and concurrently on each router.

Checking available resources during the inventory stage and upgrading as needed before turning up IS-IS in parallel with OSPF should go a long way to forestall any surprises that might appear in the middle of the migration. With all these issues in mind, the migration from OSPF should be similar to the migration from EIGRP, and the migration phases discussed earlier should be applicable here also.

Migrating from a Classful IGP to Integrated IS-IS

Migrating from a classful protocol is not any more challenging than the previous scenarios discussed. Classful protocols require deployment of flat networks by their inherent nature. The redistribution method of migration will not work well here because IS-IS being a classless protocol might carry detailed routing information that the classful protocol might not be able to handle. As you might know, classful protocols do not support VLSMs and discontiguous subnets. Classless protocols do. Also, classful protocols, such as RIPv1 and the Interior Gateway Routing Protocol (IGRP), are based on distance vector concepts, and the contents of the routing tables are directly tied to routing updates. In contrast, IS-IS generates routing information based on a complete model of the topology built on information gathered from LSPs; there, routing dynamics might differ. Also, RIP uses hop count for metrics, and IGRP uses a composite metric similar to EIGRP.

The migration from a classful protocol to Integrated IS-IS might also require a change in the physical topology if IS-IS is to be deployed with hierarchy. In most cases, however, the classful migration involves deploying a flat Level 2 IS-IS domain, and so the background method can be successfully employed with minimal challenges.

If hierarchy is required, first consider which routers form the backbone of the network. As discussed in previous chapters, Integrated IS-IS requires a contiguous backbone, which within a hierarchical topology must be a collection of Level 2 routers.

The selection of the backbone routers depends on several criteria. The primary consideration involves identifying which regions of the network are best suited to be part of the backbone. These should be core strategic locations that border other geographic regions. The layered approach discussed in Chapter 7, "General Network Design Issues," can be leveraged here.

Other criteria that must be taken into consideration, include network resources, such as bandwidth of network links, router memory, and CPU capacity. Remember that link-state protocols have to create and maintain a Link-State database, as well as the routing table and might require more memory than a distance vector protocol when deployed in comparable networks. Also, the new backbone needs to be fully redundant.

This concludes the discussion of general issues that need to be considered when migrating from a flat classful protocol to Integrated IS-IS. The next sections cover specific consideration for migrating from RIP.

Migrating from RIP to Integrated IS-IS

This section looks at migrating from the Routing Information Protocol (RIP) to Integrated IS-IS. Consider Figure 8-7, which is a flat RIP network. First, you must decide which routers need to become the backbone. This is not such a difficult decision given the current topology. Take a look at the European region: Routers RTA1, RTB1, and RTC1 are obvious candidates for backbone routers. In the USA region, routers RTB2 and RTD2 are the best candidates to be backbone routers. Finally, in the Asian region, routers RTC3 and RTD3 are the obvious choices.

Figure 8-7 *Transforming from flat to a hierarchical routing topology.*

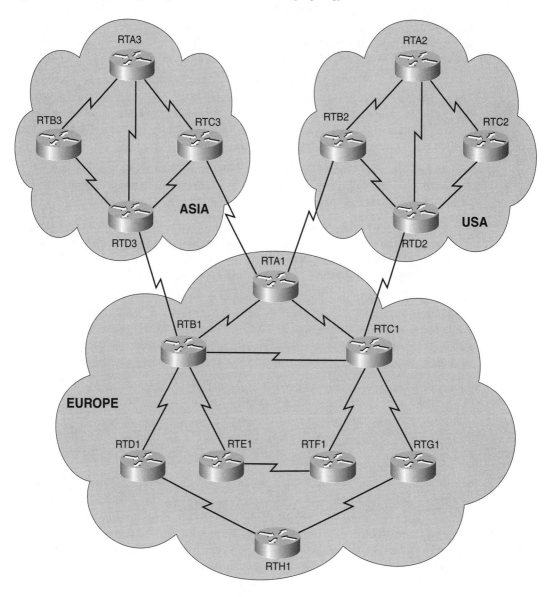

The backbone routers provide redundant connectivity to other regions. Each selected backbone router also has redundant connections into its own region. The backbone routers will certainly be excellent points for route summarization in the hierarchical topology.

The European region can be further segmented into a full three-layer hierarchy with routers RTD1, RTE1, RTF1, and RTG1 considered as the distribution routers, and RTH1 operating as an access router. Summarization can be applied at the distribution points, between the core and access layers. The distribution routers are configured as both Level 1 and Level 2, with the core being Level 2-only and the access being Level 1-only.

With all the routers assigned roles—backbone, distribution, or access—and their corresponding IS types defined, preparation for the actual migration can begin. The background migration method will be most suitable and the phases used in the migration from EIGRP can be followed. RIP has a worse default administrative distance of 120, and IS-IS has a value of 115, so the IS-IS value needs to be changed to a worse value in phase 2. Alternatively, the administrative distance for RIP can be lowered to, for example, 50 to ensure that the RIP routes remain primary.

RIP uses hop count so no special metric assignments need to be prepared ahead of time. However, if specific metric adjustments have been made by applying metric offsets to influence path selection in the RIP environment, appropriate metric adjustments need to be made this forward into IS-IS. A simple worksheet for metric conversion from the RIP environment to the IS-IS enviroment would be rightfully in place.

In phase 3, the cutover to IS-IS as primary is performed by making the IS-IS adminstrative distance better, either by removing the administrative distance of 255 from the IS-IS configuration or removing the distance of 50 from RIP if the alternate approach was used. The cutover can typically start from the edge toward the core with the **clear ip route** * command used in each router to refresh the IP routing table.

In phase 4, RIP can be disabled from the network after a reasonable level of certainty has been established that IS-IS is operating as expected and routing is fully functional.

Because RIP is a classful protocol, there might have been a potential waste of addresses in the RIP environment while assigning contiguous IP subnets to make routing work. IS-IS is more flexible with address assignment as a classless protocol and might present opportunities for more efficient address assignment in the new network. Any address changes should, however, be implemented after the migration is completed.

Migrating from IGRP to Integrated IS-IS

All the discussions for migrating from RIP are applicable to IGRP because both protocols have similar routing functionality and characteristics, such as classful addressing and distance vector routing. However, a key difference between them lies in metric definition. RIP uses hop count, and IGRP uses a composite metric based on bandwidth, delay, reliability, and MTU. Therefore, the preparations for the migration from IGRP needs to include planning of metric conversion to provide the desired path selection when IS-IS is made primary over IGRP.

In this scenario also, the background method is most suitable for the migration. The administrative distance of IGRP is 100 compared to 115 for IS-IS. This means that IGRP routes would be preferred over IS-IS routes, and no distance adjustment is required in phase 2. Making IS-IS primary will require applying a larger distance to IGRP in phase 3.

Coexisting with Other IP IGPs

Integrated IS-IS might be required to coexist with other IGPs in some networks. This can possibly happen during migration from one protocol to another, such as when using the redistribution method for migration to IS-IS. This also happens in the background approach during the cutover phase. However, there might be practical scenarios where coexistence might be needed for long-term normal operation. In this situation, IS-IS might be deployed in one region of the network and the other protocol in an adjacent region. In other situations, IS-IS might be in the core, and another less robust protocol might exist on the fringes running on routers that might not support IS-IS.

When Integrated IS-IS coexists with another IGP on a more permanent basis, mutual redistribution is required to exchange routes between the two protocol domains. Under these circumstances, the potential for routing loops because of route feedback is high. Therefore, care must be taken to ensure that redistribution occurs at only carefully selected points in the network, and route filters must also be used to reduce any potential for route feedback. Administrative distances might have to be adjusted on routers that run both protocols to ensure preference of certain routes from a specific protocol source.

As a link-state protocol, Integrated IS-IS obtains routing information through LSP exchange, and because each router must have a consistent view of the topology based on information contained in the LSPs, LSP filtering is not allowed. However, external routes can be filtered during redistribution into the IS-IS routing domain. Routes from IS-IS can also be filtered before inclusion in other protocol environments.

Using IS-IS in Dual Environments

As specified in RFC 1195, Integrated IS-IS supports routing in dual environments with both ISO CLNS and IP services. Integrated IS-IS can be used to forward both IP and CLNP packets simultaneously in such environments. This section briefly discusses requirements for using IS-IS in such enviroments and potential issues that might arise.

A critical requirement for using IS-IS in a dual environment is to keep all routers in an area consistently configured. In other words, each area must be configured to surpport either IP only or CLNP only, or both, and all routers in the area must be configured similarly. This is necessary so that all routers in the area can build a consistent level Link-State database and obtain identical views of the areas topology. However, an IP-only router can connect to another router in an area that supports both IP and CLNP and form Level 2 adjacencies with that router for sharing of IP routing information.

Figure 8-8 shows a network topology with three separate areas. Area 1 supports only ISO CLNP, and so all routers in this area must be configured for IS-IS in ISO CLNP mode only. Area 2 supports both IP and ISO CLNP, and so routers in this area must operate in dual mode. Area 3 is an IP-only area, and therefore, all routers in this area must be configured for IP only. Also, as shown in the illustration, this requirement does not apply to the backbone where Level 2 routing is performed.

Figure 8-8   *Using IS-IS in Dual IP and ISO domains.*

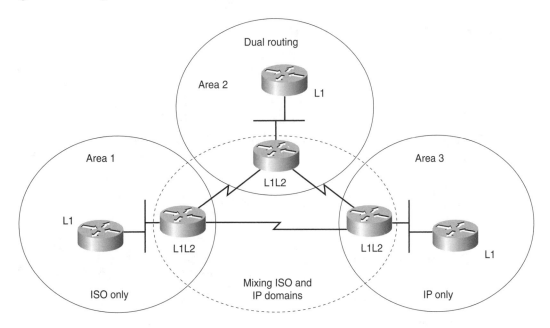

Some key points to note about using IS-IS for IP and ISO CLNP follow:

- An administrative distance of 110 is used for ISO CLNP routing and 115 for IP routing.

- CLNP static routes are automatically redistributed into IS-IS, while explicit configuration is required to carry IP static routes into IS-IS. Also, the **redistribute static** statement requires the keyword **ip** for the IP setup.

- Enabling IS-IS for IP routing automatically enables CNLS routing on the entire router. However, recent IOS releases allow CNLS to be disabled when using IS-IS for only IP routing. This can be done with the command **no clns routing**.

- IS-IS routing for IP on an inteface is enabled with the interface level IOS command **ip router isis <tag>**, whereas clns routing is enabled similarly but with the command **clns router isis <tag>**.

- Making an interface passive removes both the **ip router isis <tag>** and **clns router isis <tag>** commands from the interface configuration, and no adjacencies are formed over that interface for IP or CLNP routing. However, any IP prefixes configured on the interface are carried into the router's LSP. Because CLNP routing is completely disabled on the interface, care must be used when applying the **passive-interface** command in dual environments.

Examples 8-17 and 8-18 illustrate problems that arise when routers in the same area are configured inconsistently.

Case Study 1: Mixing ISO and IP

Example 8-17 shows a scenario in which a connection RTA and RTB is confiigured for both IP and CLNP routing on RTA but enabled for only IP routing on RTB. This configuration is not allowed in IOS because according to RFC 1195, a link between two routers in the same area must be configured identically at either end. Therefore, no adjacency is formed between RTA and RTB, as shown in the **show clns neighbors** command output.

Example 8-17 *Same Area Routers with Dual (IP and CNLP) and IP-Only Configurations*

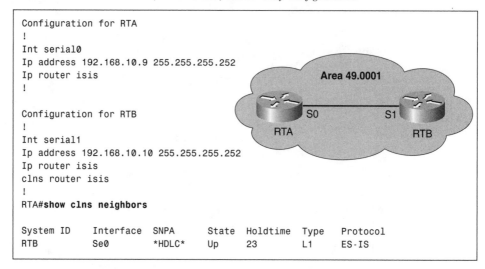

```
Configuration for RTA
!
Int serial0
Ip address 192.168.10.9 255.255.255.252
Ip router isis
!

Configuration for RTB
!
Int serial1
Ip address 192.168.10.10 255.255.255.252
Ip router isis
clns router isis
!
RTA#show clns neighbors

System ID    Interface  SNPA     State  Holdtime  Type   Protocol
RTB          Se0        *HDLC*   Up     23        L1     ES-IS
```

Case Study 2: Mixing ISO and IP

Example 8-18 shows a scenario where IS-IS is enabled for CLNP routing at one end of the connection, at RTA, and IP-only routing at RTB. This is also not allowed because both routers are in the same area, so adjacency is not formed between RTA and RTB, as shown in the **show clns neighbors** ouput.

Example 8-18 *Same Area Routers with IP-Only and CLNP-Only Configurations*

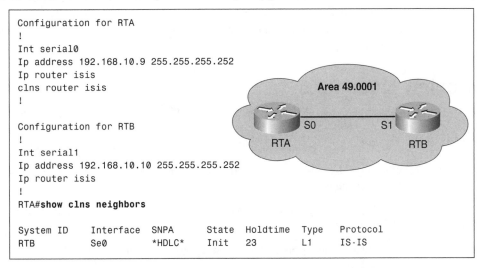

```
Configuration for RTA
!
Int serial0
Ip address 192.168.10.9 255.255.255.252
Ip router isis
clns router isis
!


Configuration for RTB
!
Int serial1
Ip address 192.168.10.10 255.255.255.252
Ip router isis
!
RTA#show clns neighbors

System ID    Interface   SNPA      State  Holdtime  Type  Protocol
RTB          Se0         *HDLC*    Init   23        L1    IS-IS
```

Summary

This chapter presents various case studies to elaborate on various network design issues when IS-IS is deployed as an IGP. The chapter starts by reviewing two migration scenarios that involve making changes in existing IS-IS configurations. The first is concerned with migration of IS-IS areas from one area ID to another, and the second deals with migration from narrow to wide metrics.

Next, IS-IS configurations are reviewed for point-to-point links and for NBMA transport deployed in ISP environments. A great amount of time is dedicated to issues relating to deploying IS-IS in NBMA environments with highly meshed PVCs. Common configuration problems and solutions are reviewed. The reviews indicate the best model for NBMA links in IS-IS networks is the point-to-point model in which point-to-point subinterface is used to model the virtual circuits as point-to-point links. IS-IS mesh groups are also suggested as a solution to address scaling issues posed by redundant flooding in highly meshed envi-ronments using the point-to-point model.

A substantial part of the chapter focuses on migrating from other IGPs to IS-IS. Two approaches are recommended: The Redistribution and Background methods. An elaborate example based on migration from EIGRP is discussed. The whole process is also summarized into four phases. Migration from OSPF is briefly discussed, and the Background method emerged here also as the recommended approach. Specific considerations for OSPF are highlighted.

The four-phase migration approach based on the Background method was also identified to be applicable for migrating from classful protocols, such as RIP and IGRP.

The final sections of the chapter were focused on two important issues, namely coexistence of IS-IS with other IP IGPs and using IS-IS in dual environments. Two case studies that were focused on configuration issues when mixing ISO CNLS and IP routing in Dual domains are presented to reinforce earlier discussions on RFC1195 requirements.

Review Questions

1 What is the main purpose and use of configuring up to three different area addresses on a single router?

2 What is the consequence of configuring more than one area address on a single router?

3 What is the purpose of the **transition** keyword when used with the **metric-style** command?

4 How many types of hello packets are used on point-to-point interfaces on Cisco routers?

5 What is the purpose of the **mesh-group blocked** command?

6 What is the default behavior of a member within a mesh group?

7 What is the purpose of the **distance** command?

8 What precautions must be taken when configuring mutual redistribution between Integrated IS-IS and other coexisting IGPs?

9 What caveat must always be adhered to when running IS-IS for CLNS and IS-IS for IP in the same area?

PART III

Configuring and Troubleshooting Integrated IS-IS

Configuring IS-IS for IP Routing on Cisco Routers

This chapter provides guidelines, procedures, and an overview of configuration commands for enabling IS-IS on Cisco routers. The Cisco implementation of the IS-IS protocol provides numerous commands for enabling various capabilities and optimization of IS-IS functionality, some of which are infrequently used in real applications. This chapter focuses on relevant capabilities, features, and related commands commonly used by network operators who run IS-IS in their networks. However, wherever possible, some less-common configuration tips are highlighted.

For the complete suite of supported features and commands, check out the Cisco IOS configuration manuals, available at www.cisco.com.

Note that this book primarily focuses on application of the IS-IS protocol in IP-only environments, such as those found in Internet service provider networks. This focus is certainly reflected in this chapter as can be discerned from the examples and related discussions.

This chapter discusses the following:

- Configuring IS-IS on point-to-point serial links
- Configuring IS-IS on broadcast links (that is, on a LAN)
- Configuring IS-IS on nonbroadcast multiaccess (NBMA) media
    - ATM point-to-point
    - ATM multipoint
    - Erame Relay point-to-point
    - Frame Relay multipoint
    - ISDN multipoint

The following specialized topics and relevant configuration examples are covered:

- Configuring IS-IS capabilities
  - Advertising the IP default route in IS-IS
  - Redistribution
  - IP route summarization
  - Secondary addresses, unnumbered interfaces, and tunneling configurations
- Authentication
- Domain-wide prefix distribution (Level 2 to Level 1 route leaking)
- IS-IS multi-area configuration
- Configuring IS-IS for optimized performance

The following two basic steps are required to enable IS-IS routing on Cisco routers running appropriate Cisco IOS releases that support IS-IS:

- Configure the routing process.
- Apply IS-IS routing to relevant interfaces.

The Cisco IOS configuration command **router isis [tag]** enables the IS-IS routing process. The tag is an optional keyword for labeling the routing process, and it has only local significance in recent versions of IOS. This means that it doesn't have to be consistent across all routers. Most service providers use the same tag on all routers in their domain for consistency. Be aware that in some older versions of IS-IS, routers might be unable to form adjacencies when the tags are mismatched. Adding an NSAP address in the router configuration level completes basic configuration for the routing process.

The command **clns routing** is automatically added to the configuration upon activation of the routing process. However, recent changes in IOS (for example, 12.0S and 12.0ST release trains) make this command relevant only in environments where ISO CLNP forwarding is required. For pure IP environments, CLNP forwarding is not required, and the entry can be removed using the negation command, **no clns routing**.

When basic IS-IS routing is enabled, a Cisco router functions as both a Level 1 and Level 2 router unless either Level 1 or Level 2 mode of operation is manually disabled. The IOS router-level command **no is-type <level-1 | level-2-only>** disables Level 1 or Level 2 routing on all interfaces.

The next step after configuring the routing process is to enable IS-IS routing on the interfaces of interest with the command **ip router isis [tag]**. As indicated previously, CLNP routing is enabled by default when the IS-IS process is activated. If the router has to operate in dual mode, routing both IP and CLNP, the interface-level command **clns router [tag]** needs to be configured. If only IP routing support is required, the **ip router [tag]** command is sufficient and the CLNP routing might be disabled globally, as explained earlier.

The interface command **[no] isis circuit type <level-1 | level-2>** can be used to specify the desired level of routing (Level 1 or Level 2) depending on the global configuration at the router level.

It is interesting to note that in the IS-IS confiuration, no IP network statements are used as in the case of other IP routing protocols. The IP subnets on IS-IS enabled interfaces are automatically placed in the IP reachability TLVs used in LSPs, which are then flooded to adjacent neighbors.

Point-to-Point Serial-Link Configuration

The IS-IS configuration for point-to-point links is the most commonly used in real networks, for point-to-point serial interfaces, as well as to NBMA point-to-point subinterfaces. The point-to-point configuration lends itself to various advantages because it provides congruency to the underlying physical topology. Figures 9-1 and 9-2 depict a simple point-to-point setup of two routers (RT1 and RT2) connected directly by a serial link. The routers are in the same IS-IS area in Figure 9-1 but in different areas in Figure 9-2.

Also shown are relevant excerpts of the IS-IS configurations on the routers. In Figure 9-1, both routers are in the same area and so share a common area prefix (49.0001). Therefore, according to the default IOS behavior, they will establish Level 1 and Level 2 adjacencies. In contrast, however, the routers in Figure 9-2 are in different areas, so they will form only a Level 2 adjacency.

Figure 9-1   *IS-IS point-to-point configuration (routers in same area).*

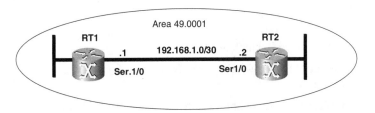

```
hostname RT1                                  hostname RT2
clns routing                                  clns routing
!                                             !
interface Loopback0                           interface Loopback0
  ip address 10.1.1.1 255.255.255.255           ip address 10.1.1.2 255.255.255.255
  ip router isis                                ip router isis
!                                             !
interface Serial0/0                           interface Serial0/0
  ip address 192.168.1.1 255.255.255.252        ip address 192.168.1.2 255.255.255.252
  ip router isis                                ip router isis
!                                             !
router isis                                   router isis
  net 49.0001.0000.0000.0001.00                 net 49.0001.0000.0000.0002.00
```

Figure 9-2   *IS-IS point-to-point configuration (routers in different areas).*

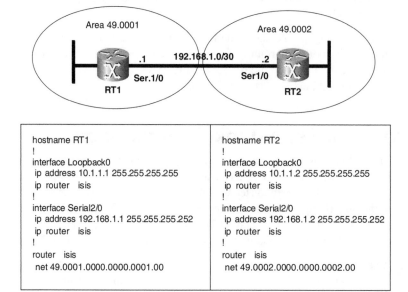

The following commands are useful for verifying proper configuration and operation of IS-IS on Cisco routers:

- **show clns protocol**—Provides a summary of the protocol state on the router (see Example 9-1)

- **show clns neighbors [detail]**—Shows adjacency state information about known neighbors (see Example 9-2)

- **show clns interface**—Shows IS-IS routing information pertaining to an interface (see Example 9-3)

- **show isis topology**—Shows path information for IS-IS nodes in the Level 1 and Level 2 topology (see Example 9-4)

- **show isis database**—Displays known LSPs in the level-1 and level-2 databases (see Example 9-5)

Examples 9-1 through 9-5 show outputs of these commands captured from the routers set up in Figure 9-2. Each example features an output from each router to show the state of either side of the connection. Because the setup is basic, most of the output is self-explanatory. Some information is provided on the **show isis database** output in Table 9-1. More information is provided on the other commands in Chapter 10, "Troubleshooting the IS-IS Routing Protocol."

Example 9-1 **show clns protocol** *Output*

```
RT1#show clns protocol
IS-IS Router: <Null Tag>
  System Id: 0000.0000.0001.00  IS-Type: level-1-2
  Manual area address(es):
        49.0001
  Routing for area address(es):
        49.0001
  Interfaces supported by IS-IS:
        Loopback0 - IP
        Serial0/0 - IP
  Redistributing:
    static
  Distance: 110
  RRR level: none
  Generate narrow metrics: level-1-2
  Accept narrow metrics:   level-1-2
  Generate wide metrics:   none
  Accept wide metrics:     none

RT2#show clns protocol
IS-IS Router: <Null Tag>
  System Id: 0000.0000.0002.00  IS-Type: level-1-2
  Manual area address(es):
        49.0002
  Routing for area address(es):
        49.0002
  Interfaces supported by IS-IS:
        Loopback0 - IP
        Serial0/0 - IP
  Redistributing:
    static
    Distance: 110
  RRR level: none
  Generate narrow metrics: level-1-2
  Accept narrow metrics:   level-1-2
  Generate wide metrics:   none
  Accept wide metrics:     none
```

Example 9-2 **show clns neighbors detail** *Command Output*

```
RT1#show clns neighbors detail

System Id    Interface   SNPA    State   Holdtime   Type   Protocol

RT2          Se0/0      *HDLC*           Up         27  L2  IS-IS
  Area Address(es): 49.0002
  IP Address(es):  192.168.1.2*
  Uptime: 00:48:46
```

continues

Example 9-2 **show clns neighbors detail** *Command Output (Continued)*

```
RT2#show clns neighbors detail

System Id      Interface    SNPA            State Holdtime Type  Protocol
RT1            Se0/0        *HDLC*          Up    26       L2    IS-IS
   Area Address(es): 49.0001
   IP Address(es):   192.168.1.1*
   Uptime: 00:52:14
```

Example 9-3 **show clns interface** *Command Output*

```
RT1#show clns interface ser 0/0
Serial0/0 is up, line protocol is up
   Checksums enabled, MTU 1500, Encapsulation HDLC
   ERPDUs enabled, min. interval 10 msec.
   RDPDUs enabled, min. interval 100 msec., Addr Mask enabled
   Congestion Experienced bit set at 4 packets
   CLNS fast switching enabled
   CLNS SSE switching disabled
   DEC compatibility mode OFF for this interface
   Next ESH/ISH in 3 seconds
   Routing Protocol: IS-IS
     Circuit Type: level-1-2
     Interface number 0x0, local circuit ID 0x100
     Level-1 Metric: 10, Priority: 64, Circuit ID: RT1.00
     Number of active level-1 adjacencies: 0
     Level-2 Metric: 10, Priority: 64, Circuit ID: RT1.00
     Number of active level-2 adjacencies: 1
     Next IS-IS Hello in 8 seconds

RT2#show clns interface serial0/0
Serial0/0 is up, line protocol is up
   Checksums enabled, MTU 1500, Encapsulation HDLC
   ERPDUs enabled, min. interval 10 msec.
   RDPDUs enabled, min. interval 100 msec., Addr Mask enabled
   Congestion Experienced bit set at 4 packets
   clns fast switching enabled
   clns SSE switching disabled
   DEC compatibility mode OFF for this interface
   Next ESH/ISH in 8 seconds
   Routing Protocol: IS-IS
     Circuit Type: level-1-2
     Interface number 0x0, local circuit ID 0x100
     Level-1 Metric: 10, Priority: 64, Circuit ID: RT2.00
     Number of active level-1 adjacencies: 0
     Level-2 Metric: 10, Priority: 64, Circuit ID: RT2.00
     Number of active level-2 adjacencies: 1
     Next IS-IS Hello in 2 seconds
```

Example 9-4   show isis topology *Command Output*

```
RT1#show isis top
IS-IS paths to level-1 routers
System Id       Metric  Next-Hop    Interface    SNPA
RT1             --


IS-IS paths to level-2 routers
System Id       Metric  Next-Hop    Interface    SNPA
RT1             --
RT2             10      RT2         Se0/0        *HDLC*

RT2#show isis topology
IS-IS paths to level-1 routers
System Id       Metric  Next-Hop    Interface    SNPA
RT2             --


IS-IS paths to level-2 routers
System Id       Metric  Next-Hop    Interface    SNPA
RT1             10      RT1         Se0/0        *HDLC*
RT2             --
```

Example 9-5   show isis database *Command Output*

```
RT1#show isis database
IS-IS Level-1 Link State Database
LSPID             LSP Seq Num   LSP Checksum  LSP Holdtime    ATT/P/OL
RT1.00-00       * 0x00000008    0x8B75        1126            1/0/0
RT1.01-00       * 0x00000001    0x459B        1131            0/0/0


IS-IS Level-2 Link State Database
LSPID             LSP Seq Num   LSP Checksum  LSP Holdtime    ATT/P/OL
RT1.00-00       * 0x0000008A    0x8FED        1126            0/0/0
RT2.00-00         0x0000001E    0xB82C        998             0/0/0

RT2#show isis database
IS-IS Level-1 Link State Database
LSPID             LSP Seq Num   LSP Checksum  LSP Holdtime    ATT/P/OL
RT2.00-00       * 0x00000019    0x3DAB        883             1/0/0
RT2.01-00       * 0x0000000D    0x339F        980             0/0/0


IS-IS Level-2 Link State Database
LSPID             LSP Seq Num   LSP Checksum  LSP Holdtime    ATT/P/OL
RT1.00-00         0x0000008A    0x8FED        931             0/0/0
RT2.00-00       * 0x0000001E    0xB82C        808             0/0/0
```

Table 9-1 describes the fields in the **show isis database** command output shown in Example 9-5.

Table 9-1   *Explanation of the Fields in the* **show isis database** *Commands*

Attribute	Comments
*	Indicates LSP is originated by the local system.
LSPID	LSP identifier. Column lists all known Level 1 and Level 2 LSPs.
LSP Seq Number	LSP sequence number for tracking the current version of LSP.
LSP Checksum	Checksum calculated at LSP origin. If it changes during storage or flooding, the LSP is corrupted and needs to be purged from the network.
LSP Holdtime	Time to expiration of LSP in seconds.
ATT	Attached bit. Set in Level 1 LSP by Level 2 routers to help Level 1 interarea traffic.
P	Partition bit. Indicates that the router supports partition repair.
OL	Overload bit. When set, it indicates resource problems, and the originating router should not be used in transit paths. Can be manually set for administrative reasons in IOS with **set-overload-bit** command.

Configuring IS-IS on Broadcast Multiaccess Links

Even though IS-IS operation on broadcast links differs a little from IS-IS operation on point-to-point links, the basic configuration is not significantly different. With broadcast links, you also activate the IS-IS routing process and then enable IS-IS routing on the interfaces where adjacencies are to be formed. In the LAN configuration example shown Figure 9-3, three routers (RT1, RT2, and RT3) are interconnected over an Ethernet link. All routers are in the same area.

A significant difference between a point-to-point scenario and this example is that, in this case, one of the routers is elected to be the designated intermediate system (DIS) to simplify database synchronization over the broadcast medium. The DIS effectively emulates the LAN as a pseudonode and uses an ID based on its system ID to represent the pseudonode. The pseudonode ID is also used by all routers connected to the LAN (including the DIS) as their circuit ID. The circuit ID associates an IS-IS interface with a link, and it is shown in the **show clns interface** output for the respective interface.

Figure 9-3   *Ethernet LAN configuration example.*

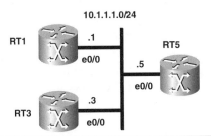

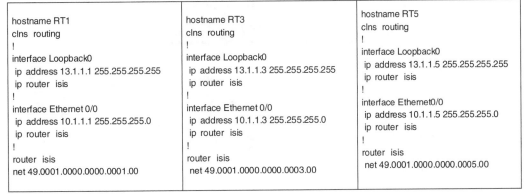

hostname RT1	hostname RT3	hostname RT5
clns routing	clns routing	clns routing
!	!	!
interface Loopback0	interface Loopback0	interface Loopback0
ip address 13.1.1.1 255.255.255.255	ip address 13.1.1.3 255.255.255.255	ip address 13.1.1.5 255.255.255.255
ip router isis	ip router isis	ip router isis
!	!	!
interface Ethernet 0/0	interface Ethernet 0/0	interface Ethernet0/0
ip address 10.1.1.1 255.255.255.0	ip address 10.1.1.3 255.255.255.0	ip address 10.1.1.5 255.255.255.0
ip router isis	ip router isis	ip router isis
!	!	!
router isis	router isis	router isis
net 49.0001.0000.0000.0001.00	net 49.0001.0000.0000.0003.00	net 49.0001.0000.0000.0005.00

Configuring IS-IS on NBMA Media

This section reviews configuration examples for popular nonbroadcast multiaccess media (NBMA), such as Asynchronous Transfer Mode (ATM), Frame Relay (FR), and Integrated Data Services Network (ISDN). IS-IS treats this media as broadcast media when they are configured as multipoint. This assumes that devices connected to such media are fully meshed with each other, which might not be always the case. When routers connecting to NBMA media are not fully meshed, routing might not work well because synchronization of the LS database might be flawed. In such cases, it is necessary to ensure that the DIS is connected to every node on the NBMA cloud, so that the periodic Complete Sequence Number Packets (CSNP) sent out by the DIS reaches every router.

The Cisco IOS Software offers an alternative for multipoint NBMA configuration. The option is known as point-to-point and allows the logical connections underlying such media (permanent virtual circuits, PVCs) to be modeled as point-to-point links. The point-to-point NBMA links simplify the NBMA topology for operation of routing protocols, by reflecting actual connectivity between network devices.

For highly meshed NMBA clouds with point-to-point setups, the IS-IS mesh group feature provides a means to reduce redundant flooding. IS-IS mesh groups are discussed in Chapter 5, "The IS-IS Link-State Database," in the section, "Flooding over NBMA Transport Media."

The following subsections feature configuration examples for ATM, FR, and ISDN. Both point-to-point and multipoint configuration examples are provided for ATM and FR.

ATM Configuration

The ATM point-to-point configuration procedure for IS-IS is similar to the serial point-to-point example discussed earlier. Figure 9-4 shows an ATM point-to-point example.

Figure 9-4   *ATM point-to-point example.*

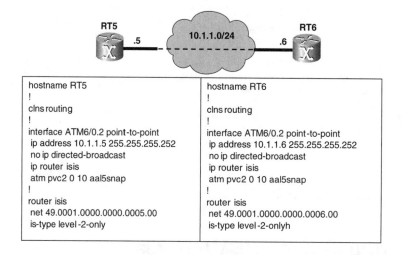

```
hostname RT5
!
clns routing
!
interface ATM6/0.2 point-to-point
 ip address 10.1.1.5 255.255.255.252
 no ip directed-broadcast
 ip router isis
 atm pvc2 0 10 aal5snap
!
router isis
 net 49.0001.0000.0000.0005.00
 is-type level-2-only
```

```
hostname RT6
!
clns routing
!
interface ATM6/0.2 point-to-point
 ip address 10.1.1.6 255.255.255.252
 no ip directed-broadcast
 ip router isis
 atm pvc2 0 10 aal5snap
!
router isis
 net 49.0001.0000.0000.0006.00
 is-type level-2-onlyh
```

If the ATM cloud is highly meshed with lots of PVC interconnections, an IS-IS mesh group configuration needs to be used to reduce the incidence of undesirable redundant flooding. Redundant flooding wastes network resources and can impact performance. The IS-IS mesh group feature is covered in Chatper 5 and also in Chapter 8, "Network Design Scenarios." The multipoint example shown in Figure 9-5 requires IP and CLNS map statements in the ATM map-list configuration section.

Figure 9-5   *ATM multipoint example.*

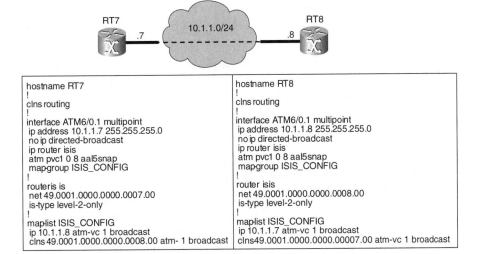

```
hostname RT7                                    hostname RT8
!                                               !
clns routing                                    clns routing
!                                               !
interface ATM6/0.1 multipoint                   interface ATM6/0.1 multipoint
ip address 10.1.1.7 255.255.255.0               ip address 10.1.1.8 255.255.255.0
no ip directed-broadcast                        no ip directed-broadcast
ip router isis                                  ip router isis
atm pvc1 0 8 aal5snap                           atm pvc1 0 8 aal5snap
mapgroup ISIS_CONFIG                            mapgroup ISIS_CONFIG
!                                               !
routeris is                                     router isis
net 49.0001.0000.0000.0007.00                   net 49.0001.0000.0000.0008.00
is-type level-2-only                            is-type level-2-only
!                                               !
maplist ISIS_CONFIG                             maplist ISIS_CONFIG
ip 10.1.1.8 atm-vc 1 broadcast                  ip 10.1.1.7 atm-vc 1 broadcast
clns 49.0001.0000.0000.0008.00 atm- 1 broadcast clns49.0001.0000.0000.00007.00 atm-vc 1 broadcast
```

Frame Relay Configuration

Just as in the case of ATM, FR setups can be configured in point-to-point or multipoint modes. The IS-IS point-to-point configuration (see Figure 9-6) is similar to the serial point-to-point example with the obvious difference being the subinterface configuration and the FR map statement.

Figure 9-6   *Frame Relay point-to-point example.*

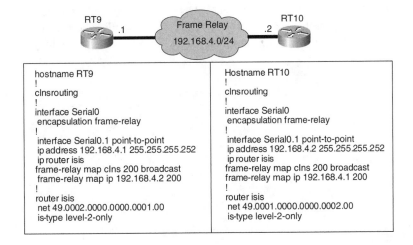

```
hostname RT9                                    Hostname RT10
!                                               !
clnsrouting                                     clnsrouting
!                                               !
interface Serial0                               interface Serial0
 encapsulation frame-relay                       encapsulation frame-relay
!                                               !
 interface Serial0.1 point-to-point              interface Serial0.1 point-to-point
ip address 192.168.4.1 255.255.255.252          ip address 192.168.4.2 255.255.255.252
ip router isis                                  ip router isis
frame-relay map clns 200 broadcast              frame-relay map clns 200 broadcast
 frame-relay map ip 192.168.4.2 200              frame-relay map ip 192.168.4.1 200
!                                               !
router isis                                     router isis
 net 49.0002.0000.0000.0001.00                   net 49.0001.0000.0000.0002.00
 is-type level-2-only                            is-type level-2-only
```

Figure 9-7 shows an FR multipoint configuration example. The point-to-point configuration is recommended over the multipoint configuration because it is maps the Layer 3 layout of the network to the underlying Layer 2 infrastructure with a clear indication of which routers have PVCs between them. This helps avoid problems with routing over a nonfully meshed multipoint cloud.

Similar to the case of ATM, the IS-IS mesh group feature must always be considered for highly meshed FR environments with point-to-point configurations. This helps limit unnecessary flooding of LSPs.

Figure 9-7 *Frame Relay multipoint example.*

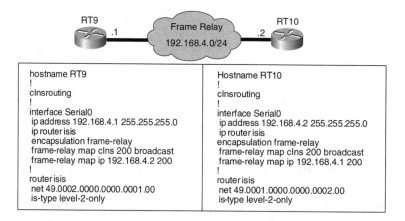

ISDN Configuration

Figure 9-8 shows a typical multipoint ISDN configuration, which follows the generic multipoint approach discussed with regard to ATM and FR. The key differences in all three cases lie in the Layer 2 configuration specifics for each technology.

Figure 9-8   *ISDN example.*

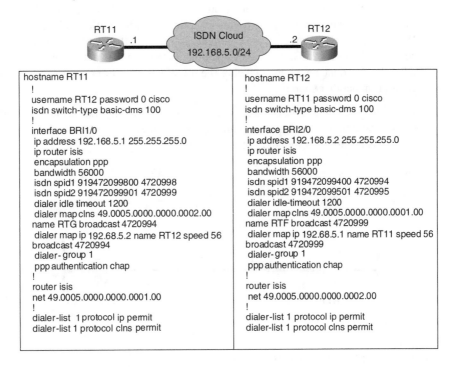

```
hostname RT11
!
  username RT12 password 0 cisco
  isdn switch-type basic-dms 100
!
  interface BRI1/0
  ip address 192.168.5.1 255.255.255.0
  ip router isis
  encapsulation ppp
  bandwidth 56000
  isdn spid1 919472099800 4720998
  isdn spid2 919472099901 4720999
  dialer idle-timeout 1200
  dialer map clns 49.0005.0000.0000.0002.00
  name RTG broadcast 4720994
  dialer map ip 192.68.5.2 name RT12 speed 56
  broadcast 4720994
  dialer- group 1
  ppp authentication chap
!
  router isis
  net 49.0005.0000.0000.0001.00
!
  dialer-list 1 protocol ip permit
  dialer-list 1 protocol clns permit
```

```
hostname RT12
!
  username RT11 password 0 cisco
  isdn switch-type basic-dms 100
!
  interface BRI2/0
  ip address 192.168.5.2 255.255.255.0
  ip router isis
  encapsulation ppp
  bandwidth 56000
  isdn spid1 919472099400 4720994
  isdn spid2 919472099501 4720995
  dialer idle-timeout 1200
  dialer map clns 49.0005.0000.0000.0001.00
  name RTF broadcast 4720999
  dialer map ip 192.68.5.1 name RT11 speed 56
  broadcast 4720999
  dialer- group 1
  ppp authentication chap
!
  router isis
  net 49.0005.0000.0000.0002.00
!
  dialer-list 1 protocol ip permit
  dialer-list 1 protocol clns permit
```

Configuring IS-IS Capabilities

The Cisco implementation of IS-IS provides numerous configuration options for enabling various IS-IS capabilities and modifying protocol parameters both globally and on a per-interface basis. This section presents some of these configuration options, such as advertising default routes, route summarization, and enabling authentication. Route leaking and IS-IS multi-area support are features recently introduced into the Cisco IS-IS implementation. The essence of these features and basic configurations are discussed briefly.

For a current and more complete list of IS-IS configuration options available in the Cisco IOS Software, see the *Cisco Configuration Guide* at www.cisco.com.

Advertising the IP Default Route in IS-IS

In the original protocol design of IS-IS, Level 1 areas are stubs and Level 1-only routers automatically install a default route to the nearest Level 1-2 router in the area. Level 1-2 routers set the ATT bit in the Level 1 LSPs they advertise into their native areas. The ATT-bit setting in LSPs provide a clue to Level 1-only routers about Level 2-capable routers in the area.

The Level 2 routers connected to the IS-IS backbone are expected to know about all routes in the IS-IS domain and do not set any automatic defaults. To advertise a default route into the IS-IS backbone requires the router-level **default-information originate** command. When configured on a router, the command inserts the IP prefix 0.0.0.0/0 as the default route into its Level 2 LSP targeted at the other Level 2 routers in the domain. The default is advertised into the backbone, whether the router has prior or no knowledge of a default route from another source.

Example 9-6, which is based on Figure 9-9, shows the configuration and application of the **default-information originate** command. Notice the default entry in the output of the **show isis database** command in Example 9-6.

Figure 9-9 *Diagram for Example 9-6.*

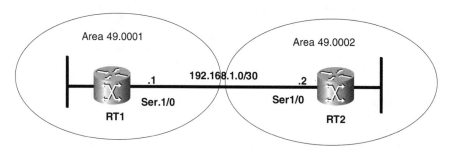

Example 9-6 *The **default-information originate** Command*

```
RT1# show running-config
[snip]
Hostname RT1
!
router isis
default-information originate
net 49.0001.0000.0000.0001.00
[snip]

RT2#show isis database detail RT1.00-00

IS-IS Level-2 LSP RT1.00-00
LSPID                   LSP Seq Num    LSP Checksum   LSP Holdtime      ATT/P/OL
RT1.00-00               0x000000E1     0x7A1E         651               0/0/0
  Area Address: 49.0001
  NLPID:       0xCC
  Hostname: RT1
  IP Address:    10.1.1.1
  Metric: 10         IS RT1.01
  Metric: 10         IS RT2.00
  Metric: 0          IP 0.0.0.0 0.0.0.0
  Metric: 10         IP 10.1.1.1 255.255.255.255
  Metric: 10         IP 192.168.1.0 255.255.255.252
```

Redistribution

Cisco IOS Software allows IP routes from other routing sources to be imported into IS-IS. Examples of the external sources are static routes, the Routing Information Protocol (RIP), and the Open Shortest Path First Protocol (OSPF). The IP external reachability TLV is used for adding external routes into the IS-IS domain. Even though RFC 1195 specifies the IP external reachability for only Level 2 LSPs, Cisco IOS Software provides a special capability for using them in Level 1 LSPs, which allows external routes into a Level 1 area.

Most service provider networks use IS-IS as the IGP in large single-area Level 1-only or Level 2-only domains. For those with Level 1-only backbones, the capability to redistribute into Level 1 provides flexibility to import external routes into the IS-IS domain. Even though this behavior is not standardized, it should not pose interoperability issues with other vendor routers because both existing IS-IS standards, ISO 10589 and RFC 1195, require IS-IS implementations to ignore unsupported or unknown optional TLVs encountered while parsing IS-IS packets.

The IOS router-level command **redistribute** enables redistribution. This command takes on other options, such as metric value, metric type, route map, and so on. In the Cisco implementation of IS-IS, CLNS static routes are automatically distributed into IS-IS. However, IP static routes are redistributed only by manual configuration.

When static IP routes need to be redistributed, the **redistribute** command requires the keyword **ip** to go with it, in addition to the other arguments previously mentioned. The metric type for external routes can be either internal or external. Internal metrics are comparable to metrics used for internal routes. External metrics require the I/E bit (bit 7) of the metric field to be set in addition to the actual metric, resulting in higher metric values. In current Cisco IOS Software releases, when using narrow metrics, bit 8 of the default metric field is set for external metrics, resulting in an increase of the metric value by 128.

By default, the internal metric type is assigned if nothing is specified in the configuration. Also, the external routes are added into Level 2 unless Level 1 is explicitly stated in the configuration. Figure 9-10 illustrates basic examples of redistribution in IS-IS. In Example 9-7, only the **ip** keyword is used with the **redistribute** command.

Figure 9-10 *Network topology for IS-IS route redistribution examples.*

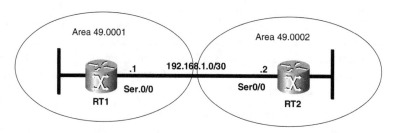

Example 9-7 *Configuring Basic Route Redistribution in IS-IS*

```
RT1#conf t
Enter configuration commands, one per line.  End with CNTL/Z.
RT1(config)#router isis
RT1(config-router)#redistribute static ip
RT1(config-router)#^Z

RT1#show running-config
[snip]
router isis
 redistribute static ip metric 0 metric-type internal level-2
 net 49.0001.0000.0000.0001.00
 !
ip route 172.16.1.0 255.255.255.0 Null0
[snip]
```

The following output from RT1 (see Example 9-8) displays the contents of its own Level 1
and Level 2 LSPs. In Example 9-7, note that *internal* metric type has been assigned by
default and the metric applied is 0. Example 9-8 shows that the external static route has
been added to only the Level 2 LSP.

Example 9-8 *LSP Contents in Case of Simple Redistribution*

```
RT1#show isis database RT1.00-00 detail

IS-IS Level-1 LSP RT1.00-00
LSPID                 LSP Seq Num  LSP Checksum  LSP Holdtime     ATT/P/OL
RT1.00-00           * 0x00000DB0   0xEB25          979              1/0/0

  Area Address: 49.0001
  NLPID:        0xCC
  Hostname: RT1
  IP Address:   10.0.0.1
  Metric: 10        IP 10.1.1.0 255.255.255.0
  Metric: 10        IP 10.0.0.1 255.255.255.255
  Metric: 10        IP 192.168.1.0 255.255.255.252
  Metric: 10        IS RT1.02
```

Example 9-8 *LSP Contents in Case of Simple Redistribution (Continued)*

```
   Metric: 10       IS RT1.01
   Metric: 0        ES RT1
IS-IS Level-2 LSP RT1.00-00
LSPID                    LSP Seq Num  LSP Checksum  LSP Holdtime    ATT/P/OL
RT1.00-00              * 0x00000E3D   0x6F45           977           0/0/0
   Area Address: 49.0001
   NLPID:        0xCC
   Hostname: RT1
   IP Address:   10.0.0.1
   Metric: 10       IS RT1.02
   Metric: 10       IS RT1.01
   Metric: 10       IS RT2.00
   Metric: 0        IP-External 172.16.1.0 255.255.255.0
   Metric: 10       IP 10.1.1.0 255.255.255.0
   Metric: 10       IP 10.0.0.1 255.255.255.255
   Metric: 10       IP 192.168.1.0 255.255.255.252
```

In Example 9-9, the metric type is explicitly set to external in the configuration, but no metric value is applied. As explained previously, the I/E bit needs to then be set for the external metric type, effectively increasing the metric value by 64. However, Cisco IOS Software sets bit 8 of the narrow metric instead of bit 7, consequently adding 128 instead to the original value of 0. The Level 2 LSP displayed in Example 9-9 shows 128 as the metric value for the external route, 172.16.1.0/24.

Example 9-9 *Configuring Redistribution with External Metrics*

```
RT1#conf t
Enter configuration commands, one per line.  End with CNTL/Z.
RT1(config)#router isis
RT1(config-router)#redistribute static ip metric-type external
RT1(config-router)#^Z

RT1#show running-config
[snip]
router isis
 redistribute static ip metric 0 metric-type external level-2
 net  49.0001.0000.0000.0001.00
!
ip route 172.16.1.0 255.255.255.0 null 0
[snip]

RT1#show isis database level-2 RT1.00-00 detail

IS-IS Level-2 LSP RT1.00-00
LSPID                    LSP Seq Num  LSP Checksum  LSP Holdtime    ATT/P/OL
RT1.00-00              * 0x00000E44   0x7FAD        703             0/0/0
   Area Address: 49.0001
   NLPID:        0xCC
```

continues

Example 9-9 *Configuring Redistribution with External Metrics (Continued)*

```
Hostname: RT1
IP Address:    10.0.0.1
Metric: 10         IS RT1.02
Metric: 10         IS RT1.01
Metric: 10         IS RT2.00
Metric: 128        IP-External 172.16.1.0 255.255.255.0
Metric: 10         IP 10.1.1.0 255.255.255.0
Metric: 10         IP 10.0.0.1 255.255.255.255
Metric: 10         IP 192.168.1.0 255.255.255.252
```

The IP routing table output from RT2 shows the external route, 172.16.1.0/24, which was redistributed from a static source into IS-IS on router RT1 (see Example 9-10). The metric entered for this route, 138, is the total of the metric on the outgoing interface from RT2 to RT1 (10) plus the metric of 128 advertised by RT1. Other routes received from RT1 (10.0.0.1/32 and 10.1.1.0/24) are registered with a metric of 20 (10 advertised by RT1 and additional 10 for the metric from RT2 to RT1).

Example 9-10 *Representation of External IS-IS Routes in the IP Routing Table*

```
RT2#show ip route
     172.16.0.0/24 is subnetted, 2 subnets
i L2    172.16.1.0 [115/138] via 192.168.1.1, Serial0/0
     10.0.0.0/8 is variably subnetted, 4 subnets, 2 masks
C        10.0.0.2/32 is directly connected, Loopback0
i L2     10.1.1.0/24 [115/20] via 192.168.1.1, Serial0/0
C        10.2.2.0/24 is directly connected, Ethernet0/0
i L2     10.0.0.1/32 [115/20] via 192.168.1.1, Serial0/0
     192.168.1.0/30 is subnetted, 1 subnets
C        192.168.1.0 is directly connected, Serial0/0
```

The **route-map** option of the **redistribute** command provides more flexibility for configuring redistribution, such as selective importation of external routes into the IS-IS environment, applying special tags, and even setting the metric of redistributed routes. When used for selective importation of routes into IS-IS, route maps provide a filtering effect by controlling which elements from an external source are allowed or denied into IS-IS. Examples 9-11a and 9-11b show redistribution with route maps. In the first example, static routes are redistributed into IS-IS while filtering through the route map TEST. Route map TEST matches the static routes against access list 1, which permits only 172.16.2.0/24 into the IS-IS environment. RT1's LSP is shown from RT2. Also shown is the routing table of RT2.

In Example 9-11b, the route map approach is used to set the metric for routes imported into IS-IS.

Example 9-11a   *Using Route Maps to Filter External Routes*

```
RT1#show running-config
!
router isis
 redistribute static ip metric 0 route-map TEST metric-type external level-2
 net 49.0001.0000.0000.0001.00
!

ip route 172.16.1.0 255.255.255.0 Null0
ip route 172.16.2.0 255.255.255.0 Null0
!
access-list 1 permit 172.16.2.0
!
route-map TEST permit 10
 match ip address 1

RT2#show isis database level-2 RT1.00-00 detail

IS-IS Level-2 LSP RT1.00-00
LSPID                   LSP Seq Num  LSP Checksum  LSP Holdtime    ATT/P/OL
RT1.00-00               0x00000E62   0x8588        1026            0/0/0
   Area Address: 49.0001
   NLPID:       0xCC
   Hostname: RT1
   IP Address:  10.0.0.1
   Metric: 10       IS RT1.02
   Metric: 10       IS RT1.01
   Metric: 10       IS RT2.00
   Metric: 128      IP-External 172.16.2.0 255.255.255.0
   Metric: 10       IP 10.1.1.0 255.255.255.0
   Metric: 10       IP 10.0.0.1 255.255.255.255
   Metric: 10       IP 192.168.1.0 255.255.255.252

RT2#show ip route
     172.16.0.0/24 is subnetted, 1 subnets
i L2    172.16.2.0 [115/138] via 192.168.1.1, Serial0/0
     10.0.0.0/8 is variably subnetted, 4 subnets, 2 masks
C       10.0.0.2/32 is directly connected, Loopback0
i L2    10.1.1.0/24 [115/20] via 192.168.1.1, Serial0/0
C       10.2.2.0/24 is directly connected, Ethernet0/0
i L2    10.0.0.1/32 [115/20] via 192.168.1.1, Serial0/0
     192.168.1.0/30 is subnetted, 1 subnets
C       192.168.1.0 is directly connected, Serial0/0
```

Example 9-11b *Setting the Metric with a Route Map*

```
RT1# show running-config
!
router isis
 redistribute static ip route-map SETMETRIC
 net 49.0001.0000.0000.0001.00
 is-type level-1
 metric-style wide
!
route-map SETMETRIC permit 10
 set metric 1000
 set level level-1

RT1#show isis database detail RT1.00-00 level-1
IS-IS Level-1 LSP RT1.00-00
LSPID                   LSP Seq Num  LSP Checksum  LSP Holdtime      ATT/P/OL
RT1.00-00         * 0x00000E56   0x0A4C             1128                      0/0/0
  Area Address: 49
  NLPID:        0xCC
  Hostname: RT1
  IP Address:   10.0.0.1
  Metric: 10        IS-Extended RT1.02
  Metric: 10        IS-Extended RT1.01
  Metric: 10        IS-Extended RT2.00
  Metric: 1000       IP 10.1.1.0 255.255.255.0
  Metric: 1000       IP 10.0.0.1 255.255.255.255
  Metric: 1000       IP 192.168.1.0 255.255.255.252
```

IP Route Summarization

An IS-IS router can be configured to summarize IP routes into Level 1, Level 2, or both, at the same time, with the following router-level configuration command: **summary-address <prefix> [level-1|level-2|level-1-2]**. By default, summaries go into Level 2 if no routing level option is indicated. An illustration of how summarization is configured and its operation is provided by the series of outputs shown in Example 9-13, which is based on Figure 9-11. The set of outputs in Example 9-12 depict the scenario where summarization is not configured yet on RT1, which has three interfaces: **loopback 0**, **Ethernet0/0**, and **Serial0/0**. Example 9-12 shows the LSP for RT1 as captured on RT2 and the routing table on RT2. The route of interest, 11.1.1.0/24, is not summarized here; however, it is summarized in Example 9-13 into 11.1.0.0/16.

Figure 9-11 *Network diagram for summarization example.*

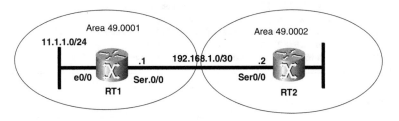

Example 9-12 *IS-IS Configuration Without Summarization*

```
RT1#show running-config

interface loopback 0
 ip address 10.0.0.1 255.255.255.255
 ip router isis
!
interface Ethernet0/0
 ip address 11.1.1.1 255.255.255.0
 ip router isis
!
interface Serial0/0
 ip address 192.168.1.1 255.255.255.252
 ip router isis

router isis
 net 49.0001.0000.0000.0001.00

RT2#show isis database level-2 RT1.00-00
IS-IS Level-2 LSP RT1.00-00
LSPID                  LSP Seq Num  LSP Checksum  LSP Holdtime     ATT/P/OL
RT1.00-00              0x00000E62   0x8588             1026                 0/0/0
  Area Address: 49.0001
  NLPID:        0xCC
  Hostname: RT1
  IP Address:   10.0.0.1
  Metric: 10       IS RT1.02
  Metric: 10       IS RT1.01
  Metric: 10       IS RT2.00
  Metric: 10       IP 11.1.1.0 255.255.255.0
  Metric: 10       IP 10.0.0.1 255.255.255.255
  Metric: 10       IP 192.168.1.0 255.255.255.252

RT2#show ip route
     10.0.0.0/8 is variably subnetted, 3 subnets, 2 masks
C       10.0.0.2/32 is directly connected, Loopback0
C       10.2.2.0/24 is directly connected, Ethernet0/0
```

continues

Example 9-12 *IS-IS Configuration Without Summarization (Continued)*

```
i L2    10.0.0.1/32 [115/20] via 192.168.1.1, Serial0/0
        11.0.0.0/24 is subnetted, 1 subnets
i L2    11.1.1.0 [115/20] via 192.168.1.1, Serial0/0
        192.168.1.0/30 is subnetted, 1 subnets
C       192.168.1.0 is directly connected, Serial0/0
```

Example 9-13 *IS-IS Configuration with Summarization*

```
RT1#show running-config
!
router isis
 summary-address 11.1.0.0 255.255.0.0
 net 49.0001.0000.0000.0001.00

RT2#show isis dat l2 RT1.00-00 det

IS-IS Level-2 LSP RT1.00-00
LSPID                 LSP Seq Num  LSP Checksum  LSP Holdtime    ATT/P/OL
RT1.00-00             0x00000E68   0x0D4A        1193            0/0/0
  Area Address: 49.0001
  NLPID:        0xCC
  Hostname: RT1
  IP Address:   10.0.0.1
  Metric: 10      IS RT1.02
  Metric: 10      IS RT1.01
  Metric: 10      IS RT2.00
  Metric: 10      IP 10.0.0.1 255.255.255.255
  Metric: 10      IP 11.1.0.0 255.255.0.0
  Metric: 10      IP 192.168.1.0 255.255.255.252

RT2#show ip route
      10.0.0.0/8 is variably subnetted, 3 subnets, 2 masks
C       10.0.0.2/32 is directly connected, Loopback0
C       10.2.2.0/24 is directly connected, Ethernet0/0
i L2    10.0.0.1/32 [115/20] via 192.168.1.1, Serial0/0
      11.0.0.0/16 is subnetted, 1 subnets
i L2    11.1.0.0 [115/20] via 192.168.1.1, Serial0/0
      192.168.1.0/30 is subnetted, 1 subnets
C       192.168.1.0 is directly connected, Serial0/0
```

Secondary Addresses, Unnumbered Interfaces, and Tunneling Configurations

This section discusses IS-IS configuration on routers with secondary IP subnets, IP unnumbered interfaces, and IP tunnel interfaces. The outputs in Examples 9-13, 9-14, and 9-15 feature the respective configurations and LSPs of the routers involved.

Configuring IS-IS on Routers with Secondary IP Subnets

No special configuration is required to advertise secondary IP subnets from IS-IS-enabled interfaces by the IS-IS process. Note that the IS-IS configuration does not require IP network statements, and IP subnets on interfaces where IS-IS routing is enabled are automatically added to LSPs by way of IP internal reachability or extended IP reachability TLVs. Example 9-14, which is based on Figure 9-12, shows the configuration of RT1 with a secondary IP subnet. Also shown is the corresponding LSP of RT1.

Figure 9-12 *Network diagram for Example 9-14.*

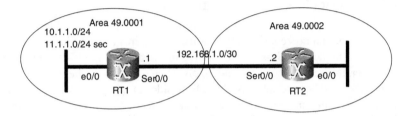

Example 9-14 *Secondary IP Subnet Configuration*

```
RT1 (config-if)#ip address 11.1.1.1 255.255.255.0 secondary
RT1 (config-if)#^Z

RT1#show running-config
[snip]
Interface Ethernet0/0
 Ip address 11.1.1.1 255.255.255.0 secondary
 Ip address 10.1.1.1 255.255.255.0
!
Interface Serial0/0
 Ip address 192.168.1.1 255.255.255.252
 No ip directed-broadcast
 Ip router Isis
!
Router Isis
 Net 49.0001.0000.0000.0001.00
!
[snip]

RT1#show Isis database level-1 RT1.00-00 detail

IS-IS Level-1 LSP RT1.00-00
LSPID                 LSP Esq. Num LSP Checksum LSP Hold time      ATT/P/OL
RT1.00-00           * 0x00000033   0x3CBB       1125               1/0/0
  Area Address: 49.0001
  NLPID:        0xCC
  Hostname: RT1
  IP Address: 10.0.0.1
```

continues

Example 9-14 *Secondary IP Subnet Configuration (Continued)*

```
Metric: 10      IP 10.1.1.0 255.255.255.0
Metric: 10      IP 11.1.1.0 255.255.255.0
Metric: 10      IP 192.168.1.0 255.255.255.252
Metric: 10      IP 10.0.0.1 255.255.255.255
Metric: 10      IS RT1.02
Metric: 10      IS RT1.01
Metric: 0       ES RT1
```

Configuring IS-IS on Routers with Unnumbered Links

IP unnumbered interfaces can be used with IS-IS without any problems. When connected interfaces are numbered, Cisco IOS Software requires that IP addresses on interfaces connected to the same link belong to the same subnet for the IS-IS adjacency to work. However, this requirement does not apply when using unnumbered interfaces on point-to-point links, either in serial or NBMA. Both sides of the point-to-point link need to be configured as unnumbered interfaces for the adjacency to be established. Figure 9-13 shows IS-IS enabled on unnumbered interfaces.

Figure 9-13 *IP unnumbered configuration.*

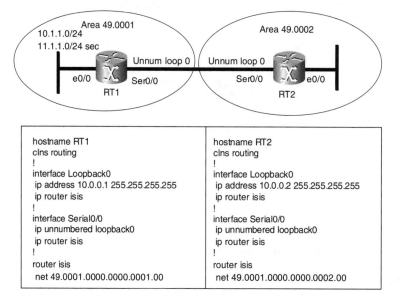

Example 9-15 shows the routing table on RT1 and RT2. Notice that each router shows the borrowed address: at the other router as the next hop of learned routes.

Example 9-15 *The IP Routing Table in an Unnumbered Environment*

```
RT1# show ip route
     10.0.0.0/8 is variably subnetted, 3 subnets, 2 masks
I L2    10.0.0.2/32 [115/20] via 10.0.0.2, Serial0/0
C       10.1.1.0/24 is directly connected, Ethernet0/0
C       10.0.0.1/32 is directly connected, Loopback0
     11.0.0.0/24 is subnetted, 1 subnets
C       11.1.1.0 is directly connected, Ethernet0/0

RT2#show ip route
     10.0.0.0/8 is variably subnetted, 4 subnets, 2 masks
C       10.0.0.2/32 is directly connected, Loopback0
i L2    10.1.1.0/24 [115/20] via 10.0.0.1, Serial0/0
C       10.2.2.0/24 is directly connected, Ethernet0/0
i L2    10.0.0.1/32 [115/20] via 10.0.0.1, Serial0/0
     11.0.0.0/24 is subnetted, 1 subnets
i L2    11.1.1.0 [115/20] via 10.0.0.1, Serial0/0
```

IS-IS over IP Tunnels

Figure 9-14 shows the configuration of IS-IS routing over an IP tunnel. The example is simplistic because in a real scenario, the tunnel would span over a cloud of non-IS-IS routers to connect two IS-IS network segments. In this scenario, IS-IS connectivity is between RT3 and RT4 only over the IP tunnel. This configuration has no relevance to virtual links, which are not supported in current Cisco IOS releases. The **show clns neighbors** outputs in Example 9-16 confirm that the adjacency is formed over the tunnel. The routing tables of RT4 show IS-IS routes are being learned over the tunnel.

Example 9-16 *IP IS-IS over Tunnel Configuration*

```
RT3#show clns neighbors
System Id      Interface   SNPA            State  Holdtime  Type Protocol
RT4            Tu0         192.168.2.2     Up     27        L2   IS-IS

RT4# show clns neighbors
System Id      Interface   SNPA            State  Holdtime  Type Protocol
RT3            Tu0         192.168.2.1     Up     25        L2   IS-IS
RT4#show ip route
     10.0.0.0/8 is variably subnetted, 3 subnets, 2 masks
C       10.1.2.0/24 is directly connected, Ethernet0/0
i L2    10.1.1.0/24 [115/20] via 10.0.0.3, Tunnel0
C       10.0.0.4/32 is directly connected, Loopback0
     11.0.0.0/24 is subnetted, 1 subnets
i L2    11.1.1.0 [115/30] via 10.0.0.3, Tunnel0
     192.168.2.0/30 is subnetted, 1 subnets
C       192.168.2.0 is directly connected, Serial0/0
```

Figure 9-14 *IS-IS over IP tunnel configuration.*

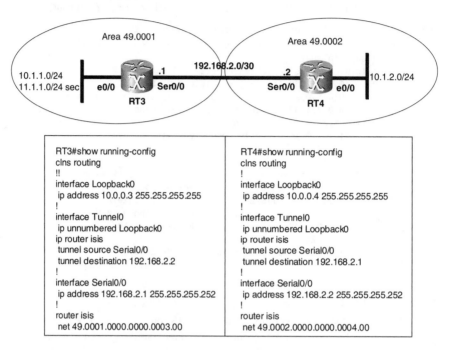

Authentication

ISO 10589 and RFC 1195 specify only simple plain-text passwords for authentication of IS-IS packets. A more recent RFC draft (IS-IS HMAC-MD5 Authentication, draft-ietf-isis-hmac-00.txt) proposes a mechanism for using the HMAC-MD5 authentication algorithm to provide a more sophisticated authentication scheme for IS-IS. Current Cisco IOS Software supports only the simple text-based passwords.

As mentioned in Chapter 3, "Integrated IS-IS Routing Protocol Concepts," IS-IS packets are not encapsulated in Layer 3 packets (IP or CLNP) as is the case of other IP routing protocols. Encapsulation over Layer 2 provides IS-IS some security advantages, in that the IS-IS process cannot be inundated by IP attacks from remote. It would require physical access to the IS-IS network to attempt an attack on the IS-IS processes running on the routers. This is certainly considered a security advantage.

Clear-text IS-IS authentication can be configured in the following three ways:

- A password can be assigned to an interface for Level 1 or Level 2 authentication. By default, the password is applied to Level 1 if Level 2 is not specified. The password is inserted in all IS-IS packets, IIHs, LSPs, CSNPs, and PSNPs for the specified level. The password is configured with the interface-level command **isis password <string>,** where **string** is the clear-text password.

- Area-level authentication can be configured with the router-level command **area-password <string>**. This causes insertion of the password into all Level 1 LSPs, CSNPs, and PSNPs.

- Domain-wide authentication is enforced by inserting passwords in Level 2 LSPs, CSNPs, and PSNPs. It is enabled with the command **domain-password <string>**.

Example 9-17, which is based on Figure 9-15, shows a configuration example and illustrates the operation of per-interface or link authentication in IS-IS. In example 9-16, a password is configured on only one side of the serial link, on RT1. Observe how the adjacency is affected, as shown in the **show clns neighbor** output.

Figure 9-15 *Network diagram for Examples 9-16 and 9-17.*

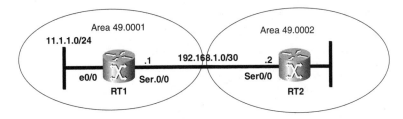

Example 9-17 *Enabling IS-IS Authentication on an Interface*

```
RT1#configure terminal
Enter configuration commands, one per line.  End with CNTL/Z.
RT1(config)#int s0/0
RT1(config-if)#isis password cisco level-2
RT1(config-if)#^Z

RT1#show clns neighbor
System Id       Interface    SNPA              State  Holdtime  Type Protocol
RT2             Se0/0        *HDLC*            Up     278            IS   ES-IS

RT2#show clns neighbor
System Id       Interface    SNPA            State  Holdtime   Type Protocol
RT1             Se0/0        *HDLC*          Init   21         L2   IS-IS
```

The outputs of the **show clns neighbor** command display the adjacency status on both routers after the password is configured on only RT1, with no matching password on router RT2. This information indicates that RT1 completely ignores the IIHs of RT2 because they could not be authenticated. RT1, however, still discovers ES-IS adjacency with RT2 by means of ISHs exchanged between them. On the other hand, RT2 is not configured for authentication, so it accepts and processes the IIHs from RT1 and then moves the status of the adjacency to *Init*. The adjacency remains in Init state because RT2 never receives an IIH from RT1 recognizing RT2 as an IS neighbor, to complete the three-way adjacency formation process.

The following output of **debug isis adj-packets** on RT1 demonstrates the authentication process between RT1 and RT2 (see Example 9-18). Configuring a password on RT2 to match the password on RT1 results in successful authentication and subsequent completion of the three-way handshake process.

Example 9-18 *Debugging Authentication Failures*

```
RT1# debug isis adj-packets
*Apr 23 04:25:36: ISIS-Adj: Rec serial IIH from *HDLC* (Serial0/0), cir type L1L2,
cir id 00, length 1499
*Apr 23 04:25:36: ISIS-Adj: Authentication failed
*Apr 23 04:25:42: ISIS-Adj: Sending serial IIH on Serial0/0, length 1499
*Apr 23 04:25:46: ISIS-Adj: Rec serial IIH from *HDLC* (Serial0/0), cir type L1L2,
cir id 00, length 1499
*Apr 23 04:25:46: ISIS-Adj: Authentication failed
*Apr 23 04:25:50: ISIS-Adj: Sending serial IIH on Serial0/0, length 1499
.
RT2#conf t
Enter configuration commands, one per line.  End with CNTL/Z.
RT2(config)#int s0/0
RT2(config-if)#isis password cisco
RT2(config-if)#^Z

RT2#show clns neighbor
System Id     Interface   SNPA          State  Holdtime  Type Protocol
RT1             Se0/0      *HDLC*        Up       21           L2   IS-IS
```

Domain-Wide Prefix Distribution (L2 to L1 Route Leaking)

RFC 2966 specifies a mechanism for domain-wide prefix distribution in an IS-IS network, effectively removing the stub-only capability specified by ISO 10589 for Level 1 areas. This feature is available in current Cisco IOS Software and it is known as IS-IS *route leaking*. The objective of route leaking is to enable interarea routes to be leaked into IS-IS Level 1 areas so that Level 1 routers have more information to make optimal interarea routing decisions. Without distributing interarea routes into Level 1, IS-IS areas function as stubs, and Level 1 routers forward traffic to destinations in other areas through the nearest Level 1-2 router. The Cisco IOS configuration for route leaking uses the router-level **redistribute** command with a newly defined option.

No special TLVs are required to advertise interarea routes from Level 2 into Level 1. The capability just allows Level 2 routes carried in TLVs 128, 130, and 135 to be injected into the various Level 1 areas in the domain. RFC 2966 specifies a procedure to prevent route feedback, which ensures that routes advertised into Level 1 from Level 2 are not advertised back into Level 2. TLV 135 features a dedicated up/down (U/D) bit (see Figure 9-16), which is set when a route is advertised from Level 2 into Level 1. RFC 2966 proposes using bit 8 in the default metric field of TLV 128 and 130 as the up/down bit to protect against routing loops when route leaking is enabled. Prefixes with the U/D bit set are never propagated from Level 1 to Level 2.

Because Cisco IOS Software sets bit 8 for external metrics when routes for external sources are advertised into IS-IS, using the same bit for route leaking might result in conflicting situations. Also note that only IS-IS routes that are Level 2 routes in the routing table are "leaked" into Level 1. Remember the following when configuring route leaking in Cisco-based IS-IS environments:

- Use wide metrics by configuring **metric-style wide** under the IS-IS router process. This allows TLV 135 to be used for carrying IP reachability information. TLV 135 has a dedicated up/down (U/D) bit.

- Do not enable the external metric type when redistributing routes from external sources into ISIS.

The following two different command-line syntaxes are supported in Cisco IOS Software for configuring route leaking. The second variant of the command is deprecated:

- 12.1, 12.0S, and 12.0ST Releases:

  ```
  redistribute isis ip level-2 into level-1 distribute-list <acl>
  ```

- 12.0S and 12.0ST Releases:

  ```
  advertise ip L2-into-L1 <acl>
  ```

Also, the IP prefixes need to be present in the routing table as the IS-IS Level 2 route for them to be advertised into Level 1.

Figure 9-16 *Up/Down (U/D) bit in IP reachability TLVs.*

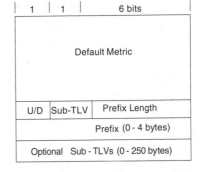

a) TLV Types 128/130   b) TLV Type 135

In the example shown in Figure 9-17, RT2 advertises 12.1.1.0/24 to RT1 through Level 2. As depicted in the configuration shown in Example 9-19, RT1 then summarizes 12.1.1.0/24 into 12.0.0.0/8 and then "leaks" it into Level 1. The route is advertised into Level 1 by adding the summary prefix to the locally generated Level 1 LSP and flooding it into area 49.0001. Example 9-19 also shows the Level 1 LSP of RT1 displayed in detail from RT5.

Figure 9-17 *Diagram for the Level 2 to Level 1 route leaking example.*

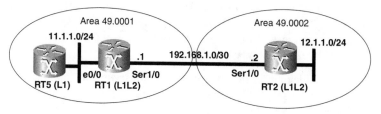

Example 9-19 *Route Leaking Example*

```
RT1#
interface Ethernet0/0
 ip address 11.1.1.1 255.255.255.0
 ip router isis
!
interface Serial0/0
 ip address 192.168.1.1 255.255.255.252
 ip router isis
!
router isis
 summary-address 12.0.0.0 255.0.0.0 level-1
 redistribute isis ip level-2 into level-1
 net 49.0001.0000.0000.0001.00


RT5#show isis data level-1 detail RT1.00-00

IS-IS Level-1 LSP RT1.00-00
LSPID                 LSP Seq Num  LSP Checksum  LSP Holdtime   ATT/P/OL
RT1.00-00             0x000000F7   0xF8AA        518            1/0/0
  Area Address: 49.0001
  NLPID:        0xCC
  Hostname: RT1
  IP Address:   10.1.1.1
  Metric: 10      IS RT1.02
  Metric: 10      IS RT1.01
  Metric: 10      IS RT5.00
  Metric: 10      IP 10.1.1.1 255.255.255.255
  Metric: 10      IP 11.1.1.0 255.255.255.0
  Metric: 10      IP 192.168.1.0 255.255.255.252
  Metric: 20      IP-Interarea  12.0.0.0 255.0.0.0
```

Multi-Area Configuration

Prior to the availability of IS-IS multi-area capability in Cisco IOS releases, each IS-IS router could be in only a single area (even when configured with multiple area IDs for multihoming). As mentioned in Chapter 4, "Addressing in Integrated IS-IS," in multihoming scenarios, the multiple areas configured are effectively merged into a single area; also, only one IS-IS process can be configured per router.

Multi-area support allows a single router to participate in up to 29 independent Level 1 areas with one of them doubling as Level 2 if necessary. The feature is designed primarily for telecommunications management networks that use IS-IS for routing. IS-IS multi-area support provides the flexibility to have one router support multiple areas in the management network in a cost-effective manner.

In essence, this feature allows up to 29 IS-IS processes to be configured on a single router, one of which can be Level 1-2 and the remainder only Level 1. Note, however, the following restrictions:

- Only one of the processes can support Level 2 interarea routing.
- Each interface cannot be in more than one area (Level 1). Subinterfaces are treated the same as regular interfaces.
- Separate areas in the same router must have unique area IDs, and individual routers in an area must have unique system IDs.
- Redistribution between processes is not allowed; however, external routing sources can be redistributed into each area independently.
- IS-IS multihoming can be used to merge multiple areas by sharing the area IDs of the areas being merged under each participating IS-IS process.

Figure 9-18 shows a multi-area scenario. In the corresponding Cisco IOS configuration output for RT1 shown in Example 9-20, three processes are running, tagged Core (Level 1-2), Access-2 (Level 1), and Access-3 (Level 1). Each process has a different area ID in its NSAP address, but they all share the same system ID (0000.0000.0001). The multi-area functionality is borrowed from the OSPF protocol and presents significant advantages for efficient network design. For more information, see the *Introduction and Configuration Guide* on IS-IS multi-area support.

Figure 9-18   *Diagram for the multi-area configuration example.*

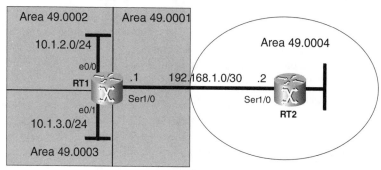

Example 9-20 *Multi-Area Configuration Example*

```
RT1#
interface Serial1/0
 ip address 192.169.1.1 255.255.255.0
 ip router isis Core

interface Ethernet0/0
 ip address 11.1.2.1 255.255.255.0
 ip router isis Access-2
interface Ethernet0/1
 ip address 11.1.3.1 255.255.255.0
 ip router isis Access-3

router isis CORE
 net 49.0001.0000.0000.0001.00
 !
router isis Access-2
 net 49.0002.0000.0000.0001.00
 is-type level-1
 !
router isis Access-3
 net 49.0003.0000.0000.0001.00
 is-type level-1
```

Configuring IS-IS for Optimized Performance

The previous sections discuss rudimentary IS-IS configuration for various scenarios, using the two basic steps required to enable IS-IS on Cisco routes: configuring the routing process and enabling IS-IS routing on interfaces. Cisco IOS Software provides numerous commands for enabling various capabilities of the IS-IS protocol and optimizing its performance. In most cases, the configuration options enabled are targeted at improving efficiency of the data-forwarding process and achieving network design objectives, such as routing stability and fast convergence. The command options can be enabled globally under the configuration of the IS-IS routing process (router-level configuration) or for specific interfaces (interface-level configuration). As you might be aware by now, the two categories of IS-IS configuration commands are interface-level commands and router-level commands.

This section discusses some commonly used (although nonessential) IS-IS commands. Example 9-21, which shows the typical configuration of an Internet router, provides the basis for discussions in this section. This configuration is for illustrative purposes only.

Example 9-21 *Internet Router IS-IS Configuration*

```
RT1#show running-config
!
clns routing
!
interface Loopback0
 ip address 172.168.123.1 255.255.255.255
 no ip directed-broadcast
!
interface Serial0/0
 ip unnumbered Loopback0
 no ip directed-broadcast
 ip router isis
 isis metric 15 level-2
 isis password cisco level-2
 isis hello-multiplier 12 level-2
 isis hello-interval 5 level-2
!
router isis
 summary-address 10.1.0.0 255.255.0.0
 passive-interface Loopback0
 net 49.0001.0002.0003.0004.0005.0006.00
 is-type level-2-only
 metric-style wide
 spf-interval 30
 no hello padding
 log-adjacency-changes
!
ip classless
!
end
```

The configuration in Example 9-21 features the following additional interface-level configuration commands:

- **isis metric**
- **isis password**
- **isis hello-interval**
- **isis hello-multiplier**

Example 9-21 also shows the following nonessential router-level commands:

- **is-type**
- **metric-style**
- **spf-interval**
- **ignore-lsp-errors**
- **no hello padding**
- **log-adjacency-changes**
- **passive-interface**
- **summary-address**

All the commands in the preceding two lists are not required to enable IS-IS. However, they are added to optimize operational efficiencies of the protocol and network design. These commands are discussed further in the following sections. The **isis password** and **summary-address** commands are covered earlier in this chapter, in the sections on authentication and summarization, respectively.

isis hello-interval and isis hello-multiplier Commands

By default, the interval between hello packets is 10 seconds, with some jittering applied to prevent network-wide synchronization. The corresponding default for the **hello multiplier** is 3. The product of these two parameters gives the holdtime for the adjacency. The holdtime is the interval after which if a hello packet has not been received from the neighbor, it will be declared "dead" and the adjacency torn down. The holdtime has a direct bearing on the speed of convergence. The holdtime can be modified by adjusting the **hello interval** and **hello multiplier**, as needed, to provide the desired effect on network stability and convergence. The holdtime value cannot be modified directly on Cisco routers. In the sample configuration shown in Example 9-21, the hello interval has been reduced to 5 and the multiplier increased to 12, resulting in a holdtime of 60 seconds rather than the 30-second default value.

isis metric and metric-style Commands

You can use the **isis metric** command to modify the default metric value for Level 1 or Level 2 separately. In both situations, the default value is 10. In the configuration shown in Example 9-21, the metric is changed to 15 for only Level 2. Notice that this router would participate only in Level 2 routing on all its active IS-IS interfaces because of the global, router-level **is-type level-2-only** command.

The **metric-style** command is a recent introduction based on the IS-IS enhancements in the IETF (IS-IS extensions for Traffic Engineering, draft-ietf-isis-traffic-02.txt), specifically to facilitate MPLS traffic engineering. The following are the current argument options for this command:

- **narrow**—Bases interpretation of the metric field in TLVs 2, 128, and 130 on ISO 10589 and RFC 1195. The router is limited to a maximum metric of 63 per interface and 1023 for an entire path.

- **transition**—Allows routers to send and receive both old and new metric formats.

- **wide**—Allows routers to use a new metric format to support large metric values.

The default is **metric-style narrow**. The **wide** option provides a lot of flexibility for metric assignment in IP networking environments. The transition option is recommended only for migration purposes and carries some overhead with it. Therefore, network operators need to avoid enabling transition mode for long-term operation. This is further discussed in Chapter 7, "General Network Design Issues," and a migration scenario is provided in Chapter 8.

isis-type Command

The **isis-type** command determines the mode of operation of all active IS-IS-enabled interfaces on a Cisco router. The argument options for this command are as follows:

- **level-1-2**—This is the default mode of operation. In this mode, the router is capable of both Level 1 and Level 2 functionality and can form either type of adjacencies with neighboring IS-IS routers.

- **level-1**—In this mode, the router can form only Level 1 adjacencies on all interface on which IS-IS is enabled. A router operating in this mode forwards all packets to other areas in the domain to the nearest Level 1-2 router in the local area.

- **level-2-only**—In this mode, the router can participate only in Level 2 routing. Routers providing extensions to the IS-IS Level 2 backbone that do not connect to any Level 1 domains could be configured to operate in this mode to conserve system resources. Some ISP networks using IS-IS as the IGP employ flat network designs with all the IS-IS routers as Level 2 only. This allows for easy migration to a hierarchical design; you can just migrate the edge to different areas and leave the core intact.

spf-interval Command

In default operation mode, the IS-IS SPF process on Cisco routers runs periodically, no more frequently than every 5 seconds. That is, by default, the normal minimum interval between two consecutive SPF calculations is 5 seconds. However, certain network changes, such as link failures, can trigger immediate runs. The SPF process might be costly in terms of CPU cycles depending on the size of the network (that is, the number of nodes, links, and prefixes involved).

The **spf-interval** command specifies the interval between SPF calculation events. A smaller interval might result in faster convergence but possibly affect the stability of the network. Typically, larger interval values are used only in stable network environments.

For example, the configuration shown in Example 9-21 is optimized for a stable environment, which is less prone to network churn; therefore, the SPF process is set to run no more frequently than every 30 seconds.

Recent IS-IS enhancements in IOS include new options for the **spf-interval** command. This change allows aggressive low intervals to be specified and provides for backoff to more conservative values when changes in the network become rampant. The backoff mechanism is also implemented for partial route calculations and also generation of LSPs. Exponential backoff is discussed in detail in Chapter 7.

The **show isis spf-log** command is a related command that enables you to view an SPF activity log. A sample output of the **show isis spf-log** command is shown in Example 9-22. The output shows various triggers that caused the running of the SPF process on this router. PERIODIC indicates periodic runs of the SPF process, whereas TLVCONTENT implies that the SPF calculation was triggered by a change in the contents of the TLV field of the LSP owned by the listed router.

Example 9-22 show isis spf-log *Command Output*

```
RT1#show isis spf-log

Level 2 SPF Log
When        Duration  Nodes  Count   Last Trigger LSP   Triggers
02:38:48    0         5      3       RT3.00-00          NEWADJ TLVCONTENT
02:31:35    0         5      1                          PERIODIC
02:22:30    0         5      2       RT1.00-00          NEWMETRIC TLVCONTENT
02:16:36    0         2      4       RT1.02-00          PERIODIC TLVSTYLE TLVCODE
02:11:27    0         2      4       RT1.00-00          NEWADJ DELADJTLVCONTENT
02:08:10    0         2      2       RT1.00-00          DELADJ TLVCONTENT
02:01:36    0         2      1                          PERIODIC
01:46:36    0         2      1                          PERIODIC
01:31:36    0         2      1                          PERIODIC
```

The following list explains the triggers shown in Example 9-22:

- **PERIODIC**—Periodic SPF process (LSPDB refresh interval)
- **NEWSYSID**—New system ID assigned
- **NEWLEVEL**—IS-IS process level changed
- **NEWMETRIC**—New metric assigned to an interface
- **TLVCODE**—LSP with a new TLV code field received

- **TLVCONTENT**—LSP with changed TLV contents received
- **NEWADJ**—New neighbor adjacency up
- **DELADJ**—Adjacency deletion

passive-interface Command

The objective of the **passive interface** command is to prevent protocol activity over a specific interface. This is a generic command applicable to all routing protocols supported in Cisco IOS Software. When configured under the IS-IS process, the **passive-interface** command prevents transmission of IIHs over the specific interface and as a result prevents formation of IS-IS adjacency over that interface. Typically, the **passive-interface** command is used when there is a need to advertise the prefix from a network interface without forming adjacencies over that interface. In Cisco IOS Software, specifying an IS-IS interface as passive removes the IS-IS configuration from that interface. The IP subnet configured on the interface is still advertised into the IS-IS environment.

The log-adjacency-changes, ignore-lsp-errors, and no hello padding Commands

The **log-adjacency-changes** command enables logging of IS-IS adjacency changes. You can use this to generate SYSLOG traps for network operations and management purposes. The logged information is also useful for troubleshooting purposes. Examples of the messages logged are shown in Example 9-23.

Example 9-23 *Tracking Adjacency Changes*

```
RT1#show log
  %CLNS-5-ADJCHANGE: ISIS: Adjacency to 0000.0000.0001 (ethernet 0)

  %CLNS-5-ADJCHANGE: ISIS: Adjacency to 0000.0000.0002 (ethernet 0)
```

The **ignore-lsp-errors** command is used in network environments prone to packet corruption. The command allows the router to ignore any corrupt LSP that would normally have triggered a purge action. A router purging another's LSP is the correct behavior of the protocol but could easily degenerate into an adverse network situation (referred to as *LSP packet corruption storms*). In this situation, a router's LSPs are repeatedly corrupted by the transport medium and are purged by other systems in the network, resulting in an SPF churn that could potentially lead to a network meltdown.

The **no hello padding** command is designed to prevent network bandwidth from being wasted by the periodic exchange of hellos over interfaces with large message transmission unit (MTU) sizes. The IS-IS protocol requires hellos to be padded to the larger of the MTU or LSP buffer size.

This would technically guarantee that systems forming adjacencies over a link can receive and process each others LSPs and other IS-IS packets over the link. However, in practice, the same MTU size is used on the interfaces of the connecting routers; therefore, padding hello packets is irrelevant in most cases. The command disables the default behavior, resulting in significant bandwidth savings, especially in situations where small hello intervals have been configured and the MTU size is reasonably large.

A global router-level variant of this command provides options to selectively disable padding on all IS-IS interfaces or all point-to-point interfaces or all multipoint interfaces (see Example 9-24). You can use an interface-level variant of the command for a single interface application, as shown in Example 9-25.

Example 9-24 *Disabling Hello Padding on Multiple Interfaces*

```
RTA(config)#router isis
RTA(config-router)#no hello padding ?
        multipoint      Pad LAN hello PDUs
        point-to-point  Pad point-to-point hello PDUs
```

Example 9-25 *Disabling Hello Padding on an Interface*

```
RTA(config)#int pos 2/0
              Rtr-A(config-if)#no isis hello padding
```

Summary

This chapter focuses on the configuration of the IS-IS routing protocol on Cisco routers. The early sections of this chapter look at enabling IS-IS routing on different network transport media types, specifically point-to-point, broadcast, and nonbroadcast multiaccess media. Specific media-dependent configurations are provided, covering point-to-point serial, ATM point-to-point, ATM multipoint subinterfaces, Frame Relay point-to-point, Frame Relay multipoint, and ISDN multipoint (BRI interface).

The chapter also explains the IS-IS configuration procedure. This involves a two-step process: configuring the IS-IS routing process and enabling IS-IS routing of the appropriate interfaces. This chapter also discusses how to enable IS-IS capabilities. Redistribution, summarization, and origination of a default route into the IS-IS environment are discussed and configuration examples are provided. Some time is spent discussing configuration of IS-IS over IP unnumbered interfaces, IP tunnels, and the use of secondary addresses.

IS-IS was originally designed to support a two-layer hierarchy with an addressing scheme that puts a whole router in one area. In the two-level hierarchy scheme, multiple stub Level 1 areas interconnect over a backbone. The stub Level 1 areas are interconnected by the Level 2 backbone. In this scheme, Level 1-only routers point default routes to Level 1-2 routers to route to other areas. This could potentially result in suboptimal routing. However, recent protocol enhancements allow leaking of interarea routes into Level 1, thus optimizing path selection for interarea destinations. This chapter also shows you how to configure the Level 2 to Level 1 route leaking capability.

Another recently added capability allows for multi-area support on a single router. The section on IS-IS multi-area support addresses the configuration requirements for this functionality.

The later sections of this chapter review a typical configuration of an IS-IS router in a service provider network and look at the various commands typically employed to optimize operation of the IS-IS process. In these sections, it is noted that the IOS command-line interface supports numerous commands that can be used to achieve network design objectives, such as scalability, fast convergence, and network stability.

This chapter is dedicated to getting the reader familiar with Cisco IOS configuration of the IS-IS protocol and discusses some "best practices" configuration options.

References

http://www.cisco.com/univercd/cc/td/doc/product/software/ios120/12cgcr/np1_c/1cprt1/1 cisis.htm#4552.

RFC 2966, "Domain-wide Prefix Distribution with Two-Level IS-IS." Li, Tony, Przygienda, Tony, Smit, Henk.

draft-ietf-isis-hmac-00.txt: IS-IS HMAC-MD5 Authentication.

draft-ietf-isis-traffic-02.txt: IS-IS extensions for Traffic Engineering.

CHAPTER 10

Troubleshooting the IS-IS Routing Protocol

This chapter covers common problems that might result in faulty operation of the IS-IS protocol, and discusses procedures to troubleshoot them. Most of the time, faulty operation results from misconfigurations, which could be easily discerned by carefully reviewing configurations of the routers involved and the output of basic CLNS- and IS-IS-related **show** commands. However, some issues might present more of a challenge. Such issues might require advanced knowledge of the IS-IS protocol architecture and capabilities, evaluation of packet captures, and complicated network-wide debugging procedures.

To quickly evaluate and resolve problems, in every case, you need a solid technical understanding of the IS-IS protocol. In addition, you need to know how to configure, debug, and interpret the various associated **show** commands available in Cisco IOS Software. The Cisco implementation of the IS-IS protocol adds many nonstandardized features and associated configuration commands, commonly referred to as *knobs*.

This chapter discusses functional problems and includes practical examples that show you how to troubleshoot IS-IS problems, from the very basic to the more advanced. The Cisco Technical Assistance Center (TAC) is the authoritative resource for service-impacting issues and outages that require immediate attention. Experience shows, however, that even when an issue is referred to the Cisco TAC, problems can be resolved faster if the person calling in the case has a good knowledge of the protocol, can describe the symptoms adequately, and can work collaboratively with the support engineer.

Link-state routing protocols, such as OSPF and IS-IS, are generally more complicated to troubleshoot than are distance-vector protocols. Compared to OSPF, however, IS-IS seems to be easier to work with by far. But this simplicity is not obvious because the operation of Integrated IS-IS in IP environments still occurs within the framework of the Connectionless Network Protocol (CLNP). This requires knowledge of CLNP, including its node-based addressing scheme, which differs from the link-based addressing scheme used in IP. Chapter 5, "The IS-IS Link-State Database," provides detailed insight into CLNP addressing and helps demystify the subject.

Before delving into the actual troubleshooting methodology, it might be useful to review some Cisco IOS **show** commands commonly used for troubleshooting IS-IS routing problems. The following is a short list of important commands:

- **show clns neighbor**—Enables you to verify the status of adjacencies

- **show clns interface**—Enables you to verify the configuration of an active CLNS interface

- **show isis database**—Enables you to check for the presence of all expected LSPs

- **show isis spf-log**—Enables you to check how frequently the SPF process is being run and the associated triggers

Some of these commands are discussed in Chapter 9, "Configuring IS-IS for IP Routing on Cisco Routers." The next section provides a detailed explanation of these key troubleshooting and monitoring commands as a prelude to the ensuing discussions on troubleshooting methodology. For example, the **show isis database** command enables you to check both the Level 1 and Level 2 databases. If you do not understand the output, however, the command is not a useful troubleshooting tool. An important point is that an IS-IS router uses only a single LSP for each level of routing. An LSP might be fragmented if there are too many TLVs to be contained in its maximum size of 1492 bytes. In most cases, however, each router generates just a single LSP for Level 1 or Level 2 routing. Because you have to deal with a single LSP, IS-IS appears to be much easier to troubleshoot than OSPF. That said, it is still important to understand all the information in an LSP.

When troubleshooting complicated problems, you might have to debug IS-IS activities on the router. The following list identifies useful IS-IS protocol debugging commands. Although debugging is generally CPU-intensive, these commands do not overburden the processor. However, always assess the routers situation before enabling any of these commands. You should enable only a single debugging command at a time, and you should capture the console screen for later review:

- **debug isis adj-packets**

- **debug isis update-packets**

- **debug spf-events**

The **log-adjacency-changes** and **ignore-lsp-errors** router-level configuration commands generate status-logging information that can prove useful in troubleshooting. The router logs can be exported to a SYSLOG server and used for management and troubleshooting purposes.

Interpreting the Output of Key IS-IS show Commands

This section details the output of some of the key troubleshooting commands discussed in the previous section. The Cisco IOS **show** commands provide information about activities occurring on the router and serve as excellent tools for diagnosing problems.

The output of the following commands are examined based on the topology and configuration of the routers in Figure 10-1:

- **show clns**
- **show clns protocol**
- **show clns neighbors**
- **show clns interface**
- **show isis database**
- **show isis topology**
- **show isis spf-log**

Figure 10-1 shows a simple topology of an IS-IS domain consisting of two areas (49.0001 and 49.0002), each with two routers. This topology provides practical significance to the output of the commands that will be studied. The router configurations are provided as well.

Figure 10-1   *Simple IS-IS domain topology.*

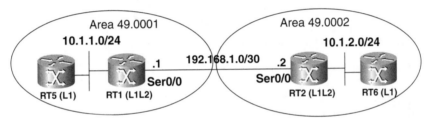

Example 10-1 *Router Configurations in Simple IS-IS Network (refer to Figure 10-1)*

```
RT5

interface Loopback0
 ip address 11.1.1.5 255.255.255.255
!
interface Ethernet0/0
 ip address 10.1.1.5 255.255.255.0
 ip router isis
!
router isis
 passive-interface Loopback0
 net 49.0001.0000.0000.0005.00
 is-type level-1
 metric-style wide
```

continues

Example 10-1 *Router Configurations in Simple IS-IS Network (refer to Figure 10-1) (Continued)*

```
RT1

interface Loopback0
 ip address 11.1.1.1 255.255.255.255
!
interface Ethernet0/0
 ip address 10.1.1.1 255.255.255.0
 ip router isis
!
interface Serial0/0
 ip address 192.168.1.1 255.255.255.252
 ip router isis
!
router isis
 passive-interface Loopback0
 net 49.0001.0000.0000.0001.00
 metric-style wide
 log-adjacency-changes

RT2

interface Loopback0
 ip address 11.1.1.2 255.255.255.255
!
interface Ethernet0/0
 ip address 10.1.2.1 255.255.255.0
 ip router isis
!
interface Serial0/0
 ip address 192.168.1.2 255.255.255.252
 ip router isis
!
router isis
 passive-interface Loopback0
 net 49.0002.0000.0000.0002.00
 metric-style wide
 log-adjacency-changes

RT6
interface Loopback0
 ip address 11.1.1.6 255.255.255.255
!
interface Ethernet0/0
 ip address 10.1.2.6 255.255.255.0
 ip router isis
!
router isis
 passive-interface Loopback0
 net 49.0002.0000.0000.0006.00
 is-type level-1
 metric-style wide
```

show clns

The IS-IS routing protocol operates within the CLNP framework even when used in pure IP environments. Therefore, to verify the operation of IS-IS routers or troubleshoot problems, often you must use IOS CLNP-related commands. The **show clns** command, which is the base of the CLNP-related **show** commands, supports several arguments that enable you to query specific attributes and status information on an IS-IS router about the ISO CLNS environment. The following are examples of these command arguments:

- **interface**—Provides CLNP interface status and configuration
- **is-neighbors**—Provides information about router adjacencies
- **neighbors**—Provides information about router and end-system adjacencies
- **protocol**—Provides information about the routing process for the CLNP protocol
- **route**—Displays routing information for CLNP prefixes
- **traffic**—Displays CLNP statistics

The output of **show clns** with some of the preceding arguments is discussed in detail later in this section. Example 10-2 shows the output of **show clns** without any arguments as issued on RT1 and RT2. The command displays concise information regarding the mode of operation and the NSAP address of an IS-IS router. The area prefix in the NSAP address is also delineated. For example, output from RT1 shows RT1 is a Level 1-2 router with 49.0001.0000.0000.0001.00 as the NSAP and 49.0001 as the area ID. The output also shows that CLNS forwarding, which in this case implies IS-IS routing, is enabled on two interfaces. This is confirmed from the configuration of RT1 in Example 10-1, which shows IS-IS is enabled on Serial0/0 and Ethernet0/0.

Example 10-2 show clns *Command Output*

```
RT1#show clns
Global CLNS Information:
  2 Interfaces Enabled for CLNS
  NET: 49.0001.0000.0000.0001.00
  Configuration Timer: 60, Default Holding Timer: 300, Packet Lifetime 64
  ERPDU's requested on locally generated packets
  Intermediate system operation enabled (forwarding allowed)
  IS-IS level-1-2 Router:
    Routing for Area: 49.0001

RT2#show clns
Global CLNS Information:
  2 Interfaces Enabled for CLNS
  NET: 49.0002.0000.0000.0002.00
  Configuration Timer: 60, Default Holding Timer: 300, Packet Lifetime 64
  ERPDU's requested on locally generated packets
  Intermediate system operation enabled (forwarding allowed)
  IS-IS level-1-2 Router:
    Routing for Area: 49.0002
```

The **show clns** command proves useful for troubleshooting problems that relate to adjacency formation. For example, it enables you to quickly verify whether a router is configured for the appropriate area. The command provides a concise snapshot of the IS-IS configuration and key parameters. Configuration timer information shown in this output pertains to both ESHs and ISHs. ESHs are related to ES-IS, which is an auxiliary protocol that supports the ISO CLNS environment.

show clns protocol

Current Cisco IOS releases offers a **show <layer 3> protocol** command for any of the Layer 3 protocols supported on Cisco routers. The **show ip protocol** command is popular and used frequently to troubleshoot IP routing problems. The **show clns protocol** command has similar importance and displays similar information for the CLNS environment. Example 10-3 shows the output of the familiar **show ip protocol** command for purposes of comparison with the output of the **show clns protocol** command shown in Example 10-3.

The **show ip protocol** command shows IP routing protocols enabled on the router and also the neighbor routers that have supplied routing information (for IS-IS in this case). The administrative distances associated with each neighbor and the last time it provided an update are also shown. As shown in Figure 10-1, the neighbors of RT1 are RT5 and RT2. Their loopback addresses to identify them.

Example 10-3 **show ip protocol** *Command Output*

```
RT1#show ip protocol
Routing Protocol is "isis"
  Invalid after 0 seconds, hold down 0, flushed after 0
  Outgoing update filter list for all interfaces is
  Incoming update filter list for all interfaces is
  Redistributing: isis
  Address Summarization:
    None
  Routing for Networks:
    Ethernet0/0
    Serial0/0
  Passive Interface(s):
    Loopback0
  Routing Information Sources:
    Gateway         Distance        Last Update
    11.1.1.2             115        00:02:25
    11.1.1.5             115        00:02:15
```

Although similar to the IP equivalent, the output of the **show clns protocol** command features slightly different content. The output in Example 10-4 shows that IS-IS is enabled without any tag associated with the IS-IS process. The mode of operation, the system ID, and the area prefixes are shown. The output also shows the system ID 0000.0000.0001.00

with the pseudonode number (00) appended. Unlike the **show clns** command, the **show clns protocol** command is explicit about which interfaces are enabled for IS-IS routing (in this case Serial0/0 and Ethernet0/0). It also shows that IS-IS is configured for IP only on these interfaces. The administrative distance of 110 pertains to IS-IS for CLNP. The default administrative distance of 115 is used for IP routing. This value is correctly shown in the output of the **show ip protocols** command in Figure 10-3.

You might recall that the notion of administrative distance is used in Cisco IOS Software to indicate the relative degree of preference between different routing information sources for the same Layer 3 protocol. The administrative distance of IP routes is 0 for connected routes, for example, 1 for static routes, 110 for OSPF routes, and 115 for IS-IS.

Some lines in the following output (the last few) pertain to the format style of IS-IS metrics, and they are displayed as a result of the **metric-style wide** command in the configuration. Wide metrics are particularly relevant for MPLS traffic engineering, which was named by Cisco as Routing with Resource Reservation (RRR) before standardization efforts started in the IETF.

Example 10-4 **show clns protocol** *Command Output*

```
RT1#show clns protocol
IS-IS Router: <Null Tag>
  System Id: 0000.0000.0001.00  IS-Type: level-1-2
  Manual area address(es):
        49.0001
  Routing for area address(es):
        49.0001
  Interfaces supported by IS-IS:
        Serial0/0 - IP
        Ethernet0/0 - IP
  Redistributing:
    static
  Distance: 110
  RRR level: none
  Generate narrow metrics: none
  Accept narrow metrics:   none
  Generate wide metrics:   level-1-2
  Accept wide metrics:     level-1-2
```

show clns neighbors

The **show clns neighbors** command is discussed in Chapter 9, where it is used to verify the proper operation of IS-IS and the status of adjacencies with directly connected IS-IS routers. The **show clns neighbors** command is syntactically similar to commands such as **show ip ospf neighbors** and **show ip eigrp neighbors**, which check the status of adjacencies in OSPF and EIGRP, respectively. However, there is no reference to a Layer 3 routing protocol in the **show clns neighbors** command.

Example 10-5 shows an output of the **show clns neighbors command**, captured from RT1 (refer to Figure 10-1). Adding the **detail** option to the command displays more information about each known neighbor, such as the area ID and IP address.

Example 10-5 **show clns neighbors** *Command Output*

```
RT1#show clns neighbors

System Id     Interface   SNPA            State  Holdtime  Type Proto
RT2           Se0/0       *HDLC*          Up     27        L2   IS-IS
RT5           Et0/0       00d0.58eb.ff01  Up     25        L1   IS-IS


RT1#show clns neighbors detail

System Id     Interface   SNPA            State  Holdtime  Type Proto
RT2           Se0/0       *HDLC*          Up     24        L2   IS-IS
  Area Address(es): 49.0002
  IP Address(es):  192.168.1.2*
  Uptime: 02:15:11
RT5           Et0/0       00d0.58eb.ff01  Up     23        L1   IS-IS
  Area Address(es): 49.0001
  IP Address(es):  10.1.1.5*
  Uptime: 02:15:11
```

Generally, the output shows the following for each neighbor:

- **System ID**—System identifier of the neighbor.
- **Interface**—Physical interface where the neighbor is connected.
- **SNPA (Subnetwork Point of Attachment)**—This is the data-link type or address (HDLC or PPP for serial and MAC address for LANs).
- **State**—State of the adjacency (up, down, or init).
- **Holdtime**—This is the interval before the adjacency expires. The holdtime is the product of the hello interval and hello multiplier. The default values of the latter two parameters are 10 and 3, respectively. The holdtime is reset to the maximum value every time a hello packet is received and decreases until the next reset.
- **Type**—The type of adjacency (Level 1, Level 2, or both).
- **Protocol**—Routing protocol source (IS-IS or ISO IGRP).

show clns interface

The **show clns interface** command is analogous to the **show ip interface** command. Both commands provide protocol information regarding specific status and parameter settings. Without any option, the **show clns interface** command spills out information about all interfaces on the router, indicating which interfaces are enabled for CLNS forwarding and which are not. An interface-specific option provides an output for only the named interface, as shown in Examples 10-6 through 10-8.

Example 10-6 *Point-to-Point Serial Interface*

```
RT2#show clns interface Serial 0/0
(1)Serial0/0 is up, line protocol is up
 (2) Checksums enabled, MTU 1500, Encapsulation HDLC
  (3) ERPDUs enabled, min. interval 10 msec.
  (4) RDPDUs enabled, min. interval 100 msec., Addr Mask enabled
  (5) Congestion Experienced bit set at 4 packets
  (6) CLNS fast switching enabled
  (7) CLNS SSE switching disabled
  (8) DEC compatibility mode OFF for this interface
  (9) Next ESH/ISH in 2 seconds
  (10) Routing Protocol: IS-IS
    (11) Circuit Type: level-1-2
    (12) Interface number 0x0, local circuit ID 0x100
    (13) Level-1 Metric: 10, Priority: 64, Circuit ID: RT2.00
    (14) Number of active level-1 adjacencies: 0
    (15) Level-2 Metric: 10, Priority: 64, Circuit ID: RT2.00
    (16) Number of active level-2 adjacencies: 1
    (17) Next IS-IS Hello in 4 seconds
```

Example 10-7 *LAN Interface*

```
RT2#show clns interface ethernet0/0
(1) Ethernet0/0 is up, line protocol is up
  (2) Checksums enabled, MTU 1497, Encapsulation SAP
  (3) ERPDUs enabled, min. interval 10 msec.
  (4) RDPDUs enabled, min. interval 100 msec., Addr Mask enabled
  (5) Congestion Experienced bit set at 4 packets
  (6) CLNS fast switching enabled
  (7) CLNS SSE switching disabled
  (8) DEC compatibility mode OFF for this interface
  (9) Next ESH/ISH in 4 seconds
  (10) Routing Protocol: IS-IS
    (11) Circuit Type: level-1-2
    (12) Interface number 0x2, local circuit ID 0x2
    (13) Level-1 Metric: 10, Priority: 64, Circuit ID: RT6.01
    (14) Number of active level-1 adjacencies: 1
    (15) Level-2 Metric: 10, Priority: 64, Circuit ID: RT6.01
    (16) Number of active level-2 adjacencies: 0
    (17) 1Next IS-IS LAN Level-1 Hello in 4 seconds
    (18) Next IS-IS LAN Level-2 Hello in 3 seconds
```

Example 10-8 *Interface Not Enabled for CLNS*

```
RT2#show clns interface FastEthernet1/0
(1) FastEthernet1/0 is administratively down, line protocol is down
  (2) CLNS protocol processing disabled
```

Example 10-6 shows the output for a point-to-point serial interface, Example 10-7 for a broadcast interface, and Example 10-8 shows the corresponding output for an interface on which IS-IS routing is not enabled. The lines in the examples are numbered. Lines 3 through 9 in Examples 10-6 and 10-7 are not particularly important for troubleshooting IS-IS in IP environments. Table 10-1 compares the lines of interest in Examples 10-6 and 10-7.

Table 10-1   *Explanation of the* **show clns interface** *Command*

Line	Example 10-6 Point-to-Point	Example 10-7 Broadcast
1	Line up, protocol up, implies working interface.	Line up, protocol up, implies working interface.
2	Encapsulation is HDLC and the default CLNS MTU is 1500, matching the default of the physical MTU.	All OSI-related protocols (CLNP, ES-IS, IS-IS) are encapsulated 802.2(SAP), limiting the MTU to 1497 bytes compared to the 1500 MTU of the physical interface.
10	IS-IS routing is enabled on this interface.	IS-IS routing is enabled on this interface.
11	Level 1 and Level 2 adjacencies can be formed on this interface.	Level 1 and Level 2 adjacencies can be formed on this interface.
12	Interface number (0x0). Assigned by configuration turns. Used as an index by SRM and SSM flags for flooding. Local circuit ID is 0x100 for serial point-to-point.	Interface number (0x2). Assigned by configuration turns. Used as an index by SRM and SSM flags for flooding. Local circuit ID is 0x2, which is the same as the interface number for LAN-type interfaces.
13	Metric and priority for Level 1 (defaults).	Metric and priority for Level 1 (defaults). The circuit ID on the LAN is the system ID of DIS + the pseudonode number (RT6.01)
14	Zero Level 1 adjacencies over this interface.	One Level 1 adjacency (with RT6).
15	Metric and priority for Level 2 (defaults).	Metric and priority for Level 2 (defaults).
16	One Level 2 adjacency (with RT1) over this interface.	Zero Level 2 adjacencies over this interface.
17	Point-to-point IIH due in four seconds.	LAN Level 1 IIH due in four seconds.
18	No entry.	LAN Level 2 IIH due in three seconds.

Use of 802.2 (SAP) Ethernet encapsulation for CLNS packets (CLNP, ES-IS, IS-IS) results in the CLNS maximum transmission unit (MTU) being three bytes shorter than the physical interface MTU. In the SAP encapsulation, one byte is used for the Destination Service Access Point (DSAP), one byte for the Source Service Access Point (SSAP), and one byte for the control fields. Table 10-1 elaborates on the key lines in the output of the **show isis clns interface** command that deserve attention when troubleshooting IS-IS adjacency problems. Certainly, the first thing to check is the status of the physical interface (lines 1 and 2). Next, check lines 10 and 11; these indicate whether IS-IS is enabled on the interfaces, as well as the adjacency count.

show isis database

Most IS-IS-related routing failures are caused either by problems with adjacency formation or route installation. The previous sections of this chapter discuss IS-IS-related commands, such as **show clns interface** and **show clns neighbors,** for troubleshooting IS-IS adjacency problems. This section focuses on the **show isis database** command, which proves useful when troubleshooting route installation problems. In Chapter 9, the **show isis database** command is mentioned as an important tool for verifying the proper operation of IS-IS.

As you might recall from previous chapters, IS-IS routers exchange LSPs with their neighbors after forming adjacencies. The LSPs received from neighbors are then grouped into Level 1 and Level 2 Link-State databases based on the type of adjacencies existing on the router. LSPs contain relevant information about the originator's routing environment, such as IP prefix information, which is held in IP reachability TLVs. One of the important steps in troubleshooting routing problems is to check the Level 1 and Level 2 Link-State databases for the presence of all expected LSPs. This is done with the **show isis database** command. Example 10-9 features a sample output of this command, which displays a summary of all known LSPs in the Level 1 and Level 2 databases. The keyword options to the command, **Level 1 (l1)** or **Level 2 (l2)**, display either of the two databases, respectively. Other command options, such as the **lsp id** and **detail,** can be used separately or combined, as in **show isis database <lsp id> detail**, to display details about a specific LSP (see Example 10-10). The details of the information in an LSP might provide clues about missing routing information. Understanding and correctly interpreting the information in an LSP is very critical to solving routing problems, such as missing or inaccurate routing information.

Example 10-9 **show isis database** *Command*

```
RT1#show isis database
IS-IS Level-1 Link State Database
LSPID             LSP Seq Num  LSP Checksum  LSP Holdtime    ATT/P/OL
RT1.00-00       * 0x000000DD   0xE942        528             1/0/0
RT1.01-00       * 0x00000087   0xA810        1039            0/0/0
RT5.00-00         0x00000F6E   0xED30        1159            0/0/0
```

continues

Example 10-9 show isis database *Command (Continued)*

```
IS-IS Level-2 Link State Database
LSPID             LSP Seq Num  LSP Checksum  LSP Holdtime    ATT/P/OL
RT1.00-00       * 0x000000E5   0x7BFA        1041            0/0/0
RT2.00-00         0x00001C9C   0x5F3E        1135            0/0/0
RT1#
```

The output in Example 10-9 is taken from RT1, which is represented in Figure 10-1. This output displays the separate Level 1 and Level 2 databases and lists all known LSPs. Various attributes, such as LSP ID, LSP checksum, and so on, are listed for each LSP. The Level 1 database lists three known LSPs, two of which are generated by RT1 (also marked by an asterisk [*]). The third is generated by RT5. That both RT1 and RT5 have LSPs in the Level 1 database is an obvious indication that they are in the same area. One of the LSPs, RT1.01-00, is a pseudonode LSP because it has a non-zero LSP number in the LSP ID. This LSP is generated by RT1, which is the designated intermediate system (DIS).

Level 2 database shows only two LSPs, one each from RT1 and RT2. This means that RT2 is the only Level 2 neighbor of RT1. This also implies that RT1 has formed only a Level 1 adjacency with RT5 and only a Level 2 adjacency with RT2. This is because RT2 is in another area and RT5 is in the same area but has been configured to be a Level 1-only router.

All routers in the same area have the same set of LSPs in their Level 1 databases. Similarly, all Level 2 routers have an identical list of Level 2 LSPs. Any inconsistency in the Level 1 database for routers in the same area or the Level 2 database for routers connected to the Level 2 backbone surely flags a problem.

Level 1 LSPs generated by Level 2-capable routers need to be checked for the ATT bit setting. The ATT bit flags a default route to Level 1 routers in the area. In Example 10-6, RT1.00-00, originated by RT1, has the ATT bit set. This indicates to RT5 that RT1 is connected to the backbone and can provide connectivity to other areas. Example 10-10 shows the contents of RT2.00-00 as displayed on RT1. The output displays all IP prefixes advertised by RT2 to other Level 2 routers and can help you to troubleshoot any potential routing problems associated with RT2.

Note that 11.1.1.6 originates from RT6 (refer to Figure 10-1), but it is advertised through Level 2 to the rest of the network by RT2. The other IP prefixes in this LSP are directly connected networks.

Example 10-10 show isis database detail *Command*

```
RT1#show isis database level-1 RT2.00-00 detail

IS-IS Level-2 LSP RT2.00-00
LSPID             LSP Seq Num  LSP Checksum  LSP Holdtime    ATT/P/OL
RT2.00-00         0x00001C9C   0x5F3E        1015            0/0/0
  Area Address: 49.0002
```

Example 10-10 show isis database detail *Command (Continued)*

```
NLPID:        0xCC
Hostname: RT2
IP Address:   11.1.1.2
Metric: 10        IS-Extended RT1.00
Metric: 10        IP 10.1.2.0/24
Metric: 0         IP 11.1.1.2/32
Metric: 10        IP 11.1.1.6/32
Metric: 10        IP 192.168.1.0/30
```

show isis topology

An output of the **show isis topology** command is shown in Example 10-11. This command provides a view of the relative location of all known routers in both the local area and the backbone. In Figure 10-2, RT5 is a Level 1 router and RT1 is a Level 1-2 router, both in area 49.0001. RT2 and RT6 are both Level 1-2 routers in area 49.0002. The Level 2 backbone expands across the largest shaded oval. The smaller ovals cover individual Level 1 areas. The output of **show isis topology** from RT1 indicates only one path to a Level 1 router (RT5) connects to Ethernet0/0 (see Example 10-11). The MAC address of RT5 is also provided. Two paths are in the backbone to Level 2 routers, both going through Serial0/0.

Figure 10-2 *The* **show isis topology** *command.*

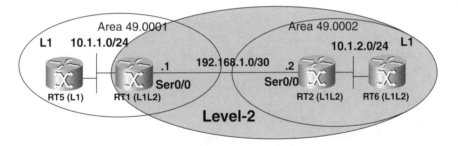

The **show isis topology** command is similar to the **show isis route** command, which provides, in essence, a Level 1 routing table for IS-IS nodes in an area. The **show isis topology** command extends **show isis route** to cover Level 2 nodes in pure IP environments and does not need the **clns router** command to be configured on IS-IS-enabled interfaces as in the case of the **show isis route** command.

Example 10-11 show isis topology *Command*

```
RT1#show isis topology

IS-IS paths to level-1 routers
System Id       Metric  Next-Hop    Interface       SNPA
RT1              --
RT5              10     RT5          Et0/0           00d0.58eb.ff01

IS-IS paths to level-2 routers
System Id       Metric  Next-Hop    Interface       SNPA
RT1              --
RT2              10     RT2          Se0/0           *HDLC*
RT6              20     RT2          Se0/0           *HDLC*
```

show isis spf-log

In most Cisco routers, a route processor is responsible for running the IS-IS protocol and calculating IS-IS-specific routing information. IS-IS routes compete with similar information from other routing protocol sources, such as static routes and OSPF if enabled, for spots in the global IP routing table of the router. The route processor runs the SPF process for IS-IS by using the IS-IS Link-State database as input to calculate IS-IS routes. The SPF process is run periodically or triggered based on network activity, such as LSP content changes or receipt of a new LSP.

The **show isis spf-log** command logs events related to the SPF process providing information such as triggers and duration of events. Reviewing the SPF log can help you to troubleshoot a churn in the network. By studying the SPF log, for example, you can determine the reason for a high spike in CPU utilization at the route processor attributable to the IS-IS SPF process. A sample output of **show isis spf-log** is shown in Example 10-12. The output shows that at 1:56:08, the SPF process was triggered by some event relating to LSP RT1.01.00. The last column of this line shows the trigger was a TLVCONTENT on RT1.01-00. In Chapter 9, the **spf-interval configuration** command is discussed and a list of SPF event triggers is provided. An augmented list of triggers is provided in Table 10-2.

Example 10-12 show isis spf-log *Command*

```
RT1#show isis spf-log

  Level 1 SPF log
  When      Duration  Nodes  Count  Last trigger LSP   Triggers
  03:40:08        0      3      1                       PERIODIC
  03:25:08        0      3      1                       PERIODIC
  03:10:07        0      3      1                       PERIODIC
  02:55:07        0      3      1                       PERIODIC
  02:40:07        0      3      1                       PERIODIC
  02:25:06        0      3      1                       PERIODIC
  02:10:06        0      3      1                       PERIODIC
```

Example 10-12 show isis spf-log *Command (Continued)*

```
01:56:08      0     2     1           RT1.01-00   TLVCONTENT
01:55:06      0     2     1                       PERIODIC
01:40:06      0     2     1                       PERIODIC
01:36:31      0     2     1           RT5.00-00   LSPEXPIRED
01:28:31      0     2     2           RT1.01-00   NEWADJ TLVCONTENT
01:28:25      0     3     1           RT5.00-00   NEWLSP
01:25:06      0     3     1                       PERIODIC
01:10:06      0     3     1                       PERIODIC
```

Table 10-2   *Event Triggers of the SPF Process*

Trigger Code	Description
AREASET	Area change
ATTACHFLAG	Attached bit setting change
CLEAR	Manual clear
CONFIG	Configuration change
DELADJ	Adjacency deletion
DIS	DIS election
ES	End system information change
HIPPITY LSPDB	Overload bit state change
IP_DEF_ORIG	Default information change
IPDOWN	Connected IP prefix down
IP_EXTERNAL	Route redistribution change
IPIA	Interarea route change
IPUP	Connected IP prefix up
NEWADJ	New neighbor adjacency up
NEWLEVEL	IS-IS process level changed
NEWMETRIC	New metric assigned to an interface
NEWSYSID	New system ID assigned
PERIODIC	Periodic SPF process (LSPDB refresh interval)
TLVCODE	LSP with a new TLV code field received
TLVCONTENT	LSP with changed TLV contents received

Other Useful IS-IS Troubleshooting Commands

Table 10-3 lists a few more IS-IS commands useful for troubleshooting. The commands are grouped by CLNS and IS-IS, IP and System. A few IS-IS and **clns clear** commands are also provided. Issuing the **clear** command usually clears data structures and resets related objects. The table also features useful debugging commands, some of which are discussed in the next section.

Consult the Cisco IOS Software command reference guides mentioned in the references at the end of this chapter for more information about the use and impact of each command before applying them on production routers (specifically references 3 and 4).

Table 10-3   *IS-IS Useful Troubleshooting Commands*

CLNS **show** commands: **show clns route** **show clns cache** **show clns traffic**	IS-IS **show** command: **show isis route**
CLNS **clear** commands: **clear clns cache** **clear clns es-neighbors** **clear clns is-neighbors** **clear clns neighbors** **clear clns route**	IS-IS **clear** command: **clear isis ***
CLNS **debug** commands: **debug clns events** **debug clns packets** **debug clns routing**	IS-IS **debug** commands: **debug isis adj-packets** **debug isis snp-packets** **debug isis spf-events** **debug isis spf-triggers** **debug isis spf-statistics** **debug isis update-packets**
System **show** commands: **show version** **show run**	IP **show** commands: **show ip protocol** **show ip route summary** **show ip traffic**

Debugging IS-IS Problems

The CLNS and IS-IS **debug** commands shown in Table 10-3 are all useful for troubleshooting IS-IS problems. However, the following three debugging commands are the most useful and are commonly used. Each is discussed in more detail in the following subsections:

- **debug isis adj-packets**
- **debug isis spf-events**
- **debug isis update-packets**

debug isis adj-packets

As the name implies, the **debug isis adj-packets** command helps debug adjacency problems by displaying information about hello packets sent and received by a router. Adjacent routers send hellos to each other to maintain the adjacency for each level of routing, which can be viewed by using the **debug isis adj-packets** command (see Example 10-13). Note also that separate hello packets are exchanged for Level 1 and Level 2.

Example 10-13 **debug isis adj-packets** *Command Output*

```
RT1#debug isis adj-packets
IS-IS Adjacency related packets debugging is on
RT1#
Mar  6 20:25:13: ISIS-Adj: Sending L2 IIH on Ethernet0/0, length 1497
Mar  6 20:25:13: ISIS-Adj: Sending L1 IIH on Ethernet0/0, length 1497
Mar  6 20:25:15: ISIS-Adj: Rec L1 IIH from 00d0.58eb.ff01 (Ethernet0/0), cir ty7
Mar  6 20:25:16: ISIS-Adj: Rec serial IIH from *HDLC* (Serial0/0), cir type L1L9
Mar  6 20:25:16: ISIS-Adj: rcvd state UP, old state UP, new state UP
Mar  6 20:25:16: ISIS-Adj: Action = ACCEPT
Mar  6 20:25:16: ISIS-Adj: Sending L2 IIH on Ethernet0/0, length 1497
Mar  6 20:25:16: ISIS-Adj: Sending L1 IIH on Ethernet0/0, length 1497
Mar  6 20:25:18: ISIS-Adj: Sending serial IIH on Serial0/0, length 1499
Mar  6 20:25:19: ISIS-Adj: Sending L1 IIH on Ethernet0/0, length 1497
Mar  6 20:25:19: ISIS-Adj: Sending L2 IIH on Ethernet0/0, length 1497
Mar  6 20:25:21: ISIS-Adj: Sending L1 IIH on Ethernet0/0, length 1497
Mar  6 20:25:22: ISIS-Adj: Sending L2 IIH on Ethernet0/0, length 1497
Mar  6 20:25:25: ISIS-Adj: Sending L2 IIH on Ethernet0/0, length 1497
Mar  6 20:25:25: ISIS-Adj: Rec L1 IIH from 00d0.58eb.ff01 (Ethernet0/0), cir ty7
Mar  6 20:25:25: ISIS-Adj: Sending L1 IIH on Ethernet0/0, length 1497
Mar  6 20:25:25: ISIS-Adj: Rec serial IIH from *HDLC* (Serial0/0), cir type L1L9
Mar  6 20:25:25: ISIS-Adj: rcvd state UP, old state UP, new state UP
Mar  6 20:25:25: ISIS-Adj: Action = ACCEPT
```

debug isis spf-events

The **debug isis spf-events** command enables debugging of events related to the SPF process. It provides a real-time output unlike the **show isis spf-log** command, which provides a history of SPF activities. Example 10-14 shows an output for the sequence of events that occur when Ethernet0/0 is shut down on RT1 (refer to Figure 10-2), causing it to flag its own LSP, and that learned from RT5, over this interface for SPF recalculation. The **debug** output also shows SPF-related events and recomputation of the Level 1 and Level 2 shortest path trees (SPTs).

Example 10-14 *Debugging SPF Events*

```
RT1#debug isis spf-events
RT1(config)#int e0/0
RT1(config-if)#shut
RT1(config-if)#^Z

Mar  6 20:17:26: ISIS-SPF: L1 LSP 1 (0000.0000.0001.00-00) flagged for recalculC
Mar  6 20:17:26: ISIS-SPF: L1 LSP 5 (0000.0000.0005.00-00) flagged for recalculC
Mar  6 20:17:28: ISIS-SPF: Compute L1 SPT
Mar  6 20:17:28: ISIS-SPF: 3 nodes for level-1
Mar  6 20:17:28: ISIS-SPF: Move 0000.0000.0001.00-00 to PATHS, metric 0
Mar  6 20:17:28: ISIS-SPF: Add 0000.0000.0001.01-00 to TENT, metric 10
Mar  6 20:17:28: ISIS-SPF: Add 0000.0000.0001 to L1 route table, metric 0
Mar  6 20:17:28: ISIS-SPF: Move 0000.0000.0001.01-00 to PATHS, metric 10
Mar  6 20:17:28: ISIS-SPF: Aging L1 LSP 1 (0000.0000.0001.00-00), version 214
Mar  6 20:17:28: ISIS-SPF: Aging L2 LSP 2 (0000.0000.0001.00-00), version 208
Mar  6 20:17:28: ISIS-SPF: Aging L1 LSP 3 (0000.0000.0001.01-00), version 207
Mar  6 20:17:28: ISIS-SPF: Aging L2 LSP 4 (0000.0000.0002.00-00), version 209
Mar  6 20:17:28: ISIS-SPF: Aging L1 LSP 5 (0000.0000.0005.00-00), version 207
Mar  6 20:17:28: ISIS-SPF: Aging L2 LSP 6 (0000.0000.0006.01-00), version 112
Mar  6 20:17:28: ISIS-SPF: Aging L2 LSP 7 (0000.0000.0006.00-00), version 114
Mar  6 20:17:28: ISIS-SPF: Aging L2 LSP 8 (0000.0000.0001.01-00), version 1
Mar  6 20:17:33: ISIS-SPF: Compute L2 SPT
Mar  6 20:17:33: ISIS-SPF: 5 nodes for level-2
Mar  6 20:17:33: ISIS-SPF: Move 0000.0000.0001.00-00 to PATHS, metric 0
Mar  6 20:17:33: ISIS-SPF: Add 49.0001 to L2 route table, metric 0
Mar  6 20:17:33: ISIS-SPF: Add 0000.0000.0001.01-00 to TENT, metric 10
Mar  6 20:17:33: ISIS-SPF: considering adj to 0000.0000.0002 (Serial0/0) metric
Mar  6 20:17:33: ISIS-SPF:    (accepted)
Mar  6 20:17:33: ISIS-SPF: Add 0000.0000.0002.00-00 to TENT, metric 10
Mar  6 20:17:33: ISIS-SPF:    Next hop 0000.0000.0002 (Serial0/0)
Mar  6 20:17:33: ISIS-SPF: Move 0000.0000.0001.01-00 to PATHS, metric 10
Mar  6 20:17:33: ISIS-SPF: Move 0000.0000.0002.00-00 to PATHS, metric 10
Mar  6 20:17:33: ISIS-SPF: Add 49.0002 to L2 route table, metric 10
Mar  6 20:17:33: ISIS-SPF: Redundant IP route 10.1.2.0/255.255.255.0, metric 20d
Mar  6 20:17:33: ISIS-SPF: Redundant IP route 11.1.1.2/255.255.255.255, metric d
Mar  6 20:17:33: ISIS-SPF: Redundant IP route 11.1.1.6/255.255.255.255, metric d
Mar  6 20:17:33: ISIS-SPF: Add 192.168.1.0/255.255.255.252 to IP route table, m0
Mar  6 20:17:33: ISIS-SPF: Next hop 0000.0000.0002/192.168.1.2 (Serial0/0) (rej)
Mar  6 20:17:33: ISIS-SPF: Aging L1 LSP 1 (0000.0000.0001.00-00), version 214
Mar  6 20:17:33: ISIS-SPF: Aging L2 LSP 2 (0000.0000.0001.00-00), version 209
```

Example 10-14 *Debugging SPF Events (Continued)*

```
Mar  6 20:17:33: ISIS-SPF: Aging L1 LSP 3 (0000.0000.0001.01-00), version 207
Mar  6 20:17:33: ISIS-SPF: Aging L2 LSP 4 (0000.0000.0002.00-00), version 210
Mar  6 20:17:33: ISIS-SPF: Aging L1 LSP 5 (0000.0000.0005.00-00), version 207
Mar  6 20:17:33: ISIS-SPF: Aging L2 LSP 6 (0000.0000.0006.01-00), version 113
Mar  6 20:17:33: ISIS-SPF: Aging L2 LSP 7 (0000.0000.0006.00-00), version 115
Mar  6 20:17:33: ISIS-SPF: Aging L2 LSP 8 (0000.0000.0001.01-00), version 2
```

debug isis update-packets

In IS-IS, update information is propagated by means of LSPs when changes occur in the network. CNSPs are sent only one time on point-to-point links after adjacency is formed, but periodically on broadcast links to compensate for unreliable advertisement of LSPs over such media. The **debug update-packets** command displays any update-related information, such as LSPs and CSNPs. The related command, **debug isis snp-packets**, displays only sequence number packets with more detail. Examples 10-15 and 10-16 show sample outputs of these debugs. Lines 1 and 2 of Example 10-15 are actually console logs for flapping Serial0/0. The debug output starts from line 3. In line 3, a new LSP is built; this line turns out to be different from the older copy. This, therefore, triggers a full SPF to be scheduled (line 5). Lines 6 and 7 show LSP exchange over Serial0/0. Lines 11 and 14 show the one-time CSNP exchange when a point-to-point link is first brought up. In lines 15, 16, 17, a PSNP is created to obtain complete LSPs for nodes 2 and 5 as a result of the CSNP exchange. In line 18, a Level 1 LSP is built apparently to set the attach bit. The change in the Level 1 LSP results in running SPF for Level 1 in line 23. In line 22, the new Level 1 LSP is sent out on Ethernet0/0 followed by a CSNP in line 23.

Example 10-15 debug isis update-packets *Command Update*

```
RT1#debug isis update-packets
(1) *Mar  2 23:25:02: %LINEPROTO-5-UPDOWN: Line protocol on Interface Serial0/0, chp
(2) *Mar  2 23:25:03: %CLNS-5-ADJCHANGE: ISIS: Adjacency to RT2 (Serial0/0) Up, newy
(3) *Mar  2 23:25:07: ISIS-Update: Building L2 LSP
(4) *Mar  2 23:25:07: ISIS-Update: TLV contents different, code 16
(5) *Mar  2 23:25:07: ISIS-Update: Full SPF required
(6) *Mar  2 23:25:07: ISIS-Update: Sending L2 LSP 0000.0000.0001.00-00, seq 160, ht0
(7) *Mar  2 23:25:07: ISIS-Update: Rec L2 LSP 0000.0000.0002.00-00, seq 1D16, ht 11,
(8) *Mar  2 23:25:07: ISIS-Update: from SNPA *HDLC* (Serial0/0)
(9) *Mar  2 23:25:07: ISIS-Update: LSP newer than database copy
(10) *Mar  2 23:25:07: ISIS-Update: No change
(11) *Mar  2 23:25:08: ISIS-SNP: Rec L2 CSNP from 0000.0000.0002 (Serial0/0)
(12) *Mar  2 23:25:08: ISIS-SNP: Rec L2 PSNP from 0000.0000.0002 (Serial0/0)
(13) *Mar  2 23:25:08: ISIS-SNP: PSNP entry 0000.0000.0001.00-00, seq 160, ht 1197
(14) *Mar  2 23:25:08: ISIS-Update: Sending L2 CSNP on Serial0/0
(15) *Mar  2 23:25:08: ISIS-Update: Build L2 PSNP entry for 0000.0000.0002.00-00, se6
(16) *Mar  2 23:25:08: ISIS-Update: Build L2 PSNP entry for 0000.0000.0006.00-00, se2
(17) *Mar  2 23:25:08: ISIS-Update: Sending L2 PSNP on Serial0/0
```

continues

Example 10-15 debug isis update-packets *Command Update (Continued)*

```
(18) *Mar  2 23:25:09: ISIS-Update: Building L1 LSP
(19) *Mar  2 23:25:09: ISIS-Update: Important fields changed
(20) *Mar  2 23:25:09: ISIS-Update: Important fields changed
(21) *Mar  2 23:25:09: ISIS-Update: Full SPF required
(22) *Mar  2 23:25:09: ISIS-Update: Sending L1 LSP 0000.0000.0001.00-00, seq 15A, ht0
(23) *Mar  2 23:25:09: ISIS-Update: Sending L1 CSNP on Ethernet0/0
```

Example 10-16 debug isis snp-packets *Command Output*

```
RT5#debug isis snp-packets
IS-IS CSNP/PSNP packets debugging is on
RT5#
Mar  6 20:02:28: ISIS-SNP: Rec L1 CSNP from 0000.0000.0001 (Ethernet0/0)
Mar  6 20:02:28: ISIS-SNP: CSNP range 0000.0000.0000.00-00 to FFFF.FFFF.FFFF.FFF
Mar  6 20:02:28: ISIS-SNP: Same entry 0000.0000.0001.00-00, seq 15D
Mar  6 20:02:28: ISIS-SNP: Same entry 0000.0000.0001.01-00, seq 104
Mar  6 20:02:28: ISIS-SNP: Same entry 0000.0000.0005.00-00, seq FEA
```

CLNS ping and traceroute

In addition to the plethora of **show** and **debug** commands available for monitoring and troubleshooting IS-IS, the **ping clns** and **traceroute clns** commands come in handy for troubleshooting forwarding problems associated with the CLNP protocol. For these commands to work in an environment with dynamic IS-IS routing, you must use the **clns router isis** command to enable CLNP forwarding on the relevant interfaces. These commands provide the CLNP equivalents of the **ping** and **traceroute** for testing node reachability in the IS-IS domain. These commands are irrelevant in IP-only environments where the **clns router isis** command is not configured on the router interfaces.

However, this is certainly a troubleshooting capability that some network operators might find useful. The CLNS **ping** and **traceroute** commands are indispensable tools for dual IP/CLNP or pure ISO CLNS environments.

Examples 10-17 through 10-19 show the configuration and CLNS routing environment of RT5. Examples 10-20 and 10-21 show the CNLS environment from the perspective of RT2, which is located in area 49.0002. This capture of the general CLNS routing environment of Figure 10-3 provides background information to help you understand the CLNS **ping** and **traceroute** from RT5 through the backbone to RT6. Examples 10-22 and 10-23 show standard and extended CLNS **ping** from RT5 to RT6. Example 10-24 is the output of the **debug clns packet** command from Example 10-23. Examples 10-25 and 10-26 demonstrate how the standard and extended CLNS **traceroute** commands work.

Figure 10-3 *Network diagram for Examples 10-17 to 10-22.*

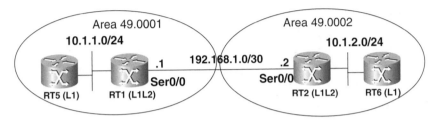

Example 10-17 *Configuration for RT5 in Figure 10-3*

```
RT5#show running-config

clns routing
!
interface Loopback0
 ip address 11.1.1.5 255.255.255.255
!
interface Ethernet0/0
 ip address 10.1.1.5 255.255.255.0
 ip router isis
 clns router isis
!
router isis
 passive-interface Loopback0
 net 49.0001.0000.0000.0005.00
 is-type level-1
 metric-style wide
```

Example 10-18 **show clns route** *from RT5*

```
RT5#show clns route
CLNS Prefix Routing Table
49.0001.0000.0000.0005.00, Local NET Entry
```

Example 10-19 **show isis route** *from RT5*

```
RT5#show isis route
IS-IS Level-1 Routing Table - version 13975
System Id     Next-Hop  Interface   SNPA            Metric  State
RT1           RT1       Et0/0       00d0.58f7.8941  10      Up    L2-IS
RT5           - -

Default route out of area - (via 1 L2-attached IS)
System Id     Next-Hop  Interface   SNPA            Metric  State
              RT1       Et0/0       00d0.58f7.8941  10      Up
```

Example 10-20 **show clns route** *from RT5*

```
RT2#show clns route
CLNS Prefix Routing Table
49.0002.0000.0000.0002.00, Local NET Entry
49.0001 [110/10]
  via RT1, IS-IS, Up, Serial0/0
49.0002 [110/0]
  via RT2, IS-IS, Up
```

Example 10-21 **show isis route** *from RT2 from Figure 10-3*

```
RT2#show isis route
IS-IS Level-1 Routing Table - version 6873
System Id       Next-Hop       Interface   SNPA            Metric  State
RT6             RT6            Et0/0       00d0.58f7.8041  10      Up
RT2             - -
```

Example 10-22 *CLNS Standard* **ping** *Command*

```
RT5#ping clns 49.0002.0000.0000.0006.00

Type escape sequence to abort.
Sending 5, 100-byte CLNS Echos with timeout 2 seconds
!!!!!
Success rate is 100 percent (5/5), round-trip min/avg/max = 4/4/4 ms
```

Example 10-23 *CLNS Extended* **ping** *Command*

```
RT5#ping
Protocol [ip]: clns
Target CLNS address: 49.0002.0000.0000.0006.00
Repeat count [5]: 2
Datagram size [100]:
Timeout in seconds [2]:
Extended commands [n]: y
Source CLNS address [49.0001.0000.0000.0005.00]:
Include global QOS option? [yes]:
Pad packet? [no]:
Validate reply data? [no]:
Data pattern [0xABCD]:
Sweep range of sizes [n]:
Verbose reply? [no]:
Type escape sequence to abort.
Sending 2, 100-byte CLNS Echos with timeout 2 seconds
!!
Success rate is 100 percent (2/2), round-trip min/avg/max = 4/4/4 ms
```

Example 10-24 *CLNS Packet Debugs During CLNS* **ping**

```
RT5#debug clns packet
Mar 10 07:50:43: CLNS: Originating packet, size 100
Mar 10 07:50:43:        from 49.0001.0000.0000.0005.00
     to 49.0002.0000.0000.0006.00
     via 0000.0000.0001 (Ethernet0/0 00d0.58f7.8941)
Mar 10 07:50:43: CLNS: Echo Reply PDU received on Ethernet0/0!

Mar 10 07:50:43: CLNS: Originating packet, size 100
Mar 10 07:50:43:        from 49.0001.0000.0000.0005.00
     to 49.0002.0000.0000.0006.00
     via 0000.0000.0001 (Ethernet0/0 00d0.58f7.8941)

Mar 10 07:50:43: CLNS: Echo Reply PDU received on Ethernet0/0!
```

Example 10-25 *CLNS Standard* **traceroute**

```
RT5#traceroute clns 49.0002.0000.0000.0006.00

Type escape sequence to abort.
Tracing the route to 49.0002.0000.0000.0006.00
  1 49.0001.0000.0000.0001.00 0 msec ! 0 msec ! 0 msec !
  2 49.0002.0000.0000.0002.00 0 msec ! 0 msec ! 0 msec !
  3 49.0002.0000.0000.0006.00 0 msec ! 0 msec ! 0 msec !
```

Example 10-26 *CLNS Extended* **traceroute** *Command*

```
RT5#traceroute
Protocol [ip]: clns
Target CLNS address: 49.0002.0000.0000.0006.00
Timeout in seconds [3]:
Probe count [3]:
Minimum Time to Live [1]:
Maximum Time to Live [30]:
Extended commands [n]: y
Source CLNS address [49.0001.0000.0000.0005.00]:
Include global QOS option? [yes]:
Pad packet? [no]:
Validate reply data? [no]:
Data pattern [0x60CD]:
Sweep range of sizes [n]:
Verbose reply? [no]:
Type escape sequence to abort.
Tracing the route to 49.0002.0000.0000.0006.00
  1 49.0001.0000.0000.0001.00 4 msec ! 0 msec ! 0 msec !
  2 49.0002.0000.0000.0002.00 0 msec ! 0 msec ! 0 msec !
  3 49.0002.0000.0000.0006.00 0 msec ! 0 msec ! 0 msec !
```

Troubleshooting IS-IS Routing Problems

The discussions in the previous sections of this chapter focus on tools and commands, ranging from simple to complex, needed for troubleshooting IS-IS problems. These sections provide a good foundation for discussing actual problems and troubleshooting methodology. Common IS-IS routing problems fall under the following two broad categories:

- Adjacency formation problems
- Route maintenance problems

During normal operation, IS-IS routers form and maintain adjacencies with each other by using hello packets. Routing information is then exchanged by flooding LSPs, which are stored in appropriate Link-State databases (Level 1 or Level 2). Sequence number packets (CSNPs and PSNPs) provide control for the flooding process and ensure database synchronization. All these processes need to occur successfully to ensure accurate dissemination of routing information in the IS-IS domain. Any failures result in inconsistencies that ultimately result in routing problems. The following sections identify problems and list the corresponding ways to isolate those problems.

IS-IS Adjacency Formation Problems

Adjacency formation problems are common IS-IS failures. They mainly occur as a result of router misconfiguration, hardware and software failures, interoperability problems between different IOS Software releases, and interoperability problems between routers from different vendors. Adjacency problems are easier to isolate than routing problems. The following list of adjacency problems are discussed in this section:

- Mismatched Level 1 and Level 2 interfaces
- Misconfigured NSAPs
- Duplicate system IDs
- Mismatched MTUs
- Misconfigured IP addresses and Subnets

Mismatched Level 1 and Level 2 Interfaces

The default mode of operation for Cisco routers running IS-IS is Level 1-2. In this mode, a router can form both Level 1 and Level 2 adjacencies with neighbors in the same area and form only Level 2 adjacencies with neighbors in different areas. Figure 10-4 diagrams such a configuration. In the output shown in Example 10-23, RT1 forms a Level 1-2 adjacency with RT5, which is in the same area (49.0001), but forms only a L2 adjacency with RT2, which is in area 49.0002. The default Level 1-2 mode can be modified for all interfaces on the router by using the router configuration-level command **IS-type** or for a specific

interface with the interface-level configuration command **isis circuit-type** *level* [**level-1** |
level-2]. If RT1 is misconfigured as a Level 1 only on Serial0/0 using any of the previously
mentioned commands, it loses the adjacency with RT2. Consequently, the domain will be
partitioned and there will be no communication between area 49.0001 and area 49.0002.
This behavior is confirmed in Example 10-27.

Figure 10-4 *Test network for studying mismatched levels of routing between connected interfaces.*

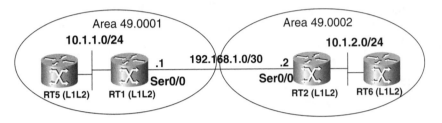

Example 10-27 **show clns neighbors** *During Normal Operation*

```
RT1#show clns neighbors

System Id    Interface   SNPA            State   Holdtime   Type Protocol
RT5          Et0/0       00d0.58eb.ff01  Up      26         L1L2 IS-IS
RT2          Se0/0       *HDLC*          Up      23         L2   IS-IS
```

Example 10-28 *Simulating Mismatched Levels of Routing on a Serial Link (refer to Figure 10-4)*

```
RT1#conf t
Enter configuration commands, one per line.  End with CNTL/Z.

RT1(config)#router isis
RT1(config-router)#is-type level-1
RT1(config-router)# ^Z


RT1#show clns neighbors

System Id    Interface   SNPA            State   Holdtime   Type Protocol
RT5          Et0/0       00d0.58eb.ff01  Up      26         L1   IS-IS
RT2          Se0/0       *HDLC*          Up      280        IS   ES-IS
```

In example 10-28, the **show clns neighbors** output shows that RT1 dropped the IS-IS
adjacency with RT2 and shows instead an ES-IS adjacency in place. This is because the
ES-IS adjacency process runs independently of IS-IS, and it is sustained by ESHs rather
than IIHs. Also because RT1 was made globally a Level 1 router with the IS-type command,
it has formed only a Level 1 IS-IS adjacency with RT5.

Misconfigured NSAPs (NETs)

Each IS-IS node must have at least one NSAP address (NET) to identify it as a network node. This NET consists of the area ID of the node, the System ID, and a 0-value NSEL. The system ID is required to be unique within the area; the NSEL value is fixed at 0x00. The area ID (also referred to as the *area prefix*) must be the same for all nodes in the same area. For nodes with multiple NETs, the system ID must be the same in all of them, and at least one of the area prefixes must be shared with another node in the same area. The effect of misconfiguring a NET is illustrated in Figure 10-5. In this example, RTE, RTF, and RTG are meant to be together in area 49.0001. They are also meant to form both Level 1 and Level 2 adjacencies.

Figure 10-5 *Test network for studying misconfigured NSAP problem.*

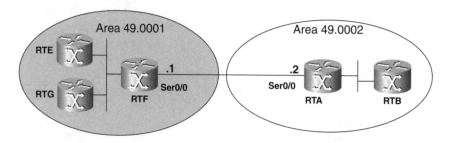

The outputs of the **show clns neighbors** command from RTE, RTF, and RTG shown in Example 10-29 indicate RTE formed only Level 2 adjacencies with RTF and RTG. However, RTF and RTG formed Level 1-2 adjacencies with each other as expected. This creates a suspicion about the configuration and operation of RTE.

Example 10-29 *Troubleshooting Misconfigured NSAPs*

```
RTE#show clns neighbors

System Id    SNPA             Interface   State   Holdtime   Type Protocol
RTF          0000.0c76.f098   Et0         Up      27         L2   IS-IS
RTG          0000.0c76.f096   Et0         Up      26         L2   IS-IS

RTF#show clns neighbors

System Id    SNPA             Interface   State   Holdtime   Type Protocol
RTB          *HDLC*           Se0         Up      27         L2   IS-IS
RTE          0000.0c76.f1fa   Et0         Up      9          L2   IS-IS
RTG          0000.0c76.f096   Et0         Up      28         L1L2 IS-IS

RTG#show clns neighbors

System Id    SNPA             Interface   State   Holdtime  Type Protocol
RTE          0000.0c76.f1fa   Et0         Up      18         L2   IS-IS
RTF          0000.0c76.f098   Et0         Up      24         L1L2 IS-IS
```

A glance at the MAC addresses under the SNPA column of Example 10-29 shows that RTE has a higher MAC address than RTF and RTG, so with each node retaining the default interface priority value, RTE should be both the Level 1 and Level 2 DIS. This is confirmed by the **show clns interface** output of RTE, shown in Example 10-30. The value of the circuit ID gives that clue. In Example 10-31, RTF points correctly to RTE as the Level 2 DIS but incorrectly to itself as the Level 1 DIS. This implies that there is a problem with Level 1 communication. Because this is a new setup and all the defaults have not been tampered with, the only factor that might dictate the type of adjacency formed is the area prefix. Further inspection of the NET configured on RTE shows that it was misconfigured with 49.0002.0000.0000.0002.00 rather than 47.0002.0000.0000.0002.00. This area ID mismatch resulted in RTF and RTG forming only Level 2 adjacencies with RTE.

Example 10-30 *Determining the DIS on the LAN (refer to Figure 10-5)*

```
RTE#show clns interface e0
Ethernet0 is up, line protocol is up
  Checksums enabled, MTU 1497, Encapsulation SAP
  ERPDUs enabled, min. interval 10 msec.
  RDPDUs enabled, min. interval 100 msec., Addr Mask enabled
  Congestion Experienced bit set at 4 packets
  CLNS fast switching enabled
  CLNS SSE switching disabled
  DEC compatibility mode OFF for this interface
     Next ESH/ISH in 4 seconds
  Routing Protocol: IS-IS
    Circuit Type: level-1-2
    Interface number 0x0, local circuit ID 0x1
    Level-1 Metric: 10, Priority: 64, Circuit ID: RTE.01
    Number of active level-1 adjacencies: 0
    Level-2 Metric: 10, Priority: 64, Circuit ID: RTE.01
    Number of active level-2 adjacencies: 2
    Next IS-IS LAN Level-1 Hello in 1 seconds
    Next IS-IS LAN Level-2 Hello in 1 seconds
```

Example 10-31 *Confirmation of DIS Conflict*

```
RTF#show clns interface
Ethernet0 is up, line protocol is up
Ethernet0 is up, line protocol is up
  Checksums enabled, MTU 1497, Encapsulation SAP
  ERPDUs enabled, min. interval 10 msec.
  RDPDUs enabled, min. interval 100 msec., Addr Mask enabled
  Congestion Experienced bit set at 4 packets
  CLNS fast switching enabled
  CLNS SSE switching disabled
  DEC compatibility mode OFF for this interface
     Next ESH/ISH in 4 seconds
```

continues

Example 10-31 *Confirmation of DIS Conflict (Continued)*

```
Routing Protocol: IS-IS
  Circuit Type: level-1-2
  Interface number 0x0, local circuit ID 0x1
  Level-1 Metric: 10, Priority: 64, Circuit ID: RTF.01
  Number of active level-1 adjacencies: 1
  Level-2 Metric: 10, Priority: 64, Circuit ID: RTE.01
  Number of active level-2 adjacencies: 2
```

Duplicate System IDs in an Area

All IS-IS nodes in an area must have the same area prefix and a unique system ID. If a node has multiple NETs configured, each address must retain the same system ID. This is a critical protocol requirement, especially because the system ID forms part of the LSPID, and uniqueness is required to identify the owners of LSPs flooded within the area. When different nodes in the area are erroneously configured with the same system ID, the problem is detected and each node logs appropriate error messages to that effect (see Example 10-32). If the nodes are directly connected, each router immediately detects the problem as it exchanges hellos to establish adjacency. Consequently, the adjacency fails. If they are not directly connected, however, they overwrite each other's LSP for some time until the IS-IS process determines, based on the frequency of occurrence, that the problem is because of duplicate system IDs and logs appropriate error messages. Example 10-33 shows the output of the **debug isis adj-packet** command for a duplicate system ID situation between directly connected neighbors.

Example 10-32 *Logging of Duplicate System ID Errors*

```
RT1#show logging
Mar 10 16:41:20: %CLNS-3-BADPACKET: ISIS: LAN L1 hello, Duplicate system ID det)
Mar 10 16:42:22: %CLNS-3-BADPACKET: ISIS: LAN L1 hello, Duplicate system ID det)
Mar 10 16:43:21: %CLNS-3-BADPACKET: ISIS: LAN L1 hello, Duplicate system ID det)
```

Example 10-33 *Debugging Duplicate System ID Scenarios*

```
RT1#debug isis adj-packet
Mar 10 16:41:53: ISIS-Adj: Sending L1 IIH on Ethernet0/0, length 1497
Mar 10 16:41:55: ISIS-Adj: Rec L1 IIH from 00d0.58eb.ff01 (Ethernet0/0), cir ty7
Mar 10 16:41:55: ISIS-Adj: Duplicate system id
Mar 10 16:41:56: ISIS-Adj: Sending L1 IIH on Ethernet0/0, length 1497
Mar 10 16:41:58: ISIS-Adj: Rec L1 IIH from 00d0.58eb.ff01 (Ethernet0/0), cir ty7
Mar 10 16:41:58: ISIS-Adj: Duplicate system id
Mar 10 16:41:59: ISIS-Adj: Sending L1 IIH on Ethernet0/0, length 1497
Mar 10 16:42:00: ISIS-Adj: Rec L1 IIH from 00d0.58eb.ff01 (Ethernet0/0), cir ty7
Mar 10 16:42:00: ISIS-Adj: Duplicate system id
```

Mismatched Interface MTUs

ISO 10589 mandates the padding of transmitted hello packets, which are used to establish and maintain adjacencies, to the maximum possible data size a router can receive and process on an interface. This provides a packet-size negotiation mechanism, which ensures adjacency forms only between systems that can receive and process the largest possible data size that the other can transmit.

Cisco IOS Software adheres to this specification by padding hellos to the full MTU size of the interface. Consequently, in the default mode of operation, IS-IS routers running Cisco IOS Software do not form adjacencies if their physical interface MTU values do not match. Verification of possible MTU mismatch should, therefore, be considered when troubleshooting adjacency problems. Examples 10-34 and 10-35, which are based on Figure 10-6, illustrate adjacency failure resulting from an MTU mismatch. Figure 10-6 shows two routers connected back-to-back over a serial link. As seen in the debug output in Examples 10-34 and 10-35, the adjacency of the serial link is dropped at approximately 20:44:16 when the MTU on RT2 is changed from 1500 to 2000. From then on, RT2 pads its hellos to 1999, which are ignored by RT1. After three hellos are ignored by RT1, the hello holdtime expires, the adjacency is dropped, and an adjacency change event is logged.

Figure 10-6 *Investigating an MTU mismatch problem.*

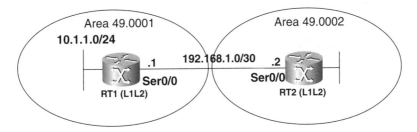

RT1 retains an ES-IS adjacency with RT2; however, RT2 receives and processes the smaller 1499-byte hellos from RT1 and puts the IS-IS adjacency in init state, hoping to complete the three-way handshake to establish full IS-IS adjacency. The IS-IS adjacency is never completed as long as the two RT2's MTU remain larger than that of RT1.

Example 10-34 *Debugging an MTU Mismatch on RT1*

```
RT1#debug isis adj-packet
IS-IS Adjacency related packets debugging is on

Mar 10 20:43:56: ISIS-Adj: Sending serial IIH on Serial0/0, length 1499
Mar 10 20:43:59: ISIS-Adj: Rec serial IIH from *HDLC* (Serial0/0), cir type L1L2
Mar 10 20:43:59: ISIS-Adj: rcvd state UP, old state UP, new state UP
Mar 10 20:43:59: ISIS-Adj: Action = ACCEPT
Mar 10 20:44:05: ISIS-Adj: Sending serial IIH on Serial0/0, length 1499
```

continues

Example 10-34 *Debugging an MTU Mismatch on RT1 (Continued)*

```
Mar 10 20:44:13: ISIS-Adj: Sending serial IIH on Serial0/0, length 1499
Mar 10 20:44:22: ISIS-Adj: Sending serial IIH on Serial0/0, length 1499
Mar 10 20:44:29: %CLNS-5-ADJCHANGE: ISIS: Adjacency to RT2 (Serial0/0) Down, hod
Mar 10 20:44:29: ISIS-Adj: L2 adj count 0
Mar 10 20:44:31: ISIS-Adj: Sending serial IIH on Serial0/0, length 1499
Mar 10 20:44:40: ISIS-Adj: Sending serial IIH on Serial0/0, length 1499
Mar 10 20:44:48: ISIS-Adj: Sending serial IIH on Serial0/0, length 1499
Mar 10 20:44:57: ISIS-Adj: Sending serial IIH on Serial0/0, length 1499
Mar 10 20:45:07: ISIS-Adj: Sending serial IIH on Serial0/0, length 1499

RT1#show clns neighbors

System Id    Interface   SNPA        State  Holdtime  Type Protocol
RT2          Se0/0       *HDLC*      Up     250       IS   ES-IS

RT1#show clns interface serial0/0
Serial0/0 is up, line protocol is up
  Checksums enabled, MTU 1500, Encapsulation HDLC
  ERPDUs enabled, min. interval 10 msec., last sent 14:13:29
  RDPDUs enabled, min. interval 100 msec., Addr Mask enabled
  Congestion Experienced bit set at 4 packets
  CLNS fast switching enabled
  CLNS SSE switching disabled
  DEC compatibility mode OFF for this interface
  Next ESH/ISH in 28 seconds
  Routing Protocol: IS-IS
    Circuit Type: level-1-2
    Interface number 0x1, local circuit ID 0x100
    Level-1 Metric: 10, Priority: 64, Circuit ID: RT1.00
    Number of active level-1 adjacencies: 0
    Level-2 Metric: 10, Priority: 64, Circuit ID: RT1.00
    Number of active level-2 adjacencies: 0
    Next IS-IS Hello in 6 seconds
```

Example 10-35 *Debugging an MTU Mismatch on RT2*

```
RT2(config)#interface s 0/0
RT2(config-if)#mtu 2000
RT2(config-if)#^Z


RT2#debug isis adj-packet
IS-IS Adjacency related packets debugging is on
RT2#
Mar 10 20:44:16: ISIS-Adj: Sending serial IIH on Serial0/0, length 1999
Mar 10 20:44:21: ISIS-Adj: Rec serial IIH from *HDLC* (Serial0/0), cir type L1L9
Mar 10 20:44:21: ISIS-Adj: rcvd state DOWN, old state UP, new state INIT
Mar 10 20:44:21: ISIS-Adj: Action = GOING DOWN
Mar 10 20:44:21: %CLNS-5-ADJCHANGE: ISIS: Adjacency to RT1 (Serial0/0) Down, nes
Mar 10 20:44:21: ISIS-Adj: L2 adj count 0
```

Example 10-35 *Debugging an MTU Mismatch on RT2 (Continued)*

```
Mar 10 20:44:21: ISIS-Adj: Sending serial IIH on Serial0/0, length 1999
Mar 10 20:44:29: ISIS-Adj: Rec serial IIH from *HDLC* (Serial0/0), cir type L1L9
Mar 10 20:44:29: ISIS-Adj: rcvd state DOWN, old state DOWN, new state INIT
Mar 10 20:44:29: ISIS-Adj: Action = GOING UP, new type = L2
Mar 10 20:44:29: ISIS-Adj: New serial adjacency
Mar 10 20:44:29: ISIS-Adj: Sending serial IIH on Serial0/0, length 1999
Mar 10 20:44:38: ISIS-Adj: Rec serial IIH from *HDLC* (Serial0/0), cir type L1L9
Mar 10 20:44:38: ISIS-Adj: rcvd state DOWN, old state INIT, new state INIT
Mar 10 20:44:38: ISIS-Adj: Action = GOING UP, new type = L2
Mar 10 20:44:38: ISIS-Adj: Sending serial IIH on Serial0/0, length 1999
Mar 10 20:44:47: ISIS-Adj: Sending serial IIH on Serial0/0, length 1999

RT2#show clns neighbors

System Id     Interface   SNPA        State  Holdtime  Type Protocol
RT1           Se0/0       *HDLC*      Init   27        L2   IS-IS

RT2#show clns interface
Serial0/0 is up, line protocol is up
  Checksums enabled, MTU 2000, Encapsulation HDLC
  ERPDUs enabled, min. interval 10 msec., last sent 12:52:30
  RDPDUs enabled, min. interval 100 msec., Addr Mask enabled
  Congestion Experienced bit set at 4 packets
  CLNS fast switching enabled
  CLNS SSE switching disabled
  DEC compatibility mode OFF for this interface
  Next ESH/ISH in 7 seconds
  Routing Protocol: IS-IS
    Circuit Type: level-1-2
    Interface number 0x0, local circuit ID 0x100
    Level-1 Metric: 10, Priority: 64, Circuit ID: RT2.00
    Number of active level-1 adjacencies: 0
    Level-2 Metric: 10, Priority: 64, Circuit ID: RT2.00
    Number of active level-2 adjacencies: 0
    Next IS-IS Hello in 7 seconds
```

Some network operators hold the notion that because default data-link capabilities are mostly standardized, known up front, and configurable, padding hellos to ensure MTU consistency unnecessarily wastes precious network bandwidth. This has prompted the introduction of a command in IOS to turn off hello padding. Two commands are available to support this capability:

[no] hello padding [multi-point| point-to-point]—Can be applied globally at the router level

[no] isis hello padding—For interface-level configuration

Example 10-36 illustrates the effect of disabling IS-IS hello padding on a serial interface and changing the MTU to 2000. The **debug isis adj-packets** command shows the size of hello packets to be only 38 bytes with padding of hellos disabled. Despite the higher MTU on one side on the link, the adjacency is retained.

Example 10-36 *Disabling Hello Padding*

```
RT1(config-router)#int se0/0
RT1(config-if)#no isis hello padding
RT1(config-if)#mtu 2000
RT1(config-if)#^Z

RT1#show clns interface Serial0/0
Serial0/0 is up, line protocol is up
  Checksums enabled, MTU 2000, Encapsulation HDLC
  ERPDUs enabled, min. interval 10 msec.
  RDPDUs enabled, min. interval 100 msec., Addr Mask enabled
  Congestion Experienced bit set at 4 packets
  CLNS fast switching enabled
  CLNS SSE switching disabled
  DEC compatibility mode OFF for this interface
  Next ESH/ISH in 40 seconds
  Routing Protocol: IS-IS
    Circuit Type: level-1-2
    Interface number 0x1, local circuit ID 0x100
    Level-1 Metric: 10, Priority: 64, Circuit ID: RT2.00
    Number of active level-1 adjacencies: 0
    Level-2 Metric: 10, Priority: 64, Circuit ID: 0000.0000.0000.00
    Number of active level-2 adjacencies: 1
    Next IS-IS Hello in 3 seconds
    No hello padding

RT1#debug isis adj-packets

*Mar  1 03:41:57: ISIS-Adj: Rec serial IIH from *HDLC* (Serial0/0), cir type L19
*Mar  1 03:41:57: ISIS-Adj: rcvd state UP, old state UP, new state UP
*Mar  1 03:41:57: ISIS-Adj: Action = ACCEPT
*Mar  1 03:41:58: ISIS-Adj: Sending serial IIH on Serial0/0, length 38
*Mar  1 03:42:06: ISIS-Adj: Rec serial IIH from *HDLC* (Serial0/0), cir type L19
*Mar  1 03:42:06: ISIS-Adj: rcvd state UP, old state UP, new state UP
*Mar  1 03:42:06: ISIS-Adj: Action = ACCEPT
*Mar  1 03:42:06: ISIS-Adj: Sending serial IIH on Serial0/0, length 38

RT1#show clns neighbors

System Id    Interface    SNPA        State  Holdtime  Type Protocol
RT2          Se0/0        *HDLC*      Up     22        L2   IS-IS
```

Misconfigured IP Addresses and Subnets

Originally, the IS-IS protocol relied on only IS-IS hellos to form and maintain adjacencies, using a three-way handshake on broadcast links and a two-way handshake on point-to-point links, all independent of the IP configuration. The increasing popularity of IS-IS for routing IP has promoted various enhancements both within the IETF and in vendor-specific implementations through feature introductions. One such feature introduced recently into Cisco IOS Software releases requires directly connected IP routers using IS-IS for routing to be also connected to the same IP subnet in order to form adjacencies.

This is not the case in older Cisco IOS Software releases, where directly connected routers could still form IS-IS adjacencies even though they were not properly configured to be on the same IP subnet. Recent changes in IOS require the source IP address of an IP neighbor to be validated before bringing up the adjacency. This behavior is implemented in Cisco IOS Software 12.0S releases, which are optimized for IP networks. This makes verification of the IP address configuration an important step in troubleshooting IS-IS adjacency problems.

The effect of IP address misconfiguration is illustrated in the following debugging and show command output (based on Figure 10-7). In Example 10-37, the IP address of RT2's serial interface is changed to 192.168.5.2/30. This erroneous entry causes adjacency to be invalidated at RT1 and logging of an adjacency change message. In this case, the IS-IS adjacency drops and it is replaced by an ES-IS adjacency. The debugging output shown in Example 10-32 includes an error, "ISIS-Adj: No usable IP interface addresses in serial IIH from 0." IP unnumbered configurations are not affected by the requirement that adjacent neighbors must be on the same subnet.

Figure 10-7 *Test network for investigating IP address and subnet misconfiguration.*

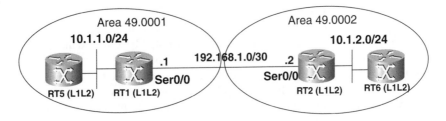

Example 10-37 *Simulating and Debugging Misconfigured IP Addresses*

```
RT2#config terminal
Enter configuration commands, one per line.  End with CNTL/Z.
RT2(config)#int s0/0
RT2(config-if)#ip address 192.168.5.2 255.255.255.252
RT2(config-if)#^Z
```

continues

Example 10-37 *Simulating and Debugging Misconfigured IP Addresses (Continued)*

```
RT2#show clns neighbors

System Id   Interface   SNPA              State  Holdtime  Type Protocol
RT1         Se0/0       *HDLC*            Up     257       IS   ES-IS
RT6         Et0/0       00d0.58f7.8041    Up     7         L1   IS-IS

RT1#show clns neighbors

System Id   Interface   SNPA              State  Holdtime  Type Protocol
RT2         Se0/0       *HDLC*            Up     284       IS   ES-IS
RT5         Et0/0       00d0.58eb.ff01    Up     26        L1   IS-IS

RT1#debug isis adj-packets

Mar 10 21:44:19: ISIS-Adj: Sending serial IIH on Serial0/0, length 1499
Mar 10 21:44:20: ISIS-Adj: Rec serial IIH from *HDLC* (Serial0/0), cir type L1L9
Mar 10 21:44:20: ISIS-Adj: No usable IP interface addresses in serial IIH from 0
Mar 10 21:44:24: %CLNS-5-ADJCHANGE: ISIS: Adjacency to RT2 (Serial0/0) Down, hod
Mar 10 21:44:24: ISIS-Adj: L2 adj count 0
Mar 10 21:44:27: ISIS-Adj: Sending serial IIH on Serial0/0, length 1499
Mar 10 21:44:30: ISIS-Adj: Rec serial IIH from *HDLC* (Serial0/0), cir type L1L9
Mar 10 21:44:30: ISIS-Adj: No usable IP interface addresses in serial IIH from 0
```

IS-IS Route Maintenance Problems

This section focuses on route maintenance problems. The adjacency formation problems discussed in the preceding section are much easier to troubleshoot and resolve than router maintenance problems, which are normally not obvious in very large networks until a specific address or subnet becomes unreachable. Obviously, most IS-IS problems relate to adjacency problems. When no adjacency issues exist, it becomes challenging to isolate routing problems; however, on Cisco routers, the routing table might be fed with routing information from multiple sources. Most routers connected to the Internet are configured with two IP routing protocols, typically BGP for interdomain routing and IS-IS or OSPF for intradomain routing. Frequently in these situations, little overlap occurs in prefixes advertised by each protocol, so there is practically no contention in populating the routing table.

The routes in the IP routing table are organized into more efficient data structures for faster route lookup. Fast packet forwarding can be achieved on Cisco routers with two basic mechanisms:

- Fast switching
- Cisco Express Forwarding

Overviews of these mechanisms are provided in Chapter 1, "Overview of IP Routing." Refer to the references provided at the end of this chapter for further details about these mechanisms. Even though very rare, route maintenance problems might relate to problems in the lookup mechanism rather than the actual source of the route. This section focuses on only IS-IS-related causes. The following are the most common causes of routing inconsistencies in IS-IS and are discussed in detail in the following sections:

- IS-IS route advertisement problems
- IS-IS route installation problem
- Discontiguous Level 2 subdomain
- Route flaps
- LSP corruption storms
- Authentication problems
- IS-IS summarization and redistribution problems

IS-IS Route Advertisement Problems

Route advertisement problems refer to the inability of accurate routing information to reach a remote destination from a specific router or section of the network. As a link-state protocol, IS-IS routing information is advertised by means of link-state packets. Troubleshooting routing basically involves inspecting the LSP of the source node at both the source and routers in the region of the network where the routes are missing.

An IS-IS router advertises routing information to the rest of the network by one of the following methods:

- The route is a subnet connected to the router, and the corresponding interface is enabled for IS-IS routing.
- Passive interface.
- External routes by means of redistribution from another routing source (static, another dynamic routing protocol such as RIP, or a connected interface).
- Route summaries.

If a route is not being heard in the rest of the area or domain, the first step in troubleshooting the problem is to make sure the procedure for introducing the route into the IS-IS process has been properly configured.

Advertising IP Subnets by Activating IS-IS on Interfaces

If the first method is used, the **ip router isis** command must be applied to the appropriate interface. Note that IS-IS does not use a network statement for advertising an IP route as is commonly done for other protocols. Instead, enabling IS-IS on an interface triggers the formation of adjacencies on that interface and also advertises the attached IP subnet in an LSP to all neighbors. The **show ip interface brief** command confirms the interface on which the route is connected, followed by a **show clns interface** command. The actual configuration of the interface can also be verified with the command **show running-config | begin interface <type and number>**, as shown in Example 10-38.

Example 10-38 *Advertising IS-IS Routing Information*

```
RT1#show run | begin interface Serial0/0

interface Serial0/0
 mtu 2000
 ip address 192.168.1.1 255.255.255.252
 no ip directed-broadcast
 ip router isis
 no ip mroute-cache
 no fair-queue
 clockrate 2000000
 no isis hello padding
```

If the interface is properly configured, the next step might be to take a look at the IP reachability information fields of the router's LSP with the command **show isis database** *level detail LSPID*. This command provides insight into the information in the LSP that is advertised to other neighbors. It is assumed that there are no adjacency problems with any of the neighbors in the direction of the network where the route is missing. The **level-1** keyword is used if the route is missing in only the local area, and the **level-2** keyword is used if the route is not present in other areas within the same domain. If no adjacency problems exist, IS-IS routing is enabled correctly on the interface where the route should be taken from, and the prefix is seen in the LSP of the local router; then the problem is complex and requires more insight. The **show isis database** *level detail LSPID* command should be used on the remote routers to check the presence and currency of the LSP in question. The **debug isis update-packet** command assists with debugging any issues with periodic database synchronization on LANs. Note that synchronization issues are absent on point-to-point links because of the reliable flooding process used on such links.

Advertising a Subnet with **passive-interface**

The **passive-interface** command is normally used when the subnet on an interface needs to be advertised without forming adjacency or sending redundant hello messages over that interface. For example, a loopback interface is normally defined as a passive interface so that its address will be advertised without wasting CPU cycles to generate unnecessary hellos to nonexistent neighbors. If a loopback address is not advertised, the configuration should be checked to make sure it is specified as a passive interface. Current Cisco IOS Software releases remove the **ip router isis** command from the interface configuration when the interface is defined as passive.

Advertising External Routes

The most complicated routing maintenance problems involve redistribution. Redistribution of static routes is manageable and related problems are easy to troubleshoot.

Problems that relate to redistribution of a dynamically learned route are far more complicated. This is primarily because no inherent loop-prevention mechanisms are associated with route redistribution. The safest way to redistribute routes without establishing loops and route feedback is to limit the points where redistribution occurs. When problems occur in such situations, it is best to troubleshoot at the points of redistribution (border routers). Redistributed IP routes are entered as externals into the LSP. The **show isis database** *level detail LSPID* command can be used to inspect the LSPs of the border routers to ensure the external reachability information reaches the LSPs correctly. When the IS-IS domain has multiple points of redistribution, more than one LSP can introduce the external routes into the IS-IS domain, requiring care to be taken so that the border routers do not point to each other as the best exit from the domain to the external destinations.

The router-level **display-route-detail** command provides knowledge about which LSPs are responsible for specific routes in the routing table. This is a useful tool for troubleshooting routing problems and tracking where the entries in the routing table originate from. Figure 10-8 demonstrates the operation of this command, and the command output is shown in Example 10-39. A partial configuration of RT1 and the output of the **show ip route isis** command executed on RT1 are included in Example 10-39. Also shown is a **show isis database** command from the same router. Each IS-IS entry in the routing table of RT1 indicates the number of the LSP from which it came. The LSP numbers are shown in brackets in the **show isis database** output. For example, 10.1.2.0/24 is learned from LSP number 4, which is RT2.00-00. The **display-route-detail** command also displays backup paths for routes, which are alternative, less-preferred paths. The following backup entry is provided for this route:

```
Backup ix/lvl/metric:9/L2/30
```

The interpretation of this backup path is as follows:

- **ix**—Index of source LSP (LSP 9)
- **lvl**—Level 1 or Level 2 (Level 2)
- **metric**—The metric value (30)

This extra information provided by the **display-route-detail** command gives more insight into the routing environment and can significantly help you to troubleshoot routing problems. In this case, 10.1.2.0/24 is learned from LSP4 (RT2.00-00) as primary, but a backup path is being advertised through LSP9 (RT4.00-00). The origins of these LSPs are obvious from the names.

Figure 10-8 *Demonstrating use of the* **display-route-detail** *command.*

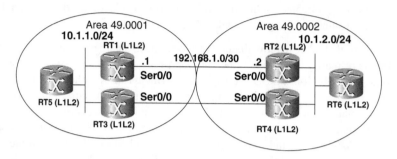

Example 10-39 **display-route-detail** *Command Example*

```
RT1#show running-config
[snip]
router isis
 passive-interface Loopback0
 default-information originate
 net 49.0001.0000.0000.0001.00
 metric-style wide
 log-adjacency-changes
 display-route-detail


RT1#show ip route isis
     10.0.0.0/8 is variably subnetted, 3 subnets, 2 masks
i L2 10.1.2.0/24 [115/20] via 192.168.1.2, Serial0/0, from LSP 4
        Backup ix/lvl/metric:  9/L2/30
     11.0.0.0/32 is subnetted, 6 subnets
i L1    11.1.1.3 [115/10] via 10.1.1.3, Ethernet0/0, from LSP 7
        Backup ix/lvl/metric:  8/L2/10
i L2    11.1.1.2 [115/10] via 192.168.1.2, Serial0/0, from LSP 4
        Backup ix/lvl/metric:  9/L2/30
i L2    11.1.1.6 [115/20] via 192.168.1.2, Serial0/0, from LSP 4
        Backup ix/lvl/metric:  9/L2/30
i L1    11.1.1.5 [115/10] via 10.1.1.5, Ethernet0/0, from LSP 5
        Backup ix/lvl/metric:  8/L2/20
i L2    11.1.1.4 [115/20] via 192.168.1.2, Serial0/0, from LSP 9
        Backup ix/lvl/metric:  4/L2/20
     192.168.2.0/30 is subnetted, 1 subnets
i L1    192.168.2.0 [115/20] via 10.1.1.3, Ethernet0/0, from LSP 7
        Backup ix/lvl/metric:  4/L2/30  8/L2/110  */L2/120



RT1#show isis data
IS-IS Level-1 Link State Database
LSPID            LSP Seq Num  LSP Checksum  LSP Holdtime     ATT/P/OL
RT1.00-00      * 0x000000FA   0xAF5F        661              1/0/0  (1)
```

Example 10-39 display-route-detail *Command Example (Continued)*

```
RT1.01-00      * 0x000000F4    0x40FC        349         0/0/0  (3)
RT3.00-00        0x0000119B    0xCA8D        668         1/0/0  (7)
RT5.00-00        0x000000EC    0x1E90        434         0/0/0  (5)


IS-IS Level-2 Link State Database
LSPID            LSP Seq Num   LSP Checksum  LSP Holdtime   ATT/P/OL
RT1.00-00      * 0x00000101    0x9FB7        563         0/0/0  (2)
RT1.01-00      * 0x0000000D    0x8D30        1193        0/0/0  (6)
RT2.00-00        0x00001FC0    0x1F57        739         0/0/0  (4)
RT2.01-00        0x00000001    0xBA0C        730         0/0/0  (10)
RT3.00-00        0x0000119D    0x01F4        714         0/0/0  (8)
RT4.00-00        0x00001191    0x06F3        834         0/0/0  (9)
```

Advertising Summary Routes

Frequently, network operators attempt to summarize routing information by representing a set of routes with one or a fewer number of prefixes than in the original set. This is good practice and helps save on system resources, such as memory and network bandwidth. If many smaller prefixes are summarized into one prefix, less space is required in the LSP to advertise those prefixes, and, therefore, less bandwidth is needed to flood the smaller LSP throughout the area. When routes are summarized, they might become part of an aggregate. Therefore, troubleshooting missing routes in such environments should involve checking whether they are represented accurately by the summaries as intended.

IS-IS Route Installation Problems

Route installation problems involve situations where an LSP from a remote router is properly received, but a route in the LSP is not installed in the routing table as expected. IS-IS does not have any complicated schemes for installing routes that are determined by the SPF process to be the best path. For example, OSPF external link-state advertisements have a forwarding address when non-zero has to be learned through OSPF for a routing bit that controls insertion into the routing table to be set appropriately. IS-IS has no concept of a routing bit. The most plausible reason why an IS-IS route should not make it into the routing table is because there is a similar route from another routing source with a better administrative distance than IS-IS. Route installation problems are rare in IS-IS, and when they do occur, the reason is most certainly a software failure or an interoperability issue.

You can use the following commands to isolate route installation problems:

- **show ip route [isis]**
- **show isis database** *level detail LSPID*

The **show ip route** *prefix* command determines the absolute absence of the prefix from the routing table. If the route is present but from another source, the administrative distance should be lower; otherwise, there's an issue. The **isis** keyword lists only all IS-IS routes in the IP routing table. This might prove useful to confirm whether only a specific route from IS-IS is affected.

If a route is not in the routing table as expected, the **show isis database** command specifying the routing level, the LSPID of the source LSP, and the detail keyword should be used to probe further into the contents of the LSP. Help from an expert might be required to confirm the problem.

Unstable IS-IS Routes

Route instability means that the route is available only intermittently. This is usually described as a *route flap*. Route flap might result just from an unstable link or possibly because of a more complex underlying condition, such as an intermittent routing loop.

Typically, at the point where the flap is seen, the LSP that contains the route is periodically advertised and withdrawn, or newer versions are continuously being received. Route flaps can also have a devastating effect on the routing environment if a large number of LSPs and routers are affected. This might cause the SPF process to run for prolonged periods, resulting in potentially dangerous levels of CPU utilization on the affected routers.

If the network changes affect only IP prefixes, only partial route calculation (PRC) might be performed by the IS-IS SPF process. Other situations might require scheduling of a "full" SPF. The latter is more CPU-intensive.

By far, the most common causes of route flaps are unstable links. Another well-known cause is corruption of an LSP in a network device as it is being flooded through the network. LSP corruption storms are discussed later in this chapter.

In a large network, the **display-route-detail** command discussed in the preceding section can determine the LSP associated with the unstable route (refer to Example 10-35). The focus of problem isolation can then be placed on the source of the LSP.

In most cases, a route flap problem can be quickly confirmed by looking at the sequence numbers of LSPs in the same link state database. The **show isis database output** in Example 10-40 features a far higher sequence number for the LSP with ID RT2.00-00 than for the other known LSPs. The huge discrepancy signals either problems at the source or somewhere in between the source and the point of observation. If the source and the router at which the problem is being observed are directly connected, you can use standard procedures to troubleshoot the physical and data link layers. The **show interface** or **show clns interface** command can provide link status information and some leads might be available in the logs. Because the problem might be adjacency related, the **debug isis adj-packet** debugging option can be enabled to observe the problem further. At the source of the LSP, the **debug isis spf-log** command provides information regarding events affecting the locally sourced LSP and, therefore, some clues to the problem (refer to Example 10-12 and Table 10-2).

Example 10-40 *Troubleshooting Unstable Routes*

```
RT1#show isis database
IS-IS Level-1 Link State Database
LSPID              LSP Seq Num  LSP Checksum  LSP Holdtime    ATT/P/OL
RT1.00-00        * 0x00000093   0x7EF7        438             1/0/0
RT1.01-00        * 0x0000008B   0xA014        838             0/0/0
RT5.00-00          0x00000085   0xEC29        1107            0/0/0

IS-IS Level-2 Link State Database
LSPID              LSP Seq Num  LSP Checksum  LSP Holdtime    ATT/P/OL
RT1.00-00        * 0x00000095   0xA819        1082            0/0/0
RT2.00-00          0x00001F57   0xE0FE        781             0/0/0
```

LSP Corruption Storms

LSP corruption storms occur when LSPs are corrupted by a network device as the LSPs are flooded. When a router receives a corrupted LSP, it purges it from the network by setting its remaining lifetime to 0 and flooding it back into the network. Corrupted LSPs are determined through checksum matching. When a corrupted LSP is purged, the source regenerates another copy and re-advertises it back into the network. This advertise-and-purge activity will likely occur until the source of the corruption is removed from the network. Corruption storms consume network resources, such as CPU and bandwidth, and can seriously impact network performance. LSP corruption storms can be eliminated with the router-level command **ignore-lsp-errors**.

Discontiguous Level 2 Subdomains

IS-IS requires the Level 2 backbone that interconnects the various areas to be contiguous. This condition can easily be violated by bad network design or router misconfiguration, as shown in Figure 10-9. Cisco routers function as Level 1-2 by default and caution should be exercised in turning off Level 2 routing until the impact is well understood. The Level 1-only router in area 49.0002 disrupts the continuity of the Level 2 path, preventing areas 49.0001 and 49.0003 from reaching each other.

Figure 10-9 *Case study for fragmented Level 2 backbone.*

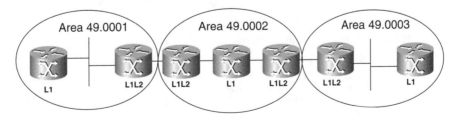

Authentication Problems

IS-IS specifications (ISO 10589 [1] and RFC 1195 [2]) provide a simple password scheme for authentication. Three kinds of authentication methods that use simple password are supported on Cisco routers, as discussed in Chapter 9.

- Link authentication
- Area authentication
- Domain authentication

When authentication is configured, a clear-text password is inserted into IS-IS packets, such as LSPs, CSNPs, and PSNPs, as are also hellos (link authentication only). The password is verified before a packet is accepted for processing. Clearly, a password mismatch between the source of the packet and the recipient could create both adjacency and routing maintenance problems, depending on the type of authentication enabled. Example 10-41 shows a **debug adj-packet** output for a link authentication failure.

Example 10-41 *Debugging Authentication Failures*

```
RT1# debug isis adj-packets
*Apr 23 04:25:36: ISIS-Adj: Rec serial IIH from *HDLC* (Serial0/0), cir type L1L2,
cir id 00, length 1499
*Apr 23 04:25:36: ISIS-Adj: Authentication failed
*Apr 23 04:25:42: ISIS-Adj: Sending serial IIH on Serial0/0, length 1499
*Apr 23 04:25:46: ISIS-Adj: Rec serial IIH from *HDLC* (Serial0/0), cir type L1L2,
cir id 00, length 1499
*Apr 23 04:25:46: ISIS-Adj: Authentication failed
*Apr 23 04:25:50: ISIS-Adj: Sending serial IIH on Serial0/0, length 1499
```

IS-IS Error Logging

The errors logged by Cisco IOS Software frequently provide information about problems occurring on the router or the network in general and should always be checked for pertinent clues when troubleshooting problems. Example 10-42 shows an IS-IS-related logged error that indicates that an address prefix that had a length of 135 bytes was detected, which is more than the expected maximum size. This log information also provides the ID of the LSP carrying the malformed TLV with the bad information. Example 10-43 shows that a hello packet is received from an ATM VC with a length of 51 bytes rather than the expected 53 bytes.

Example 10-44 shows information logged for an adjacency change.

Example 10-42 *IS-IS Logging for Malformed Packets on PoS Link*

```
Mar 10 11:59:46.171: %CLNS-3-BADPACKET: ISIS: L1 LSP, option 1 address prefix
   length 135 > max NSAP length (21), ID 0000.0000.04B7.00-00, seq 25948, ht 1115
   from *PPP* (POS6/0).
```

Example 10-43 *IS-IS Logging for Malformed Packet on ATM PVC*

```
Nov 16 02:18:04.848 EDT: %CLNS-4-BADPACKET: ISIS: P2P hello, option 8 length 53
  remaining bytes (51) from VC 2 (ATM4/0.2)
```

Example 10-44 *Logs for Adjacency Changes*

```
RT1#show log
  %CLNS-5-ADJCHANGE: ISIS: Adjacency to 0000.0000.0001 (ethernet 0)
  %CLNS-5-ADJCHANGE: ISIS: Adjacency to 0000.0000.0002 (ethernet 0)
```

Summary

The network engineer should have a good understanding of the concepts behind a network protocol and be able to apply that knowledge in troubleshooting scenarios, logical and practical, in the real world. This chapter focuses on the application of the concepts discussed in the previous chapters for troubleshooting IS-IS routing problems. The practical material covered in Chapter 9 is heavily leveraged, and every effort is made to present practical examples for the reader. The material presented categorizes IS-IS failures into two main groups: adjacency problems and route maintenance problems.

The discussion about troubleshooting tools, such as **show** commands and **debug** commands, show you how to review specific problems and examples. The various command and debug output examples enable you to build up expertise in troubleshooting IS-IS routing problems and also serve as an excellent reference source.

Review Questions

1 List the two main categories of IS-IS problems discussed in this chapter and provide examples of each.

2 List two **show** commands that are useful for troubleshooting adjacency problems.

3 List a **debug** command that provides help in troubleshooting IS-IS adjacency problems.

4 What are LSP corruption storms, and how do they impact a network's performance.

5 Describe the methodology for troubleshooting an LSP corruption storm.

References

Callon, Ross. "Use of OSI IS-IS for Routing in TCP/IP and Dual Environments." IETF RFC 1195. 1990.

http://www.cisco.com/univercd/cc/td/doc/product/software/ios121/121cgcr/switch_c/xcprt2/xcdcef.htm.

Integrated IS-IS Commands.
http://www.cisco.com/univercd/cc/td/doc/product/software/ios122/122cgcr/fiprrp_r/1rfisis.htm.

Intra-domain Routing Information Exchange Protocol for Use in Conjunction with the Protocol for Providing the Connectionless-mode Network Service (ISO 8473). ISO/IEC 10589. 1992.

IP routing Protocol Commands.
http://www.cisco.com/univercd/cc/td/doc/product/software/ios100/rpcr/66004.htm.

IS-IS intra-domain routing information exchange protocol (ISO10589, p.37).

PART IV

Appendixes

IS-IS Packet Formats

IS-IS Packet Fields (Alphabetical Order)

- **ATT**—Attachment Bits (Flags attachment to other areas)
- **Checksum**—Checksum of contents of LSP from source ID field to the end
- **Circuit Type**—Defines whether link is Level-1 and Level-2
- **End LSP**—LSP ID of last LSP in CSNP
- **Holding Time**—Defines how long to wait for a hello from this system before clearing the adjacency
- **ID Length**—Length of the System ID field in an NSAP(NET)
- **Intradomain Routing Protocol Discriminator**—Network layer protocol identifier
- **IS Type**—Defines type of router, Level-1 or Level-2
- **LAN ID**—LAN Identifier, Consists of the System ID of the designated intermediate system plus a unique number
- **Length Indicator**—Length of the fixed header of the packet in bytes
- **Local Circuit ID**—Unique identifier for a link
- **LSP ID**—Identifier for router's LSP, consisting of the System ID of the router, fragment number, and a nonzero octet for pseudonode number in case of pseudonode LSP
- **Maximum Area Addresses**—Number of areas permitted
- **OL**—LSP overload bit (also represented as LSPDBOL)
- **P**—Partition repair bit
- **PDU Length**—Length of packet (PDU) in bytes
- **PDU Type**—Type of packet
- **Priority**—Priority for node for DIS arbitration
- **R**—See Reserved

- **Remaining Lifetime**—Remaining time for an LSP to expire
- **Reserved**—Unspecified fields, transmitted as 0s and ignored on receipt
- **Sequence Number**—Sequence number of LSP
- **Source ID**—Same as system identifier (SysID)
- **TLV Fields**—Type (or code), Length and Value fields, also known as variable-length fields
- **Version/Protocol ID Extension**—Of the IS-IS protocol (defined as 1)

Hello Packets

Figure A-1 *LAN Level-1 hello packet format (PDU Type 15).*

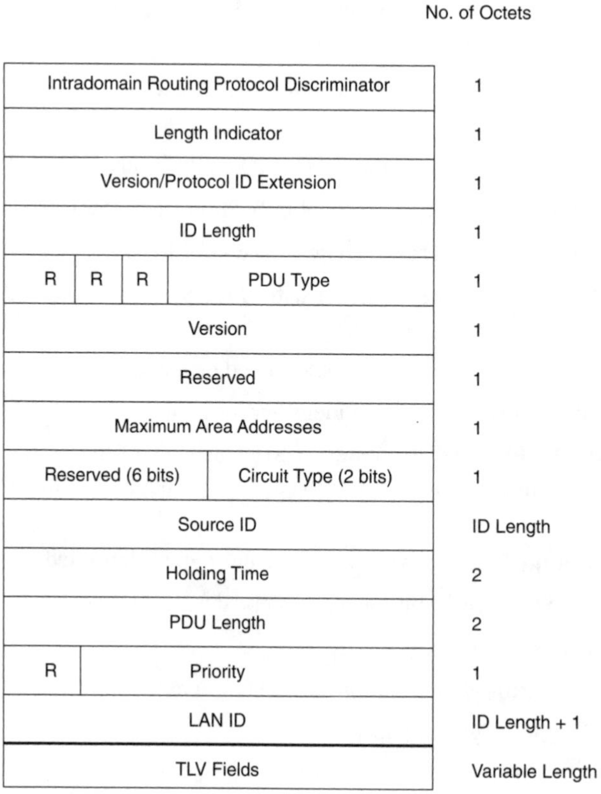

No. of Octets

Intradomain Routing Protocol Discriminator	1
Length Indicator	1
Version/Protocol ID Extension	1
ID Length	1
R R R PDU Type	1
Version	1
Reserved	1
Maximum Area Addresses	1
Reserved (6 bits) Circuit Type (2 bits)	1
Source ID	ID Length
Holding Time	2
PDU Length	2
R Priority	1
LAN ID	ID Length + 1
TLV Fields	Variable Length

Example A-1 *Analyzer Capture: LAN Level-1 Hello Packet*

```
        ADDR  HEX                                                          ASCII
       0000: 01 80 c2 00 00 14 00 d0 58 f7 89 41 05 dc fe fe ¦ .ÓÂ....DX÷&A.Üww
       0010: 03 83 1b 01 00 0f 01 00 00 03 00 00 00 00 00 01 ¦ .ƒ..............
       0020: 00 0a 05 d9 40 00 00 00 00 00 01 01 81 01 cc 01 ¦ ...Ù@.........Ì.
       0030: 04 03 49 00 01 84 04 0a 01 01 01 06 0c 00 d0 58 ¦ ..I..„........DX
       0040: eb f8 41 00 d0 58 eb ff 01 08 ff 00 00 00 00 00 ¦ ëøA.DXëÿ..ÿ.....
       0050: 00 00 00 00 00 00 00 00 00 00 00 00 00 00 00 00 ¦ ................
       0060: 00 00 00 00 00 00 00 00 00 00 00 00 00 00 00 00 ¦ ................
       0070: 00 00 00 00 00 00 00 00 00 00 00 00 00 00 00 00 ¦ ................
       0080: 00 00 00 00 00 00 00 00 00 00 00 00 00 00 00 00 ¦ ................
       0090: 00 00 00 00 00 00 00 00 00 00 00 00 00 00 00 00 ¦ ................
       00a0: 00 00 00 00 00 00 00 00 00 00 00 00 00 00 00 00 ¦ ................
       00b0: 00 00 00 00 00 00 00 00 00 00 00 00 00 00 00 00 ¦ ................
       00c0: 00 00 00 00 00 00 00 00 00 00 00 00 00 00 00 00 ¦ ................
       00d0: 00 00 00 00 00 00 00 00 00 00 00 00 00 00 00 00 ¦ ................
       00e0: 00 00 00 00 00 00 00 00 00 00 00 00 00 00 00 00 ¦ ................
       00f0: 00 00 00 00 00 00 00 00 00 00 00 00 00 00 00 00 ¦ ................
       0100: 00 00 00 00 00 00 00 00 00 00 00 00 00 00 00 00 ¦ ................
       0110: 00 00 00 00 00 00 00 00 00 00 00 00 00 00 00 00 ¦ ................
       0120: 00 00 00 00 00 00 00 00 00 00 00 00 00 00 00 00 ¦ ................
       0130: 00 00 00 00 00 00 00 00 00 00 00 00 00 00 00 00 ¦ ................
       0140: 00 00 00 00 00 00 00 00 00 00
```

Example A-2 *Decode of Example A-1 (Part 1)*

```
DLC:  ----- DLC Header -----
      DLC:
      DLC:  Frame 1 arrived at  19:03:01.2025; frame size is 1514 (05EA hex) bytes.
      DLC:  Destination = Multicast 0180C2000014
      DLC:  Source      = Station 00D058F78941
      DLC:  802.3 length = 1500
      DLC:
LLC:  ----- LLC Header -----
      LLC:
      LLC:  DSAP Address = FE, DSAP IG Bit = 00 (Individual Address)
      LLC:  SSAP Address = FE, SSAP CR Bit = 00 (Command)
      LLC:  Unnumbered frame: UI
```

Example A-3 *Decode of Example A-1 (Part 2)*

```
IS-IS: ----- ISO Network Layer Header -----
       IS-IS:
       IS-IS: Protocol ID = 83 (Intermediate System Routing Exchange Protocol)
       IS-IS: Header length = 27
       IS-IS: Version / Protocol ID Extension = 1
       IS-IS: ID Length = 0, Indicates 6 Octets
```

continues

Example A-3 *Decode of Example A-1 (Part 2) (Continued)*

```
IS-IS: PDU type = 15   (Hello, LAN Level 1)
IS-IS: Version = 1
IS-IS: Reserved = 0
IS-IS: Maximum Area Addesses = 0
IS-IS: Circuit Type = 3   (Both level 1 and level 2 routing)
IS-IS: Source ID = 000000000001
IS-IS: Holding time is 10 second(s)
IS-IS: Frame length is 1497 byte(s)
IS-IS: Designated Intermediate System for Level 1
IS-IS:   Priority = 64
IS-IS:   Address = 000000000001
IS-IS:   ID = 01
```

Example A-4 *Decode of Example A-1 (Part 3)*

```
IS-IS: ----- ISO Network Layer Variable Fields -----
   IS-IS:
   IS-IS: Variable field:
   IS-IS:   Field Code = 129   (Protocols Supported)
   IS-IS:   Field length = 1
   IS-IS:   NLPID'sfor protocols within this IS:
   IS-IS:     NLPID = CC (Internet IP)
   IS-IS: Variable field:
   IS-IS:   Field Code = 1   (Manual Area Addresses)
   IS-IS:   Field length = 4
   IS-IS:   Manual Area Address:
   IS-IS:     Length  = 3
   IS-IS:     Format  = 49 (Local Binary)
   IS-IS:     Address = 490001
   IS-IS: Variable field:
   IS-IS:   Field Code = 132   (IP Interface Address)
   IS-IS:   Field length = 4
   IS-IS:   IP Interface Address:
   IS-IS:     IP Address = [10.1.1.1]
   IS-IS: Variable field:
   IS-IS:   Field Code = 6   (System Neighbors)
   IS-IS:   Field length = 12
   IS-IS:   Neighbor = 00D058EBF841
   IS-IS:   Neighbor = 00D058EBFF01
   IS-IS: Variable field:
   IS-IS:   Field Code = 8   (Padding)
   IS-IS:   Field length = 255
```

Figure A-2 *LAN Level-2 hello packets (PDU Type 16).*

No. of Octets

Intradomain Routing Protocol Discriminator	1
Length Indicator	1
Version/Protocol ID Extension	1
ID Length	1
R R R PDU Type	1
Version	1
Reserved	1
Maximum Area Addresses	1
Reserved (6 bits) Circuit Type (2 bits)	1
Source ID	ID Length
Holding Time	2
PDU Length	2
R Priority	1
LAN ID	ID Length + 1
TLV Fields	Variable Length

Example A-5 *Analyzer Capture: LAN Level-2 Hello Packet*

```
                                                                  ASCII
      ADDR  HEX
0000: 01 80 c2 00 00 15 00 d0 58 f7 89 41 05 dc fe fe¦ .ÓÂ....DX÷&A.Üww
0010: 03 83 1b 01 00 10 01 00 00 03 00 00 00 00 00 01 ¦ .ƒ..............
0020: 00 0a 05 d9 40 00 00 00 00 00 01 01 81 01 cc 01 ¦ ...Ù@.......?.Ì.
0030: 04 03 49 00 01 84 04 0a 01 01 01 06 06 00 d0 58 ¦ ..I..„........DX
0040: eb f8 41
```

Example A-6   *Decode of Example A-5 (LAN Level-2 Hello Packet)*

```
IS-IS: -----ISO Network Layer Header -----
       IS-IS:
       IS-IS: Protocol ID = 83 (Intermediate System Routing Exchange Protocol)
       IS-IS: Header length = 27
       IS-IS: Version / Protocol ID Extension = 1
       IS-IS: ID Length = 0, Indicates 6 Octets
       IS-IS: PDU type = 16  (Hello, LAN Level 2)
       IS-IS: Version = 1
       IS-IS: Reserved = 0
       IS-IS: Maximum Area Addesses = 0
       IS-IS: Circuit Type = 3  (Both level 1 and level 2 routing)
       IS-IS: Source ID = 000000000001
       IS-IS: Holding time is 10 second(s)
       IS-IS: Frame length is 1497 byte(s)
       IS-IS: Designated Intermediate System for Level 2
       IS-IS:   Priority = 64
       IS-IS:   Address = 000000000001
       IS-IS:   ID = 01
```

Figure A-3   *Point-to-point hello packets (PDU Type 17).*

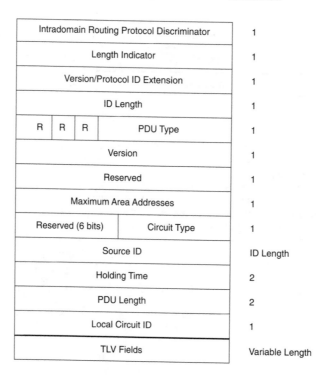

Link-State Packets

Figure A-4 *Level-1 link-state packets (PDU Type 18).*

No. of Octets

	No. of Octets
Intradomain Routing Protocol Discriminator	1
Length Indicator	1
Version/Protocol ID Extension	1
ID Length	1
R | R | R | PDU Type	1
Version	1
Reserved	1
Maximum Area Addresses	1
PDU Length	2
Remaining Lifetime	2
LSP ID	ID Length + 2
Sequence Number	4
Checksum	2
P | ATT | OL | IS Type	1
TLV Fields	

Example A-7 *Analyzer Capture: Level-1 LSP*

```
      ADDR  HEX                                              ASCII
      0000: 01 80 c2 00 00 14 00 d0 58 f7 89 41 00 67 fe fe ¦ .ÓÂ....DX÷%A.gww
      0010: 03 83 1b 01 00 12 01 00 00 00 64 04 af 00 00 00 ¦ .ƒ........d.¯...
      0020: 00 00 01 00 00 00 00 18 3b e6 cf 0b 01 04 03 49 ¦ ........;æÏ....I
      0030: 00 01 81 01 cc 89 03 52 54 31 84 04 0b 01 01 01 ¦ ...Ì‰.RT1„......
      0040: 87 1a 00 00 00 0a 18 0a 01 01 00 00 00 0a 1e c0 ¦ ‡..............À
      0050: a8 01 00 00 00 00 00 20 0b 01 01 01 16 0b 00 00 ¦ ¨...... ........
      0060: 00 00 00 01 01 00 00 0a 00 03 0a 00 80 80 80 00 ¦ ............óóó.
      0070: 00 00 00 00 01                                  ¦ .....
```

Example A-8 *Decode of Example A-7 (Level-1 LSP Part 1)*

```
DLC:  ----- DLC Header -----
      DLC:
      DLC:  Frame 318 arrived at  18:50:53.1251; frame size is 117 (0075 hex) bytes.
      DLC:  Destination = Multicast 0180C2000014
      DLC:  Source      = Station 00D058F78941
      DLC:  802.3 length = 103
      DLC:
LLC:  ----- LLC Header -----
      LLC:
      LLC:  DSAP Address = FE, DSAP IG Bit = 00 (Individual Address)
      LLC:  SSAP Address = FE, SSAP CR Bit = 00 (Command)
      LLC:  Unnumbered frame: UI
```

Example A-9 *Decode of Example A-7 (Level-1 LSP Part 2)*

```
IS-IS:  -----ISO Network Layer Header -----
IS-IS:
IS-IS: Protocol ID = 83 (Intermediate System Routing Exchange Protocol)
IS-IS: Header length = 27
IS-IS: Version / Protocol ID Extension = 1
IS-IS: ID Length = 0, Indicates 6 Octets
IS-IS: PDU type = 18  (Link State, Level 1)
IS-IS: Version = 1
IS-IS: Reserved = 0
IS-IS: Maximum Area Addesses = 0
IS-IS: Frame length is 100 byte(s)
IS-IS: Remaining life is 1199 second(s)
IS-IS: Link State Frame ID:
IS-IS:   Source ID     = 000000000001
IS-IS:   Pseudo-node   = 00   (Not a pseudo-node)
IS-IS:   Link frame no. = 0
IS-IS: Frame Sequence = 6203
IS-IS: Checksum = E6CF
IS-IS: Attributes = 0B
IS-IS: 0... .... = Partition repair not supported
IS-IS: .0.. .... = Not attached using error metric
IS-IS: ..0. .... = Not attached using expense metric
IS-IS: ...0 .... = Not attached using delay metric
IS-IS: .... 1... = Attached using default metric
IS-IS: .... .0.. = No LSP Database Overload
IS-IS: .... ..11  = Level 2 intermediate system
```

Example A-10 *Decode of Example A-7 (Level-1 LSP Part 3)*

```
IS-IS: ----- ISO Network Layer Variable Fields -----
      IS-IS:
      IS-IS: Variable field:
      IS-IS:   Field Code = 1  (Manual Area Addresses)
      IS-IS:   Field length = 4
      IS-IS:   Manual Area Address:
      IS-IS:     Length  = 3
      IS-IS:     Format  = 49 (Local Binary)
      IS-IS:     Address = 490001
      IS-IS: Variable field:
      IS-IS:   Field Code = 129  (Protocols Supported)
      IS-IS:   Field length = 1
      IS-IS:   NLPID's for protocols within this IS:
      IS-IS:     NLPID = CC (Internet IP)
      IS-IS: Variable field:
      IS-IS:   Field Code = 137  (Dynamic Hostname)
      IS-IS:   Field length = 3
      IS-IS: Variable field:
      IS-IS:   Field Code = 132  (IP Interface Address)
      IS-IS:   Field length = 4
      IS-IS:   IP Interface Address:
      IS-IS:     IP Address = [11.1.1.1]
```

Example A-11 *Decode of Example A-7 (Level-1 LSP Part 3 Continued)*

```
IS-IS: ----- ISO Network Layer Variable Fields -----
IS-IS: Variable field:
      IS-IS:   Field Code = 135  (Extended IP Reachability)
      IS-IS:   Field length = 26
      IS-IS: Variable field:
      IS-IS:   Field Code = 22  (Extended IS Reachability)
      IS-IS:   Field length = 11
      IS-IS: Variable field:
      IS-IS:   Field Code = 3  (Neighboring End Systems)
      IS-IS:   Field length = 10
      IS-IS:   Default metric = 0
      IS-IS:   Delay metric   = Not supported
      IS-IS:   Expense metric = Not supported
      IS-IS:   Error metric   = Not supported
      IS-IS:   Neighbor ID    = 000000000001
```

Figure A-5 *Level-2 link-state packets (PDU Type 20).*

No. of Octets

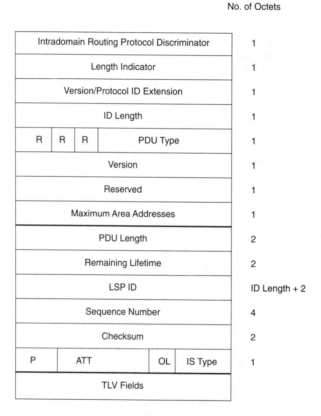

Example A-12 *Analyzer Capture: Level-2 LSP*

```
        ADDR  HEX                                                    ASCII
0000: 01 80 c2 00 00 15 00 d0 58 f7 89 41 05 dc fe fe ¦ .ÓÂ....DX÷&A.Üww
0010: 03 83 1b 01 00 10 01 00 00 03 00 00 00 00 00 01 ¦ .f..............
0020: 00 0a 05 d9 40 00 00 00 00 00 01 01 81 01 cc 01 ¦ ...Ù@.........Ì.
0030: 04 03 49 00 01 84 04 0a 01 01 01 06 06 00 d0 58 ¦ ..I..„........DX
0040: eb f8 41
```

Example A-13 *Decode of Example A-12 (Level-2 LSP Part 1)*

```
IS-IS: ----- ISO Network Layer Header -----
       IS-IS:
       IS-IS: Protocol ID = 83 (Intermediate System Routing Exchange Protocol)
       IS-IS: Header length = 27
       IS-IS: Version / Protocol ID Extension = 1
       IS-IS: ID Length = 0, Indicates 6 Octets
```

Example A-13 *Decode of Example A-12 (Level-2 LSP Part 1) (Continued)*

```
IS-IS: PDU type = 20   (Link State, Level 2)
IS-IS: Version = 1
IS-IS: Reserved = 0

IS-IS: Maximum Area Addesses = 0
IS-IS: Frame length is 131 byte(s)
IS-IS: Remaining life is 1199 second(s)
IS-IS: Link State Frame ID:
IS-IS:   Source ID      = 000000000001
IS-IS:   Pseudo-node    = 00    (Not a pseudo-node)
IS-IS:   Link frame no. = 0
IS-IS: Frame Sequence = 6188
IS-IS: Checksum = E72A
IS-IS: Attributes = 03
IS-IS:  0... .... = Partition repair not supported
IS-IS:  .0.. .... = Not attached using error metric
IS-IS:  ..0. .... = Not attached using expense metric
IS-IS:  ...0 .... = Not attached using delay metric
IS-IS:  .... 0... = Not attached using default metric
IS-IS:  .... .0.. = No LSP Database Overload
IS-IS:  .... ..11 = Level 2 intermediate system
```

Example A-14 *Decode of Example A-12 (Level-2 LSP Part 2)*

```
IS-IS: ----- ISO Network Layer Variable Fields -----
IS-IS: Variable field:
IS-IS:   Field Code = 1  (Partition Area Addresses)
IS-IS:   Field length = 4
IS-IS:   Partition Area Address:
IS-IS:     Length  = 3
IS-IS:     Format  = 49 (Local Binary)
IS-IS:     Address = 490001
IS-IS: Variable field:
IS-IS:   Field Code = 129  (Protocols Supported)
IS-IS:   Field length = 1
IS-IS:   NLPID'sfor protocols within this IS:
IS-IS:     NLPID = CC (Internet IP)
IS-IS: Variable field:
IS-IS:   Field Code = 137  (Dynamic Hostname)
IS-IS:   Field length = 3
IS-IS: Variable field:
IS-IS:   Field Code = 132  (IP Interface Address)
IS-IS:   Field length = 4
IS-IS:   IP Interface Address:
IS-IS:     IP Address = [11.1.1.1]
IS-IS: Variable field:
IS-IS:   Field Code = 22  (Extended IS Reachability)
IS-IS:   Field length = 22
IS-IS: Variable field:
IS-IS:   Field Code = 135  (Extended IP Reachability)
IS-IS:   Field length = 58
```

Sequence Number Packets

Figure A-6 *Level-1 complete sequence number packets (PDU Type 24).*

No. of Octets

Field	Octets
Intradomain Routing Protocol Discriminator	1
Length Indicator	1
Version/Protocol ID Extension	1
ID Length	1
R | R | R | PDU Type	1
Version	1
Reserved	1
Maximum Area Addresses	1
PDU Length	2
Source ID	ID Length + 1
Start LSP ID	ID Length + 2
End LSP ID	ID Length + 2
TLV Fields	

Example A-15 *Analyzer Capture: Level-1 CSNP*

```
      ADDR  HEX                                                    ASCII
0000: 01 80 c2 00 00 14 00 d0 58 f7 89 41 00 66 fe fe  ¦  .ÓÂ....DX÷‰A.fww
0010: 03 83 21 01 00 18 01 00 00 00 63 00 00 00 00 00  ¦  .ƒ!.......c.....
0020: 01 00 00 00 00 00 00 00 00 00 ff ff ff ff ff ff  ¦  .........ÿÿÿÿÿÿ
0030: ff ff 09 40 04 a6 00 00 00 00 00 01 00 00 00 00  ¦  ÿÿ.@.¦..........
0040: 18 33 f6 c7 04 1b 00 00 00 00 00 01 01 00 00 00  ¦  .3öÇ...........
0050: 18 13 a5 61 04 a8 00 00 00 00 00 03 00 00 00 00  ¦  ..¥a.¨..........
0060: 28 be 06 12 04 77 00 00 00 00 00 05 00 00 00 00  ¦  (p...w..........
0070: 05 fd ec ab                                      ¦  .ýì«
```

Example A-16 *Decode of Example A-15 (Level-1 CSNP Part 1)*

```
DLC:  ----- DLC Header -----
      DLC:  Frame 75 arrived at  18:48:07.8401; frame size is 116 (0074 hex) bytes.
      DLC:  Destination = Multicast 0180C2000014
      DLC:  Source      = Station 00D058F78941
      DLC:  802.3 length = 102
LLC:  ----- LLC Header -----
LLC:  DSAP Address = FE, DSAP IG Bit = 00 (Individual Address)
      LLC:  SSAP Address = FE, SSAP CR Bit = 00 (Command)
      LLC:  Unnumbered frame: UI
      LLC:
IS-IS: ----- ISO Network Layer Header -----
      IS-IS: Protocol ID = 83 (Intermediate System Routing Exchange Protocol)
      IS-IS: Header length = 33
      IS-IS: Version / Protocol ID Extension = 1
      IS-IS: ID Length = 0, Indicates 6 Octets
      IS-IS: PDU type = 24  (Complete Sequence Numbers, Level 1)
      IS-IS: Version = 1
      IS-IS: Reserved = 0
      IS-IS: Maximum Area Addesses = 0
      IS-IS: Frame length is 99 byte(s)
      IS-IS: Source:
      IS-IS:   ID          = 000000000001
      IS-IS:   Pseudo-node = 00   (Not a pseudo-node)
      IS-IS: Start Link State ID = 000000000000-00-00
      IS-IS: End Link State ID   = FFFFFFFFFFFF-FF-FF
```

Example A-17 *Decode of Example A-15 (Level-1 CSNP Part 2)*

```
IS-IS: ----- ISO Network Layer Variable Fields -----
IS-IS: Variable field:
IS-IS:   Field Code = 9  (Link State Frame Entries)
IS-IS:   Field length = 64
IS-IS:   Link State Frame Data:
IS-IS:     Remaining Life is 1190 second(s)
IS-IS:     Link State Frame ID:
IS-IS:       Source ID    = 000000000001
IS-IS:       Pseudo-node  = 00   (Not a pseudo-node)
IS-IS:       Link frame no. = 0
IS-IS:     Frame Sequence  = 6195
IS-IS:     Checksum        = F6C7
IS-IS:   Link State Frame Data:
IS-IS:     Remaining Life is 1051 second(s)
IS-IS:     Link State Frame ID:
IS-IS:       Source ID    = 000000000001
IS-IS:       Pseudo-node  = 01
IS-IS:       Link frame no. = 0
IS-IS:     Frame Sequence  = 6163
IS-IS:     Checksum        = A561
```

continues

Example A-17 *Decode of Example A-15 (Level-1 CSNP Part 2) (Continued)*

```
IS-IS:   Link State Frame Data:
IS-IS:     Remaining Life is 1192 second(s)
IS-IS:     Link State Frame ID:
IS-IS:       Source ID      = 000000000003
IS-IS:       Pseudo-node    = 00   (Not a pseudo-node)
IS-IS:       Link frame no. = 0
IS-IS:     Frame Sequence   = 10430
IS-IS:     Checksum         = 0612
[snip]
```

Figure A-7 *Level-2 complete sequence number packets (PDU Type 25).*

No. of Octets

Field	No. of Octets
Intradomain Routing Protocol Discriminator	1
Length Indicator	1
Version/Protocol ID Extension	1
ID Length	1
R R R PDU Type	1
Version	1
Reserved	1
Maximum Area Addresses	1
PDU Length	2
Source ID	ID Length + 1
Start LSP ID	ID Length + 2
End LSP ID	ID Length + 2
TLV Fields	

Figure A-8 *Level-1 partial sequence number packets (PDU Type 26).*

No. of Octets

Field	Octets
Intradomain Routing Protocol Discriminator	1
Length Indicator	1
Version/Protocol ID Extension	1
ID Length	1
R R R PDU Type	1
Version	1
Reserved	1
Maximum Area Addresses	1
Reserved (6 bits) / Circuit Type	1
Source ID	ID Length
Holding Time	2
PDU Length	2
Local Circuit ID	1
TLV Fields	Variable Length

Example A-18 *Analyzer Capture: Level-1 PSNP*

```
       ADDR  HEX                                                        ASCII
      0000: 01 80 c2 00 00 14 00 d0 58 eb f8 41 00 56 fe fe ¦ .ÓÂ....DXëøA.Vww
      0010: 03 83 11 01 00 1a 01 00 00 00 53 00 00 00 00 00 ¦ .f........S.....
      0020: 03 00 09 40 04 af 00 00 00 00 00 01 00 00 00 00 ¦ ...@.¯..........
      0030: 00 00 00 00 04 af 00 00 00 00 00 01 01 00 00 00 ¦ .....¯..........
      0040: 00 00 00 00 04 aa 00 00 00 00 00 03 00 00 00 00 ¦ .....ª..........
      0050: 00 02 ed 19 04 af 00 00 00 00 00 05 00 00 00 00 ¦ ..í..¯..........
      0060: 00 00 00 00                                     ¦ ....
```

Example A-19 *Decode of Example A-18 (Level-1 PSNP Part 1)*

```
DLC:  ----- DLC Header -----
      DLC:
      DLC: Frame 103 arrived at  19:04:39.3473; frame size is 100 (0064 hex) bytes.
      DLC: Destination = Multicast 0180C2000014
      DLC: Source      = Station 00D058EBF841
      DLC: 802.3 length = 86
      DLC:
LLC:  ----- LLC Header -----
      LLC:
      LLC: DSAP Address = FE, DSAP IG Bit = 00 (Individual Address)
      LLC: SSAP Address = FE, SSAP CR Bit = 00 (Command)
      LLC: Unnumbered frame: UI
      LLC:
IS-IS: ----- ISO Network Layer Header -----
      IS-IS:
      IS-IS: Protocol ID = 83 (Intermediate System Routing Exchange Protocol)
      IS-IS: Header length = 17
      IS-IS: Version / Protocol ID Extension = 1
      IS-IS: ID Length = 0, Indicates 6 Octets
      IS-IS: PDU type = 26  (Partial Sequence Numbers, Level 1)
      IS-IS: Version = 1
      IS-IS: Reserved = 0
      IS-IS: Maximum Area Addesses = 0
      IS-IS: Frame length is 83 byte(s)
      IS-IS: Source:
      IS-IS:   ID        = 000000000003
      IS-IS:   Pseudo-node = 00   (Not a pseudo-node)
```

Example A-20 *Decode of Example A-18 (Level-1 PSNP Part 2)*

```
IS-IS: ----- ISO Network Layer Variable Fields -----
      IS-IS:
      IS-IS: Variable field:
      IS-IS:   Field Code = 9  (Link State Frame Entries)
      IS-IS:   Field length = 64
      IS-IS:   Link State Frame Data:
      IS-IS:     Remaining Life is 1199 second(s)
      IS-IS:     Link State Frame ID:
      IS-IS:       Source ID   = 000000000001
      IS-IS:       Pseudo-node = 00   (Not a pseudo-node)
      IS-IS:       Link frame no. = 0
      IS-IS:     Frame Sequence  = 0
      IS-IS:     Checksum    = 0000   (No checksum sent)
      IS-IS:   Link State Frame Data:
      IS-IS:     Remaining Life is 1199 second(s)
      IS-IS:     Link State Frame ID:
      IS-IS:       Source ID   = 000000000001
      IS-IS:       Pseudo-node = 01
      IS-IS:       Link frame no. = 0
```

Example A-20 *Decode of Example A-18 (Level-1 PSNP Part 2)*

```
IS-IS:    Frame Sequence  = 0
IS-IS:    Checksum        = 0000   (No checksum sent)-
IS-IS:  Link State Frame Data:
IS-IS:    Remaining Life is 1194 second(s)
IS-IS:    Link State Frame ID:
IS-IS:      Source ID     = 000000000003
IS-IS:      Pseudo-node   = 00   (Not a pseudo-node)
IS-IS:      Link frame no. = 0
IS-IS:    Frame Sequence  = 2
IS-IS:    Checksum        = ED19
```

Figure A-9 *Partial sequence number packets (PDU Type 27).*

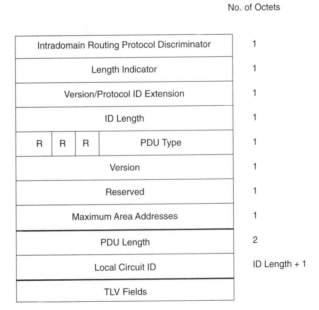

Answers to Review Questions

Chapter 1

1 Name the two planes of operation in a modern router.

The two planes of operation are Control and Data planes.

2 IP forwarding and IP routing are related concepts. What is the difference between them?

IP forwarding is the process by which a router moves a packet from the ingress port to the egress port. This process is sometimes called packet switching or routing. However, IP routing involves more than just switching of packets. IP routing is the much broader process of exchanging routing information in a domain to build the routing tables required to make the forwarding decisions.

3 Name the three common classifications of IP routing protocols.

The three common classifications are classless and classful; intradomain and interdomain; and distance vector and link state.

4 Name three basic packet-switching mechanisms supported in Cisco IOS Software.

Process switching, fast switching, and Cisco Express Forwarding.

5 What is the critical shortcoming of the IPv4 architecture that IPv6 tries to address and how is it addressed?

IPv6 is intended to provide a larger address space than IPv4. IPv6 addresses are 128-bits long compared to the 32-bit IPv4 addresses.

Chapter 2

1 Name the three network layer protocols that support the ISO CLNS.

The three network layer protocols are CLNP, ES-IS, and IS-IS.

2 In comparing the layers of the TCP/IP protocols suite and the ISO CLNS architecture, describe how the Internet Protocol (IP) differs from the ISO Connectionless Network Protocol (CLNP).

In TCP/IP, the Internet Protocol is the only network layer protocol. CLNP coexists with other protocols such as ES-IS and IS-IS in the ISO CLNS architecture.

3 What is the use of the Intradomain Routing Protocol Discriminator in the ISO network layer protocol packet headers?

It plays the role of network layer protocol identifier and allows differentiation between the multiple ISO network layer protocols.

4 What was IS-IS originally designed for?

IS-IS was intended to be used as a dynamic routing protocol for routing Connectionless Network Protocol packets in the ISO CLNS environment.

5 How is IS-IS used in an IP network?

The IS-IS uses Type Length Value (TLV) fields for carrying routing information in IS-IS protocol packets. RFC 1195 specifies additional TLVs for carrying IP information in IS-IS packets, thus providing support for IP routing.

6 Describe any similarities or differences between the ES-IS protocol and IP ARP.

Both ARP and ES-IS are network host-level protocols for discovering adjacencies on connected media and provide network layer to data link layer address mapping.

IP ARP is used on only broadcast media and multipoint network media, whereas ES-IS also works over point-to-point links. Unlike ARP, Layer 3 to Layer 2 address mapping is a subset of the functionality provided by ES-IS. Other functions of ES-IS in the ISO CLNS environment are redirection and autoconfiguration.

Chapter 3

1 How many levels of hierarchy does the IS-IS routing protocol support and describe their significance?

Two levels, Level 1 and Level 2, are specified by ISO 10589 and adopted by RFC 1195. Hierarchical routing allows control over the spread of routing updates, which is a key requirement for network stability and scalability.

2 What is the reason for suboptimal, interarea routing in the ISO 10589 architecture?

In the ISO 10589 architecture, the Level 1 routing areas are stubs and do not have a complete view of the domain that is necessary for making optimal exit decisions out of their local area. Instead, Level 1 routers point defaults to the nearest Level 2 router, which might not necessarily be on the best path to a specific destination outside the area.

3 Name the two categories of IS-IS protocol functions and describe the services they provide.

The two categories are the subnetwork-dependent functions and the subnetwork-independent functions. The former is primarily responsible for the adjacency formation process, and the latter for managing the routing information update and maintenance processes.

4 What is the general layout of IS-IS packet formats?

All IS-IS packets are composed of a header and variable-length TLV fields.

5 List the TLVs specified by ISO 10589.

See Table 3.1.

6 List the TLVs specified by RFC 1195 and describe their significance.

See Table 3.2. The TLVs specified by RFC 1195 allow the IS-IS protocol, which was originally designed for routing ISO CLNP packets, to be used for IP routing.

7 How does the TLV Type 133 specified by RFC 1195 differ from the original authentication TLV 10 specified by IS0 10589?

TLV Type 133 does not place any restriction on the length of the authentication TLV (255 octets in TLV 10). Also, it does not specify authentication Type 255 for routing domain private authentication as in TLV 10.

8 Describe any differences between the adjacency formation processes on point-to-point and broadcast links.

Point-to-point adjacency formation is preceded by detection of ISHs; also, reliability is not built into the process because of the lack of an IS Neighbor TLV field in point-to-point hellos. A reliable three-way adjacency for point-to-point links has been proposed in the IETF for standardization.

9 Describe the three-way adjacency formation process that has been proposed in the IETF to enhance the method for forming adjacencies on point-to-point links.

The method allows for introduction of a new TLV field (240), which will include IS neighbor information in point-to-point hellos. This information can then be used for a three-way handshake in the adjacency formation process.

10 What is the relevance of the pseudonode functionality?

The pseudonode functionality is provided on broadcast media as a way to control flooding in such environments. LSPs are multicast to neighbors on such links, and the DIS that acts as the pseudonode facilitates database synchronization over the LAN by periodically multicasting summaries of all known LSPs. This allows use of a less reliable but periodic mechanism to alleviate the challenges of reliably advertising LSPs among the many possible adjacencies on multiaccess or broadcast links.

11 Briefly describe the DIS election and replacement process.

DIS election is by highest interface priority with the highest SNPA (MAC address) as the tie breaker. Election also is pre-emptive and any newly connected router can take over the DIS functions if it better qualifies to be the DIS, according to this criteria.

12 Explain why no backup DIS exists.

A backup DIS is unnecessary because of the periodic database synchronization on LAN media and the shorter hello interval used by the DIS, which allows for fast detection of any failures and subsequent replacement.

Chapter 4

1 What does the acronym NSAP stand for and what is an NSAP used for?

NSAP means network service access point. This is OSI terminology for a network layer address. NSAP addresses provide the foundation for routing datagrams in a CLNP network, and IS-IS functions are designed around NSAPs. Therefore, IP routers need to be configured with NSAPs when using IS-IS for IP routing.

2 What are the three major components of an NSAP? Describe the significance of each.

The three components are area address (area ID), system ID (SysID), and the NSAP selector (NSEL). The area address identifies the native area of a network node and helps determine the type of adjacencies one node forms with another. The SysID is a unique identifier of a node within an IS-IS area. The NSEL determines the higher level user of the network service that packets must be delivered to for processing at a node. The value of the NSEL is 0x00 for the routing layer.

3 What is the maximum length of an NSAP, and what is the minimum length that can be configured on a Cisco router?

The maximum length of an NSAP is 160 bits (20 bytes). The minimum size that can be configured on a Cisco router is 8 bytes. The 8 bytes includes 1 byte of NSEL, 6 bytes of SysID, and 1 byte of area ID. However, it is recommended that the AFI stands apart from the actual area value in the area ID. Therefore, 9 bytes makes more sense where 2 bytes are allocated for the area, one of which is the AFI.

4 What's the AFI field in an NSAP, and what is its significance?

AFI stands for address and format identifier. The AFI designates the top-level address domain to which the NSAP belongs and also defines the syntax (binary, decimal, or character) of the domain-specific part of the NSAP.

5 How many OSI top-layer address domains exist? List them.

There are seven top-layer OSI addressing domains:

- **X.121—International plan for public data networks**
- **ISO DCC—Data country code**
- **F.69—Telex**
- **E.163—Public Switched Telephone network**
- **E.164—ISDN**
- **ISO 6523—International code designator (ICD) for organizations**
- **Local—For local use only within a network domain**

6 Associate the following addresses with one of these top-level address domains:

1 39.0005.1100.2200.432A.26CD.00

2 47.0001.2211.3311.5566.ACD7.2351.00AC.210700

You can associate an NSAP address with one top-level domain from the value of its AFI, which is the leftmost byte in the address:

1 AFI value of 39 is ISO DCC.

2 AFI value of 47 is ISO 6523(ICD).

7 How many bytes of the NSAP are allocated to the SysID on a Cisco router? What is the value specified by ISO 10589?

Cisco follows the convention specified by the US GOSIP version 2 standard, which requires 6 bytes for the system ID field. ISO 10589 specifies a range of 1 to 8 bytes.

8   IS-IS has two levels of routing, Level 1 and Level 2. Elaborate on the relevance of the major fields of the NSAP to these routing levels in the ISO CLNS environment.

Level 1 routing is based on only the System ID field in the NSAP, whereas Level 2 routing uses only the Area field. On a Cisco router, the combined length of the System ID and N-Selector fields is always 7 bytes, so the area address can easily be discerned as the remainder of the NSAP after stripping the trailing 7 bytes.

9   List some of the requirements and caveats for defining the system ID on a device.

The system ID of all nodes in the routing domain must have the same length. On Cisco routers, the system ID length must be 6 bytes.

Each node in an area must have a unique system ID.

10   How many NSAPs can you have per router according to ISO 10589? What is the purpose of having more than one NSAP per router?

According to ISO 10589, a router can have up to three NSAPs, all of which must use the same system ID and 0x00 for the N-selector but different area prefixes. Multiple NSAPs per router might be necessary for renumbering NSAPs in an area or domain, partitioning an area or merging different areas in a network domain.

11   What does SNPA stand for and what is its relevance in the IS-IS routing environment?

SNPA stands for subnetwork point of attachment. It has no relevance to the Subnetwork Access Point (SNAP) field associated with the Ethernet 802.3 SNAP frame format. SNPA is the ISO name for a data-link address, such as a MAC or a Frame Relay DLCI address. Layer 3 routes point to an outgoing data-link interface that is also described by its address, the SNPA.

12   Identify the area address, SysID, and NSEL values in the following address:

47.005.8001.443E.AB11.BD48.0C1F.00

The NSAP address components are as follows:

Area: 47.005.8001.443E

System ID: AB11.BD48.0C1F

N-selector: 00

Chapter 5

1   What type of information is stored in an IS-IS Link-State database and how is this information collected?

There are two types of Link-State databases in IS-IS, Level 1 and Level 2. These databases store link-state packets, which are generated by routers in an area or the backbone, respectively, and spread out by a process called flooding.

2 Describe the use of the Link-State database in IS-IS.

As a link-state protocol, IS-IS requires each router in an area to have the same view of the area's topology. The Link-State database contains LSPs from other routers in the area and describes the topology of the area. Each router bases its route calculation on the information in the Link-State database. The route calculation is done using the shortest path first (Dikjstra) algorithm.

3 What is the difference between Level 1 and Level 2 Link-State databases?

The Level 1 Link-State database describes a single IS-IS area. It contains only LSPs from the routers in that area. A separate Level 1 Link-State database exists for each area in an IS-IS domain (if more than one exists).

An IS-IS domain with multiple areas has a backbone, which interconnects the areas. The Level 2 database describes the backbone and consists of Level 2 LSPs from the routers connected to the backbone.

4 What is the meaning of Link-State database synchronization?

Link-State database synchronization is the process of using reliable or periodic flooding mechanisms to ensure that routers in the same area or the backbone have identical Level 1 or Level 2 databases, respectively.

5 Describe the general format of a link-state packet.

A link-state packet is composed of a 27-byte header and variable-length TLV fields.

6 List the four fields in the LSP header that adequately describe the LSP.

LSP ID, Sequence Number, Remaining Lifetime, and Checksum fields.

7 What are TLVs?

TLV stands for Type, Length, and Value. TLVs are special information fields that are appended as necessary to the header of an IS-IS packet. Every type of IS-IS packet supports a specific set of TLVs. The same TLV type can be used in different IS-IS packet types.

8 List five TLVs that carry metric information and where they are originally specified.

IS-neighbor TLV (ISO 10589)

Internal IP Reachability TLV (RFC 1195)

External IP Reachability TLV (RFC 1195)

Extended IS Reachability TLV (RFC Draft)

Extended IP Reachability TLV (RFC Draft)

9 What is the format of the LSP identifier (LSPID)? Give an example.

The LSPID is composed of the system ID of the originating router, a pseudonode number, and an LSP fragment number.

Example: 000.0000.0001.00-00 or RTA.00-00, where the first 6 bytes represent the system ID, the seventh byte is the pseudonode number, and the last byte is the LSP fragment number. If ISIS dynamic name resolution is enabled on the router or CLNS host names are configured, the system ID is replaced by the host name of the source router.

10 Name the types of metric information specified by ISO 10589.

ISO 10589 specifies four types of metrics: default, reliability, monetary cost, and delay.

11 What are the limitations of the default metric specified by ISO 10589?

Only 7 bits are dedicated to the value of the default metric, allowing a maximum value of only 63 units.

In addition, the maximum metric for an entire path is 1023 units. Even though the default metric has a connotation of bandwidth, it is not assigned automatically based on the interface bandwidth of a router.

12 How are the metric limitations of ISO 10589 addressed by TLVs Type 22 and Type 135 recently proposed in the IETF IS-IS Working Group?

Because all widely deployed IS-IS implementations use only the default metric, TLV Types 22 and 135 propose the extension of the default metric field with the fields of the unused metric types. The extended default metric field allows larger metric values and provide more flexibility to network administrators in designing and expanding their networks.

13 What are sequence number packets? List all types.

Sequence number packets contain LSP summary TLVs and aid the flooding process, as well as database synchronization. Two types of sequence number packets exist: complete sequence number packets (CSNP) and partial sequence number packets (PSNPs). CSNPs contain summaries of all known LSPs. They are exchanged on point-to-point links only once after the adjacency is brought up. However, they are advertised periodically on broadcast links by the DIS. PSNPs that normally contain summaries of a subset of known LSPs in the area are used to request complete copies of LSPs on both point-to-point links and broadcast links. PSNPs are also used as acknowledgments on point-to-point links to support reliable flooding.

14 What are IS-IS mesh groups?

IS-IS mesh groups are used to limit redundant flooding in NBMA environments with point-to-point subinterfaces and highly meshed underlying PVCs.

15 What is maxage and maximum LSP regeneration interval? List the Cisco IOS commands that can be used to change their values.

Maxage specifies the maximum life span of an LSP, from the time it is generated at the source until it expires.

The IOS router-level command max-lsp-interval is used to modify the value of maxage. The default value in Cisco IOS is 20 minutes (120 seconds).

Maximum LSP regeneration interval, also known as the LSP refresh interval, is the periodic interval between the times at which a router must refresh its LSP throughout the whole network. LSP refresh occurs before maxage is reached. The IOS router-level command lsp-refresh-interval is used to modify this timer.

16 Can two routers in the same area have the same system ID? Briefly describe what happens when two routers in the same area are configured with the same system ID.

No. All routers in the same area must have different system IDs to make them unique so that packets sourced from them (Hellos, LSPs, SNPs) can be uniquely identified. When two or more routers in the same area share the same system ID, their LSPs get mixed up and each router sees incorrect information in what seems to be its LSP. The routers, therefore, continuously try to update each others LSP creating unnecessary resource consuming churn in the network. An error is logged if LSP regeneration exceeds a frequency threshold.

Chapter 6

1 What is the basic application of the SPF algorithm?

The SPF algorithm was designed to find the shortest distance between two points in any problem that can be modeled as a graph.

2 What is a directed graph, and how is an internetwork modeled as a directed graph?

A directed graph or digraph consists of the set of vertices and the set of interconnections between the vertices referred to as arcs or directed edges. An internetwork is modeled as a directed graph by representing the network nodes or routers as vertices and the network links (adjacencies) as arcs. Bidirectional traffic flow is depicted by parallel opposite arrows.

3 Name the three tables used in the operation of the Dijkstra algorithm for computing IS-IS routes.

Paths, Tentative, and Unknown.

4 What is the estimated processing cost of the Dijkstra algorithm?

The computational cost directly dependent on the complexity of execution of Dijkstra algorithm, which is of the order, $O(Llog N)$, where L is the number of links and N is the number of nodes.

5 What is the difference between a full SPF and a partial route calculation (PRC)?

A full SPF is a complete computation of the shortest path tree (SPT) caused by an adjacency change. PRC is a partial computation of the SPF algorithm and performed when only an IP prefix change is reported in a new LSP.

Chapter 8

1 What is the main purpose and use of configuring up to three different area addresses on a single router?

You configure multiple area addresses within a transition period when migrating from one area address to another.

2 What is the consequence of configuring more than one area address on a single router?

The Link-State databases of the two areas are merged, consequently merging the areas into one.

3 What is the purpose of the **transition** keyword when used with the **metric-style** command?

It enables the router to advertise and accept both old- and new-style TLVs.

4 How many types of hello packets are used on point-to-point interfaces on Cisco routers?

Only a single hello packet

5 What is the purpose of the **mesh-group blocked** command?

It blocks LSP flooding on the applicable interface.

6 What is the default behavior of a member within a mesh group?

Within the mesh group, an LSP received from a member is not forwarded to other members of the same group but forwarded to nonmembers.

7 What is the purpose of the **distance** command?

The distance command places an administrative weight, referred to as administrative distance, on routes from a particular routing protocol. The administrative distance is used to discriminate between multiple instances of the same route received from multiple routing protocol sources. The route with the lowest administrative distance is preferred for insertion into the routing table.

8 What precautions must be taken when configuring mutual redistribution between Integrated IS-IS and other coexisting IGPs?

Configure route filters to stop redistribution feedback and eliminate any possibility of routing loops.

9 What caveat must always be adhered to when running IS-IS for CLNS and IS-IS for IP in the same area?

All routers within the area must be configured in a consistent manner so that they are IP-only, CLNS-only, or operating in dual mode—both IP and CLNS. They are applied on a per-router basis and not per-interface basis.

Chapter 10

1 List the two main categories of IS-IS problems discussed in this chapter and provide examples of each.

Adjacency formation problems (for example, misconfigured IP interface addresses) and route maintenance problems (for example, route advertisement problems).

2 List two **show** commands that are useful for troubleshooting adjacency problems.

show clns neighbors and show clns interface

3 List a **debug** command that provides help in troubleshooting IS-IS adjacency problems.

debug isis adj-packet

4 What are LSP corruption storms, and how do they impact a network's performance?

LSP corruption storms occur when LSPs are continuously corrupted by a malfunctioning device in the network; the corrupted LSPs are purged from the network and then reflooded by their sources. This flooding and purging leads to a waste of network bandwidth and might cause high CPU utilization in the routers. If CPU is continuously pegged high levels, the routers might eventually run out of processing resources leading to disruption of network services.

5 Describe the methodology for troubleshooting an LSP corruption storm.

Because the routers in the network might already be overloaded, debugging is used as a last resort. You can use the show process cpu command to track CPU utilization, and you can use show isis spf log to determine the LSPs responsible for any SPF churns. A trail can then be followed to determine the location of the culprit device that is corrupting LSPs.

INDEX

Numerics

0xFEFE protocol, 33

A

access layer, 158
    devices, 164
addressing, 61
    duplicate system IDs, 133
    node-based
        Area ID, 40
        NET, 41
        N-selector, 40
        SysID, 40
structure, 165–167
adjacencies
    DIS election process, 58–59
    error logging, 340
    ES-IS, forming, 48
    establishing fast convergence, 190–192
    formation, troubleshooting, 322
    IS-IS
        forming, 49–50
        over multiaccess media, forming, 54–56
    Level 1, forming, 57
    Level 2, forming, 57
    logging changes in, 295
    maintenance, IS-IS versus OSPF, 205
    point-to-point, forming, 51– 54
    problems, debugging, 315
    reachability information, displaying, 333–334
    statistics, displaying, 305, 306
    subnetwork-dependent functions (routing
      layer), 48
    two-way communication, 57
    virtual adjacencies, 100
Adjacency database, 23
administrative distances, 61, 305
    default, 234

advertising
    external routes, 335–337
    interarea routes, 286
    subnets, 333–334
AFI (Authority and Format Identifier), 70
aggregation, CIDR, 12
ANSI (American National Standards Institute),
    NSAP address registration, 75
arc, 140
Area Addresses TLV (LAN hellos), 45, 52, 56, 104
Area ID field
    NSAP addresses, 69, 72
    simplified NSAP addresses, 73
Area ID, 40
area-level authentication, 285
area-password command, 285
areas, 40, 162–164
    addressing scheme, 41
    adjacencies, two-way communication, 57
    duplicate system IDs, troubleshooting, 326
    IS-IS as an IGP, 168
        IP prefix advertisement restrictions, 170
        metric limitations, 169
    IS-IS versus OSPF, 215
    L1 to L2 route leaking, 286–288
    Level 1 adjacencies
        forming, 57
        routers, 41
        routing table, displaying, 311
    Level 1-2 routers, 41
    Level 2
        adjacencies, 53, 57
        routers, 41
    merging, 80
    multi-area configuration, 289
    nonhierarchical design, 174–175
    splitting, 80
AS (autonomous system), 39, 73. *See also* areas
AS Path attribute (BGP), 16
ASICs (application-specific integrated circuits), 22
assigning
    metrics, 172
    passwords to interfaces, 284
ATM, point-to-point configuration, 268

K–L

M

N

O

P

S

T

Hey, you've got enough worries.

Don't let IT training be one of them.

Get on the fast track to IT training at InformIT,
your total Information Technology training network.

 | **www.informit.com** |

■ Hundreds of timely articles on dozens of topics ■ Discounts on IT books from all our publishing partners, including Cisco Press ■ Free, unabridged books from the InformIT Free Library ■ "Expert Q&A"—our live, online chat with IT experts ■ Faster, easier certification and training from our Web- or classroom-based training programs ■ Current IT news ■ Software downloads ■ Career-enhancing resources

Train with authorized Cisco Learning Partners.

Discover all that's possible on the Internet.

One of the biggest challenges facing networking professionals is how to stay current with today's ever-changing technologies in the global Internet economy. Nobody understands this better than Cisco Learning Partners, the only companies that deliver training developed by Cisco Systems.

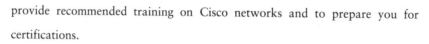

Just go to **www.cisco.com/go/training_ad**. You'll find more than 120 Cisco Learning Partners in over 90 countries worldwide.* Only Cisco Learning Partners have instructors that are certified by Cisco to provide recommended training on Cisco networks and to prepare you for certifications.

To get ahead in this world, you first have to be able to keep up. Insist on training that is developed and authorized by Cisco, as indicated by the Cisco Learning Partner or Cisco Learning Solutions Partner logo.

Visit **www.cisco.com/go/training_ad** today.

CCIE Professional Development

Cisco BGP-4 Command and Configuration Handbook

William R. Parkhurst, Ph. D., CCIE

1-58705-017-X • AVAILABLE NOW

Cisco BGP-4 Command and Configuration Handbook is a clear, concise, and complete source of documentation for all Cisco IOS Software BGP-4 commands. If you are preparing for the CCIE exam, this book can be used as a laboratory guide to learn the purpose and proper use of every BGP command. If you are a network designer, this book can be used as a ready reference for any BGP command.

Cisco LAN Switching

Kennedy Clark, CCIE; Kevin Hamilton, CCIE

1-57870-094-9 • AVAILABLE NOW

This volume provides an in-depth analysis of Cisco LAN switching technologies, architectures, and deployments, including unique coverage of Catalyst network design essentials. Network designs and configuration examples are incorporated throughout to demonstrate the principles and enable easy translation of the material into practice in production networks.

Routing TCP/IP, Volume I

Jeff Doyle, CCIE

1-57870-041-8 • AVAILABLE NOW

This book takes the reader from a basic understanding of routers and routing protocols through a detailed examination of each of the IP interior routing protocols. Learn techniques for designing networks that maximize the efficiency of the protocol being used. Exercises and review questions provide core study for the CCIE Routing and Switching exam.

Routing TCP/IP, Volume II

Jeff Doyle, CCIE, Jennifer DeHaven Carroll, CCIE

1-57870-089-2 • AVAILABLE NOW

Routing TCP/IP, Volume II, provides you with the expertise necessary to understand and implement BGP-4, multicast routing, NAT, IPv6, and effective router management techniques. Designed not only to help you walk away from the CCIE lab exam with the coveted certification, this book also helps you to develop the knowledge and skills essential to a CCIE.

Cisco Press

ciscopress.com

Cisco Press Solutions

Enhanced IP Services for Cisco Networks

Donald C. Lee, CCIE

1-57870-106-6 • **AVAILABLE NOW**

This is a guide to improving your network's capabilities by understanding the new enabling and advanced Cisco IOS services that build more scalable, intelligent, and secure networks. Learn the technical details necessary to deploy Quality of Service, VPN technologies, IPsec, the IOS firewall and IOS Intrusion Detection. These services will allow you to extend the network to new frontiers securely, protect your network from attacks, and increase the sophistication of network services.

Developing IP Multicast Networks, Volume I

Beau Williamson, CCIE

1-57870-077-9 • **AVAILABLE NOW**

This book provides a solid foundation of IP multicast concepts and explains how to design and deploy the networks that will support appplications such as audio and video conferencing, distance-learning, and data replication. Includes an in-depth discussion of the PIM protocol used in Cisco routers and detailed coverage of the rules that control the creation and maintenance of Cisco mroute state entries.

Designing Network Security

Merike Kaeo

1-57870-043-4 • **AVAILABLE NOW**

Designing Network Security is a practical guide designed to help you understand the fundamentals of securing your corporate infrastructure. This book takes a comprehensive look at underlying security technologies, the process of creating a security policy, and the practical requirements necessary to implement a corporate security policy.

Cisco Press

ciscopress.com

Cisco Press Solutions

EIGRP Network Design Solutions
Ivan Pepelnjak, CCIE
1-57870-165-1 • AVAILABLE NOW

EIGRP Network Design Solutions uses case studies and real-world configuration examples to help you gain an in-depth understanding of the issues involved in designing, deploying, and managing EIGRP-based networks. This book details proper designs that can be used to build large and scalable EIGRP-based networks and documents possible ways each EIGRP feature can be used in network design, implmentation, troubleshooting, and monitoring.

Top-Down Network Design
Priscilla Oppenheimer
1-57870-069-8 • AVAILABLE NOW

Building reliable, secure, and manageable networks is every network professional's goal. This practical guide teaches you a systematic method for network design that can be applied to campus LANs, remote-access networks, WAN links, and large-scale internetworks. Learn how to analyze business and technical requirements, examine traffic flow and Quality of Service requirements, and select protocols and technologies based on performance goals.

Cisco IOS Releases: The Complete Reference
Mack M. Coulibaly
1-57870-179-1 • AVAILABLE NOW

Cisco IOS Releases: The Complete Reference is the first comprehensive guide to the more than three dozen types of Cisco IOS releases being used today on enterprise and service provider networks. It details the release process and its numbering and naming conventions, as well as when, where, and how to use the various releases. A complete map of Cisco IOS software releases and their relationships to one another, in addition to insights into decoding information contained within the software, make this book an indispensable resource for any network professional.

Cisco Press

ciscopress.com

Cisco Press Solutions

Residential Broadband, Second Edition

George Abe

1-57870-177-5 • AVAILABLE NOW

This book will answer basic questions of residential broadband networks such as:
Why do we need high speed networks at home? How will high speed residential
services be delivered to the home? How do regulatory or commercial factors affect
this technology? Explore such networking topics as xDSL, cable, and wireless.

Internetworking Technologies Handbook, Third Edition

Cisco Systems, et al.

1-58705-001-3 • AVAILABLE NOW

This comprehensive reference provides a foundation for understanding and
implementing contemporary internetworking technologies, providing you with
the necessary information needed to make rational networking decisions. Master
terms, concepts, technologies, and devices that are used in the internetworking
industry today. You also learn how to incorporate networking technologies into
a LAN/WAN environment, as well as how to apply the OSI reference model to
categorize protocols, technologies, and devices.

OpenCable Architecture

Michael Adams

1-57870-135-X • AVAILABLE NOW

Whether you're a television, data communications, or telecommunications
professional, or simply an interested business person, this book will help
you understand the technical and business issues surrounding interactive
television services. It will also provide you with an inside look at the combined
efforts of the cable, data, and consumer electronics industries' efforts to develop
those new services.

Performance and Fault Management

Paul Della Maggiora, Christopher Elliott, Robert Pavone, Kent Phelps, James
Thompson

1-57870-180-5 • AVAILABLE NOW

This book is a comprehensive guide to designing and implementing effective strategies
for monitoring performance levels and correctng problems in Cisco networks. It
provides an overview of router and LAN switch operations to help you understand
how to manage such devices, as well as guidance on the essential MIBs, traps, syslog
messages, and show commands for managing Cisco routers and switches.

Cisco Press

ciscopress.com

Cisco Press

Committed to being your long-term learning resource while you grow as a Cisco Networking Professional

Help Cisco Press **stay connected** to the issues and challenges you face on a daily basis by registering your product and filling out our brief survey. Complete and mail this form, or better yet …

Register online and enter to win a FREE book!

Jump to **www.ciscopress.com/register** and register your product online. Each complete entry will be eligible for our monthly drawing to win a FREE book of the winner's choice from the Cisco Press library.

May we contact you via e-mail with information about **new releases, special promotions,** and **customer benefits**?

❏ Yes   ❏ No

E-mail address _____

Name _____

Address _____

City _____ State/Province _____

Country _____ Zip/Post code _____

Where did you buy this product?

❏ Bookstore   ❏ Computer store/Electronics store   ❏ Direct from Cisco Systems
❏ Online retailer   ❏ Direct from Cisco Press   ❏ Office supply store
❏ Mail order   ❏ Class/Seminar   ❏ Discount store
❏ Other _____

When did you buy this product? _____ **Month** _____ **Year**

What price did you pay for this product?

❏ Full retail price   ❏ Discounted price   ❏ Gift

Was this purchase reimbursed as a company expense?

❏ Yes   ❏ No

How did you learn about this product?

❏ Friend   ❏ Store personnel   ❏ In-store ad   ❏ cisco.com
❏ Cisco Press catalog   ❏ Postcard in the mail   ❏ Saw it on the shelf ❏ ciscopress.com
❏ Other catalog   ❏ Magazine ad   ❏ Article or review
❏ School   ❏ Professional organization ❏ Used other products
❏ Other _____

What will this product be used for?

❏ Business use   ❏ School/Education
❏ Certification training   ❏ Professional development/Career growth
❏ Other _____

How many years have you been employed in a computer-related industry?

❏ less than 2 years   ❏ 2–5 years   ❏ more than 5 years

Have you purchased a Cisco Press product before?

❏ Yes   ❏ No

CISCO SYSTEMS

Cisco Press

ciscopress.com

How many computer technology books do you own?
❏ 1   ❏ 2–7   ❏ more than 7

Which best describes your job function? (check all that apply)
❏ Corporate Management   ❏ Systems Engineering   ❏ IS Management   ❏ Cisco Networking
❏ Network Design   ❏ Network Support   ❏ Webmaster   Academy Program
❏ Marketing/Sales   ❏ Consultant   ❏ Student   Instuctor
❏ Professor/Teacher   ❏ Other _____

Do you hold any computer certifications? (check all that apply)
❏ MCSE   ❏ CCNA   ❏ CCDA
❏ CCNP   ❏ CCDP   ❏ CCIE   ❏ Other _____

Are you currently pursuing a certification? (check all that apply)
❏ MCSE   ❏ CCNA   ❏ CCDA
❏ CCNP   ❏ CCDP   ❏ CCIE   ❏ Other _____

On what topics would you like to see more coverage?

_____
_____

Do you have any additional comments or suggestions?

_____
_____

Thank you for completing this survey and registration. Please fold here, seal, and mail to Cisco Press.

IS-IS Network Design Solutions ISBN: 1-57870-220-8

Cisco Press
Customer Registration—CP050227
P.O. Box #781046
Indianapolis, IN 46278-8046

Place
Stamp
Here

Cisco Press
201 West 103rd Street
Indianapolis, IN 46290
ciscopress.com

CISCO SYSTEMS/PACKET MAGAZINE
ATTN: C. Glover
170 West Tasman, Mailstop SJ8-2
San Jose, CA 95134-1706

Place
Stamp
Here

☐ **YES!** I'm requesting a **free** subscription to *Packet*™ magazine.

☐ No. I'm not interested at this time.

☐ Mr.
☐ Ms.

First Name (Please Print) | Last Name

Title/Position (Required)

Company (Required)

Address

City | State/Province

Zip/Postal Code | Country

Telephone (Include country and area codes) | Fax

E-mail

Signature (Required) | Date

☐ I would like to receive additional information on Cisco's services and products by e-mail.

1. Do you or your company:
- A ☐ Use Cisco products
- B ☐ Resell Cisco products
- C ☐ Both
- D ☐ Neither

2. Your organization's relationship to Cisco Systems:
- A ☐ Customer/End User
- B ☐ Prospective Customer
- C ☐ Cisco Reseller
- D ☐ Cisco Distributor
- E ☐ Integrator
- F ☐ Non-Authorized Reseller
- G ☐ Cisco Training Partner
- I ☐ Cisco OEM
- J ☐ Consultant
- K ☐ Other (specify):

3. How many people does your entire company employ?
- A ☐ More than 10,000
- B ☐ 5,000 to 9,999
- c ☐ 1,000 to 4,999
- D ☐ 500 to 999
- E ☐ 250 to 499
- f ☐ 100 to 249
- G ☐ Fewer than 100

4. Is your company a Service Provider?
- A ☐ Yes
- B ☐ No

5. Your involvement in network equipment purchases:
- A ☐ Recommend
- B ☐ Approve
- C ☐ Neither

6. Your personal involvement in networking:
- A ☐ Entire enterprise at all sites
- B ☐ Departments or network segments at more than one site
- C ☐ Single department or network segment
- F ☐ Public network
- D ☐ No involvement
- E ☐ Other (specify):

7. Your Industry:
- A ☐ Aerospace
- B ☐ Agriculture/Mining/Construction
- C ☐ Banking/Finance
- D ☐ Chemical/Pharmaceutical
- E ☐ Consultant
- F ☐ Computer/Systems/Electronics
- G ☐ Education (K–12)
- U ☐ Education (College/Univ.)
- H ☐ Government—Federal
- I ☐ Government—State
- J ☐ Government—Local
- K ☐ Health Care
- L ☐ Telecommunications
- M ☐ Utilities/Transportation
- N ☐ Other (specify):

CPRESS

PACKET

Packet magazine serves as the premier publication linking customers to Cisco Systems, Inc. Delivering complete coverage of cutting-edge networking trends and innovations, *Packet* is a magazine for technical, hands-on users. It delivers industry-specific information for enterprise, service provider, and small and midsized business market segments. A toolchest for planners and decision makers, *Packet* contains a vast array of practical information, boasting sample configurations, real-life customer examples, and tips on getting the most from your Cisco Systems' investments. Simply put, *Packet* magazine is straight talk straight from the worldwide leader in networking for the Internet, Cisco Systems, Inc.

We hope you'll take advantage of this useful resource. I look forward to hearing from you!

Cecelia Glover
Packet Circulation Manager
packet@external.cisco.com
www.cisco.com/go/packet

PACKET